THE DIARY OF

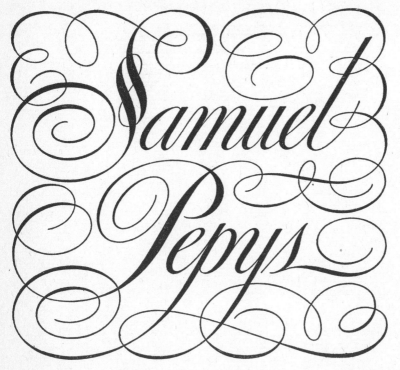

Samuel Pepys

FOR THE YEAR A.D. 1660

TRANSCRIBED BY THE REV. MYNORS BRIGHT
FROM THE SHORTHAND MANUSCRIPT IN THE
PEPYSIAN LIBRARY AT MAGDALENE COLLEGE
CAMBRIDGE AND EDITED WITH ADDITIONS
BY HENRY B. WHEATLEY, F.S.A.

THE LIMITED EDITIONS CLUB
New York, 1942

THE EDITOR'S
Preface

ALTHOUGH the Diary of Samuel Pepys has been in the hands of the public for nearly seventy years, it has not hitherto appeared in its entirety. In the original edition of 1825 scarcely half of the manuscript was printed. Lord Braybrooke added some passages as the various editions were published, but in the preface to his last edition he wrote:—"there appeared indeed no necessity to amplify or in any way to alter the text of the Diary beyond the correction of a few verbal errors and corrupt passages hitherto overlooked."

The public knew nothing as to what was left unprinted, and there was therefore a general feeling of gratification when it was announced some eighteen years ago that a new edition was to be published by the Rev. Mynors Bright, with the addition of new matter equal to a third of the whole. It was understood that at last the Diary was to appear in its entirety, but there was a passage in Mr. Bright's preface which suggested a doubt respecting the necessary completeness. He wrote: "It would have been tedious to the reader if I had copied from the Diary the account of his daily work at the office."

As a matter of fact, Mr. Bright left roughly speaking about one-fifth of the whole Diary still unprinted, although he transcribed the whole, and bequeathed his transcript to Magdalene College.

It has now been decided that the whole of the Diary shall be made public, with the exception of a few passages which cannot possibly be printed. It may be thought by some that these omissions are due to an unnecessary squeamishness, but it is not really so, and readers are therefore asked to have faith in the judgment of the editor. Where any passages have been omitted marks of omission are added, so that in all cases readers will know where anything has been left out.

Lord Braybrooke made the remark in his "Life of Pepys," that "the cipher employed by him greatly resembles that known by the name of 'Rich's system'." When Mr. Bright came to decipher the MS., he discovered that the shorthand system used by Pepys was an earlier one than Rich's, viz., that of Thomas Shelton, who made his system public in 1620.[1]

In his various editions Lord Braybrooke gave a large number of valuable notes, in the collection and arrangement of which he was assisted by the late Mr. John Holmes of the British Museum, and the late Mr. James Yeowell, sometime sub-editor of "Notes and Queries." Where these notes are left unaltered in the present edition the letter "B." has been affixed to them, but in many instances the notes have been altered and added to from later information, and in these cases no mark is affixed. A large number of additional notes are now supplied, but still much has had to be left unexplained. Many persons are mentioned in the Diary who were little known in the outer world, and in some instances it has been impossible to identify them. In other cases, however, it has been possible to throw light upon these persons by reference to different portions of the Diary itself. I would here ask the kind assistance of any reader who is able to illustrate passages that have been left unnoted. I have received much assistance from the various books in which the Diary is quoted. Every writer on the period covered by the Diary has been pleased to illustrate his subject by quotations from Pepys, and from these books it has often been possible to find information which helps to explain difficult passages in the Diary.

Much illustrative matter of value was obtained by Lord Braybrooke from the "Diurnall" of Thomas Rugge, which is preserved

---

[1] Shelton's work was frequently reprinted, and the edition of 1691 is in the Pepysian Library. The late Mr. John E. Bailey read a very interesting paper on "The Cipher of Pepys's Diary," before the Manchester Literary Club, on December 14th, 1875, an abstract of which has been printed.

in the British Museum (Add. MSS. 10,116, 10,117). The following is the description of this interesting work as given by Lord
Braybrooke:—

"MERCURIUS POLITICUS REDIVIVUS;
or, A Collection of the most materiall occurrances and transactions in Public
Affairs since Anno Dñi, 1659, untill 28 March, 1672,
serving as an annuall diurnall for future satisfaction and information,
BY THOMAS RUGGE.

Est natura hominum novitatis avida. — *Plinius.*

"This MS. belonged, in 1693, to Thomas Grey, second Earl of Stamford. It
has his autograph at the commencement, and on the sides are his arms (four
quarterings) in gold. In 1819, it was sold by auction in London, as part of the
collection of Thomas Lloyd, Esq. (No. 1465), and was then bought by Thomas
Thorpe, bookseller. Whilst Mr. Lloyd was the possessor, the MS. was lent to
Dr. Lingard, whose note of thanks to Mr. Lloyd is preserved in the volume.
From Thorpe it appears to have passed to Mr. Heber, at the sale of whose
MSS. in Feb. 1836, by Mr. Evans, of Pall Mall, it was purchased by the
British Museum for £8 8s.

"Thomas Rugge was descended from an ancient Norfolk family, and two
of his ancestors are described as Aldermen of Norwich. His death has been
ascertained to have occurred about 1672; and in the Diary for the preceding
year he complains that on account of his declining health, his entries will be
but few. Nothing has been traced of his personal circumstances beyond the
fact of his having lived for fourteen years in Covent Garden, then a fashionable locality."

Another work I have found of the greatest value is the late Mr.
J. E. Doyle's "Official Baronage of England" (1886), which contains a mass of valuable information not easily to be obtained
elsewhere. By reference to its pages I have been enabled to correct
several erroneous dates in previous notes caused by a very natural confusion of years in the case of the months of January,
February, and March, before it was finally fixed that the year
should commence in January instead of March. More confusion
has probably been introduced into history from this than from
any other cause of a like nature. The reference to two years, as in
the case of, say, Jan. 5, 1661-62, may appear clumsy, but it is the
only safe plan of notation. If one year only is mentioned, the
reader is never sure whether or not the correction has been made.
It is a matter for sincere regret that the popular support was
withheld from Mr. Doyle's important undertaking, so that the
author's intention of publishing further volumes, containing the
Baronies not dealt with in those already published, was frus-
trated.

My labours have been much lightened by the kind help which I have received from those interested in the subject. Lovers of Pepys are numerous, and I have found those I have applied to ever willing to give me such information as they possess. It is a singular pleasure, therefore, to have an opportunity of expressing publicly my thanks to these gentlemen, and among them I would especially mention Messrs. Fennell, Danby P. Fry, J. Eliot Hodgkin, Henry Jackson, J. K. Laughton, Julian Marshall, John Biddulph Martin, J. E. Matthew, Philip Norman, Richard B. Prosser, and Hugh Callendar, Fellow of Trinity College, who verified some of the passages in the manuscript. To the Master and Fellows of Magdalene College, also I am especially indebted for allowing me to consult the treasures of the Pepysian Library, and more particularly my thanks are due to Mr. Arthur G. Peskett, the Librarian.

H. B. W.

LONDON, 1893

Samuel Pepys

T HE FAMILY of Pepys is one of considerable antiquity in the east of England, and the Hon. Walter Courtenay Pepys[1] says that the first mention of the name that he has been able to find is in the Hundred Rolls (Edw. I., 1273), where Richard Pepis and John Pepes are registered as holding lands in the county of Cambridge. In the next century the name of William Pepis is found in deeds relating to lands in the parish of Cottenham, co. Cambridge, dated 1329 and 1340 respectively (Cole MSS., British Museum, vol. i., p. 56; vol. xlii., p. 44). According to the Court Roll of the manor of Pelhams, in the parish of Cottenham, Thomas Pepys was "bayliffe of the Abbot of Crowland in 1434,"

---

[1] Mr. W. C. Pepys has paid great attention to the history of his family, and in 1887 he published an interesting work entitled "Genealogy of the Pepys Family, 1273-1887," London, George Bell and Sons, which contains the fullest pedigrees yet issued.

but in spite of these references, as well as others to persons of the same name at Braintree, Essex, Depedale, Norfolk, &c., the first ancestor of the existing branches of the family from whom Mr. Walter Pepys is able to trace an undoubted descent, is "William Pepis the elder, of Cottenham, co. Cambridge," whose will is dated 20th March, 1519.[1]

In 1852 a curious manuscript volume, bound in vellum, and entitled "Liber Talboti Pepys de instrumentis ad Feoda pertinentibus exemplificatis," was discovered in an old chest in the parish church of Bolney, Sussex, by the vicar, the Rev. John Dale, who delivered it to Henry Pepys, Bishop of Worcester, and the book is still in the possession of the family. This volume contains various genealogical entries, and among them are references to the Thomas Pepys of 1434 mentioned above, and to the later William Pepys. The reference to the latter runs thus:—

"A Noate written out of an ould Booke of my uncle William Pepys."

"William Pepys, who died at Cottenham, 10 *H*. 8, was brought up by the Abbat of Crowland, in Huntingdonshire, and he was borne in Dunbar, in Scotland, a gentleman, whom the said Abbat did make his Bayliffe of all his lands in Cambridgeshire, and placed him in Cottenham, which William aforesaid had three sonnes, Thomas, John, and William, to whom Margaret was mother naturallie, all of whom left issue."

In illustration of this entry we may refer to the Diary of June 12th, 1667, where it is written that Roger Pepys told Samuel that "we did certainly come out of Scotland with the Abbot of Crowland." The references to various members of the family settled in Cottenham and elsewhere, at an early date already alluded to, seem to show that there is little foundation for this very positive statement.

With regard to the standing of the family, Mr. Walter Pepys writes:—

"The first of the name in 1273 were evidently but small copy-holders. Within 150 years (1420) three or four of the name had entered the priesthood, and others had become connected with the monastery of Croyland as bailiffs, &c. In 250 years (1520) there were certainly two families: one at Cottenham, co. Cambridge, and another at Braintree, co. Essex, in comfortable circumstances as yeomen farmers. Within fifty years more (1563), one of the family, Thomas, of Southcreeke, co. Norfolk, had entered the ranks of the gentry sufficiently to have his coat-of-arms recognized by the Herald Cooke,

[1] "Genealogy," pp. 17, 18.

who conducted the Visitation of Norfolk in that year. From that date the majority of the family have been in good circumstances, with perhaps more than the average of its members taking up public positions."[1]

There is a very general notion that Samuel Pepys was of plebeian birth because his father followed the trade of a tailor, and his own remark, "But I believe indeed our family were never considerable,"[2] has been brought forward in corroboration of this view, but nothing can possible be more erroneous, and there can be no doubt that the Diarist was really proud of his descent. This may be seen from the inscription on one of his book-plates, where he is stated to be—

"Samuel Pepys of Brampton in Huntingdonshire, Esq., Secretary of the Admiralty to his Ma^{ty} King Charles the second: Descended from ye antient family of Pepys of Cottenham in Cambridgeshire."

Many members of the family have greatly distinguished themselves since the Diarist's day, and of them Mr. Foss wrote ("Judges of England," vol. vi., p. 467):—

"In the family of Pepys is illustrated every gradation of legal rank from Reader of an Inn of Court to Lord High Chancellor of England."

The William Pepys of Cottenham who commences the pedigree had three sons and three daughters; from the eldest son (Thomas) descended the first Norfolk branch, from the second son (John Pepys of Southcreeke) descended the second Norfolk branch, and from the third son (William) descended the Impington branch. The latter William had four sons and two daughters; two of these sons were named Thomas, and as they were both living at the same time one was distinguished as "the black" and the other as "the red." Thomas the red had four sons and four daughters. John, born 1601, was the third son, and he became the father of Samuel the Diarist. Little is known of John Pepys, but we learn when the Diary opens that he was settled in London as a tailor. He does not appear to have been a successful man, and his son on August 26th, 1661, found that there was only £45 owing to him, and that he owed about the same sum. He was a citizen of London in 1650, when his son Samuel was admitted

---

[1] "Genealogy," p. 16.
[2] February 10th, 1661-62.

to Magdalene College, but at an earlier period he appears to have had business relations with Holland.[1]

In August, 1661, John Pepys retired to a small property at Brampton (worth about £80 per annum),[2] which had been left to him by his eldest brother, Robert Pepys, where he died in 1680.[3] His wife Margaret,[4] whose maiden name has not been discovered,

---

[1] "We went through Horslydown, where I never was since a little boy, that I went to enquire after my father, whom we did give over for lost coming from Holland."—Diary, Jan. 24th, 1665-66. John Pepys appears, from the State Papers to have visited Holland as late as 1656.

"That passes be graunted to goe beyond ye seas to ye persons following, vizt, To John Pepys and his man, with necessaryes for Holland, being on the desire of Mr Samll Pepys.

"Ordered by the Council, Thursday, 7th August, 1656."

[2] See Diary, June 17th, 1666.

[3] The following is a copy of John Pepys's will:—

"MY FATHER'S WILL.
[Indorsement by S. Pepys.]

"Memorandum. That I, John Pepys of Ellington, in the county of Huntingdon, Gentn, doe declare my mind in the disposall of my worldly goods as followeth:

"First, I desire that my lands and goods left mee by my brother, Robert Pepys, deceased, bee delivered up to my eldest son, Samuell Pepys, of London, Esqr, according as is expressed in the last Will of my brother Robert aforesaid.

"Secondly, As for what goods I have brought from London, or procured since, and what moneys I shall leave behind me or due to me, I desire may be disposed of as followeth:

"Imprimis, I give to the stock of the poore of the parish of Brampton, in which church I desire to be enterred, five pounds.

"Item. I give to the poore of Ellington forty shillings.

"Item. I desire that my two grandsons, Samuell and John Jackson, have ten pounds a piece.

"Item. I desire that my daughter, Paulina Jackson, may have my largest silver tankerd.

"Item. I desire that my son John Pepys may have my gold seale-ring.

"Lastly. I desire that the remainder of what I shall leave be equally distributed between my sons Samuel and John Pepys and my daughter Paulina Jackson.

"All which I leave to the care of my eldest son Samuel Pepys, to see performed, if he shall think fit.

"In witness hereunto I set my hand."

[4] Pepys tells us (Diary, Dec. 31st, 1664) that his father and mother were married at Newington in Surrey, on October 15th, 1626, but although the register of marriages of St. Mary, Newington, has been searched, the certificate of the marriage has not been found, and the maiden name of Mrs. John Pepys is still

x

died on the 25th March, 1667, also at Brampton. The family of these two consisted of six sons and five daughters: John (born 1632, died 1640), Samuel (born 1633, died 1703), Thomas (born 1634, died 1664), Jacob (born 1637, died young), Robert (born 1638, died young), and John (born 1641, died 1677); Mary (born 1627), Paulina (born 1628), Esther (born 1630), Sarah (born 1635; these four girls all died young), and Paulina (born 1640, died 1680), who married John Jackson of Brampton, and had two sons, Samuel and John. The latter was made his heir by Samuel Pepys.

Samuel Pepys was born on the 23rd February, 1632-3, but the place of birth is not known with certainty. Samuel Knight, D.D., author of the "Life of Colet," who was a connection of the family (having married Hannah Pepys, daughter of Talbot Pepys of Impington), says positively that it was at Brampton. His statement cannot be corroborated by the registers of Brampton church, as these records do not commence until the year 1654.

Samuel's early youth appears to have been spent pretty equally between town and country. When he and his brother Tom were children they lived with a nurse (Goody Lawrence) at Kingsland,[1] and in after life Samuel refers to his habit of shooting with bow and arrow in the fields around that place.[2] He then went to school at Huntingdon,[3] from which he was transferred to St. Paul's School in London. He remained at the latter place until 1650, early in which year his name was entered as a sizar on the boards of Trinity Hall, Cambridge.[4] He was admitted on the 21st

---

unknown. Mr. Osmund Airy suggests, in the "Encyclopædia Britannica," the possibility that her maiden name may have been Perkins, and refers to an uncle and aunt Perkins who lived in poverty in the Fens near Wisbeach. I believe, however, that these Perkins were connections on the father's rather than on the mother's side. Jane Pepys, youngest sister of Samuel's father, married J. Perkin. The suggestion, nevertheless, is useful, as it draws attention to the possibility of some of the cousins and aunts to whom we can find no clue, having been relations on the mother's side.

[1] Diary, April 25th, 1664.

[2] May 12th, 1667.

[3] March 15th, 1659-60.

[4] Lord Braybrooke says Trinity *College*, but his statement does not agree with the information given in the extracts from the Magdalene College register books quoted in the note on p. xii, where we find the words, "in Aulâ Trin."

June, but subsequently he transferred his allegiance to Magdalene College, where he was admitted a sizar on the 1st October of this same year. He did not enter into residence until March 5th, 1650-51,[1] but in the following month he was elected to one of Mr. Spendluffe's scholarships, and two years later (October 14th, 1653) he was preferred to one on Dr. John Smith's foundation.[2]

Little or nothing is known of Pepys's career at college, but soon after obtaining the Smith scholarship he got into trouble, and, with a companion, was admonished for being drunk.[3] His time, however, was not wasted, and there is evidence that he carried into his busy life a fair stock of classical learning and a true love of letters. Throughout his life he looked back with pleasure to the time he spent at the university, and his college was remembered in his will when he bequeathed his valuable library. In this same

I have made inquiries in order to settle this point, but the result is only negative. The Master of Trinity Hall has been so good as to inform me that the registers of his college do not go back so far as this date, and through the kindness of Mr. J. W. L. Glaisher, F.R.S., Fellow of Trinity College, I learn that Pepys's name does not occur in the registers of that college, and that there is no reason to suspect any omissions in the registers. As there is thus much evidence against his admission at Trinity College, it seems but fair to accept the evidence of the books of Magdalene College until they are proved to be incorrect.

[1] "Went to reside in Magl. Coll. Camb., and did put on my gown first, March 5, 1650-51."—Diary, Dec. 31st, 1664.

[2] Mr. Mynors Bright has printed the following extracts from the entry and register books of Magdalene College, which refer to these movements:—

"Oct. 1, 1650. Samuell Peapys filius Johannis Peapys civis Londinensis, annos natus—è scholâ Paulina admissus est Sizator, Tutore D^{no} Morland.

"Mem, eū prius admissū fuisse in Aulâ Trin: 21 die Junii ejusdem añi, ut patet ex testif. M^{ri} Twells ibidem Socio, dat. Mar. 4 1650-1, quo die etiā in ordinē transijt Pensionariorum apud nos."

"Aprilis 3°, 1651. Ego Samuel Pepys electus fui et admissus in discipulum hujus Collegij pro Magistro Spenluff."

"Octob. 4°, 1653. Ego Samuel Pepys electus fui et admissus in discipulum hujus Collegij pro Magistro Johanne Smyth."

These entries are also printed in the Appendix to the "Fifth Report of the Historical MSS. Commission," p. 484.

[3] October 21st, 1653. "Memorandum: that Peapys and Hind were solemnly admonished by myself and Mr. Hill, for having been scandalously over-served with drink ye night before. This was done in the presence of all the Fellows then resident, in Mr. Hill's chamber.—JOHN WOOD, Registrar." (*From the Registrar's-Book of Magdalene College.*)

year, 1653, he graduated B.A.[1] On the 1st of December, 1655, when he was still without any settled means of support, he married Elizabeth St. Michel, a beautiful and portionless girl of fifteen. Her father, Alexander Marchant, Sieur de St. Michel, was of a good family in Anjou, being son of the High Sheriff of Bauge (in Anjou). Having turned Huguenot at the age of twenty-one, when in the German service, his father disinherited him, and he also lost the reversion of some £20,000 sterling which his uncle, a rich French canon, intended to bequeath to him before he left the Roman Catholic church. He came over to England in the retinue of Henrietta Maria on her marriage with Charles I., but the queen dismissed him on finding that he was a Protestant and did not attend mass. Being a handsome man, with courtly manners, he found favour in the sight of the widow of an Irish squire (daughter of Sir Francis Kingsmill), who married him against the wishes of her family. After the marriage, Alexander St. Michel and his wife having raised some fifteen hundred pounds, started for France in the hope of recovering some part of the family property. They were unfortunate in all their movements, and on their journey to France were taken prisoners by the Dunkirkers, who stripped them of all their property. They now settled at Bideford in Devonshire, and here or near by were born Elizabeth and the rest of the family. At a later period St. Michel served against the Spaniards at the taking of Dunkirk and Arras, and settled at Paris. He was an unfortunate man throughout life, and his son Balthasar says of him: "My father at last grew full of whimsies and propositions of perpetual motion, &c., to kings, princes and others, which soaked his pocket, and brought all our family so low by his not minding anything else, spending all he had got and getting no other employment to bring in more."

While he was away from Paris, some "deluding papists" and "pretended devouts" persuaded Madame St. Michel to place her daughter in the nunnery of the Ursulines. When the father heard

---

[1] There is no information at the registry of the university which throws any light upon the question whether Pepys was first entered at Trinity College or Trinity Hall, but Mr. Charles E. Grant has kindly informed me that "Sam: Peapys" matriculated as a pensioner at Magdalene on July 4th, 1651, and was a B.A. of 1653.

of this, he hurried back, and managed to get Elizabeth out of the nunnery after she had been there twelve days. Thinking that France was a dangerous place to live in, he removed his family to England, where soon afterwards his daughter was married, although, as Lord Braybrooke remarks, we are not told how she became acquainted with Pepys.

St. Michel was greatly pleased that his daughter had become the wife of a true Protestant, and she herself said to him, kissing his eyes: "Dear father, though in my tender years I was by my low fortune in this world deluded to popery, by the fond dictates thereof I have now (joined with my riper years, which give me some understanding) a man to my husband too wise and one too religious to the Protestant religion to suffer my thoughts to bend that way any more."[1]

Alexander St. Michel kept up his character for fecklessness through life, and took out patents for curing smoking chimneys, purifying water, and moulding bricks. In 1667 he petitioned the king, asserting that he had discovered King Solomon's gold and silver mines, and the Diary of the same date contains a curious commentary upon these visions of wealth:—

"March 29, 1667. 4s. a week which his (Balty St. Michel's) father receives of the French church is all the subsistence his father and mother have, and about £20 a year maintains them."

As already noted, Pepys was married on December 1st, 1655. This date is given on the authority of the Registers of St. Margaret's Church, Westminster,[2] but strangely enough Pepys himself supposed his wedding day to have been October 10th.[3] Lord Braybrooke remarks on this,—

"It is notorious that the registers in those times were very ill kept, of which

---

[1] These particulars are obtained from an interesting letter from Balthasar St. Michel to Pepys, dated "Deal, Feb. 8, 1673-4," and printed in "Life, Journals, and Correspondence of Samuel Pepys," 1841, vol. i., pp. 146-53.

[2] The late Mr. T. C. Noble kindly communicated to me a copy of the original marriage certificate, which is as follows: "Samuell Peps of this parish Gent. & Elizabeth De Snt Michell of Martins in the ffields Spinster. Published October 19th, 22nd, 29th [1655], and were married by Richard Sherwin Esqr one of the Justices of the Peace of the Cittie and Lyberties of Westmr December 1st. (Signed) Ri. Sherwin."

[3] See Diary, Oct. 10th, 1661; Oct. 10th, 1664; Oct. 10th, 1666.

we have here a striking instance. . . . Surely a man who kept a diary could not have made such a blunder."

What is even more strange than Pepys's conviction that he was married on October 10th is Mrs. Pepys's agreement with him. On October 10th, 1666, we read,—

"So home to supper, and to bed, it being my wedding night, but how many years I cannot tell; but my wife says ten."

Here Mrs. Pepys was wrong, as it was eleven years; so she may have been wrong in the day also. In spite of the high authority of Mr. and Mrs. Pepys on a question so interesting to them both, we must accept the register as conclusive on this point until further evidence of its incorrectness is forthcoming.

Sir Edward Montagu (afterwards Earl of Sandwich), who was Pepys's first cousin one remove (Pepys's grandfather and Montagu's mother being brother and sister), was a true friend to his poor kinsman, and he at once held out a helping hand to the imprudent couple, allowing them to live in his house. John Pepys does not appear to have been in sufficiently good circumstances to pay for the education of his son, and it seems probable that Samuel went to the university under his influential cousin's patronage. At all events he owed his success in life primarily to Montagu, to whom he appears to have acted as a sort of agent.

On March 26th, 1658, he underwent a successful operation for the stone, and we find him celebrating each anniversary of this important event of his life with thanksgiving. He went through life with little trouble on this score, but when he died at the age of seventy a nest of seven stones was found in his left kidney.[1]

In June, 1659, Pepys accompanied Sir Edward Montagu in the "Naseby," when the Admiral of the Baltic Fleet and Algernon Sidney went to the Sound as joint commissioners. It was then that Montagu corresponded with Charles II., but he had to be very secret in his movements on account of the suspicions of Sidney. Pepys knew nothing of what was going on, as he confesses in the Diary:—

---

[1] "June 10th, 1669. I went this evening to London, to carry Mr. Pepys to my brother Richard, now exceedingly afflicted with the stone, who had been successfully cut, and carried the stone, as big as a tennis ball, to show him and encourage his resolution to go thro' the operation."—Evelyn's *Diary*.

"I do from this raise an opinion of him, to be one of the most secret men in the world, which I was not so convinced of before."[1]

On Pepys's return to England he obtained an appointment in the office of Mr., afterwards Sir George Downing, who was one of the Four Tellers of the Receipt of the Exchequer. He was clerk to Downing when he commenced his diary on January 1st, 1660, and then lived in Axe Yard, close by King Street, Westminster, a place on the site of which was built Fludyer Street. This, too, was swept away for the Government offices in 1864-65. His salary was £50 a year.[2] Downing invited Pepys to accompany him to Holland, but he does not appear to have been very pressing, and a few days later in this same January he got him appointed one of the Clerks of the Council, but the recipient of the favour does not appear to have been very grateful. A great change was now about to take place in Pepys's fortunes, for in the following March he was made secretary to Sir Edward Montagu in his expedition to bring about the restoration of Charles II., and on the 23rd he went on board the "Swiftsure" with Montagu. On the 30th they transferred themselves to the "Naseby." Owing to this appointment of Pepys we have in the Diary a very full account of the daily movements of the fleet until, events having followed their natural course, Montagu had the honour of bringing Charles II. to Dover, where the King was received with great rejoicing. Several of the ships in the fleet had names which were obnoxious to Royalists, and on the 23rd May the King came on board the "Naseby" and altered there—the "Naseby" to the "Charles," the "Richard" to the "Royal James," the "Speaker" to the "Mary," the "Winsby" to the "Happy Return," the "Wakefield" to the "Richmond," the "Lambert" to the "Henrietta," the "Cheriton" to the "Speedwell," and the "Bradford" to the "Success."[3] This portion of the Diary is of particular interest, and the various excursions in Holland which the Diarist made are described in a very amusing manner.

When Montagu and Pepys had both returned to London, the

---

[1] Nov. 7th, 1660. See also Diary, March 8th, 1662-63.

[2] Diary, Jan. 30th, 1659-60: "I taking my £12 10s. od. due to me for my last quarter's salary."

[3] A List of such Shipps as were at Sceaueling in attending on his Ma^ty at his returne to England, with an Account of the then Commanders in each

former told the latter that he had obtained the promise of the office of Clerk of the Acts for him. Many difficulties occurred before Pepys actually secured the place, so that at times he was inclined to accept the offers which were made to him to give it up. General Monk was anxious to get the office for Mr. Turner, who was Chief Clerk in the Navy Office, but in the end Montagu's influence secured it for Pepys. Then Thomas Barlow, who had been appointed Clerk of the Acts in 1638, turned up, and appeared likely to become disagreeable. Pepys bought him off with an annuity of £100, which he did not have to pay for any length of time, as Barlow died in February, 1664-65. It is not in human

Ship, as also an Account of the Gratuity. [*From a paper in the British Museum.* (June 19th, 1660.)]

Names	Commanders	Men	Guns	Gratuities		
Naseby, *alias* Charles	Roger Cuttance	500	80	801	19	6
London	John Lawson	360	64	580	13	6
Swiftsure	Sir Richd Stayner	300	40	444	13	6
Speaker, *alias* Mary	Rob. Clarke	220	52	295	17	0
Centurion	John Parke	150	40	209	17	0
Plymouth	Jo. Haywarde	260	54	298	7	10
Cherriton, *alias* Speedwell	Henry Cuttance	90	20	122	15	6
Dartmouth	Richd Rooth	100	22	134	4	2
Lark	Tho. Levidge	40	10	57	6	8
Hinde	Richd Country	35	6	55	15	8
Nonsuch frigate	John Parker	120	34	194	18	0
Norwich	Mich. Untton	100	22	133	0	0
Winsby, Happy Return	Joseph Ames	160	44	173	6	9
Royal James	John Stoakes	400	70	369	4	3
Lamport, *alias* Henrietta	John Coppin	210	50	274	1	4
Essex	Tho. Bunn	200	48	210	2	2
Portsmouth	Rob. Sansum	130	38	155	6	3
Yarmouth	Cha. Wager	160	44	215	2	0
Assistance	Thos Sparling	140	40	160	17	4
Foresight	Peter Mootham	140	40	176	19	4
Elias	Mark Harrison	110	36	172	10	3
Bradford, Success	Peter Bower	100	24			
Hampshire	Henry Terne	130	38	171	9	1
Greyhound	Jerem. Country	85	20	95	15	10
Francis	Willm Dale	45	10	37	15	6
Lilly	John Pearce	35	6	46	9	9
Hawk	And^w Ashford	35	8	48	16	3
Richmond, formerly Wakefield	John Pointz	100	22	118	2	0
Martin	Wm Burrowes	50				
Merlyn	Edw. Grove			34	16	0
Roe, ketch	Tho. Bowry			51	8	0

nature to be greatly grieved at the death of one to whom you have to pay an annuity, and Pepys expresses his feelings in a very naive manner:—

"For which God knows my heart I could be as sorry as is possible for one to be for a stranger by whose death he gets £100 per annum, he being a worthy honest man; but when I come to consider the providence of God by this means unexpectedly to give me £100 a-year in my estate, I have cause to bless God, and do it from the bottom of my heart."[1]

This office was one of considerable importance, for not only was the holder the secretary or registrar of the Navy Board, but he was also one of the principal officers of the navy, and, as member of the board, of equal rank with the other commissioners. This office Pepys held during the whole period of the Diary, and we find him constantly fighting for his position, as some of the other members wished to reduce his rank merely to that of secretary. In his contention Pepys appears to have been in the right, and a valuable MS. volume in the Pepysian Library contains an extract from the Old Instructions of about 1649, in which this very point is argued out. The volume appears to have been made up by William Penn the Quaker, from a collection of manuscripts on the affairs of the navy found in his father's, "Sir William Penn's closet." It was presented to Charles II., with a dedication ending thus:—

"I hope enough to justify soe much freedome with a Prince that is so easie to excuse things well intended as this is
"By,
"Great Prince,
"Thy faithfull subject,
"WM. PENN."
"London, the 22 of the Mo. called June, 1680."

It does not appear how the volume came into Pepys's possession. It may have been given him by the king, or he may have taken it as a perquisite of his office. The book has an index, which was evidently added by Pepys; in this are these entries, which show his appreciation of the contents of the MS.:—

"Clerk of the Acts,
his duty,
his necessity and usefulness."

---

[1] Diary, Feb. 9th, 1664-65.

The following description of the duty of the Clerk of the Acts shows the importance of the office, and the statement that if the clerk is not fitted to act as a commissioner he is a blockhead and unfit for his employment is particularly racy, and not quite the form of expression one would expect to find in an official document: —

"CLERKE OF THE ACTS.

"The clarke of the Navye's duty depends principally upon rateing (by the Board's approbation) of all bills and recording of them, and all orders, contracts & warrants, making up and casting of accompts, framing and writing answers to letters, orders, and commands from the Councell, Lord High Admirall, or Commissioners of the Admiralty, and he ought to be a very able accomptant, well versed in Navall affairs and all inferior officers dutyes.

"It hath been objected by some that the Clarke of the Acts ought to be subordinate to the rest of the Commissioners, and not to be joyned in equall power with them, although he was so constituted from the first institution, which hath been an opinion only of some to keep him at a distance, least he might be thought too forward if he had joynt power in discovering or argueing against that which peradventure private interest would have concealed; it is certaine no man sees more of the Navye's Transactions than himselfe, and possibly may speak as much to the project if required, or else he is a blockhead, and not fitt for that imployment. But why he should not make as able a Commissioner as a shipp wright lett wise men judge."

In Pepys's patent the salary is stated to be £33 6s. 8d., but this was only the ancient "fee out of the Exchequer," which had been attached to the office for more than a century. Pepys's salary had been previously fixed at £350 a-year.

Neither of the two qualifications upon which particular stress is laid in the above Instructions was possessed by Pepys. He knew nothing about the navy, and so little of accounts that he learned the multiplication table for the first time in July, 1662. We see from the particulars given in the Diary how hard he worked to obtain the knowledge required in his office, and in consequence of his assiduity he soon became a model official. When Pepys became Clerk of the Acts he took up his residence at the Navy Office, a large building situated between Crutched Friars and Seething Lane, with an entrance in each of those places. On July 4th, 1660, he went with Commissioner Pett to view the houses, and was very pleased with them, but he feared that the more influential officers would jockey him out of his rights. His fears were not well grounded, and on July 18th he records the fact that he dined in his own apartments, which were situated in the Seething Lane front.

On July 23rd, 1660, Pepys was sworn in as Lord Sandwich's deputy for a Clerkship of the Privy Seal. This office, which he did not think much of at first, brought him in for a time £3 a day. In June, 1660, he was made Master of Arts by proxy, and soon afterwards he was sworn in as a Justice of the Peace for Middle-sex, Essex, Kent, and Hampshire, the counties in which the chief dockyards were situated.

Pepys's life is written large in the Diary, and it is not neces-sary here to do more than catalogue the chief incidents of it in chronological order. In February, 1661-62, he was chosen a Younger Brother of the Trinity House, and in April, 1662, when on an official visit to Portsmouth Dockyard, he was made a burgess of the town. In August of the same year he was appointed one of the commissioners for the affairs of Tangier. Soon after-wards Thomas Povy, the treasurer, got his accounts into a muddle, and showed himself incompetent for the place, so that Pepys replaced him as treasurer to the commission.

In March, 1663-64, the Corporation of the Royal Fishery was appointed, with the Duke of York as governor, and thirty-two as-sistants, mostly "very great persons." Through Lord Sandwich's influence Pepys was made one of these.

The time was now arriving when Pepys's general ability and devotion to business brought him prominently into notice. Dur-ing the Dutch war the unreadiness of the ships, more particularly in respect to victualling, was the cause of great trouble. The Clerk of the Acts did his utmost to set things right, and he was appointed Surveyor-General of the Victualling Office. The kind way in which Mr. Coventry proposed him as "the fittest man in England" for the office, and the Duke of York's expressed ap-proval, greatly pleased him.

During the fearful period when the Plague was raging, Pepys stuck to his business, and the chief management of naval affairs devolved upon him, for the meetings at the Navy Office were but thinly attended. In a letter to Coventry he wrote:—

"The sickness in general thickens round us, and particularly upon our neighbourhood. You, sir, took your turn of the sword; I must not, therefore, grudge to take mine of the pestilence."

xx

At this time his wife was living at Woolwich, and he himself with his clerks at Greenwich; one maid only remained in the house in London.

Pepys rendered special service at the time of the Fire of London. He communicated the king's wishes to the Lord Mayor, and he saved the Navy Office by having up workmen from Woolwich and Deptford Dockyards to pull down the houses around, and so prevent the spread of the flames.

When peace was at length concluded with the Dutch, and people had time to think over the disgrace which the country had suffered by the presence of De Ruyter's fleet in the Medway, it was natural that a public inquiry into the management of the war should be undertaken. A Parliamentary Committee was appointed in October, 1667, to inquire into the matter. Pepys made a statement which satisfied the committee, but for months afterwards he was continually being summoned to answer some charge, so that he confesses himself as mad to "become the hackney of this office in perpetual trouble and vexation that need it least."[1]

At last a storm broke out in the House of Commons against the principal officers of the navy, and some members demanded that they should be put out of their places. In the end they were ordered to be heard in their own defence at the bar of the House. The whole labour of the defence fell upon Pepys, but having made out his case with great skill, he was rewarded by a most unexpected success. On the 5th March, 1667-68, he made the great speech of his life, and spoke for three hours, with the effect that he so far removed the prejudice against the officers of the Navy Board, that no further proceedings were taken in parliament on the subject. He was highly praised for his speech, and he was naturally much elated at his brilliant success.

About the year 1664 we first hear of a defect in Pepys's eyesight. He consulted the celebrated Cocker, and began to wear green spectacles, but gradually this defect became more pronounced, and on the 31st of May, 1669, he wrote the last words in his Diary:—

"And thus ends all that I doubt I shall ever be able to do with my own eyes

[1] Diary, Feb. 11th, 1667-68.

in the keeping of my Journal, I being not able to do it any longer, having done now as long as to undo my eyes almost every time that I take a pen in my hand."

He feared blindness and was forced to desist, to his lasting regret and our great loss.

At this time he obtained leave of absence from the duties of his office, and he set out on a tour through France and Holland accompanied by his wife. In his travels he was true to the occupation of his life, and made collections respecting the French and Dutch navies. Some months after his return he spoke of his journey as having been "full of health and content," but no sooner had he and his wife returned to London than the latter became seriously ill with a fever. This disease took a fatal turn, and on the 10th of November, 1669, Elizabeth Pepys died at the early age of twenty-nine years, to the great grief of her husband. She died at their house in Crutched Friars, and was buried at St. Olave's Church, Hart Street, where Pepys erected a monument to her memory with this inscription:—

H. S. E.

Cui

Cunas dedit SOMERSETIA, Octob: 23, 1640.

Patrem e præclarâ familiâ	Matrem e nobili Stirpe
de St Michel,	Cliffodorum,
ANDEGAVIA,	CUMBRIA,

ELIZABETHA PEPYS,

Samuelis Pepys (Classi Regiæ ab Actis) Uxor.
Quæ in Cænobio primum, Aulâ dein educata Gallicâ.
Utriusque unà claruit virtutibus,
Formâ, Artibus, Linguis, cultissima.
Prolem enixa, quia parem non potuit, nullam.
Huic demum placidè cum valedixerat
(Confecto per amæniora ferè Europæ itinere)
Potiorem abiit redux lustratura mundum.
Obiit 10 Novembris,

Anno { Ætatis 29.
Conjugii 15.
Domini 1669.

Arms.—Sable, on a Bend Or, between two Nags' Heads erased Argent, three Fleurs de Lis of the first; impaling Ermine, three Roses.

Pepys's successful speech at the bar of the House of Commons made him anxious to become a member, and the Duke of York and Sir William Coventry heartily supported him in his resolution. An opening occurred in due course, at Aldborough, in Suffolk, owing to the death of Sir Robert Brooke in 1669,[1] but, in consequence of the death of his wife, Pepys was unable to take part in the election. His cause was warmly espoused by the Duke of York and by Lord Henry Howard (afterwards Earl Norwich and sixth Duke of Norfolk), but the efforts of his supporters failed, and the contest ended in favour of John Bruce, who represented the popular party. In November, 1673, Pepys was more successful, and was elected for Castle Rising on the elevation of the member, Sir Robert Paston, to the peerage as Viscount Yarmouth. His unsuccessful opponent, Mr. Offley, petitioned against the return, and the election was determined to be void by the Committee of Privileges. The Parliament, however, being prorogued the following month without the House's coming to any vote on the subject, Pepys was permitted to retain his seat. A most irrelevant matter was introduced into the inquiry, and Pepys was charged with having a crucifix in his house, from which it was inferred that he was "a papist or popishly inclined." The charge was grounded upon reported assertions of Sir John Banks and the Earl of Shaftesbury, which they did not stand to when examined on the subject, and the charge was not proved to be good.[2] It will be seen from the extracts from the Journals of the

[1] Sir Robert Brooke, Lord of the Manor of Wanstead from 1662 to 1667, M.P. for Aldborough 1660, 1661-69. He retired to France in bad circumstances, and from a letter among the Pepys MSS. it appears that he was drowned in the river at Lyons.

[2] "The House then proceeding upon the debate touching the Election for Castle Rising, between Mr. Pepys and Mr. Offley, did, in the first place, take into consideration what related personally to Mr. Pepys. Information being given to the House that they had received an account from a person of quality, that he saw an Altar with a Crucifix upon it, in the house of Mr. Pepys; Mr. Pepys, standing up in his place, did heartily and flatly deny that he ever had any Altar or Crucifix, or the image or picture of any Saint whatsoever in his house, from the top to the bottom of it; and the Members being called upon to name the person that gave them the information, they were unwilling to declare it without the order of the House; which, being made, they named the Earl of Shaftesbury; and the House being also informed that Sir J. Banks did likewise see the Altar, he was ordered to attend the Bar of the House, to declare what he knew of this matter. 'Ordered that Sir William Coventry, Sir Thomas Meeres, and Mr. Garraway do attend Lord Shaftesbury on the like occasion, and receive what information his Lordship can give on this matter'." —Journals of the House of Commons, vol. ix., p. 306.—"13th February, Sir W. Coventry reports that they attended the Earl of Shaftesbury, and received

House of Commons given in the note that Pepys denied ever having had an altar or crucifix in his house. In the Diary there is a distinct statement of his possession of a crucifix, but it is not clear from the following extracts whether it was not merely a varnished engraving of the Crucifixion which he possessed:—

July 20, 1666. "So I away to Lovett's, there to see how my picture goes on to be varnished, a fine crucifix which will be very fine." August 2. "At home find Lovett, who showed me my crucifix, which will be very fine when done." Nov. 3. "This morning comes Mr. Lovett and brings me my print of the Passion, varnished by him, and the frame which is indeed very fine, though not so fine as I expected; however pleases me exceedingly."

Whether he had or had not a crucifix in his house was a matter for himself alone, and the interference of the House of Commons was a gross violation of the liberty of the subject.

In connection with Lord Shaftesbury's part in this matter, the late Mr. W. D. Christie found the following letter to Sir Thomas Meres among the papers at St. Giles's House, Dorsetshire:—

"Exeter House, February 10th, 1674.

"Sir,—That there might be no mistake, I thought best to put my answer in writing to those questions that yourself, Sir William Coventry, and Mr. Garroway were pleased to propose to me this morning from the House of Commons, which is that I never designed to be a witness against any man for what I either heard or saw, and therefore did not take so exact notice of things inquired of as to be able to remember them so clearly as is requisite to do in a testimony upon honour or oath, or to so great and honourable a body as the House of Commons, it being some years' distance since I was at Mr. Pepys his lodging. Only that particular of an altar is so signal that I must needs have

from him the account which they had put in writing. The Earl of Shaftesbury denieth that he ever saw an Altar in Mr. Pepys's house or lodgings; as to the Crucifix, he saith he hath some imperfect memory of seeing somewhat which he conceived to be a Crucifix. When his Lordship was asked the time, he said it was before the burning of the Office of the Navy. Being asked concerning the manner, he said he could not remember whether it were painted or carved, or in what manner the thing was; and that his memory was so very imperfect in it, that if he were upon his oath he could give no testimony."—*Ibid.*, vol. ix., p. 309.—"16th February—Sir John Banks was called in—The Speaker desired him to answer what acquaintance he had with Mr. Pepys, and whether he used to have recourse to him to his house, and had ever seen there any Altar or Crucifix, or whether he knew of his being a Papist, or Popishly inclined. Sir J. Banks said that he had known and had been acquainted with Mr. Pepys several years, and had often visited him and conversed with him at the Navy Office, and at his house there upon several occasions; and that he never saw in his house there any Altar or Crucifix, and that he does not believe him to be a Papist, or that way inclined in the least, nor had any reason or ground to think or believe it."—*Ibid.*, vol. ix., p. 310.

remembered it had I seen any such thing, which I am sure I do not. This I desire you to communicate with Sir William Coventry and Mr. Garroway to be delivered as my answer to the House of Commons, it being the same I gave you this morning.

"I am, Sir,
"Your most humble servant,
"SHAFTESBURY."

After reading this letter Sir William Coventry very justly remarked, "There are a great many more Catholics than think themselves so, if having a crucifix will make one." Mr. Christie resented the remarks on Lord Shaftesbury's part in this persecution of Pepys made by Lord Braybrooke, who said, "Painful indeed is it to reflect to what length the bad passions which party violence inflames could in those days carry a man of Shaftesbury's rank, station, and abilities." Mr. Christie observes, "It is clear from the letter to Meres that Shaftesbury showed no malice and much scrupulousness when a formal charge, involving important results, was founded on his loose private conversations."[1] This would be a fair vindication if the above attack upon Pepys stood alone, but we shall see later on that Shaftesbury was the moving spirit in a still more unjustifiable attack.

Lord Sandwich died heroically in the naval action in Southwold Bay, and on June 24th, 1672, his remains were buried with some pomp in Westminster Abbey. There were eleven earls among the mourners, and Pepys, as the first among "the six Bannerolles," walked in the procession.

About this time Pepys was called from his old post of Clerk of the Acts to the higher office of Secretary of the Admiralty. His first appointment was a piece of favouritism, but it was due to his merits alone that he obtained the secretaryship. In the summer of 1673, the Duke of York having resigned all his appointments on the passing of the Test Act, the King put the Admiralty into commission, and Pepys was appointed Secretary for the Affairs of the Navy.[2] He was thus brought into more intimate connection

---

[1] Christie's "Life of the First Earl of Shaftesbury," 1871, vol. ii., pp. 195-197.

[2] The office generally known as Secretary of the Admiralty dates back many years, but the officer who filled it was sometimes Secretary to the Lord High Admiral, and sometimes to the Commission for that office. "His Majesties Letters Patent for ye erecting the office of Secretary of ye Admiralty of England, and creating Samuel Pepys, Esq., first Secretary therein," is dated June 10th, 1684.

with Charles II., who took the deepest interest in shipbuilding and all naval affairs. The Duke of Buckingham said of the King:—

"The great, almost the only pleasure of his mind to which he seemed addicted was shipping and sea affairs, which seemed to be so much his talent for knowledge as well as inclination, that a war of that kind was rather an entertainment than any disturbance to his thoughts."[1]

When Pepys ceased to be Clerk of the Acts he was able to obtain the appointment for his clerk, Thomas Hayter, and his brother, John Pepys, who held it jointly. The latter does not appear to have done much credit to Samuel. He was appointed Clerk to the Trinity House in 1670 on his brother's recommendation, and when he died in 1677 he was in debt £300 to his employers, and this sum Samuel had to pay. In 1676 Pepys was Master of the Trinity House, and in the following year Master of the Cloth-workers' Company, when he presented a richly-chased silver cup, which is still used at the banquets of the company. On Tuesday, 10th September, 1677, the Feast of the Hon. Artillery Company was held at Merchant Taylors' Hall, when the Duke of York, the Duke of Somerset, the Lord Chancellor, and other distinguished persons were present. On this occasion Viscount Newport, Sir Joseph Williamson, and Samuel Pepys officiated as stewards.[2]

About this time it is evident that the secretary carried himself with some haughtiness as a ruler of the navy, and that this was resented by some. An amusing instance will be found in the "Parliamentary Debates." On May 11th, 1678, the King's verbal message to quicken the supply was brought in by Mr. Secretary Williamson, when Pepys spoke to this effect:—

"When I promised that the ships should be ready by the 30th of May, it was upon the supposition of the money for 90 ships proposed by the King and voted by you, their sizes and rates, and I doubt not by that time to have 90 ships, and if they fall short it will be only from the failing of the Streights ships coming home and those but two. . . .

"Sir Robert Howard then rose and said, 'Pepys here speaks rather like an Admiral than a Secretary, "I" and "we." I wish he knows half as much of the Navy as he pretends'."[3]

Pepys was chosen by the electors of Harwich as their member

[1] Jesse's "Stuarts," vol. iii., p. 326.

[2] Raikes's "Hon. Artillery Company," vol. i., p. 196.

[3] Cobbett's "Parliamentary History," vol. iv., cols. 975, 976.

in the short Parliament that sat from March to July, 1679, his colleague being Sir Anthony Deane, but both members were sent to the Tower in May on a baseless charge, and they were superseded in the next Parliament that met on the 17th October, 1679.

The high-handed treatment which Pepys underwent at this time exhibits a marked instance of the disgraceful persecution connected with the so-called Popish plot. He was totally unconnected with the Roman Catholic party, but his association with the Duke of York was sufficient to mark him as a prey for the men who initiated this "Terror" of the seventeenth century. Sir Edmund Berry Godfrey came to his death in October, 1678, and in December Samuel Atkins, Pepys's clerk, was brought to trial as an accessory to his murder.[1] Shaftesbury and the others not having succeeded in getting at Pepys through his clerk, soon afterwards attacked him more directly, using the infamous evidence of Colonel Scott. Much light has lately been thrown upon the underhand dealings of this miscreant by Mr. G. D. Scull, who printed privately in 1883 a valuable work entitled, "Dorothea Scott, otherwise Gotherson, and Hogben of Egerton House, Kent, 1611-1680."

John Scott (calling himself Colonel Scott) ingratiated himself into acquaintance with Major Gotherson, and sold to the latter

---

[1] In Sir G. F. Duckett's "Naval Commissioners, 1660-1760" (privately printed, 1889), there are several particulars as to the life of Samuel Atkins. He was the son of "a colonel on the Parliament side in the late Rebellion," and from 1670 to 1672 was clerk to Colonel Middleton, one of the Commissioners of the Navy, who died in the latter year. He was then clerk in Chatham Dockyard, and in 1674 "he went as junior clerk ... under Mr. Hewer," and afterwards chief or head-clerk under Pepys, to whom he is said to have been devoted. He was examined before a Committee of the House of Lords, and several times remanded back to Newgate touching the murder of Sir Edmund Berry Godfrey. He was eventually acquitted, and having influential friends he subsequently obtained several good appointments. He was a Commissioner of the Navy from 1694 to 1702, and in 1700 he was one of five Commissioners appointed by the House of Lords to state the accounts due to the Army. He died in 1706. An account of Atkins's case, and other documents connected with Godfrey's murder, will be found among the Rawlinson MSS. in the Bodleian Library, A. 173. References to Atkins are given in the House of Lords MSS. ("Historical MSS. Commission," 11th Report, Appendix, part 2, pp. 49-51). Mr. J. R. Tanner communicated an interesting article on "Pepys and the Popish Plot" to the April number (1892) of the "English Historical Review." He shows how the *alibi* which caused the jury to acquit Atkins without leaving the box was prepared by Pepys himself.

large tracts of land in Long Island, to which he had no right whatever. Dorothea Gotherson, after her husband's death, took steps to ascertain the exact state of her property, and obtained the assistance of Colonel Francis Lovelace, Governor of New York. Scott's fraud was discovered, and a petition for redress was presented to the King. The result of this was that the Duke of York commanded Pepys "to collect evidence against Scott, and he accordingly brought together a great number of depositions and information as to his dishonest proceedings in New England, Long Island, Barbadoes, France, Holland, and England,"[1] and these papers are preserved among the Rawlinson Manuscripts in the Bodleian. Scott had his revenge, and accused Pepys of betraying the navy by sending secret particulars to the French Government, and of a design to dethrone the king and extirpate the Protestant religion. Pepys and Sir Anthony Deane were committed to the Tower under the Speaker's warrant on May 22nd, 1679, and Pepys's place at the Admiralty was filled by the appointment of Thomas Hayter. When the two prisoners were brought to the bar of the King's Bench on the 2nd of June, the Attorney-General refused bail, but subsequently they were allowed to find security for £30,000.[2]

---

[1] Scull's "Dorothea Scott," pp. 16, 17.

[2] In connection with this period of disgrace the following is of interest:

Extract from a paper without date.

[Endorsed—"The Coffee-House-Paper, wherein ye scandalous intelligence touching Mr Pepys."]

"On Tuesday last, Mr Peeps went to Windsor, having ye confidence yt he might kisse ye King's hand; and being at Court, mett the Lord Chamberlain and made his complent to his Lordshipp. But his Lordshipp told him yt he wondered he should presume to come to Court before he had cleared himselfe, being charged with treason; whose answer was, his innocency was such, that he valued not any thing he was charged with; soe parted with his Lordshipp; but by the favour of some courtiers, he was brought into ye King's presence: but so soon as his Majtie saw him, he frowned and turned aside, showing his dislike of seeing him there."

The following contradiction to this statement appeared in "The Domestic Intelligencer, and News from Town and Country," 15th and 26th September, 1679: "These are to give notice that all and every part of the relation published in 'The Domestic Intelligencer' the 9th of this instant September, is, as to the matter, and every particular circumstance therein mentioned, altogether false and scandalous, there having no such passage happened, nor any thing that might give occasion to that report."

Pepys was put to great expense in collecting evidence against Scott and obtaining witnesses to clear himself of the charges brought against him. He employed his brother-in-law, Balthasar St. Michel, to collect evidence in France, as he himself explains in a letter to the Commissioners of the Navy:—

"His Majesty of his gracious regard to me, and the justification of my innocence, was then pleased at my humble request to dispence with my said brother goeing (with yᵉ shippe about that time designed for Tangier) and to give leave to his goeing into France (the scene of yᵉ villannys then in practice against me), he being the only person whom (from his relation to me, together with his knowledge in the place and language, his knowne dilligence and particular affection towards mee) I could at that tyme and in soe greate a cause pitch on, for committing the care of this affaire of detecting the practice of my enemies there."[1]

In the end Scott refused to acknowledge to the truth of his original deposition, and the prisoners were relieved from their bail on February 12th, 1679-80. John James, a butler previously in Pepys's service,[2] confessed on his deathbed in 1680 that he had trumped up the whole story relating to his former master's change of religion at the instigation of Mr. William Harbord, M.P. for Thetford.

Pepys wrote on July 1st, 1680, to Mrs. Skinner:—

"I would not omit giving you the knowledge of my having at last obtained what with as much reason I might have expected a year ago, my full discharge from the bondage I have, from one villain's practice, so long lain under."[3]

William Harbord, of Cadbury, co. Somerset, second son of Sir Charles Harbord, whom he succeeded in 1682 as Surveyor-General of the Land Revenues of the Crown, was Pepys's most persistent enemy. Several papers referring to Harbord's conduct were found at Scott's lodging after his flight, and are now preserved among the Rawlinson MSS. in the Bodleian. One of these was the following memorandum, which shows pretty plainly Pepys's opinion of Harbord:—

"That about the time of Mr. Pepys's surrender of his employment of Secretary of the Admiralty, Capt. Russell and myself being in discourse about

---

[1] Scull's "Dorothea Scott," pp. 21, 22.

[2] John James, of Glentworth, co. Lincoln, had been servant to Sir William Coventry, and was recommended to Pepys by Sir R. Mason. James's evidence against Pepys is given in Grey's "Debates," vol. vii., p. 304.

[3] "Pepys's Life, Journals, and Correspondence," 1841, vol. i., p. 216.

Mr. Pepys, Mr. Russell delivered himself in these or other words to this pur-
port: That he thought it might be of advantage to both, if a good understanding
were had between his brother Harbord and Mr. Pepys, asking me to propose
it to Mr. Pepys, and he would to his brother, which I agreed to, and went immediately from him to Mr. Pepys, and telling him of this discourse, he gave
me readily this answer in these very words: That he knew of no service Mr.
Harbord could doe him, or if he could, he should be the last man in England
he would receive any from."[1]

Besides Scott's dishonesty in his dealings with Major Gotherson, it came out that he had cheated the States of Holland out of
£7,000, in consequence of which he was hanged in effigy at the
Hague in 1672. In 1682 he fled from England to escape from the
law, as he had been guilty of wilful murder by killing George
Butler, a hackney coachman, and he reached Norway in safety,
where he remained till 1696. In that year some of his influential
friends obtained a pardon for him from William III., and he returned to England.[2]

In October, 1680, Pepys attended on Charles II. at New-
market, and there he took down from the King's own mouth the
narrative of his Majesty's escape from Worcester, which was
first published in 1766 by Sir David Dalrymple (Lord Hailes)
from the MS., which now remains in the Pepysian Library both
in shorthand and in longhand.[3] It is creditable to Charles II. and
the Duke of York that both brothers highly appreciated the abilities of Pepys, and availed themselves of his knowledge of naval
affairs.

In the following year there was some chance that Pepys might
retire from public affairs, and take upon himself the headship of
one of the chief Cambridge colleges. On the death of Sir Thomas
Page, the Provost of King's College, in August, 1681, Mr. S.
Maryon, a Fellow of Clare Hall, recommended Pepys to apply
to the King for the appointment, being assured that the royal
mandate if obtained would secure his election. He liked the idea,
but replied that he believed Colonel Legge (afterwards Lord

---

[1] William Harbord sat as M.P. for Thetford in several parliaments. In 1689
he was chosen on the Privy Council, and in 1690 became Vice-Treasurer for
Ireland. He was appointed Ambassador to Turkey in 1692, and died at Bel-
grade in July of that year.

[2] Scull's "Dorothea Scott," p. 74.

[3] It is included in the "Boscobel Tracts," published with "Grammont's Memoirs" in Bohn's Standard Library (Bell and Sons).

Dartmouth) wanted to get the office for an old tutor. Nothing further seems to have been done by Pepys, except that he promised if he were chosen to give the whole profit of the first year, and at least half of that of each succeeding year, to "be dedicated to the general and public use of the college." In the end Dr. John Coplestone was appointed to the post.

On May 22nd, 1681, the Rev. Dr. Milles, rector of St. Olave's, who is so often mentioned in the Diary, gave Pepys a certificate as to his attention to the services of the Church. It is not quite clear what was the occasion of the certificate, but probably the Diarist wished to have it ready in case of another attack upon him in respect to his tendency towards the Church of Rome:—

"I, Daniel Milles, Doctor in Divinity, present (and for above twenty yeares last past) Rector of the Parish of St. Olave's, Hart Street, London, doe hereby certify that Samuel Pepys, Esq., some time one of the principall Officers and Commissioners of his Majestie's Navy, and since Secretary of the Admiralty of England, became (with his family) an inhabitant of the said Parish, about the month of June, in the yeare of our Lord 1660, and so continued (without intermission) for the space of thirteen yeares—viz., untill about the same month in the year 1673, when he was called thence to attend his Majesty in his said Secretaryship: during all which time, the said Mr. Pepys and his whole family were constant attendants upon the public worship of God and his holy Ordinances, (under my ministration,) according to the Doctrine and Discipline of the Church of England, established by Law, without the least appearance or suggestion had of any inclination towards Popery, either in himself or any of his family; his Lady receiving the Holy Sacrament (in company with him, the said Mr. Pepys, her husband, and others) from my hand, according to the rites of the Church of England, upon her death-bed, few houres before her decease, in the yeare 1669.

"And I doe hereby further certify, that the said Mr. Pepys hath, from the determination of his said residence in this parish, continued to receive the Holy Communion with the inhabitants thereof, to this day; so that I verily believe, hee never failed, within the whole space of one and twenty yeares last past (viz., from June, 1660,) to this instant 22d of May, (being Whitsunday in the same yeare 1681,) of communicating publickly in the Sacrament of the Lord's Supper with the inhabitants of the Parish, from my hand, at any of the solemn Feasts of Christmas, Easter, and Pentecost, (besides his frequent monthly communicatings therein,) saving on Whitsunday, 1679, when, being a prisoner in the Tower, he appears to have received it in the publick Chappell there; and at Easter last, when, by a violent sickness, (which confined him to his bed,) he was, to my particular knowledge, rendered incapable of attending it. Witnesse my Hand, the day and the yeare above written.

"D. Milles, D.D., Rectʳ of Sᵗ Olave,
"Hart Street, Lond."

Early in 1682 Pepys accompanied the Duke of York to Scot-

land, and narrowly escaped shipwreck by the way. Before letters could arrive in London to tell of his safety, the news came of
the wreck of the "Gloucester" (the Duke's ship), and of the loss
of many lives. His friends' anxiety was relieved by the arrival of
a letter which Pepys wrote from Edinburgh to Hewer on May
8th, in which he detailed the particulars of the adventure. The
Duke invited him to go on board the "Gloucester" frigate, but he
preferred his own yacht (the "Catherine"), in which he had
more room, and in consequence of his resolution he saved himself from the risk of drowning. On May 5th the frigate struck
upon the sand called "The Lemon and Oar," about sixteen
leagues from the mouth of the Humber. This was caused by the
carelessness of the pilot, to whom Pepys imputed "an obstinate
over-weening in opposition to the contrary opinions of Sir I.
Berry, his master, mates, Col. Legg, the Duke himself, and several others, concurring unanimously in not being yet clear of the
sands." The Duke and his party escaped, but numbers were
drowned in the sinking ship, and it is said that had the wreck
occurred two hours earlier, and the accompanying yachts been
at the distance they had previously been, not a soul would have
escaped.

Pepys stayed in Edinburgh for a short time, and the Duke of
York allowed him to be present at two councils. He then visited,
with Colonel George Legge, some of the principal places in the
neighbourhood, such as Stirling, Linlithgow, Hamilton, and
Glasgow. The latter place he describes as "a very extraordinary
town indeed for beauty and trade, much superior to any in Scotland."[1]

Pepys had now been out of office for some time, but he was soon
to have employment again. Tangier, which was acquired at the
marriage of the King to Katharine of Braganza, had long been an
incumbrance, and it was resolved at last to destroy the place.
Colonel Legge (now Lord Dartmouth) was in August, 1683, constituted Captain-General of his Majesty's forces in Africa, and
Governor of Tangier, and sent with a fleet of about twenty sail to
demolish and blow up the works, destroy the harbour, and bring

---

[1] Pepys to Hewer, May 10th, 1682 ("Pepys's Life, Journals, and Correspondence," 1841, vol. i., p. 295).

home the garrison. Pepys received the King's commands to accompany Lord Dartmouth on his expedition, but the latter's instructions were secret, and Pepys therefore did not know what had been decided upon. He saw quite enough, however, to form a strong opinion of the uselessness of the place to England. Lord Dartmouth carried out his instructions thoroughly, and on March 29th, 1684, he and his party (including Pepys) arrived in the English Channel.[1]

The King himself now resumed the office of Lord High Admiral, and appointed Pepys Secretary of the Admiralty, with a salary of £500 per annum. In the Pepysian Library is the original patent, dated June 10th, 1684: "His Majesty's Letters Patent for yᵉ erecting the office of Secretary of yᵉ Admiralty of England, and creating Samuel Pepys, Esq., first Secretary therein." In this office the Diarist remained until the period of the Revolution, when his official career was concluded.

A very special honour was conferred upon Pepys in this year, when he was elected President of the Royal Society in succession to Sir Cyril Wyche, and he held the office for two years. Pepys had been admitted a fellow of the society on February 15th, 1664-65, and from Birch's "History" we find that in the following month he made a statement to the society:—

[1] Pepys's true friend, Mr. Houblon, gave him the following letter of credit when he set out on the expedition:—

"London, August 8, 1683.

"Mr. Richard Gough—This goes by my deare friend Mr. Pepys, who is embarked on board the Grafton man-of-warr, commanded by our Lord Dartmouth, who is Admiral of the King's Fleet for this Expedition. If Mr. Pepys's occasions draw him to Cadiz, you know what love and respect I bear him, so that I need not use arguments with you for to serve him there, which I am sure you will do to the utmost of your power. And wherein you find yourself deficient either for want of language or knowing the country, oblige your friends to help you, that he may have all the pleasure and divertisement there that Cales can afford him. And if his occasions require any money, you will furnish him what he desires, placing it to my account. I shall write you per next post concerning other matters. I am, your loving friend,

"JAMES HOUBLON."
—*Rawlinson MS.*

Pepys kept a journal of his proceedings at Tangier, which is now preserved among the Rawlinson MSS. in the Bodleian Library, Oxford. It was deciphered and published by the Rev. John Smith, in his "Life, Journals, and Correspondence of Pepys," 1841.

"Mr. Pepys gave an account of what information he had received from the Master of the Jersey ship which had been in company with Major Holmes in the Guinea voyage concerning the pendulum watches (March 15th, 1664-5)."[1]

The records of the society show that he frequently made himself useful by obtaining such information as might be required in his department. After he retired from the presidency, he continued to entertain some of the most distinguished members of the society on Saturday evenings at his house in York Buildings. Evelyn expressed the strongest regret when it was necessary to discontinue these meetings on account of the infirmities of the host.

In 1685 Charles II. died, and was succeeded by James, Duke of York. From his intimate association with James it might have been supposed that a long period of official life was still before Pepys, but the new king's bigotry and incapacity soon made this a practical impossibility. At the coronation of James II. Pepys marched in the procession immediately behind the king's canopy, as one of the sixteen barons of the Cinque Ports.

In the year 1685 a new charter was granted to the Trinity Company, and Pepys was named in it the first master, this being the second time that he had held the office of master. Evelyn specially refers to the event in his Diary, and mentions the distinguished persons present at the dinner on July 20th.

It is evident that at this time Pepys was looked upon as a specially influential man, and when a parliament was summoned to meet on May 19th, 1685, he was elected both for Harwich and for Sandwich. He chose to serve for Harwich, and Sir Philip Parker was elected to fill his place at Sandwich. This parliament was dissolved by proclamation July 2nd, 1687, and on August 24th the king declared in council that another parliament should be summoned for November 27th, 1688, but great changes took place before that date, and when the Convention Parliament was called together in January and February, 1689-90, Pepys found no place in it. The right-hand man of the exiled monarch was not likely to find favour in the eyes of those who were now in possession. When the election for Harwich came on, the electors refused to return him, and the streets echoed to the cry of "No

---

[1] Birch's "History of the Royal Society," vol. ii., p. 23.

Tower men, no men out of the Tower!" They did not wish to be represented in parliament by a disgraced official.

We have little or no information to guide us as to Pepys's proceedings at the period of the Revolution. We know that James II. just before his flight was sitting to Kneller for a portrait intended for the Secretary to the Admiralty, and that Pepys acted in that office for the last time on 20th February, 1688-89, but between those dates we know nothing of the anxieties and troubles that he must have suffered. On the 9th March an order was issued from the Commissioners of the Admiralty for him to deliver up his books, &c., to Phineas Bowles, who superseded him as secretary.

Pepys had many firm friends upon whom he could rely, but he had also enemies who lost no opportunity of worrying him. On June 10th, 1690, Evelyn has this entry in his Diary, which throws some light upon the events of the time:—

"Mr. Pepys read to me his Remonstrance, shewing with what malice and injustice he was suspected with Sir Anth. Deane about the timber of which the thirty ships were built by a late Act of Parliament, with the exceeding danger which the fleete would shortly be in, by reason of the tyranny and incompetency of those who now managed the Admiralty and affairs of the Navy, of which he gave an accurate state, and shew'd his greate ability."

On the 25th of this same month Pepys was committed to the Gatehouse at Westminster on a charge of having sent information to the French Court of the state of the English navy. There was no evidence of any kind against him, and at the end of July he was allowed to return to his own house on account of ill-health. Nothing further was done in respect to the charge, but he was not free till some time after, and he was long kept in anxiety, for even in 1692 he still apprehended some fresh persecution.

Sir Peter Palavicini, Mr. James Houblon, Mr. Blackburne, and Mr. Martin bailed him, and he sent them the following circular letter:—

"October 15, 1690.

"Being this day become once again a free man in every respect, I mean but that of my obligation to you and the rest of my friends, to whom I stand indebted for my being so, I think it but a reasonable part of my duty to pay you and them my thanks for it in a body; but know not how otherwise to compass it than by begging you, which I hereby do, to take your share with them and me here, to-morrow, of a piece of mutton, which is all I dare promise you, besides that of being ever,

"Your most bounden and faithful humble servant,

"S. P."

He employed the enforced idleness caused by being thrust out of his employment in the collection of the materials for the valuable work which he published in 1690, under the title of "Memoirs of the Navy." Little more was left for him to do in life, but as the government became more firmly established, and the absolute absurdity of the idea of his disloyalty was proved, Pepys held up his head again as a man to be respected and consulted, and for the remainder of his life he was looked upon as the Nestor of the Navy.

There is little more to be told of Pepys's life. He continued to keep up an extended correspondence with his many friends, and as Treasurer of Christ's Hospital he took very great interest in the welfare of that institution. He succeeded in preserving from impending ruin the mathematical foundation which had been originally designed by him, and through his anxious solicitations endowed and cherished by Charles II. and James II. One of the last public acts of his life was the presentation of the portrait of the eminent Dr. John Wallis, Savilian Professor of Geometry, to the University of Oxford. In 1701 he sent Sir Godfrey Kneller to Oxford to paint the portrait, and the University rewarded him with a Latin diploma containing in gorgeous language the expression of thanks for his munificence.[1]

---

[1] *The Diploma sent by the University of Oxford to Mr. Pepys,*
Upon his presenting the Portrait of Dr. Wallis to their Picture Gallery,
October, 1702.

"Ornatissimo, Optimoque, Viro SAMUELI PEPYS, Armigero, Regibus Carolo Secundo et Jacobo Secundo a Secretis Admiraliæ, Universitas Oxoniensis.

"Te de litteris optimè mereri (Vir ornatissime!) si non multis aliis, hoc uno argumento probari possit, quod litteratorum honori tam impensè faves: certe ante oculos gratissimum simul atque splendidissimum munificentiæ vestræ atque in nos benevolentiæ exemplum quotidie cum laude tuâ observabitur, neque in doctissimi Professoris imagine ipsam quasi depictam mathematicen, insolitamque animi vestri descriptam benignitatem satis unquam mirabimur. Et quidem præclaræ indolis est posse magnum Wallisium in pretio habere, qui nihil unquam vulgare aut sapuit aut fecit, tendit in altos multâ curâ litterarum tractus, sublimesque aperit mathematum vias, cœlis proximus quos metitur et sideribus stellisque quorum numerus ejus arithmeticæ patet, omnesque nisi Lynceum atque Aquilinum oculum fugit. Tu solertissimus tam

On the 26th May, 1703, Samuel Pepys, after long continued suffering, breathed his last in the presence of the learned Dr. George Hickes, the nonjuring Dean of Worcester, and the following letter from John Jackson to his uncle's lifelong friend Evelyn contains particulars as to the cause of death:—

Mr. Jackson to Mr. Evelyn.

"Clapham, May 28th, 1703.
"Friday night.

"Honoured Sir,

" 'Tis no small addition to my grief, to be obliged to interrupt the quiet of your happy recess with the afflicting tidings of my Uncle Pepys's death: knowing how sensibly you will partake with me herein. But I should not be

cœlestis ingenii æstimator, dum tantum in alio meritum suspicis, et dum tam eximii, tam perspicacis in rebus abstrusissimis Viri similitudinem nobis proponis, egregiæ mentis tuæ erigis immortalitatem: non illius formæ atque titulis tantum, verum famæ etiam nomen tuum inscribis, et quantus sis non obscurè inde judicare possumus, quod talem Virum Genti nostræ, et litterati Orbis tam grande ornamentum, in amicum tibi cooptasti; pulchrè similes unit amor, atque in eâdem tabulâ in secula juncti vivatis, utrique perpetuis nostris encomiis dignissimi, quorum alter Academiam exornat, alter ipsum ornantem. At non a solâ istius tabulæ diuturnitate utriusque immortalitas æstimanda est. Illum Motûs Leges et quicquid uspiam cœli terrarumque ab humanâ mente capi, quædam quæ a solâ Wallisianâ inveniri possunt non morituris descripta voluminibus omnium temporum admirationi consecravere; patet vero in laudes tuas ipse Oceanus, quem illâ tam bene instructâ classe contravisti, quæ et potentissimorum hostium, et voracissimorum fluctuum iras potuit contemnere. Tu felicioribus quam ullus unquam Dædalus armamentis naves tuas firmasti, ut navigantium non tantum gloriæ fuerint, vèrum etiam saluti. Tu certè Ligneis Muris Britanniam munivisti, et quod ad utrumque Polum (sive quiddam novi exploraturi, sive victoriam circumferentes) vela nostri explicare potuissent, sola tua cura effecit. Alii res arduas mari aggredi ausi sunt, tuum vero profundius ipso Oceano ingenium audaces reddidit; quod mirâ arte, sive passis velis sive contractis agt, excogitavit, ut id tuto poterant præstare. Aliorum virtuti forsan debemus, ut res magnæ agerentur, sed ut agi potuissent, propria gloria est industriæ tuæ. Fruere ergo felix hâc parte laudis tuæ, quæ tamdiu duratura est, quamdiu erit in usu Pyxis nautica, aut cursus suos peragent Sidera: quam quidem (omissis aliis rebus a quibus immortali gloria viges) ideo tantum memoramus, ne sis nescius probè nos scire quanto a Viro benevolentia ista in nos conferatur, quam gratis animis amplectimur ut non plus debeant artes atque scientiæ Wallisio, neque Reges et Britannia tibi, quam ob hoc præclarum munus nos tibi obæratos læti sentimus, atque optamus ut hoc gratitudinis nostræ testimonium observatissimæ in te nostræ mentis viva imago parem cum vestrâ famâ perennitatis circulum describat, atque adeo sit æterna.

"Datum in Domo Convocationis, Vicesimo tertio die Mensis Octobris, Anno Domini millesimo septingesimo secundo.

"Sigillat: in Domo Convocationis, Vicesimo nono ejusdem Mensis Octobris Annoque Domini supradict."

xxxvii

faithful to his desires, if I did not beg your doing the honour to his memory of accepting mourning from him, as a small instance of his most affectionate respect and honour for you. I have thought myself extremely unfortunate to be out of the way at that only time when you were pleased lately to touch here, and express so great a desire of taking your leave of my Uncle; which could not but have been admitted by him as a most welcome exception to his general orders against being interrupted; and I could most heartily wish that the circumstances of your health and distance did not forbid me to ask the favour of your assisting in the holding up of the pawll at his interment, which is intended to be on Thursday next; for if the manes are affected with what passes below, I am sure this would have been very grateful to his.

"I must not omit acquainting you, sir, that upon opening his body, (which the uncommonness of his case required of us, for our own satisfaction as well as public good,) there was found in his left kidney a nest of no less than seven stones, of the most irregular figures your imagination can frame, and weighing together four ounces and a half, but all fast linked together, and adhering to his back; whereby they solve his having felt no greater pains upon motion, nor other of the ordinary symptoms of the stone. Some lesser defects there also were in his body, proceeding from the same cause. But his stamina, in general, were marvellously strong, and not only supported him, under the most exquisite pains, weeks beyond all expectations; but, in the conclusion, contended for nearly forty hours (unassisted by any nourishment) with the very agonies of death, some few minutes excepted, before his expiring, which were very calm.

"There remains only for me, under this affliction, to beg the consolation and honour of succeeding to your patronage, for my Uncle's sake; and leave to number myself, with the same sincerity he ever did, among your greatest honourers, which I shall esteem as one of the most valuable parts of my inheritances from him; being also, with the faithfullest wishes of health and a happy long life to you,

"Honoured Sir,

"Your most obedient and

"Most humble Servant,

"J. JACKSON.

"Mr. Hewer, as my Uncle's Executor, and equally your faithful Servant, joins with me in every part hereof.

"The time of my Uncle's departure was about three-quarters past three on Wednesday morning last."[1]

Evelyn alludes in his Diary to Pepys's death and the present

---

[1] Communicated to Lord Braybrooke by the late Mr. William Upcott. It appears, from the Evelyn Papers in the British Museum (bought at Mr. Upcott's sale), that in September, 1705, Mr. John Jackson made a proposal of marriage to one of Evelyn's grand-daughters, through their common friend, William Hewer. The alliance was declined solely on account of Jackson's being unable to make an adequate settlement on the young lady; whilst Evelyn (the draught of whose answer is preserved) courteously acknowledged the respect entertained by him for Pepys's memory, and his sense of his nephew's extraordinary accomplishments. Mr. Jackson married Anne, daughter of the

to him of a suit of mourning. He speaks in very high terms of his friend:—

"1703, May 26th. This day died Mr. Sam Pepys, a very worthy, industrious, and curious person, none in England exceeding him in knowledge of the navy, in which he had passed thro' all the most considerable offices, Clerk of the Acts and Secretary of the Admiralty, all which he performed with great integrity. When K. James II. went out of England, he laid down his office, and would serve no more, but withdrawing himselfe from all public affaires, he liv'd at Clapham with his partner Mr. Hewer, formerly his clerk, in a very noble and sweete place, where he enjoy'd the fruits of his labours in greate prosperity. He was universally belov'd, hospitable, generous, learned in many things, skill'd in music, a very greate cherisher of learned men of whom he had the conversation. . . . Mr. Pepys had been for neere 40 yeeres so much my particular friend that Mr. Jackson sent me compleat mourning, desiring me to be one to hold up the pall at his magnificent obsequies, but my indisposition hinder'd me from doing him this last office."

The body was brought from Clapham and buried in St. Olave's Church, Hart Street, on the 5th June, at nine o'clock at night, in a vault just beneath the monument to the memory of Mrs. Pepys. Dr. Hickes performed the last sad offices for his friend, as described in the following letter:—

Extract of a Letter from Dr. Hickes to Dr. Charlett.

"June 5, 1703.

"Last night, at 9 o'clock, I did the last office for your and my good friend, Mr Pepys, at St Olave's Church, where he was laid in a vault of his own makeing, by his wife and brother.

"The greatness of his behaviour, in his long and sharp tryall before his death, was in every respect answerable to his great life; and I believe no man ever went out of this world with greater contempt of it, or a more lively faith in every thing that was revealed of the world to come. I administered the Holy Sacrament twice in his illness to him, and had administered it a third time, but for a sudden fit of illness that happened at the appointed time of administering of it. Twice I gave him the absolution of the Church, which he desired, and received with all reverence and comfort; and I never attended any sick or dying person that dyed with so much Christian greatnesse of mind, or a more lively sense of immortality, or so much fortitude and patience, in so long and sharp a tryall, or greater resignation to the will, which he most devoutly acknowledged to be the wisdom of God; and I doubt not but he is now

Rev. John Edgerley, Vicar of Wandsworth, Prebendary of St. Paul's, and Archdeacon, by Anne, daughter of ——— Blackburn, William Hewer's uncle, often mentioned in the Diary. Mr. Jackson left two sons (at whose death, s. p., the male line became extinct) and five daughters, the youngest of whom married John Cockerell, of Bishop's Hull, Somerset, and the present representatives are the family of Pepys Cockerell.

a very blessed spirit, according to his motto, MENS CUJUSQUE IS EST QUISQUE.

"GEORGE HICKES."[1]

Pepys's faithful friend, Hewer, was his executor, and his nephew, John Jackson, his heir. Mourning was presented to forty persons, and a large number of rings to relations, godchildren, servants, and friends, also to representatives of the Royal Society, of the Universities of Cambridge and Oxford, of the Admiralty, and of the Navy Office. The bulk of the property was bequeathed to Jackson, but the money which was left was much less than might have been expected, for at the time of Pepys's death there was a balance of £28,007 2s. 1 1/4d. due to him from the Crown, and none of this was ever paid. The books and other collections were left to Magdalene College, Cambridge, but Jackson was to have possession of them during his lifetime. These were the most important portion of Pepys's effects, for with them was the manuscript of the immortal Diary. The following are the directions for the disposition of the library, taken from Harl. MS., No. 7301:—

"For the further settlement and preservation of my said library, after the death of my nephew John Jackson, I do hereby declare, That could I be sure of a constant succession of heirs from my said nephew, qualified like himself for the use of such a library, I should not entertain a thought of its ever being alienated from them. But this uncertainty considered, with the infinite pains, and time, and cost employed in my collecting, methodising and reducing the same to the state it now is, I cannot but be greatly solicitous that all possible provision should be made for its unalterable preservation and perpetual security against the ordinary fate of such collections falling into the hands of an incompetent heir, and thereby being sold, dissipated, or embezzled. And since it has pleased God to visit me in a manner that leaves little appearance of being myself restored to a condition of concerting the necessary measures for attaining these ends, I must and do with great confidence rely upon the sincerity and direction of my executor and said nephew for putting in execution the powers given them, by my forementioned will relating hereto, requiring that the same be brought to a determination in twelve months after my decease, and that special regard be had therein to the following particu-

---

[1] From the original in the Bodleian Library:—

"London, June 5. Yesterday, in the evening, were performed the obsequies of Samuel Pepys, Esq., in Crutched-Friars' Church; whither his corpse was brought in a very honourable and solemn manner from Clapham, where he departed this life the 26th day of the last month."—*Post Boy*, No. 1257, June 5, 1703.

"June 4th, 1703.—Samuel Peyps, Esqre, buried in a vault by ye Comunion Table."—*Register of St. Olave's, Hart Street.*

lars which I declare to be my present thoughts and prevailing inclinations in this matter, viz.:—

"1. That after the death of my said nephew, my said library be placed and for ever settled in one of our universities, and rather in that of Cambridge than Oxford.

"2. And rather in a private college there, than in the public library.

"3. And in the colleges of Trinity or Magdalen preferably to all others.

"4. And of these too, *cæteris paribus,* rather in the latter, for the sake of my own and my nephew's education therein.

"5. That in which soever of the two it is, a fair roome be provided therein.

"6. And if in Trinity, that the said roome be contiguous to, and have communication with, the new library there.

"7. And if in Magdalen, that it be in the new building there, and any part thereof at my nephew's election.

"8. That my said library be continued in its present form and no other books mixed therein, save what my nephew may add to them of his own collecting, in distinct presses.

"9. That the said room and books so placed and adjusted be called by the name of 'Bibliotheca Pepysiana.'

"10. That this 'Bibliotheca Pepysiana' be under the sole power and custody of the master of the college for the time being, who shall neither himself convey, nor suffer to be conveyed by others, any of the said books from thence to any other place, except to his own lodge in the said college, nor there have more than ten of them at a time; and that of those also a strict entry be made and account kept, at the time of their having been taken out and returned, in a book to be provided, and remain in the said library for that purpose only.

"11. That before my said library be put into the possession of either of the said colleges, that college for which it shall be designed, first enter into covenants for performance of the foregoing articles.

"12. And that for a yet further security herein, the said two colleges of Trinity and Magdalen have a reciprocal check upon one another; and that college which shall be in present possession of the said library, be subject to an annual visitation from the other, and to the forfeiture thereof to the life, possession, and use of the other, upon conviction of any breach of their said covenants.

"S. PEPYS."

The library and the original book-cases were not transferred to Magdalene College until 1773, when Jackson died, and there they have been preserved in safety ever since.

A large number of Pepys's manuscripts appear to have remained unnoticed in York Buildings for some years. They never came into Jackson's hands, and were thus lost to Magdalene College. Dr. Rawlinson afterwards obtained them, and they were included in the bequest of his books to the Bodleian Library.

Pepys was partial to having his portrait taken, and he sat to Savill, Hales, Lely, and Kneller. Hales's portrait, painted in 1666, is now in the National Portrait Gallery, and an etching

xli

from it appears in the demy 8vo edition of the Diary. The portrait by Lely is in the Pepysian Library. Of the three portraits by Kneller, one is in the hall of Magdalene College, another at the Royal Society, and the third was lent to the First Special Exhibition of National Portraits, 1866, by the late Mr. Andrew Pepys Cockerell. Several of the portraits have been engraved, but the most interesting of these are those used by Pepys himself as book-plates. These were both engraved by Robert White, and taken from paintings by Kneller:—

"1. Portrait in a carved oval frame, bearing inscription 'SAM. PEPYS. CAR. ET. JAC. ANGL. REGIB. A. SECRETIS. ADMIRALIAE.' Motto under the frame, 'Mens cujusque is est quisque.' Large book-plate.

"2. Portrait in a medallion on a scroll of paper. Motto over the head, 'Mens cujusque is est quisque'; underneath the same inscription as on No. 1. Small book-plate."

The church of St. Olave, Hart Street, is intimately associated with Pepys both in his life and in his death, and for many years the question had been constantly asked by visitors, "Where is Pepys's monument?" On Wednesday, July 5th, 1882, a meeting was held in the vestry of the church, when an influential committee was appointed, upon which all the great institutions with which Pepys was connected were represented by their masters, presidents, or other officers, with the object of taking steps to obtain an adequate memorial of the Diarist. Mr. (now Sir) Alfred Blomfield, architect of the church, presented an appropriate design for a monument, and sufficient subscriptions having been obtained for the purpose, he superintended its erection. On Tuesday afternoon, March 18th, 1884, the monument, which was affixed to the wall of the church where the gallery containing Pepys's pew formerly stood, was unveiled in the presence of a large concourse of visitors. The Earl of Northbrook, First Lord of the Admiralty, consented to unveil the monument, but he was at the last moment prevented by public business from attending. The late Mr. Russell Lowell, then the American Minister, took Lord Northbrook's place, and made a very charming and appreciative speech on the occasion, from which the following passages are extracted:—

"It was proper," his Excellency said, "that he should read a note he had received from Lord Northbrook. This was dated that day from the Admiralty, and was as follows:—

" 'My dear Mr. Lowell,

" 'I am very much annoyed that I am prevented from assisting at the ceremony to-day. It would be very good if you would say that nothing but very urgent business would have kept me away. I was anxious to give my testimony to the merits of Pepys as an Admiralty official, leaving his literary merits to you. He was concerned with the administration of the Navy from the Restoration to the Revolution, and from 1673 as secretary. I believe his merits to be fairly stated in a contemporary account, which I send.

" 'Yours very truly,
" 'NORTHBROOK.'

"The contemporary account, which Lord Northbrook was good enough to send him, said:—

" 'Pepys was, without exception, the greatest and most useful Minister that ever filled the same situations in England, the acts and registers of the Admiralty proving this beyond contradiction. The principal rules and establishments in present use in these offices are well known to have been of his introducing, and most of the officers serving therein since the Restoration of his bringing-up. He was a most studious promoter and strenuous asserter of order and discipline. Sobriety, diligence, capacity, loyalty, and subjection to command were essentials required in all whom he advanced. Where any of these were found wanting, no interest or authority was capable of moving him in favour of the highest pretender. Discharging his duty to his Prince and country with a religious application and perfect integrity, he feared no one, courted no one, and neglected his own fortune.'

"That was a character drawn, it was true, by a friendly hand, but to those who were familiar with the life of Pepys, the praise hardly seemed exaggerated. As regarding his official life, it was unnecessary to dilate upon his peculiar merits, for they all knew how faithful he was in his duties, and they all knew, too, how many faithful officials there were working on in obscurity, who were not only never honoured with a monument but who never expected one. The few words, Mr. Lowell went on to remark, which he was expected to say upon that occasion, therefore, referred rather to what he believed was the true motive which had brought that assembly together, and that was by no means the character of Pepys either as Clerk of the Acts or as Secretary to the Admiralty. This was not the place in which one could go into a very close examination of the character of Pepys as a private man. He would begin by admitting that Pepys was a type, perhaps, of what was now called a 'Philistine.' We had no word in England which was equivalent to the French adjective *Bourgeois*; but, at all events, Samuel Pepys was the most perfect type that ever existed of the class of people whom this word described. He had all its merits as well as many of its defects. With all those defects, however—perhaps in consequence of them—Pepys had written one of the most delightful books that it was man's privilege to read in the English language or in any other. Whether Pepys intended this Diary to be afterwards read by the general public or not—and this was a doubtful question when it was considered that he had left, possibly by inadvertence, a key to his cypher behind him—it was certain that he had left with us a most delightful picture, or rather he had left the power in our hands of drawing for ourselves some of the most delight-

xliii

ful pictures, of the time in which he lived. There was hardly any book which was analogous to it. . . . If one were asked what were the reasons for liking Pepys, it would be found that they were as numerous as the days upon which he made an entry in his Diary, and surely that was sufficient argument in his favour. There was no book, Mr. Lowell said, that he knew of, or that occurred to his memory, with which Pepys's Diary could fairly be compared, except the journal of L'Estoile, who had the same anxious curiosity and the same commonness, not to say vulgarity of interest, and the book was certainly unique in one respect, and that was the absolute sincerity of the author with himself. Montaigne is conscious that we are looking over his shoulder, and Rousseau secretive in comparison with him. The very fact of that sincerity of the author with himself argued a certain greatness of character. Dr. Hickes, who attended Pepys at his death-bed, spoke of him as 'this great man,' and said he knew no one who died so greatly. And yet there was something almost of the ridiculous in the statement when the 'greatness' was compared with the garrulous frankness which Pepys showed towards himself. There was no parallel to the character of Pepys, he believed, in respect of *naiveté*, unless it were found in that of Falstaff, and Pepys showed himself, too, like Falstaff, on terms of unbuttoned familiarity with himself. Falstaff had just the same *naiveté*, but in Falstaff it was the *naiveté* of conscious humour. In Pepys it was quite different, for Pepys's *naiveté* was the inoffensive vanity of a man who loved to see himself in the glass. Falstaff had a sense, too, of inadvertent humour, but it was questionable whether Pepys could have had any sense of humour at all, and yet permitted himself to be so delightful. There was probably, however, more involuntary humour in Pepys's Diary than there was in any other book extant. When he told his readers of the landing of Charles II. at Dover, for instance, it would be remembered how Pepys chronicled the fact that the Mayor of Dover presented the Prince with a Bible, for which he returned his thanks and said it was the 'most precious Book to him in the world.' Then, again, it would be remembered how, when he received a letter addressed 'Samuel Pepys, *Esq.*,' he confesses in the Diary that this pleased him mightily. When, too, he kicked his cookmaid, he admits that he was not sorry for it, but was sorry that the footboy of a worthy knight with whom he was acquainted saw him do it. And the last instance he would mention of poor Pepys's *naiveté* was when he said in the Diary that he could not help having a certain pleasant and satisfied feeling when Barlow died. Barlow, it must be remembered, received during his life the yearly sum from Pepys of £100. The value of Pepys's book was simply priceless, and while there was nothing in it approaching that single page in St. Simon where he described that thunder of courtierly red heels passing from one wing of the Palace to another as the Prince was lying on his death-bed, and favour was to flow from another source, still Pepys's Diary was unequalled in its peculiar quality of amusement. The lightest part of the Diary was of value, historically, for it enabled one to see London of 200 years ago, and, what was more, to see it with the eager eyes of Pepys. It was not Pepys the official who had brought that large gathering together that day in honour of his memory: it was Pepys the Diarist."

In concluding this account of the chief particulars of Pepys's life it may be well to add a few words upon the pronunciation of his name. Various attempts appear to have been made to represent this phonetically. Lord Braybrooke, in quoting the entry of death from St. Olave's Registers, where the spelling is "Peyps," wrote, "This is decisive as to the proper pronunciation of the name." This spelling may show that the name was pronounced as a monosyllable, but it is scarcely conclusive as to anything else, and Lord Braybrooke does not say what he supposes the sound of the vowels to have been. At present there are three pronunciations in use—*Peps*, which is the most usual; *Peeps*, which is the received one at Magdalene College, and *Peppis*, which I learn from Mr. Walter C. Pepys is the one used by other branches of the family. Mr. Pepys has paid particular attention to this point, and in his valuable "Genealogy of the Pepys Family" (1887) he has collected seventeen varieties of spelling of the name, which are as follows, the dates of the documents in which the form appears being attached:—1. Pepis (1273); 2. Pepy (1439); 3. Pypys (1511); 4. Pipes (1511); 5. Peppis (1518); 6. Peppes (1519); 7. Pepes (1520); 8. Peppys (1552); 9. Peaps (1636); 10. Pippis (1639); 11. Peapays (1653); 12. Peps (1655); 13. Pypes (1656); 14. Peypes (1656); 15. Peeps (1679); 16. Peepes (1683); 17. Peyps (1703). Mr. Walter Pepys adds:—

"The accepted spelling of the name 'Pepys' was adopted generally about the end of the seventeenth century, though it occurs many years before that time. There have been numerous ways of pronouncing the name, as 'Peps,' 'Peeps,' and 'Peppis.' The Diarist undoubtedly pronounced it 'Peeps,' and the lineal descendants of his sister Paulina, the family of 'Pepys Cockerell' pronounce it so to this day. The other branches of the family all pronounce it as 'Peppis,' and I am led to be satisfied that the latter pronunciation is correct by the two facts that in the earliest known writing it is spelt 'Pepis,' and that the French form of the name is 'Pepy'."

The most probable explanation is that the name in the seventeenth century was either pronounced *Pĕps* or *Pāpes;* for both the forms *ea* and *ey* would represent the latter pronunciation. The general change in the pronunciation of the spelling *ea* from *ai* to *ee* took place in a large number of words at the end of the seventeenth and beginning of the eighteenth century, and three words at least (yea, break, and great) keep this old pronunciation still. The present Irish pronunciation of English is really the same as the English pronunciation of the seventeenth century, when the most extensive settlement of Englishmen in Ireland took place, and the Irish always pronounce *ea* like *ai* (as, He gave him a nate bating=neat beating). Again, the *ey* of *Peyps* would rhyme with they and obey. English literature is full of illustrations of the old pronunciation of *ea*, as in "Hudibras,"—

> "Doubtless the pleasure is as great
> In being cheated as to cheat,"—

which was then a perfect rhyme. In the "Rape of the Lock" tea (tay) rhymes with obey, and in Cowper's verses on Alexander Selkirk sea rhymes with survey.[1] It is not likely that the pronunciation of the name was fixed, but there is every reason to suppose that the spellings of *Peyps* and *Peaps* were intended to represent the sound *Pāpes* rather than *Peeps*.

In spite of all the research which has brought to light so many incidents of interest in the life of Samuel Pepys, we cannot but feel how dry these facts are when placed by the side of the living details of the Diary. It is in its pages that the true man is displayed, and it has therefore not been thought necessary here to do more than set down in chronological order such facts as are known of the life outside the Diary. A fuller "appreciation" of the man must be left for some future occasion.

H. B. W.

---

[1] See Ellis's "Early English Pronunciation," part iv., pp. 1230-1243.

THE DIARY OF
SAMUEL PEPYS
1659-60

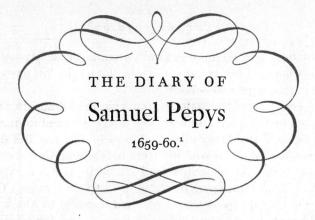

THE DIARY OF
Samuel Pepys
1659-60.[1]

BLESSED BE GOD, AT THE END OF THE LAST YEAR
I was in very good health, without any sense of my old pain, but
upon taking of cold.[2] I lived in Axe Yard[3] having my wife, and

---

[1] The year did not legally begin in England before the 25th March until the
act for altering the style fixed the 1st of January as the first day of the year,
and previous to 1752 the year extended from March 25th to the following
March 24th. Thus since 1752 we have been in the habit of putting the two
dates for the months of January and February and March 1 to 24 in all years
previous to 1752. Practically, however, many persons considered the year to
commence with January 1st, as it will be seen Pepys did. The 1st of January
was considered as New Year's day long before Pepys's time. The fiscal year has
not been altered, and the national accounts are still reckoned from old Lady
Day, which falls on the 6th of April.

[2] Pepys was successfully cut for the stone on March 26th, 1658. See March
26th below. Although not suffering from this cause again until the end of his
life, there are frequent references in the Diary to pain whenever he caught
cold. In a letter from Pepys to his nephew Jackson, April 8th, 1700, there is
a reference to the breaking out three years before his death of the wound
caused by the cutting for the stone: "It has been my calamity for much the
greatest part of this time to have been kept bedrid, under an evil so rarely
known as to have had it matter of universal surprise and with little less
general opinion of its dangerousness; namely, that the cicatrice of a wound
occasioned upon my cutting for the stone, without hearing anything of it in
all this time, should after more than 40 years' perfect cure, break out again."
At the post-mortem examination a nest of seven stones, weighing four and a
half ounces, was found in the left kidney, which was entirely ulcerated.

[3] Pepys's house was on the south side of King Street, Westminster; it is singular that when he removed to a residence in the city, he should have settled
close to another Axe Yard. Fludyer Street stands on the site of Axe Yard,
which derived its name from a great messuage or brew-house on the west side
of King Street, called "The Axe," and referred to in a document of the 23rd
of Henry VIII.—B.

3

servant Jane, and no more in family than us three. My wife . . .
gave me hopes of her being with child, but on the last day of the
year . . . [the hope was belied].

The condition of the State was thus; viz. the Rump, after being
disturbed by my Lord Lambert,[1] was lately returned to sit again.
The officers of the Army all forced to yield. Lawson[2] lies still in
the river, and Monk[3] is with his army in Scotland. Only my Lord
Lambert is not yet come into the Parliament, nor is it expected
that he will without being forced to it. The new Common Council of the City do speak very high; and had sent to Monk their
sword-bearer, to acquaint him with their desires for a free and
full Parliament, which is at present the desires, and the hopes,
and expectation of all. Twenty-two of the old secluded mem-

---

[1] John Lambert, major-general in the Parliamentary army. The title Lord
was not his by right, but it was frequently given to the republican officers.
He was born in 1619, at Calton Hall, in the parish of Kirkby-in-Malham-Dale,
in the West Riding of Yorkshire. In 1642 he was appointed captain of horse
under Fairfax, and acted as major-general to Cromwell in 1650 during the
war in Scotland. After this Parliament conferred on him a grant of lands in
Scotland worth £1,000 per annum. He refused to take the oath of allegiance
to Cromwell, for which the Protector deprived him of his commission. After
Cromwell's death he tried to set up a military government. The Commons
cashiered Lambert, Desborough, and other officers, October 12th, 1659, but
Lambert retaliated by thrusting out the Commons, and set out to meet Monk.
His men fell away from him, and he was sent to the Tower, March 3rd, 1660,
but escaped. In 1662 he was tried on a charge of high treason and condemned,
but his life was spared. It is generally stated that he passed the remainder of
his life in the island of Guernsey, but this is proved to be incorrect by a MS.
in the Plymouth Athenæum, entitled "Plimmouth Memoirs collected by
James Younge, 1684." This will be seen from the following extracts quoted by
Mr. R. J. King, in "Notes and Queries," 1st S., iv. 340: "1667 Lambert the
arch-rebel brought to this island [St. Nicholas, at the entrance of Plymouth
harbour]." "1683 Easter day Lambert that olde rebell dyed this winter on
Plimmouth Island where he had been prisoner 15 years and more."

[2] Sir John Lawson, the son of a poor man at Hull, entered the navy as a
common sailor, rose to the rank of admiral, and distinguished himself during
the Protectorate. Though a republican, he readily closed with the design of
restoring the King. He was vice-admiral under the Earl of Sandwich, and
commanded the "London" in the squadron which conveyed Charles II. to
England. He was mortally wounded in the action with the Dutch off Harwich, June, 1665. He must not be confounded with another John Lawson, the
Royalist, of Brough Hall, in Yorkshire, who was created a Baronet by Charles
II., July 6th, 1665.

[3] George Monk, born 1608, created Duke of Albemarle, 1660, married Ann
Clarges, March, 1654, died January 3rd, 1676.

bers[1] having been at the House-door the last week to demand entrance, but it was denied them; and it is believed that [neither] they nor the people will be satisfied till the House be filled. My own private condition very handsome, and esteemed rich, but indeed very poor; besides my goods of my house, and my office, which at present is somewhat uncertain. Mr. Downing master of my office.[2]

[Jan. 1st] (Lord's day). This morning (we living lately in the garret,) I rose, put on my suit with great skirts, having not lately worn any other clothes but them. Went to Mr. Gunning's[3]

[1] "The City sent and invited him [Monk] to dine the next day at Guildhall, and there he declared for the members whom the army had forced away in year forty-seven and forty-eight, who were known by the names of secluded members."—Burnet's *Hist. of his Own Time*, book i.

[2] George Downing was one of the Four Tellers of the Receipt of the Exchequer, and in his office Pepys was a clerk. He was the son of Emmanuel Downing of the Inner Temple, afterwards of Salem, Massachusetts, and of Lucy, sister of Governor John Winthrop. He is supposed to have been born in August, 1623. He and his parents went to New England in 1638, and he was the second graduate of Harvard College. He returned to England about 1645, and acted as Colonel Okey's chaplain before he entered into political life. Anthony à Wood (who incorrectly describes him as the son of Dr. Calybute Downing, vicar of Hackney) calls Downing a sider with all times and changes: skilled in the common cant, and a preacher occasionally. He was sent by Cromwell to Holland in 1657, as resident there. At the Restoration, he espoused the King's cause, and was knighted and elected M.P. for Morpeth, in 1661. Afterwards, becoming Secretary to the Treasury and Commissioner of the Customs, he was in 1663 created a Baronet of East Hatley, in Cambridgeshire, and was again sent Ambassador to Holland. His grandson of the same name, who died in 1749, was the founder of Downing College, Cambridge. The title became extinct in 1764, upon the decease of Sir John Gerrard Downing, the last heir-male of the family. Sir George Downing's character will be found in Lord Clarendon's "Life," vol. iii. p. 4. Pepys's opinion seems to be somewhat of a mixed kind. He died in July, 1684.

[3] Peter Gunning, afterwards Master of St. John's College, Cambridge, and successively Bishop of Chichester and Ely. He had continued to read the Liturgy at the chapel at Exeter House when the Parliament was most predominant, for which Cromwell often rebuked him. Evelyn relates that on Christmas Day, 1657, the chapel was surrounded with soldiers, and the congregation taken prisoners, he and his wife being among them. There are several notices of Dr. Gunning in Evelyn's Diary. When he obtained the mastership of St. John's College upon the ejection of Dr. Tuckney, he allowed that Noncomformist divine a handsome annuity during his life. He was a great controversialist, and a man of great reading. Burnet says he "was a very honest sincere man, but of no sound judgment, and of no prudence in affairs" ("Hist. of his Own Time"). He died July 6th, 1684, aged seventy-one.

chapel at Exeter House,[1] where he made a very good sermon upon these words:—"That in the fulness of time God sent his Son, made of a woman," &c.; showing, that, by "made under the law," is meant his circumcision, which is solemnized this day. Dined at home in the garret, where my wife dressed the remains of a turkey, and in the doing of it she burned her hand. I staid at home all the afternoon, looking over my accounts; then went with my wife to my father's, and in going observed the great posts which the City have set up at the Conduit in Fleet-street.[2] Supt at my father's, where in came Mrs. The. Turner[3] and Madame Morrice, and supt with us. After that my wife and I went home with them, and so to our own home.

[2nd]. In the morning before I went forth old East brought me a dozen of bottles of sack, and I gave him a shilling for his pains. Then I went to Mr. Sheply,[4] who was drawing of sack in the wine cellar to send to other places as a gift from my Lord, and told me that my Lord had given him order to give me the dozen of bottles. Thence I went to the Temple to speak with Mr. Calthropp about the £60 due to my Lord,[5] but missed of him, he being abroad. Then I went to Mr. Crew's[6] and borrowed £10 of Mr. Andrewes

[1] Exeter House, which stood on the north side of the Strand, to the east of Bedford House, was built by Sir William Cecil, Lord Burghley, whose eldest son was created first Earl of Exeter. It was also known as Cecil and Burleigh House. Exeter Street and Burleigh Street mark the site of the house.
[2] The conduit was situated near the north end of Salisbury Square. Monk's lodgings were close by.
[3] Theophila Turner, daughter of Sergeant John and Jane Turner, who married Sir Arthur Harris, Bart. She died 1686.
[4] W. Shepley was a servant of Admiral Sir Edward Montagu (afterwards Earl of Sandwich), with whom Pepys was frequently brought in contact. He was steward at Hinchinbroke.
[5] Sir Edward Montagu, born 1625, son of Sir Sidney Montagu, by Paulina, daughter of John Pepys of Cottenham, married Jemima, daughter of John Crew of Stene. He died in action against the Dutch in Southwold Bay, May 28th, 1672. The title of "My Lord" here applied to Montagu before he was created Earl of Sandwich is of the same character as that given to General Lambert.
[6] John Crew, born 1598, eldest son of Sir Thomas Crew, Sergeant-at-Law and Speaker of the House of Commons. He sat for Brackley in the Long Parliament. Created Baron Crew of Stene, in the county of Northampton, at the coronation of Charles II. He married Jemima, daughter and co-heir of Edward Walgrave (or Waldegrave) of Lawford, Essex. His house was in Lincoln's Inn Fields. He died December 12th, 1679.

6

for my own use, and so went to my office, where there was nothing to do. Then I walked a great while in Westminster Hall, where I heard that Lambert was coming up to London; that my Lord Fairfax[1] was in the head of the Irish brigade, but it was not

[1] Thomas, Lord Fairfax, Generalissimo of the Parliament forces. After the Restoration, he retired to his country seat, where he lived in private till his death, 1671. In a volume (autograph) of Lord Fairfax's Poems, preserved in the British Museum, 11744, f. 42, the following lines occur upon the 30th of January, on which day the King was beheaded. It is believed that they have never been printed.

> "O let that day from time be bloted quitt,
>   And beleef of 't in next age be waved,
> In depest silence that act concealed might,
>   That so the creadet of our nation might be saved;
> But if the powre devine hath ordered this,
> His will's the law, and our must aquiess."

These wretched verses have obviously no merit; but they are curious as showing that Fairfax, who had refused to act as one of Charles I.'s judges, continued long afterwards to entertain a proper horror for that unfortunate monarch's fate. It has recently been pointed out to me, that the lines were not originally composed by Fairfax, being only a poor translation of the spirited lines of Statius (Sylvarum lib. v. cap. ii. l. 88):—

7

certain what he would declare for. The House was to-day upon
finishing the act for the Council of State, which they did; and for
the indemnity to the soldiers; and were to sit again thereupon in
the afternoon. Great talk that many places have declared for a
free Parliament; and it is believed that they will be forced to fill
up the House with the old members. From the Hall I called at
home, and so went to Mr. Crew's (my wife she was to go to her
father's), thinking to have dined, but I came too late, so Mr.
Moore[1] and I and another gentleman went out and drank a cup
of ale together in the new market,[2] and there I eat some bread and
cheese for my dinner. After that Mr. Moore and I went as far as
Fleet-street together and parted, he going into the City, I to find
Mr. Calthrop, but failed again of finding him, so returned to Mr.
Crew's again, and from thence went along with Mrs. Jemimah[3]
home, and there she taught me how to play at cribbage.[4] Then I
went home, and finding my wife gone to see Mrs. Hunt, I went
to Will's,[5] and there sat with Mr. Ashwell talking and singing

"Excidat illa dies ævo, ne postera credant
Secula, nos certè taceamus; et obruta multâ
Nocte tegi propriæ patiamur crimina gentis."

These verses were first applied by the President de Thou to the massacre
of St. Bartholomew, 1572; and in our day, by Mr. Pitt, in his memorable
speech in the House of Commons, January, 1793, after the murder of Louis
XVI.–B.

[1] This gentleman was a connection of Sir Edward Montagu's, whose daughter
Jemima he wanted to marry, but he was not received with favour by her
(see January 17th, 1659-60).

[2] Clare Market, named after John Holles, Earl of Clare, was at first known as
New Market. John Willis's "Mnemonica, or the Art of Memory," was pub-
lished in 1661, by "Leonard Sowerby at the Turnstile near New Market in
Lincoln's Inn Fields."

[3] Mrs. Jemimah, or Mrs. Jem, was Jemima, eldest daughter of Sir Edward
Montagu. At this time she and her sister, Mrs. Ann, seem to have been
living alone with their maids in London, and Pepys's duty was to look after
them.

[4] Pepys does not appear to have made any progress in learning the game, for
on May 15th he writes that he cannot play it. "The game at cribbidge" is
described in the "Complete Gamester," 1677, and subsequent editions.

[5] Pepys constantly visited "Will's" about this time; but this could not be
the famous coffee-house in Covent Garden, because he mentions visiting there
for the first time, February 3rd, 1663-64. It was most probably the house of
William Joyce, who kept a place of entertainment at Westminster (see Jan.
29th).

till nine o'clock, and so home, there, having not eaten anything but bread and cheese, my wife cut me a slice of brawn which I received from my Lady,[1] which proves as good as ever I had any. So to bed, and my wife had a very bad night of it through wind and cold.

[3rd]. I went out in the morning, it being a great frost, and walked to Mrs. Turner's[2] to stop her from coming to see me to-day, because of Mrs. Jem's coming, thence I went to the Temple to speak with Mr. Calthrop, and walked in his chamber an hour, but could not see him, so went to Westminster, where I found soldiers in my office to receive money, and paid it them. At noon went home, where Mrs. Jem, her maid, Mr. Sheply, Hawly, and Moore dined with me on a piece of beef and cabbage, and a collar of brawn. We then fell to cards till dark, and then I went home with Mrs. Jem, and meeting Mr. Hawly got him to bear me company to Chancery Lane, where I spoke with Mr. Calthrop, he told me that Sir James Calthrop was lately dead, but that he would write to his Lady, that the money may be speedily paid. Thence back to White Hall, where I understood that the Parliament had passed the act for indemnity to the soldiers and officers that would come in, in so many days, and that my Lord Lambert should have benefit of the said act. They had also voted that all vacancies in the House, by the death of any of the old members, shall be filled up; but those that are living shall not be called in. Thence I went home, and there found Mr. Hunt and his wife, and Mr. Hawly, who sat with me till ten at night at cards, and so broke up and to bed.

[4th]. Early came Mr. Vanly[3] to me for his half-year's rent, which I had not in the house, but took his man to the office and there paid him. Then I went down into the Hall and to Will's,

[1] Jemima, wife of Sir Edward Montagu, daughter of John Crew of Stene, afterwards Lord Crew.

[2] Jane, daughter of John Pepys of South Creake, Norfolk, married to John Turner, Sergeant-at-law, Recorder of York; their only child, Theophila, frequently mentioned as The. or Theoph., became the wife of Sir Arthur Harris, Bart., of Stowford, Devon, and died 1686, s. p.

[3] Mr. Vanley appears to have been Pepys's landlord; he is mentioned again in the Diary on September 20th, 1660.

where Hawly brought a piece of his Cheshire cheese, and we were merry with it. Then into the Hall again, where I met with the Clerk and Quarter Master of my Lord's troop, and took them to the Swan[1] and gave them their morning's draft,[2] they being just come to town. Mr. Jenkins shewed me two bills of exchange for money to receive upon my Lord's and my pay. It snowed hard all this morning, and was very cold, and my nose was much swelled with cold. Strange the difference of men's talk! Some say that Lambert must of necessity yield up; others, that he is very strong, and that the Fifth-monarchy-men[3] [will] stick to him, if he declares for a free Parliament. Chillington was sent yesterday to him with the vote of pardon and indemnity from the Parliament. From the Hall I came home, where I found letters from Hinchinbroke[4] and news of Mr. Sheply's going thither the next week. I dined at home, and from thence went to Will's to Shaw, who promised me to go along with me to Atkinson's about some money, but I found him at cards with Spicer[5] and D. Vines,[6] and could not get him along with me. I was vext at this, and went and walked in the Hall, where I heard that the Parliament spent this

---

[1] Pepys visited several Swan taverns, so that it is impossible to say which one is here referred to. It might have been either the one in the Palace Yard or the one in King Street, Westminster.

[2] It was not usual at this time to sit down to breakfast, but instead a morning draught was taken at a tavern.

[3] The rising of the Fifth Monarchy men is described later on.

[4] Hinchinbroke was Sir Edward Montagu's seat, from which he afterwards took his second title. Hinchinbroke House, so often mentioned in the Diary, stood about half a mile to the westward of the town of Huntingdon. It was erected late in the reign of Elizabeth, by Sir Henry Cromwell, on the site of a Benedictine nunnery, granted at the Dissolution, with all its appurtenances, to his father, Richard Williams, who had assumed the name of Cromwell, and whose grandson, Sir Oliver, was the uncle and godfather of the Protector. The knight, who was renowned for his hospitality, had the honour of entertaining King James at Hinchinbroke, but, getting into pecuniary difficulties, was obliged to sell his estates, which were conveyed, July 28th, 1627, to Sir Sidney Montagu of Barnwell, father of the first Earl of Sandwich, in whose descendant they are still vested. On the morning of the 22nd January, 1830, during the minority of the seventh Earl, Hinchinbroke was almost entirely destroyed by fire, but the pictures and furniture were mostly saved, and the house has been rebuilt in the Elizabethan style, and the interior greatly improved, under the direction of Edward Blore, Esq., R.A.—B.

[5] Dick Spicer, afterwards a brother clerk with Pepys of the Privy Seal.

[6] Dick Vines.

day in fasting and prayer; and in the afternoon came letters from
the North, that brought certain news that my Lord Lambert his
forces were all forsaking him, and that he was left with only fifty
horse, and that he did now declare for the Parliament himself;
and that my Lord Fairfax did also rest satisfied, and had laid
down his arms, and that what he had done was only to secure the
country against my Lord Lambert his raising of money, and free
quarter. I went to Will's again, where I found them still at cards,
and Spicer had won 14s. of Shaw and Vines. Then I spent a little
time with G. Vines[1] and Maylard at Vines's at our viols.[2] So
home, and from thence to Mr. Hunt's, and sat with them and Mr.
Hawly at cards till ten at night, and was much made of by them.
Home and so to bed, but much troubled with my nose, which was
much swelled.

[5th]. I went to my office, where the money was again expected
from the Excise office, but none brought, but was promised to be
sent this afternoon. I dined with Mr. Sheply, at my Lord's lodgings, upon his turkey-pie. And so to my office again; where the
Excise money was brought, and some of it told to soldiers till it
was dark. Then I went home, and after writing a letter to my
Lord and told him the news that the Parliament hath this night
voted that the members that were discharged from sitting in the
years 1648 and 49, were duly discharged; and that there should
be writs issued presently for the calling of others in their places,
and that Monk and Fairfax were commanded up to town, and
that the Prince's lodgings[3] were to be provided for Monk at Whitehall. Then my wife and I, it being a great frost, went to Mrs.
Jem's, in expectation to eat a sack-posset, but Mr. Edward[4] not
coming it was put off; and so I left my wife playing at cards with
her, and went myself with my lanthorn to Mr. Fage, to consult

---

[1] George Vines.

[2] It was usual to have a "chest of viols," which consisted of six, viz., two
trebles, two tenors, and two basses (see note in North's "Memoirs of Musick,"
ed. Rimbault, p. 70). The bass viol was also called the *viola da gamba*, because
it was held between the legs.

[3] Later on (January 9th) it is said that Bradshaw's lodgings were being prepared for Monk.

[4] Edward Montagu, son of Sir Edward, and afterwards Lord Hinchinbroke.

concerning my nose, who told me it was nothing but cold, and after that we did discourse concerning public business; and he told me it is true the City had not time enough to do much, but they are resolved to shake off the soldiers; and that unless there be a free Parliament chosen, he did believe there are half the Common Council will not levy any money by order of this Parliament. From thence I went to my father's, where I found Mrs. Ramsey and her grandchild, a pretty girl, and staid a while and talked with them and my mother, and then took my leave, only heard of an invitation to go to dinner to-morrow to my cosen Thomas Pepys.[1] I went back to Mrs. Jem, and took my wife and Mrs. Sheply, and went home.

[6th]. This morning Mr. Sheply and I did eat our breakfast at Mrs. Harper's, (my brother John[2] being with me,) upon a cold turkey-pie and a goose. From thence I went to my office, where we paid money to the soldiers till one o'clock, at which time we made an end, and I went home and took my wife and went to my cosen, Thomas Pepys, and found them just sat down to dinner, which was very good; only the venison pasty was palpable beef, which was not handsome. After dinner I took my leave, leaving my wife with my cozen Stradwick,[3] and went to Westminster to Mr. Vines, where George[4] and I fiddled a good while, Dick and his wife (who was lately brought to bed) and her sister being there, but Mr. Hudson not coming according to his promise, I went away, and calling at my house on the wench, I took her and the lanthorn with me to my cosen Stradwick, where, after a good supper, there being there my father, mother, brothers, and sister, my

---

[1] Thomas Pepys, probably the son of Thomas Pepys of London (born 1595), brother of Samuel's father, John Pepys.

[2] John Pepys was born in 1641, and his brother Samuel took great interest in his welfare, but he did not do any great credit to his elder. He took orders in 1666, and in 1670 was, through the influence of his brother Samuel, appointed Clerk to the Trinity House. In 1674 he was appointed joint Clerk of the Acts with Thomas Hayter. He died in March, 1676-77, leaving some debts which Samuel paid.

[3] Elizabeth, daughter of Richard Pepys, Lord Chief Justice of Ireland, and wife of Thomas Stradwick.

[4] George Vines and Dick Vines.

cosen Scott[1] and his wife, Mr. Drawwater and his wife, and her brother, Mr. Stradwick, we had a brave cake brought us, and in the choosing, Pall[2] was Queen, and Mr. Stradwick was King. After that my wife and I bid adieu and came home, it being still a great frost.

[7th]. At my office as I was receiving money of the probate of wills, in came Mrs. Turner, Theoph., Madame Morrice, and Joyce,[3] and after I had done I took them home to my house, and Mr. Hawly came after, and I got a dish of steaks and a rabbit for them, while they were playing a game or two at cards. In the middle of our dinner a messenger from Mr. Downing came to fetch me to him, so leaving Mr. Hawly there, I went and was forced to stay till night in expectation of the French Embassador,[4] who at last came, and I had a great deal of good discourse with one of his gentlemen concerning the reason of the difference between the zeal of the French and the Spaniard. After he was gone I went home, and found my friends still at cards, and after that I went along with them to Dr. Whores (sending my wife to Mrs. Jem's to a sack-posset), where I heard some symphony and songs of his own making, performed by Mr. May,[5] Harding,[6] and Mallard. Afterwards I put my friends into a coach, and went to Mrs. Jem's, where I wrote a letter to my Lord by the post, and had my part of the posset which was saved for me, and so we went home, and put in at my Lord's lodgings, where we staid late, eating of part of his turkey-pie, and reading of Quarles' Emblems.[7] So home and to bed.

---

[1] J. Scott was husband of Judith, another daughter of Chief Justice Richard Pepys.

[2] Paulina, sister of Samuel, who was born 1640, and married John Jackson of Brampton, co. Hunts. She had two sons, Samuel and John, the second being heir to his uncle Samuel.

[3] This was probably Joyce Norton, who was cousin to the Turners as well as to Pepys. She was the daughter of Richard Norton of South Creake and his wife, Barbara Pepys.

[4] Antoine de Neuville, Seigneur de Bordeaux.

[5] Probably Hugh May, who after 1662 was established as an architect.

[6] John Harding was one of the Gentlemen of the King's Private Music in 1674.

[7] The "Emblems, Divine and Moral" of Francis Quarles was first published in 1635. There is no copy of this book now in the Pepysian Library.

[8th] (Sunday). In the morning I went to Mr. Gunning's, where a good sermon, wherein he showed the life of Christ, and told us good authority for us to believe that Christ did follow his father's trade, and was a carpenter till thirty years of age. From thence to my father's to dinner, where I found my wife, who was forced to dine there, we not having one coal of fire in the house, and it being very hard frosty weather. In the afternoon my father, he going to a man's to demand some money due to my Aunt Bell,[1] my wife and I went to Mr. Mossum's,[2] where a strange doctor made a very good sermon. From thence sending my wife to my father's, I went to Mrs. Turner's, and staid a little while, and then to my father's, where I found Mr. Sheply, and after supper went home together. Here I heard of the death of Mr. Palmer, and that he was to be buried at Westminster to-morrow.

[9th]. For these two or three days I have been much troubled with thoughts how to get money to pay them that I have borrowed money of, by reason of my money being in my uncle's hands. I rose early this morning, and looked over and corrected my brother John's speech, which he is to make the next apposition,[3] and after that I went towards my office, and in my way met with W. Simons,[4] Muddiman, and Jack Price, and went with them to Harper's and in many sorts of talk I staid till two of the clock in the afternoon. I found Muddiman a good scholar, an arch rogue; and owns that though he writes new[s] books for the Parliament, yet he did declare that he did it only to get money; and did talk very basely of many of them. Among other things, W. Simons told me how his uncle Scobell[5] was on Saturday last called to the bar, for entering in the journal of the House, for the year 1653,

---

[1] Mrs. Bell; she died of the plague.

[2] Dr. Robert Mossum, author of several sermons preached in London, and printed about the time of the Restoration, who was in 1666 made Bishop of Derry. In the title-page of his "Apology in behalf of the Sequestered Clergy," printed in 1660, he calls himself "Preacher of God's word at St. Peter's, Paul's Wharf, London," and at the end, "one of the sequestered clergy." This pamphlet is reprinted in "Somers Tracts," vol. vii. p. 237, edit. 1812.

[3] Declamations at St. Paul's School, in which there were opponents and respondents.

[4] William Simons.

[5] Henry Scobell was Clerk to the House of Commons.

these words: "This day his Excellence the Lord G[eneral] Cromwell dissolved this House"; which words the Parliament voted a forgery, and demanded of him how they came to be entered. He answered that they were his own handwriting, and that he did it by virtue of his office, and the practice of his predecessor;[1] and that the intent of the practice was to let posterity know how such and such a Parliament was dissolved, whether by the command of the King, or by their own neglect, as the last House of Lords was; and that to this end, he had said and writ that it was dissolved by his Excellence the Lord G[eneral]; and that for the word dissolved, he never at the time did hear of any other term; and desired pardon if he would not dare to make a word himself when it was six years after, before they came themselves to call it an interruption; but they were so little satisfied with this answer, that they did chuse a committee to report to the House, whether this crime of Mr. Scobell's did come within the act of indemnity or no. Thence I went with Muddiman to the Coffee-House,[2] and gave 18d. to be entered of the Club. Thence into the Hall, where I heard for certain that Monk was coming to London, and that Bradshaw's[3] lodgings were preparing for him. Thence to Mrs. Jem's, and found her in bed, and she was afraid that it would prove the small-pox. Thence back to Westminster Hall, where I heard how Sir H. Vane[4] was this day voted out of the House, and to sit no more there; and that he would retire himself to his house at Raby,[5] as also all the rest of the nine officers that had their commissions formerly taken away from them, were commanded to their farthest houses from London during the pleasure of the Parliament. Here I met with the Quarter Master of my Lord's

---

[1] Henry Elsynge, born at Battersea, appointed Clerk of the House of Commons through the influence of Archbishop Laud, resigned in 1648 to avoid taking part in the proceedings against Charles I. He retired to Hounslow, where he died 1654.

[2] Miles's Coffee House in Old Palace Yard, where was held the Rota Club, founded by James Harrington, which is referred to again further on.

[3] John Bradshaw (born 1602), President of the Council of State, died at the Deanery, Westminster, on October 31st, 1659.

[4] Sir Harry Vane the younger, an inflexible republican. He was executed in 1662, on a charge of conspiring the death of Charles I.

[5] Raby Castle in Durham, now the seat of Sir Harry Vane's descendant, Lord Barnard.

troop, and his clerk Mr. Jennings,[1] and took them home, and gave
them a bottle of wine, and the remainder of my collar of brawn,
and so good night. After that came in Mr. Hawly, who told me
that I was mist this day at my office, and that to-morrow I must
pay all the money that I have, at which I was put to a great loss
how I should get money to make up my cash, and so went to bed
in great trouble.

[10th]. Went out early, and in my way met with Greatorex,[2] and
at an alehouse he shewed me the first sphere of wire that ever he
made, and indeed it was very pleasant; thence to Mr. Crew's, and
borrowed £10, and so to my office, and was able to pay my
money. Thence into the Hall, and meeting the Quarter Master,
Jenings, and Captain Rider, we four went to a cook's to dinner.
Thence Jenings and I into London (it being through heat of the

---

[1] Mr. Jennings is mentioned again August 8th, 1660.
[2] Ralph Greatorex, the well-known mathematical instrument maker of his
day. He is frequently mentioned by Pepys.

sun a great thaw and dirty) to show our bills of return, and coming back drank a pint of wine at the Star in Cheapside.[1] So to Westminster, overtaking Captain Okeshott[2] in his silk cloak, whose sword got hold of many people in walking. Thence to the Coffee-house, where were a great confluence of gentlemen; viz. Mr. Harrington,[3] Poultny,[4] chairman, Gold,[5] Dr. Petty,[6] &c., where admirable discourse till 9 at night. Thence with Doling[7] to Mother Lam's, who told me how this day Scott[8] was made Intelligencer, and that the rest of the members that were objected against last night, their business was to be heard this day se'nnight. Thence I went home and wrote a letter, and went to Har-

[1] There are two tokens of the Star Tavern in Cheapside, one dated 1648 and the other 1652 (see "Boyne's Trade Tokens," ed. Williamson, vol. i. 1889, pp. 562, 563).

[2] Captain Okeshott is not mentioned again in the Diary.

[3] James Harrington, the political writer, born January, 1611, author of "Oceana," and founder of a club called The Rota, in 1659, which met at Miles's coffee-house in Old Palace Yard, and lasted only a few months. He attended Charles I. on the scaffold. In 1661 he was sent to the Tower, on suspicion of treasonable designs, and was removed from thence to St. Nicholas Island, near Plymouth, but his intellect having failed his friends obtained his discharge on giving security for his behaviour. He died September 11th, 1667. Henry Nevill and Harrington "had every night a meeting at the (then) Turke's Head, in the New Palace Yard, where they take water, the next house to the Staires, at one Miles's, where was made purposely a large oval table, with a passage in the middle, for Miles to deliver his coffee. About it sate his disciples and the virtuosi."—Aubrey's *Bodleian Letters*, 1813, vol. ii. pt. 2, p. 371.

[4] Sir William Poultny, or Pulteney, subsequently M.P. for Westminster, and a Commissioner of the Privy Seal under King William. Died 1671. Grandfather to William Earl of Bath.

[5] Edward Gold, the merchant. His name occurs among the Governors of Sir Roger Cholmley's school at Highgate.

[6] William Petty, M.D., an eminent physician and the founder of Political Economy (or Political Arithmetic, as he called it), born May 16th, 1623. He was elected Professor of Music at Gresham College by the interest of Captain John Graunt. Knighted in 1661. He died December 16th, 1687. His widow was created Baroness Shelburne in the Peerage of Ireland, and their eldest son succeeded to the title.

[7] Thomas Doling.

[8] Thomas Scott, M.P., was made Secretary of State to the Commonwealth on the 17th of this same January. He signed the death warrant of Charles I., for which he was executed at Charing Cross, October 16th, 1660. He gloried in his offence, and desired to have written on his tombstone, "Thomas Scott who adjudged to death the late king."

per's, and staid there till Tom[1] carried it to the postboy at White-hall. So home to bed.

[11th]. Being at Will's with Captain Barker, who hath paid me £300 this morning at my office, in comes my father, and with him I walked, and leave him at W. Joyce's, and went myself to Mr. Crew's, but came too late to dine, and therefore after a game at shittle-cocks[2] with Mr. Walgrave[3] and Mr. Edward, I returned to my father, and taking him from W. Joyce's, who was not abroad himself, we inquired of a porter, and by his direction went to an alehouse, where after a cup or two we parted. I went towards London, and in my way went in to see Crowly, who was now grown a very great loon and very tame. Thence to Mr. Steven's with a pair of silver snuffers, and bought a pair of shears to cut silver, and so homeward again. From home I went to see Mrs. Jem, who was in bed, and now granted to have the small-pox. Back again, and went to the Coffee-house, but tarried not, and so home.

[12th]. I drink my morning at Harper's with Mr. Sheply and a seaman, and so to my office, where Captain Holland[4] came to see me, and appointed a meeting in the afternoon. Then wrote letters to Hinchinbroke and sealed them at Will's, and after that went home, and thence to the Half Moon, where I found the Captain and Mr. Billingsly and Newman, a barber, where we were very merry, and had the young man that plays so well on the Welsh harp. Billingsly paid for all. Thence home, and finding my letters this day not gone by the carrier I new sealed them, but my broth-er Tom coming we fell into discourse about my intention to feast the Joyces. I sent for a bit of meat for him from the cook's, and forgot to send my letters this night. So I went to bed, and in dis-course broke to my wife what my thoughts were concerning my design of getting money by, &c.

---

[1] Thomas Pepys, Samuel's brother, born 1634 and died 1664. He carried on his father's business as a tailor.

[2] The game of battledore and shuttlecock was formerly much played even in tennis courts, and was a very violent game.

[3] Edward Walgrave, or Waldegrave, of Lawford, Essex, father of Mrs. Crew.

[4] Captain Philip Holland, at one time captain of "Assurance" (see December 11th, 1660); he renewed his commission on June 3rd, 1660.

[13th]. Coming in the morning to my office, I met with Mr. Fage and took him to the Swan.[1] He told me how high Haselrigge,[2] and Morly,[3] the last night began at my Lord Mayor's[4] to exclaim against the City of London, saying that they had forfeited their charter. And how the Chamberlain of the City did take them down, letting them know how much they were formerly beholding to the City, &c. He also told me that Monk's letter that came to them by the sword-bearer was a cunning piece, and that which they did not much trust to; but they were resolved to make no more applications to the Parliament, nor to pay any money, unless the secluded members be brought in, or a free Parliament chosen. Thence to my office, where nothing to do. So to Will's with Mr. Pinkney,[5] who invited me to their feast at his Hall the next Monday. Thence I went home and took my wife and dined at Mr. Wade's, and after that we went and visited Catan.[6] From thence home again, and my wife was very unwilling to let me go forth, but with some discontent would go out if I did, and I going forth towards Whitehall, I saw she followed me, and so I staid and took her round through Whitehall, and so carried her home angry. Thence I went to Mrs. Jem, and found her up and merry, and that it did not prove the small-pox, but only the swine-pox; so I played a game or two at cards with her. And so to Mr. Vines, where he and I and Mr. Hudson played half-a-dozen things, there being there Dick's wife and her sister. After that I went home and

[1] The Swan tavern in Fenchurch Street.

[2] Sir Arthur Haselrigge, Bart., of Nosely, co. Leicester, and M.P. for that county. He brought forward the Bill in the House of Commons for the attainder of the Earl of Strafford, and he was one of the five members charged with high treason by Charles I. in 1642. Colonel of a regiment in the Parliament army, and much esteemed by Cromwell. In March, 1659-60, he was committed to the Tower by Monk, where he died, January, 1660-61. Although one of the King's judges, he did not sign the death-warrant.

[3] Colonel Morley, one of the Council of State, Lieutenant of the Tower. John Evelyn attempted to bring him over to the King's side, but he hesitated, and lost the honour of restoring the King.

[4] The Lord Mayor was Thomas Allen, created a baronet at the Restoration.

[5] Leonard Pinckney was one of the four tellers of the Receipt of the Exchequer, and he acted as Clerk of the Kitchen at Charles II.'s Coronation feast. His son, William Pinckney, was admitted into his place of Teller in 1661.

[6] Catan Stirpin, a girl who afterwards married a Monsieur Petit (see October 23rd, 1660). She is called Kate Sterpin on March 6th, 1659-60.

found my wife gone abroad to Mr. Hunt's, and came in a little after me. So to bed.

[14th]. Nothing to do at our office. Thence into the Hall, and just as I was going to dinner from Westminster Hall with Mr. Moore (with whom I had been in the lobby to hear news, and had spoke with Sir Anthony Ashley Cooper[1] about my Lord's lodgings) to his house, I met with Captain Holland, who told me that he hath brought his wife to my house, so I posted home and got a dish of meat for them. They staid with me all the afternoon, and went hence in the evening. Then I went with my wife, and left her at market and went myself to the Coffee-house, and heard exceeding good argument against Mr. Harrington's assertion, that overbalance of propriety [i.e. property] was the foundation of government. Home, and wrote to Hinchinbroke, and sent that and my other letter that missed of going on Thursday last. So to bed.

[15th]. Having been exceedingly disturbed in the night with the barking of a dog of one of our neighbours that I could not sleep for an hour or two, I slept late, and then in the morning took physic, and so staid within all day. At noon my brother John came to me, and I corrected as well as I could his Greek speech to say at the Apposition, though I believe he himself was as well able to do it as myself. After that we went to read in the great Officiale about the blessing of bells in the Church of Rome.[2] After that my wife and I in pleasant discourse till night, then I went to supper, and after that to make an end of this week's notes in this

---

[1] Sir Anthony Ashley Cooper was born July 22nd, 1621, and received his early instruction from Puritan private tutors. He was admitted into the Society of Lincoln's Inn, February 18th, 1638, and was elected Member of Parliament for Tewkesbury in 1640. For a time he favoured the royal cause, but soon transferred his services to the Commonwealth. He had taken his seat for Downton on the 7th of this January. He was created Baron Ashley in 1661, and Earl of Shaftesbury in 1672.

[2] "Baronius informs us that Pope John XIII. in 968 consecrated a very large new cast bell in the Lateran Church, and gave it the name of John. This is the first instance I meet with of what has been since called 'The baptizing of bells,' a superstition which the reader may find ridiculed in the 'Beehive of the Romish Church,' 1579." A list of the ceremonies is quoted, and instance given of the practice in 14 Hen. VII., when Sir William Symys, Richard Clech, and Maistres Smyth were godfathers and godmother to a bell at Reading. See Brand's "Popular Antiquities," ed. Hazlitt, vol. ii. pp. 239-240.

book, and so to bed. It being a cold day and a great snow my physic did not work so well as it should have done.

[16th]. In the morning I went up to Mr. Crew's, and at his bed-side he gave me direction to go to-morrow with Mr. Edward to Twickenham, and likewise did talk to me concerning things of state; and expressed his mind how just it was that the secluded members should come to sit again. I went from thence, and in my way went into an alehouse and drank my morning draft with Matthew Andrews and two or three more of his friends, coach-men. And of one of them I did hire a coach to carry us to-morrow to Twickenham. From thence to my office, where nothing to do; but Mr. Downing he came and found me all alone; and did mention to me his going back into Holland, and did ask me whether I would go or no, but gave me little encouragement, but bid me consider of it; and asked me whether I did not think that Mr. Hawly could perform the work of my office alone or no. I confess I was at a great loss, all the day after, to bethink myself how to carry this business. At noon, Harry Ethall came to me and went along with Mr. Maylard by coach as far as Salsbury Court, and there we set him down, and we went to the Clerks, where we came a little too late, but in a closet we had a very good dinner by Mr. Pinkny's courtesy, and after dinner we had pretty good singing, and one, Hazard, sung alone after the old fashion, which was very much cried up, but I did not like it. Thence we went to the Green Dragon, on Lambeth Hill,[1] both the Mr. Pink-ney's, Smith, Harrison, Morrice, that sang the bass, Sheply and I, and there we sang of all sorts of things, and I ventured with good success upon things at first sight, and after that I played on my flageolet,[2] and staid there till nine o'clock, very merry and drawn on with one song after another till it came to be so late. After that Sheply, Harrison and myself, we went towards West-minster on foot, and at the Golden Lion, near Charing Cross, we went in and drank a pint of wine, and so parted, and thence home, where I found my wife and maid a-washing. I staid up

---

[1] There is a token of the Green Dragon on Lambeth Hill, dated 1651 (see "Boyne's Trade Tokens," ed. Williamson, vol. i., 1889, p. 650).

[2] The flageolet is a small flute à bec.

till the bell-man came by with his bell just under my window as I was writing of this very line, and cried, "Past one of the clock, and a cold, frosty, windy morning." I then went to bed, and left my wife and the maid a-washing still.

[17th]. Early I went to Mr. Crew's, and having given Mr. Edward money to give the servants, I took him into the coach that waited for us and carried him to my house, where the coach waited for me while I and the child went to Westminster Hall, and bought him some pictures. In the Hall I met Mr. Woodfine, and took him to Will's and drank with him. Thence the child and I to the coach, where my wife was ready, and so we went towards Twickenham. In our way, at Kensington we understood how that my Lord Chesterfield[1] had killed another gentleman about half an hour before, and was fled. We went forward and came about one of the clock to Mr. Fuller's[2] but he was out of town, so we had a dinner there, and I gave the child 40s. to give to the two ushers. After that we parted and went homewards, it being market day at Brainford [Brentford]. I set my wife down and went with the coach to Mr. Crew's, thinking to have spoke

---

[1] Philip Stanhope, second Earl of Chesterfield, ob. 1713, æt. suæ 80. We learn, from the memoir prefixed to his "Printed Correspondence," that he fought three duels, disarming and wounding his first and second antagonists, and killing the third. The name of the unfortunate gentleman who fell on this occasion was Woolly. Lord Chesterfield, absconding, went to Breda, where he obtained the royal pardon from Charles II. He acted a busy part in the eventful times in which he lived, and was remarkable for his steady adherence to the Stuarts. Lord Chesterfield's letter to Charles II., and the King's answer granting the royal pardon, occur in the Correspondence published by General Sir John Murray, in 1829.

"Jan 17th, 1659. The Earl of Chesterfield and Dr. Woolly's son of Hammersmith, had a quarrel about a mare of eighteen pounds price: the quarrel would not be reconciled, insomuch that a challenge passed between them. They fought a duel on the backside of Mr. Colby's house at Kensington, where the Earl and he had several passes. The Earl wounded him in two places, and would fain have then ended, but the stubbornness and pride of heart of Mr. Woolly would not give over, and the next pass [he] was killed on the spot. The Earl fled to Chelsea, and there took water and escaped. The jury found it chance-medley."—Rugge's *Diurnal*, Addit. MSS., British Museum. —B.

[2] William Fuller, of Magdalen Hall, Oxford, was a schoolmaster at Twickenham during the Rebellion, and at the Restoration became Dean of St. Patrick's, and, in 1663, Bishop of Limerick, from which see, in 1667, he was translated to Lincoln. He died April 23rd, 1675.

with Mr. Moore and Mrs. Jem, he having told me the reason of his melancholy was some unkindness from her after so great expressions of love, and how he had spoke to her friends and had their consent, and that he would desire me to take an occasion of speaking with her, but by no means not to heighten her discontent or distaste whatever it be, but to make it up if I can. But he being out of doors, I went away and went to see Mrs. Jem, who was now very well again, and after a game or two at cards, I left her. So I went to the Coffee Club, and heard very good discourse; it was in answer to Mr. Harrington's answer, who said that the state of the Roman government was not a settled government and so it was no wonder that the balance of propriety [*i.e.* property] was in one hand, and the command in another, it being therefore always in a posture of war; but it was carried by ballot, that it was a steady government, though it is true by the voices it had been carried before that it was an unsteady government; so to-morrow it is to be proved by the opponents that the balance lay in one hand, and the government in another. Thence I went to Westminster, and met Shaw and Washington,[1] who told me how this day Sydenham[2] was voted out of the House for sitting any more this Parliament, and that Salloway[3] was voted out likewise and sent to the Tower, during the pleasure of the House. Home and wrote by the Post, and carried to Whitehall, and coming back turned in at Harper's, where Jack Price was, and I drank with him and he told me, among other things, how much the Protector[4] is altered, though he would

---

[1] Mr. Washington the purser, see July 2nd, 1660.

[2] Colonel William Sydenham had been an active officer during the Civil Wars, on the Parliament side; M.P. for Dorsetshire, Governor of Melcombe, and one of the Committee of Safety. He was the elder brother of the celebrated physician of that name.—B.

[3] In the Journals of that date, Major Richard Salwey. Colonel Calway is mentioned as a prisoner in the Tower, 1663-4, in Bayley's "History of the Tower of London," 1830, p. 590.

[4] Richard Cromwell, third son of Oliver Cromwell, born October 4th, 1626, admitted a member of Lincoln's Inn, May 27th, 1647, fell into debt and devoted himself to hunting and field sports. His succession to his father as Protector was universally accepted at first, but the army soon began to murmur because he was not a general. Between the dissensions of various parties he fell, and the country was left in a state of anarchy. He went abroad

seem to bear out his trouble very well, yet he is scarce able to
talk sense with a man; and how he will say that "Who should
a man trust, if he may not trust to a brother and an uncle;" [1] and
"how much those men have to answer before God Almighty,
for their playing the knave with him as they did." He told me
also, that there was £100,000 offered, and would have been
taken for his restitution, had not the Parliament come in as they
did again; and that he do believe that the Protector will live to
give a testimony of his valour and revenge yet before he dies,
and that the Protector will say so himself sometimes. Thence I
went home, it being late and my wife in bed.

[18th]. To my office and from thence to Will's, and there Mr.
Sheply brought me letters from the carrier and so I went home.
After that to Wilkinson's,[2] where we had a dinner for Mr. Talbot, Adams, Pinkny and his son, but his son did not come. Here
we were very merry, and while I was here Mr. Fuller came
thither and staid a little while. After that we all went to my
Lord's, whither came afterwards Mr. Harrison, and by chance
seeing Mr. Butler[3] coming by I called him in and so we sat
drinking a bottle of wine till night. At which time Mistress Ann[4]
came with the key of my Lord's study for some things, and so
we all broke up and after I had gone to my house and inter-

---

early in the summer of 1660, and lived abroad for some years, returning to
England in 1680. After his fall he bore the name of John Clarke. Died at
Cheshunt, July 12th, 1712.

[1] Fleetwood and Desborough played a double game. John Desborough, born
1608, second son of James Disbrowe, married, 1636, Jane, sister to Oliver
Cromwell; Major-General, 1648. Charles Fleetwood, son of Sir William
Fleetwood, Cup-bearer to James I. and Charles I.; Lord Deputy of Ireland
(for a time being succeeded by Henry Cromwell), became Cromwell's son-in-
law by his marriage with Ireton's widow, and a member of the Council of
State. He seemed disposed to have espoused Charles II.'s interests, but had not
resolution enough to execute his design. At the Restoration, he was excepted
out of the Act of Indemnity, and spent the remainder of his life in retirement
at Stoke Newington. He died 1692.

[2] Mr. Wilkinson was landlord of the Crown in King Street, Westminster.

[3] Mr. Butler is usually styled by Pepys Mons. l'Impertinent.

[4] Probably Mrs. (afterwards Lady) Anne Montagu, daughter of Sir Edward
Montagu, and sister to Mrs. Jem.

preted my Lord's letter by his character[1] I came to her again and went with her to her lodging and from thence to Mr. Crew's, where I advised with him what to do about my Lord's lodgings and what answer to give to Sir Ant. Cooper and so I came home and to bed. All the world is at a loss to think what Monk will do: the City saying that he will be for them, and the Parliament saying he will be for them.

[19th]. This morning I was sent for to Mr. Downing, and at his bed side he told me, that he had a kindness for me, and that he thought that he had done me one; and that was, that he had got me to be one of the Clerks of the Council; at which I was a little stumbled, and could not tell what to do, whether to thank him or no; but by and by I did; but not very heartily, for I feared that his doing of it was but only to ease himself of the salary[2] which he gives me. After that Mr. Shepley staying below all this time for me went thence and met Mr. Pierce,[3] so at the Harp and Ball drank our morning draft and so to Whitehall where I met with Sir. Ant. Cooper and did give him some answer from my Lord and he did give us leave to keep the lodgings still. And so we did determine thereupon that Mr. Shepley might now go into the country and would do so to-morrow. Back I went by Mr. Downing's order and staid there till twelve o'clock in expectation of one to come to read some writings, but he came not, so I staid all alone reading the answer of the Dutch Ambassador to our State,[4] in answer to the reasons of my Lord's coming home, which he gave for his coming, and did labour herein to contradict my Lord's arguments for his coming home. Thence to my office and so with Mr. Shepley and Moore, to dine upon a turkey with Mrs. Jem, and after that Mr. Moore and I

---

[1] The making of ciphers was a popular amusement about this time. Pepys made several for Montagu, Downing, and others.

[2] This salary appears to have been £50 a year. See 30th of this month.

[3] Pepys had two friends named Pierce, one the surgeon and the other the purser; he usually (but not always) distinguishes them. The one here alluded to was probably the surgeon, and husband of pretty Mrs. Pierce. After the Restoration James Pearse or Pierce became Surgeon to the Duke of York, and he was also Surgeon-General of the Fleet.

[4] Nieuport, who is described by Evelyn as "a judicious, crafty, and wise man."

went to the French Ordinary, where Mr. Downing this day feasted Sir Arth. Haselrigge, and a great many more of the Parliament, and did stay to put him in mind of me. Here he gave me a note to go and invite some other members to dinner to-morrow. So I went to White Hall, and did stay at Marsh's, with Simons, Luellin, and all the rest of the Clerks of the Council, who I hear are all turned out, only the two Leighs, and they do all tell me that my name was mentioned the last night, but that nothing was done in it. Hence I went and did leave some of my notes at the lodgings of the members and so home. To bed.

[20th]. In the morning I went to Mr. Downing's bedside and gave him an account what I had done as to his guests, and I went thence to my Lord Widdrington[1] who I met in the street, going to seal the patents for the Judges to-day, and so could not come to dinner. I called upon Mr. Calthrop about the money due to my Lord. Here I met with Mr. Woodfine and drank with him at the Sun in Chancery Lane and so to Westminster Hall, where at the lobby I spoke with the rest of my guests and so to my office. At noon went by water with Mr. Maylard and Hales to the Swan in Fish Street[2] at our Coal Feast, where we were very merry at our Jole of Ling, and from thence after a great and good dinner

---

[1] Sir Thomas Widdrington was admitted a member of Gray's Inn in 1618. As Recorder of Berwick he addressed a loyal speech to Charles I. in 1633, when he expressed the wish that his throne might be "established before the Lord for ever." He afterwards distinguished himself as a zealous Presbyterian, and in 1648 he was appointed a Commissioner of the Great Seal. When the trial of the King was arranged, he and his fellow Commissioner (Whitelocke) kept out of the way, so that they should have nothing to do with that criminal proceeding. Having declined to serve further as Commissioner, he was made Sergeant for the Commonwealth in 1650, and member of the Council of State in 1651. In 1654 he was again appointed Commissioner of the Great Seal, but was dismissed in 1655. He was elected in 1656 for York and for Northumberland, and chose to sit for the county. He was Speaker of this Parliament, which was dissolved in 1658. He was appointed Lord Chief Baron, but soon after was transferred to his former office of Commissioner of the Great Seal. He had the benefit of the Act of Indemnity at the Restoration, and was the first named of the re-appointed sergeants. He died May 13th, 1664, and was buried in the chancel of the church of St. Giles's-in-the-Fields.

[2] The Swan in Old Fish Street was an old tavern, as it is mentioned in 1413 as the Swan on the Hoop, at the south-east corner of old Fish Street and Bread Street. There is a token of the house. (See "Boyne's Trade Tokens," ed. Williamson, vol. i., 1889, p. 691.)

Mr. Falconberge[1] would go drink a cup of ale at a place where I had like to have shot at a scholar that lay over the house of office. Thence calling on Mr. Stephens and Wootton (with whom I drank) about business of my Lord's I went to the Coffee Club where there was nothing done but choosing of a Committee for orders. Thence to Westminster Hall where Mrs. Lane[2] and the rest of the maids had their white scarfs, all having been at the burial of a young bookseller in the Hall.[3] Thence to Mr. Sheply's and took him to my house and drank with him in order to his going to-morrow. So parted and I sat up late making up my accounts before he go. This day three citizens of London went to meet Monk from the Common Council.[4]

---

[1] Mr. Falconberge (or Falconbridge, as sometimes spelt) appears to have been a clerk in the Exchequer. Mrs. Barker, Mrs. Pepys's woman, was previously in the service of Mr. Falconberge.

[2] Mrs. Betty Lane, a haberdasher or seamstress who occupied a stall in the Hall. She is frequently mentioned in the Diary.

[3] These stationers and booksellers, whose shops disfigured Westminster Hall down to a late period, were a privileged class. In the statutes for appointing licensers and regulating the press, there is a clause exempting them from the pains and penalties of these obnoxious laws. The exception in the 14 Car. II, cap. 33, sec. xx., runs thus: "Provided alsoe . . . that neither this act, nor any therein contained, shall be construed to prohibit any person or persons to sell books or papers who have sold books or papers within Westminster Hall, the Palace of Westminster, or in any shopp or shopps within twenty yards of the Great Gate of Westminster Hall aforesaid before the said 20th November, 1661, but they and every of them may sell books and papers as they have or did before the said 20th November, 1661, within the said Hall, Pallace, and twenty yards aforesaid, and not elsewhere, anything in this act to the contrary in any wise notwithstanding."

[4] "Jan. 20th. Then there went out of the City, by desire of the Lord Mayor and Court of Aldermen, Alderman Fowke and Alderman Vincett, *alias* Vincent, and Mr. Broomfield, to compliment General Monk, who lay at Harborough Town, in Leicestershire."

"Jan. 21st. Because the Speaker was sick, and Lord General Monk so near London, and everybody thought that the City would suffer for their affronts to the soldiery, and because they had sent the sword-bearer to the General without the Parliament's consent, and the three Aldermen were gone to give him the welcome to town, these four lines were in almost everybody's mouth:—

'Monk under a hood, not well understood,
   The City pull in their horns;
The Speaker is out, and sick of the gout,
   And the Parliament sit upon thorns.' "—Rugge's *Diurnal.*—B.

27

[21st]. Up early in finishing my accounts and writing to my Lord and from thence to my Lord's and took leave of Mr. Sheply and possession of all the keys and the house. Thence to my office for some money to pay Mr. Sheply and sent it him by the old man. I then went to Mr. Downing who chid me because I did not give him notice of some of his guests failed him but I told him that I sent our porter to tell him and he was not within, but he told me that he was within till past twelve o'clock. So the porter or he lied. Thence to my office where nothing to do. Then with Mr. Hawly, he and I went to Mr. Crew's and dined there. Thence into London to Mr. Vernon's and I received my £25 due by bill for my troopers' pay. Then back again to Steadman's. At the Mitre,[1] in Fleet-street, in our way calling on Mr. Fage, who told me how the City have some hopes of Monk. Thence to the Mitre, where I drank a pint of wine, the house being in fitting for Banister to come hither from Paget's. Thence to Mrs. Jem and gave her £5. So home and left my money and to White-hall where Luellin and I drank and talked together an hour at Marsh's and so up to the clerks' room, where poor Mr. Cook, a black man, that is like to be put out of his clerk's place, came and railed at me for endeavouring to put him out and get myself in, when I was already in a good condition. But I satisfied him and after I had wrote a letter there to my Lord, wherein I gave him an account how this day Lenthall[2] took his chair again, and [the House] resolved a declaration to be brought in on

---

[1] The Mitre in Fleet Street was opposite St. Dunstan's Church, and stood on the site of part of Messrs. Hoare's banking house. It is said to have dated back to Shakespeare's day. There is a token of "Will. Pagget at the Miter in Fleet Street." Pagget appears to have succeeded John Bayly, who died January, 1648-9. Mitre Tavern, Mitre Court, is another tavern. (See "Boyne's Trade Tokens," ed. Williamson, vol. i., 1889, p. 604.)

[2] William Lenthall, born June, 1591, called to the bar at Lincoln's Inn in 1616. He was chosen Speaker of Charles I.'s second parliament of 1640, but was forced to vacate his chair by Cromwell's forcible expulsion of the members from the House, 1653. He retired to the Rolls, having been sworn in Master of the Rolls in 1643. He was chosen Speaker of Cromwell's second parliament in 1654. Cromwell made him one of his Lords, but when the Long Parliament resumed its sittings, he was induced again to take his seat as Speaker. He was three times Keeper of the Great Seal for short periods of time. After the Restoration he was in fear for his safety, but eventually he obtained the royal pardon, and died September 3rd, 1662.

Monday next to satisfy the world what they intend to do. So home and to bed.

[22nd]. I went in the morning to Mr. Messum's,[1] where I met with W. Thurburn and sat with him in his pew. A very eloquent sermon about the duty of all to give good example in our lives and conversation, which I fear he himself was most guilty of not doing. After sermon, at the door by appointment my wife met me, and so to my father's to dinner, where we had not been to my shame in a fortnight before. After dinner my father shewed me a letter from Mr. Widdrington,[2] of Christ's College, in Cambridge, wherein he do express very great kindness for my brother, and my father intends that my brother shall go to him. To church in the afternoon to Mr. Herring,[3] where a lazy poor sermon. And so home with Mrs. Turner and sitting with her a while we went to my father's where we supt very merry, and so home. This day I began to put on buckles to my shoes, which I have bought yesterday of Mr. Wotton.

[23rd]. In the morning called out to carry £20 to Mr. Downing, which I did and came back, and finding Mr. Pierce, the surgeon, I took him to the Axe[4] and gave him his morning draft. Thence to my office and there did nothing but make up my balance. Came home and found my wife dressing of the girl's head, by which she was made to look very pretty. I went out and paid Wilkinson what I did owe him, and brought a piece of beef home for dinner. Thence I went out and paid Waters, the vint-

---

[1] Dr. Robert Mossum (afterwards Bishop of Derry). See *ante*, January 8th, 1659-60. His name is sometimes written Mossum and sometimes Messum in the Diary.

[2] Dr. Ralph Widdrington, Lady Margaret's Professor and Public Orator, having been ejected from his fellowship by the Master and Fellows of Christ's College, Cambridge, October 28th, 1661, sued out a mandamus to be restored to it; and the matter being referred to commissioners—"The Bishop of London, the Lord Chancellor, and some of the judges"—he obtained restitution.— Kennett's *Register*, p. 552.

[3] John Herring, a Presbyterian minister, who was afterwards ejected from St. Bride's, Fleet Street. His farewell sermon is described in the Diary under date August 17th, 1662.

[4] Probably the Axe on the west side of King Street, Westminster, from the predecessor of which tavern Axe Yard where Pepys lived, took its name.

ner, and went to see Mrs. Jem, where I found my Lady Wright,[1] but Scott was so drunk that he could not be seen. Here I staid and made up Mrs. Ann's bills, and played a game or two at cards, and thence to Westminster Hall, it being very dark. I paid Mrs. Michell,[2] my bookseller, and back to Whitehall, and in the garden, going through to the Stone Gallery[3] I fell into a ditch, it being very dark. At the Clerk's chamber I met with Simons and Luellin, and went with them to Mr. Mount's chamber at the Cock Pit, where we had some rare pot venison, and ale to abundance till almost twelve at night, and after a song round we went home. This day the Parliament sat late, and resolved of the declaration to be printed for the people's satisfaction, promising them a great many good things.

[24th]. In the morning to my office, where, after I had drank my morning draft at Will's with Ethell and Mr. Stevens, I went and told part of the excise money till twelve o'clock, and then called on my wife and took her to Mr. Pierce's, she in the way being exceedingly troubled with a pair of new pattens, and I vexed to go so slow, it being late. There when we came we found Mrs. Carrick very fine, and one Mr. Lucy, who called one another husband and wife, and after dinner a great deal of mad stir. There was pulling of Mrs. bride's and Mr. bridegroom's ribbons,[4] with a great deal of fooling among them that I and my

---

[1] Anne, daughter of John, first Lord Crew, married to Sir Harry Wright, Bart., M.P. She was sister to Lady Montagu. Lived till 1708.

[2] Mrs. Michell, to whose shop in the Hall Pepys was a frequent visitor.

[3] The Stone Gallery was a long passage between the Privy Garden and the river. It led from the Bowling Green to the Court of the Palace.

[4] The scramble for ribbons, here mentioned by Pepys in connection with weddings (see also January 26th, 1660-61, and February 8th, 1662-3), doubtless formed part of the ceremony of undressing the bridegroom, which, as the age became more refined, fell into disuse. All the old plays are silent on the custom; the earliest notice of which occurs in the old ballad of the wedding of Arthur O'Bradley, printed in the Appendix to "Robin Hood," 1795, where we read—

> "Then got they *his points and his garters,*
> *And cut them in pieces like martyrs;*
> And then they all did play
> For the honour of Arthur O'Bradley."

Sir Winston Churchill also observes ("Divi Britannici," p. 340) that James I.

wife did not like. Mr. Lucy and several other gentlemen coming in after dinner, swearing and singing as if they were mad, only he singing very handsomely. There came in afterwards Mr. Sotherne,[1] clerk to Mr. Blackburne, and with him Lam-

was no more troubled at his querulous countrymen robbing him than a bridegroom at the losing of his points and garters. Lady Fanshawe, in her "Memoirs," says, that at the nuptials of Charles II. and the Infanta, "the Bishop of London declared them married in the name of the Father, the Son, and the Holy Ghost; and then they caused the ribbons her Majesty wore to be cut in little pieces; and as far as they would go, every one had some." The practice still survives in the form of wedding favours.

A similar custom is still of every day's occurrence at Dieppe. Upon the morrow after their marriage, the bride and bridegroom perambulate the streets, followed by a numerous cortege, the guests at the wedding festival, two and two; each individual wearing two bits of narrow ribbon, about two inches in length, of different colours, which are pinned crossways upon the breast. These morsels of ribbons originally formed the garters of the bride and bridegroom, which had been divided amidst boisterous mirth among the assembled company, the moment the happy pair had been formally installed in the bridal bed.—Ex. inf. Mr. William Hughes, Belvedere, Jersey.—B.

[1] Robert Blackburne was Secretary to the Admiralty Committee, with a salary of £250 a year, until the appointment of the Duke of York as Lord High Ad-

bert,[1] lieutenant of my Lord's ship, and brought with them the declaration that came out to-day from the Parliament, wherein they declare for law and gospel, and for tythes; but I do not find people apt to believe them. After this taking leave I went to my father's, and my wife staying there, he and I went to speak with Mr. Crumlum[2] (in the meantime, while it was five o'clock, he being in the school, we went to my cozen Tom Pepys' shop,[3] the turner in Paul's Churchyard, and drank with him a pot of ale); he gave my father directions what to do about getting my brother an exhibition, and spoke very well of my brother. Thence back with my father home, where he and I spoke privately in the little room to my sister Pall about stealing of things as my wife's scissars and my maid's book, at which my father was much troubled. Hence home with my wife and so to Whitehall, where I met with Mr. Hunt and Luellin, and drank with them at Marsh's, and afterwards went up and wrote to my Lord by the post. This day the Parliament gave order that the late Committee of Safety should come before them this day se'nnight, and all their papers, and their model of Government that they had made, to be brought in with them. So home and talked with my wife about our dinner on Thursday.

[25th]. Called up early to Mr. Downing; he gave me a Character, such a one as my Lord's, to make perfect, and likewise gave me his order for £500 to carry to Mr. Frost, which I did and so to my office, where I did do something about the character till twelve o'clock. Then home and found my wife and the maid at my Lord's getting things ready against to-morrow. I went by

---

miral in July, 1660. James Sotherne, his clerk (afterwards clerk to Sir William Coventry), was Clerk of the Acts from 1677 till 1690, when he was appointed Secretary to the Admiralty.

[1] Lieutenant Lambert was appointed captain of the "Norwich" in June, 1661. His death is mentioned by Pepys under date September 14th, 1665.

[2] Samuel Cromleholme (or Crumlum), born in Wiltshire in 1618; Surmaster of St. Paul's School, 1647; High Master in 1657. He was a good scholar, and lost a valuable library when the school was burnt in the Great Fire. Died July 21st, 1672.

[3] Tom Pepys the turner was son of Thomas Pepys, the elder brother of Samuel's father. He had a shop in Bartholomew Fair in 1667.

water to my Uncle White's[1] to dinner, where I met my father, where we alone had a fine jole of Ling to dinner. After dinner I took leave, and coming home heard that in Cheapside there had been but a little before a gibbet set up, and the picture of Huson[2] hung upon it in the middle of the street. I called at Paul's Churchyard, where I bought Buxtorf's Hebrew Grammar;[3] and read a declaration of the gentlemen of Northampton which came out this afternoon.[4] Thence to my father's, where I staid with my mother a while and then to Mr. Crew's about a picture to be sent into the country, of Mr. Thomas Crew,[5] to my Lord. So [to] my Lady Wright to speak with her, but she was abroad, so Mr. Evans, her butler, had me into his buttery, and gave me sack and a lesson on his lute, which he played very well. Thence I went to my Lord's and got most things ready against to-morrow, as fires and laying the cloth, and my wife was making of her tarts and larding of her pullets till eleven o'clock. This evening Mr. Downing sent for me, and gave me order to go to Mr. Jessop[6] for his papers concerning his dispatch to Holland which were not ready, only his order for a ship to

---

[1] Pepys's uncle and aunt Wight are frequently mentioned in the Diary.

[2] John Hewson, who, from a low origin, became a colonel in the Parliament army, and sat in judgment on the King: he escaped hanging by flight, and died in 1662, at Amsterdam. A curious notice of Hewson occurs in Rugge's "Diurnal," December 5th, 1659, which states that "he was a cobbler by trade, but a very stout man, and a very good commander; but in regard of his former employment, they [the city apprentices] threw at him old shoes, and slippers, and turnip-tops, and brick-bats, stones, and tiles." . . . "At this time [January, 1659-60] there came forth, almost every day, jeering books: one was called 'Colonel Hewson's Confession; or, a Parley with Pluto,' about his going into London, and taking down the gates of Temple-Bar." He had but one eye, which did not escape the notice of his enemies.—B.

[3] "Johannis Buxtorfii Thesaurus Grammaticus Linguæ Sanctæ Hebrææ," 1651, is in the Pepysian Library.

[4] "Address to the King by his loyal subjects of the County of Northampton, 24 January, 1661." Declarations came in from the nobility, knights, and gentry of the several counties, and most of these Declarations appeared before this one from Northampton. These broadsides are in the Library of the British Museum.

[5] Thomas Crew, afterwards knighted, eldest son of John, afterwards Lord Crew, whom he succeeded in that title as second Lord. He died 1697.

[6] William Jessop was Clerk of the Council under the Commonwealth, and Secretary to the Commissioners of Parliament for Accounts.

transport him he gave me. To my Lord's again and so home with my wife, tired with this day's work.

[26th]. To my office for £20 to carry to Mr. Downing, which I did and back again. Then came Mr. Frost to pay Mr. Downing his £500, and I went to him for the warrant and brought it Mr. Frost. Called for some papers at Whitehall for Mr. Downing, one of which was an Order of the Council for £1,800 per annum, to be paid monthly; and the other two, Orders to the Commissioners of Customs, to let his goods pass free. Home from my office to my Lord's lodgings where my wife had got ready a very fine dinner — viz. a dish of marrow bones; a leg of mutton; a loin of veal; a dish of fowl, three pullets, and two dozen of larks all in a dish; a great tart, a neat's tongue, a dish of anchovies; a dish of prawns and cheese. My company was my father, my uncle Fenner,[1] his two sons, Mr. Pierce, and all their wives, and my brother Tom. We were as merry as I could frame myself to be in the company, W. Joyce talking after the old rate and drinking hard, vexed his father and mother and wife. And I did perceive that Mrs. Pierce her coming so gallant, that it put the two young women quite out of courage. When it became dark they all went away but Mr. Pierce, and W. Joyce, and their wives and Tom, and drank a bottle of wine afterwards, so that Will did heartily vex his father and mother by staying. At which I and my wife were much pleased. Then they all went and I fell to writing of two characters for Mr. Downing, and carried them to him at nine o'clock at night, and he did not like them but corrected them, so that to-morrow I am to do them anew. To my Lord's lodging again and sat by the great log, it being now a very good fire, with my wife, and ate a bit and so home. The news this day is a letter that speaks absolutely Monk's concurrence with this Parliament, and nothing else, which yet I hardly believe. After dinner to-day my father showed me a letter from my

---

[1] Fenner lived in Old Bailey. Pepys's aunt Fenner died August 19th, 1661, after twenty-eight years of married life, and his uncle married again in January, 1661-62; see January 19th. Uncle Fenner himself died May 24th, 1664. Their daughter Kate married Anthony Joyce.

Uncle Robert,[1] in answer to my last, concerning my money which I would have out of my Coz. Beck's[2] hand, wherein Beck desires it four months longer, which I know not how to spare.

[27th]. Going to my office I met with Tom Newton, my old comrade, and took him to the Crown in the Palace,[3] and gave him his morning draft. And as he always did, did talk very high what he would do with the Parliament, that he would have what place he would, and that he might be one of the Clerks to the Council if he would. Here I staid talking with him till the offices were all shut, and then I looked in the Hall, and was told by my bookseller, Mrs. Michell, that Mr. G. Montagu[4] had inquired there for me. So I went to his house, and was forced by him to dine with him, and had a plenteous brave dinner and the greatest civility that ever I had from any man. Thence home and so to Mrs. Jem, and played with her at cards, and coming home again my wife told me that Mr. Hawly had been there to speak with me, and seemed angry that I had not been at the office that day, and she told me she was afraid that Mr. Downing may have a mind to pick some hole in my coat. So I made haste to him, but found no such thing from him, but he sent me to Mr. Sherwin's[5] about getting Mr. Squib to come to him to-morrow, and I carried him an answer. So home and fell a writing the characters for Mr. Downing, and about nine at night Mr. Hawly came, and after he was gone I sat up till almost twelve writing, and wrote two of them. In the morning up early and wrote another, my wife lying in bed and reading to me.

[28th]. I went to Mr. Downing and carried him three char-

---

[1] Robert Pepys of Brampton, whose will was proved August 23rd, 1661, uncle of Samuel.

[2] Ellenor Pepys (baptized 1598) married George Becke of Lolworth, co. Cambridge. This cousin was probably one of their children.

[3] The Crown was in Palace Yard.

[4] George Montagu, fifth son of Henry, first Earl of Manchester, afterwards M.P. for Dover, and father of the first Earl of Halifax. He was youngest brother of Lord Manchester.

[5] Mr. Sherwin was afterwards clerk to the Tangier Committee, see January 17th, 1664-65.

acters, and then to my office and wrote another, while Mr. Frost staid telling money. And after I had done it Mr. Hawly came into the office and I left him and carried it to Mr. Downing, who then told me that he was resolved to be gone for Holland this morning. So I to my office again, and dispatch my business there, and came with Mr. Hawly to Mr. Downing's lodging, and took Mr. Squib from White Hall in a coach thither with me, and there we waited in his chamber a great while, till he came in; and in the mean time, sent all his things to the barge that lay at Charing-Cross Stairs. Then came he in, and took a very civil leave of me, beyond my expectation, for I was afraid that he would have told me something of removing me from my office; but he did not, but that he would do me any service that lay in his power. So I went down and sent a porter to my house for my best fur cap, but he coming too late with it I did not present it to him. Thence I went to Westminster Hall, and bound up my cap at Mrs. Michell's, who was much taken with my cap, and endeavoured to overtake the coach at the Exchange and to give it him there, but I met with one that told me that he was gone, and so I returned and went to Heaven,[1] where Luellin and I dined on a breast of mutton all alone, discoursing of the changes that we have seen and the happiness of them that have estates of their own, and so parted, and I went by appointment to my office and paid young Mr. Walton £500; it being very dark he took £300 by content. He gave me half a piece and carried me in his coach to St. Clement's, from whence I went to Mr. Crew's and made even with Mr. Andrews, and took in all my notes and gave him one for all. Then to my Lady Wright and gave her my Lord's letter which he bade me give her privately. So home and then to Will's for a little news, then came home again and wrote to my Lord, and so to Whitehall and gave them to the post-boy. Back again home and to bed.

---

[1] A place of entertainment within or adjoining Westminster Hall. It is called in "Hudibras," "False Heaven, at the end of the Hall." There were two other alehouses near Westminster Hall, called Hell and Purgatory.

> "Nor break his fast
> In Heaven and Hell."
> Ben Jonson's *Alchemist*, act v. sc. 2.

[29th]. In the morning I went to Mr. Gunning's, where he made an excellent sermon upon the 2d of the Galatians, about the difference that fell between St. Paul and St. Peter (the feast day of St. Paul being a day or two ago), whereby he did prove, that, contrary to the doctrine of the Roman Church, St. Paul did never own any dependance, or that he was inferior to St. Peter, but that they were equal, only one a particular charge of preaching to the Jews, and the other to the Gentiles. Here I met with Mr. Moore, and went home with him to dinner to Mr. Crew's, where Mr. Spurrier being in town did dine with us. From thence I went home and spent the afternoon in casting up my accounts, and do find myself to be worth £40 and more, which I did not think, but am afraid that I have forgot something. To my father's to supper, where I heard by my brother Tom how W. Joyce would the other day have Mr. Pierce and his wife to the tavern after they were gone from my house, and that he had so little manners as to make Tom pay his share notwithstanding that he went upon his account, and by my father I understand that my uncle Fenner and my aunt were much pleased with our entertaining them. After supper home without going to see Mrs. Turner.

[30th]. This morning, before I was up, I fell a-singing of my song, "Great, good, and just," &c.[1] and put myself thereby in mind that this was the fatal day, now ten years since, his Majesty died. Scull the waterman came and brought me a note from the Hope[2] from Mr. Hawly with direction, about his money, he tarrying there till his master be gone. To my office, where I received money of the excise of Mr. Ruddyer, and after we

---

[1] This is the beginning of the Marquis of Montrose's verses on the execution of Charles I., which Pepys had set to music:—

> "Great, good, and just, could I but rate
> My grief and thy too rigid fate,
> I'd weep the world to such a strain
> That it should deluge once again.
> But since thy loud-tongued blood demands supplies
> More from Briareus' hands, than Argus' eyes,
> I'll sing thy obsequies with trumpet sounds,
> And write thy epitaph with blood and wounds."

[2] This may be the Hope Tavern, or more probably the reach of the Thames.

had done went to Will's and staid there till 3 o'clock and then I taking my £12 10s. 0d. due to me for my last quarter's salary, I went with them by water to London to the house where Sign^r Torriano[1] used to be and staid there awhile with Mr. Ashwell, Spicer and Ruddier. Then I went and paid £12 17s. 6d. due from me to Captⁿ Dick Matthews according to his direction the last week in a letter. After that I came back by water playing on my flageolette and not finding my wife come home again from her father's I went and sat awhile and played at cards with Mrs. Jem, whose maid had newly got an ague and was ill thereupon. So homewards again, having great need to do my business, and so pretending to meet Mr. Shott the wood monger of Whitehall I went and eased myself at the Harp and Ball, and thence home where I sat writing till bed-time and so to bed. There seems now to be a general cease of talk, it being taken for granted that Monk do resolve to stand to the Parliament, and nothing else. Spent a little time this night in knocking up nails for my hat and cloaks in my chamber.

[31st]. In the morning I fell to my lute till 9 o'clock. Then to my Lord's lodgings and set out a barrel of soap to be carried to Mrs. Ann. Here I met with Nick Bartlet, one that had been a servant of my Lord's at sea and at Harper's gave him his morning draft. So to my office where I paid £1,200 to Mr. Frost and at noon went to Will's to give one of the Excise office a pot of ale that came to-day to tell over a bag of his that wanted £7 in it, which he found over in another bag. Then home and dined with my wife when in came Mr. Hawly newly come from ship-board from his master, and brought me a letter of direction what to do in his lawsuit with Squib about his house and office. After dinner to Westminster Hall, where all we clerks had orders to wait upon the Committee, at the Star Chamber that is to try Colonel Jones,[2] and were to give an account what money we

---

[1] Gio. Torriano, M.A., a teacher of Italian in London, who edited a new edition of Florio's "Italian Dictionary." His "Piazza Universale di Proverbi Italiani," published in 1666, is exceedingly rare, as the greater part of the impression was burnt in the Fire of London.

[2] Colonel John Jones, impeached, with General Ludlow and Miles Corbet, for treasonable practices in Ireland.

had paid him; but the Committee did not sit to-day. Hence to Will's, where I sat an hour or two with Mr. Godfrey Austin, a scrivener in King Street. Here I met and afterwards bought the answer to General Monk's letter, which is a very good one, and I keep it by me. Thence to Mrs. Jem, where I found her maid in bed in a fit of the ague, and Mrs. Jem among the people below at work and by and by she came up hot and merry, as if they had given her wine, at which I was troubled, but said nothing; after a game at cards, I went home and wrote by the post and coming back called in at Harper's and drank with Mr. Pulford, servant to Mr. Waterhouse,[1] who tells me, that whereas my Lord Fleetwood should have answered to the Parliament to-day, he wrote a letter and desired a little more time, he being a great way out of town. And how that he is quite ashamed of himself, and confesses how he had deserved this, for his baseness to his brother. And that he is like to pay part of the money, paid out of the Exchequer during the Committee of Safety, out of his own purse again, which I am glad of. Home and to bed, leaving my wife reading in Polixandre.[2] I could find nothing in Mr. Downing's letter, which Hawly brought me, concerning my office; but I could discern that Hawly had a mind that I would get to be Clerk of the Council, I suppose that he might have the greater salary; but I think it not safe yet to change this for a public employment.

[February 1st]. In the morning went to my office where afterwards the old man brought me my letters from the carrier. At noon I went home and dined with my wife on pease porridge and nothing else. After that I went to the Hall and there met with Mr. Swan and went with him to Mr. Downing's Coun-

---

[1] Probably Edward Waterhouse, an heraldic and miscellaneous writer, styled by Lloyd "as the learned, industrious, and ingenious E. W. of Sion College." His portrait was engraved by Loggan, and inserted in a book of his, entitled "Fortescue Illustratus," folio, 1663; he died in 1670.

[2] "Polexandre," by Louis Le Roy de Gomberville, was first published in 1632. "The History of Polexander" was "done into English by W. Browne," and published in folio, London, 1647. It was the earliest of the French heroic romances, and it appears to have been the model for the works of Calprenede and Mdlle. de Scuderi; see Dunlop's "History of Fiction" for the plot of the romance.

sellor, who did put me in very little hopes about the business between Mr. Downing and Squib, and told me that Squib would carry it against him, at which I was much troubled, and with him went to Lincoln's Inn and there spoke with his attorney, who told me the day that was appointed for the trial. From thence I went to Sir Harry Wright's[1] and got him to give me his hand for the £60 which I am to-morrow to receive from Mr. Calthrop and from thence to Mrs. Jem and spoke with Madam Scott[2] and her husband who did promise to have the thing for her neck done this week. Thence home and took Gammer East, and James the porter, a soldier, to my Lord's lodgings, who told me how they were drawn into the field to-day, and that they were ordered to march away to-morrow to make room for General Monk; but they did shut their Colonel Fitch,[3] and the rest of the officers out of the field, and swore they would not go without their money, and if they would not give it them, they would go where they might have it, and that was the City. So the Colonel went to the Parliament, and commanded what money could be got, to be got against to-morrow for them, and all the rest of the soldiers in town, who in all places made a mutiny this day, and do agree together. Here I took some bedding to send to Mrs. Ann for her to lie in now she hath her fits of the ague. Thence I went to Will's and staid like a fool there and played at cards till 9 o'clock and so came home, where I found Mr. Hunt and his wife who staid and sat with me till 10 and so good night.

[2nd]. Drank at Harper's with Doling, and so to my office, where I found all the officers of the regiments in town, waiting to receive money that their soldiers might go out of town, and what was in the Exchequer they had. At noon after dining at home I called at Harper's for Doling, and he and I met with

---

[1] Sir Harry Wright, M.P. for Harwich; created a baronet by Cromwell, 1658, and by Charles II., 1660. He married Anne, daughter of the first Lord Crew, and sister to Sir E. Montagu's wife, and resided at Dagenham, Essex.

[2] Probably Judith Pepys, wife of J. Scott; see January 6th, 1659-60.

[3] Thomas Fitch, colonel of a regiment of foot in 1658, M.P. for Inverness; also Lieutenant of the Tower.

Luellin and drank with him at the Exchequer at Charing Cross, and thence he and I went to the Temple to Mr. Calthrop's chamber, and from thence had his man by water to London Bridge to Mr. Calthrop, a grocer, and received £60 for my Lord. In our way we talked with our waterman, White,[1] who told us how the watermen had lately been abused by some that had a desire to get in to be watermen to the State, and had lately presented an address of nine or ten thousand hands to stand by this Parliament, when it was only told them that it was to a petition against hackney coaches; and that to-day they had put out another to undeceive the world and to clear themselves, and that among the rest Cropp, my waterman and one of great practice, was one that did cheat them thus. After I had received the money we went to the Bridge Tavern and drank a quart of wine and so back by water, landing Mr. Calthrop's man at the Temple and we went homewards, but over against Somerset House, hearing the noise of guns, we landed and found the Strand full of soldiers. So I took my money and went to Mrs. Johnson, my Lord's sempstress, and giving her my money to lay up, Doling and I went up stairs to a window, and looked out and see the foot face the horse and beat them back, and stood bawling and calling in the street for a free Parliament and money. By and by a drum was heard to beat a march coming towards them, and they got all ready again and faced them, and they proved to be of the same mind with them; and so they made a great deal of joy to see one another. After all this, I took my money, and went home on foot and laying up my money, and changing my stockings and shoes, I this day having left off my great skirt suit, and put on my white suit with silver lace coat, and went over to Harper's, where I met with W. Simons, Doling, Luellin and three merchants, one of which had occasion to use a porter, so they sent for one, and James the soldier came, who told us how they had been all day and night upon their guard at St. James's, and that through the whole town they did resolve to stand to what they had began, and that to-morrow he did believe they would go into the City, and be received there. After all this we went to a sport

---

[1] Waterman White went to sea in May, 1661, and Pepys tried to get his place for Waterman Payne.

called, selling of a horse for a dish of eggs and herrings, and sat talking there till almost twelve o'clock and then parted, they were to go as far as Aldgate. Home and to bed.

[3rd]. Drank my morning draft at Harper's, and was told there that the soldiers were all quiet upon promise of pay. Thence to St. James's Park, and walked there to my place for my flageolet and then played a little, it being a most pleasant morning and sunshine. Back to Whitehall, where in the guard-chamber I saw about thirty or forty 'prentices of the City, who were taken at twelve o'clock last night and brought prisoners hither. Thence to my office, where I paid a little more money to some of the soldiers under Lieut.-Col. Miller (who held out the Tower against the Parliament after it was taken away from Fitch by the Committee of Safety, and yet he continued in his office). About noon Mrs. Turner came to speak with me, and Joyce, and I took them and shewed them the manner of the Houses sitting, the doorkeeper very civilly opening the door for us. Thence with my cozen Roger Pepys,[1] it being term time, we took him out of the Hall to Prior's,[2] the Rhenish wine-house, and there had a pint or two of wine and a dish of anchovies, and bespoke three or four dozen bottles of wine for him against his wedding. After this done he went away, and left me order to call and pay for all that Mrs. Turner would have. So we called for nothing more there, but went and bespoke a shoulder of mutton at Wilkinson's to be roasted as well as it could be done, and sent a bottle of wine home to my house. In the meantime she and I and Joyce went walking all over White Hall, whither General Monk was newly come, and we saw all his forces march by in very good plight and stout officers. Thence to my house where we dined, but with

---

[1] Roger Pepys, son of Talbot Pepys of Impington, a barrister of the Middle Temple, M.P. for Cambridge, 1661-78, and Recorder of that town, 1660-88. He married, for the third time, Parnell, daughter and heiress of John Duke, of Workingham, co. Suffolk, and this was the wedding for which the posy ring was required.

[2] There were several Rhenish wine-houses in different parts of London. There was one in Cannon Row, and another on the east side of King Street, Westminster. This latter was about the middle of the street. There is a token of "John Garrew at ye old Renishe Wine house, King Street, Westminster," 1668 (see "Boyne's Trade Tokens," ed. Williamson, vol. i., 1889, p. 648).

a great deal of patience, for the mutton came in raw, and so we were fain to stay the stewing of it. In the meantime we sat studying a Posy[1] for a ring for her which she is to have at Roger Pepys his wedding. After dinner I left them and went to hear news, but only found that the Parliament House was most of them with Monk at White Hall, and that in his passing through the town he had many calls to him for a free Parliament, but

little other welcome. I saw in the Palace Yard how unwilling some of the old soldiers were yet to go out of town without their money, and swore if they had it not in three days, as they were promised, they would do them more mischief in the country than if they had staid here; and that is very likely, the country being all discontented. The town and guards are already full of

---

[1] It is supposed that the fashion of having mottoes inscribed on rings was of Roman origin. In the fourteenth and fifteenth centuries the posy was inscribed on the outside of the ring, and in the sixteenth and seventeenth centuries it was placed inside. A small volume was published in 1674, entitled "Love's Garland: or Posies for Rings, Handkerchers and Gloves, and such pretty tokens that Lovers send their Loves."

Monk's soldiers. I returned, and it growing dark I and they went to take a turn in the park, where Theoph. (who was sent for to us to dinner) outran my wife and another poor woman, that laid a pot of ale with me that she would outrun her. After that I set them as far as Charing Cross, and there left them and my wife, and I went to see Mrs. Ann, who began very high about a flock bed I sent her, but I took her down. Here I played at cards till 9 o'clock. So home and to bed.

[4th]. In the morning at my lute an hour, and so to my office, where I staid expecting to have Mr. Squib come to me, but he did not. At noon walking in the Hall I found Mr. Swan and got him and Captain Stone together, and there advised about Mr. Downing's business. So to Will's, and sat there till three o'clock and then to Mr. Swan's, where I found his wife in very genteel mourning for her father, and took him out by water to the Counsellor at the Temple, Mr. Stephens, and from thence to Gray's Inn, thinking to speak with Sotherton Ellis, but found him not, so we met with an acquaintance of his in the walks, and went and drank, where I ate some bread and butter, having ate nothing all day, while they were by chance discoursing of Marriot, the great eater, so that I was, I remember, ashamed to eat what I would have done. Here Swan shewed us a ballad to the tune of Mardike which was most incomparably wrote in a printed hand, which I borrowed of him, but the song proved but silly, and so I did not write it out. Thence we went and leaving Swan at his master's, my Lord Widdrington, I met with Spicer, Washington, and D. Vines in Lincoln's Inn Court, and they were buying of a hanging-jack to roast birds on of a fellow that was there selling of some. I was fain to slip from there and went to Mrs. Crew's to her and advised about a maid to come and be with Mrs. Jem while her maid is sick, but she could spare none. Thence to Sir Harry Wright's, but my lady not being within I spoke to Mrs. Carter about it, who will get one against Monday. So with a linkboy to Scott's, where Mrs. Ann was in a heat, but I spoke not to her, but told Mrs. Jem what I had done, and after that went home and wrote letters into the country by the post, and then played awhile on my lute, and so done, to supper and then to bed. All the news

44

to-day is, that the Parliament this morning voted the House to be made up four hundred forthwith. This day my wife killed her turkeys that Mr. Sheply gave her, that came out of Zealand with my Lord, and could not get her maid Jane by no means at any time to kill anything.

[5th] (Lord's day). In the morning before church time Mr. Hawly, who had for this day or two looked something sadly, which methinks did speak something in his breast concerning me, came to me telling me that he was out £24 which he could not tell what was become of, and that he do remember that he had such a sum in a bag the other day, and could not tell what he did with it, at which I was very sorry but could not help him. In the morning to Mr. Gunning, where a stranger, an old man, preached a good honest sermon upon "What manner of love is this that we should be called the sons of God." After sermon I could not find my wife, who promised to be at the gate against my coming out, and waited there a great while; then went to my house and finding her gone I returned and called at the Chequers, thinking to dine at the ordinary with Mr. Chetwind and Mr. Thomas, but they not being there I went to my father and found her there, and there I dined. To their church in the afternoon, and in Mrs. Turner's pew my wife took up a good black hood and kept it. A stranger preached a poor sermon, and so I read over the whole book of the story of Tobit. After sermon home with Mrs. Turner, staid with her a little while, then she went into the court to a christening and we to my father's, where I wrote some notes for my brother John to give to the Mercers[1] to-morrow, it being the day of their apposition. After supper home, and before going to bed I staid writing of this day its passages, while a drum came by, beating of a strange manner of beat, now and then a single stroke, which my wife and I wondered at, what the meaning of it should be. This afternoon at church I saw Dick Cumberland[2] newly come out of the country from his living, but did not speak to him.

---

[1] The Mercers Company as the patrons of St. Paul's School.
[2] Richard Cumberland, of St. Paul's School, in his seventeenth year, was admitted a pensioner of Magdalene College in 1649, and in 1653 he was elected

[6th]. Before I went to my office I went to Mr. Crew's and paid Mr. Andrews the same £60 that he had received of Mr. Calthrop the last week. So back to Westminster and walked with him thither, where we found the soldiers all set in the Palace Yard, to make way for General Monk to come to the House.[1] At the Hall we parted, and meeting Swan, he and I to the Swan and drank our morning draft. So back again to the Hall, where I stood upon the steps and saw Monk go by, he making observance to the judges as he went along. At noon my father dined with me upon my turkey that was brought from Denmark, and after dinner he and I to the Bull Head Tavern, where we drank half a pint of wine and so parted. I to Mrs. Ann, and Mrs. Jem being gone out of the chamber she and I had a very high bout, I rattled her up, she being in her bed, but she becoming more cool, we parted pretty good friends. Thence I went to Will's, where I staid at cards till 10 o'clock, losing half a crown, and so home to bed.

[7th]. In the morning I went early to give Mr. Hawly notice of my being forced to go into London, but he having also business we left our office business to Mr. Spicer and he and I walked as far as the Temple, where I halted a little and then went to Paul's School, but it being too soon, went and drank my morning draft with my cozen Tom Pepys the turner,[2] and saw his house and shop, thence to school, where he that made the speech for the seventh form in praise of the founder, did show a book which

a Fellow of the College. In 1658 he got possession of the rectory of Brampton, but he was not legally instituted till 1661. He was presented to the rectory of All Saints, Stamford, in 1668. See Diary, March 18th, 1667, where Pepys writes: "The truth is, if he would accept of my sister's fortune, I should give £100 more with him than to a man able to settle her four times as much as, I fear, he is able to do." He dedicated his work on Jewish measures, 1686, to the Hon. S. Pepys, "for that good affection being begun in your youth thirty years ago in Magdalene College, Cambridge." He was made Bishop of Peterborough 1691, and died 1719, aged 86.

[1] "Feb. 6th. General Monk being in his lodgings at Whitehall, had notice that the House had a desire to see him. He came into the Court of Wards, and being there, the Sergeant-at-Arms went to meet him with the mace, and his Lordship attended the Sergeant, who went before him with the mace on his shoulder, being accompanied with Mr. Scott and Mr. Robinson."—Rugge's Diurnal.

[2] His shop was in St. Paul's Churchyard. See ante, January 24th, 1659-60.

Mr. Crumlum had lately got, which is believed to be of the Founder's own writing.[1] After all the speeches, in which my brother John came off as well as any of the rest, I went straight home and dined, then to the Hall, where in the Palace I saw Monk's soldiers abuse Billing[2] and all the Quakers, that were at a meeting-place there, and indeed the soldiers did use them very roughly and were to blame. So after drinking with Mr. Spicer, who had received £600 for me this morning, I went to Capt. Stone and with him by coach to the Temple Gardens (all the way talking of the disease of the stone), where we met Mr. Squib, but would do nothing till to-morrow morning. Thence back on foot home, where I found a letter from my Lord in character, which I construed, and after my wife had shewn me some ribbon and shoes that she had taken out of a box of Mr. Montagu's which formerly Mr. Kipps had left here when his master was at sea, I went to Mr. Crew and advised with him about it, it being concerning my Lord's coming up to Town, which he desires upon my advice the last week in my letter. Thence calling upon Mrs. Ann I went home, and wrote in character to my Lord in answer to his letter. This day Mr. Crew told me that my Lord St. John[3] is for a free Parliament, and that he is very

---

[1] John Colet, Dean of St. Paul's, born 1466, died September 16th, 1519.

[2] "Fox, or some other 'weighty' friend, on hearing of this, complained to Monk, who issued the following order, dated March 9th: 'I do require all officers and soldiers to forbear to disturb peaceable meetings of the Quakers, they doing nothing prejudicial to the Parliament or the Commonwealth of England. George Monk.' This order, we are told, had an excellent effect on the soldiers."—A. C. Bickley's *George Fox and the Early Quakers*, London, 1884, p. 179. The Quakers were at this time just coming into notice. The first preaching of George Fox, the founder, was in 1648, and in 1655 the preachers of the sect numbered seventy-three. Fox computed that there were seldom less than a thousand quakers in prison. The statute 13 and 14 Car. II, cap. i. (1662) was "An act for preventing the mischiefs and dangers that may arise by certain persons called quakers and others, refusing to take lawful oaths." Billing is mentioned again on July 22nd, 1667, when he addressed Pepys in Westminster Hall.

[3] Oliver St. John, born about 1598; called to the Bar as a member of Lincoln's Inn, 1626; M.P. for Totnes, 1640; Solicitor-General, January, 1640-41; Chief Justice of the Common Pleas, 1648, and afterwards Lord Chief Justice of the Upper Bench. He died December 31st, 1673. His first wife, Johanna Altham, was aunt to Oliver Cromwell and to John Hampden. His second wife was Elizabeth Cromwell, first cousin to Oliver.

great with Monk, who hath now the absolute command and power to do anything that he hath a mind to do. Mr. Moore told me of a picture hung up at the Exchange of a great pair of buttocks shooting of a turd into Lawson's mouth, and over it was wrote "The thanks of the house." Boys do now cry "Kiss my Parliament," instead of "Kiss my [rump]," so great and general a contempt is the Rump come to among all the good and bad.

[8th]. A little practice at my flageolet, and afterwards walking in my yard to see my stock of pigeons, which begin now with the spring to breed very fast. I was called on by Mr. Fossan,[1] my fellow pupil at Cambridge, and took him to the Swan in the Palace yard, and drank together our morning draft. Thence to my office, where I received money, and afterwards Mr. Carter,[2] my old friend at Cambridge, meeting me as I was going out of my office I took him to the Swan, and in the way I met with Captain Lidcott, and so we three went together and drank there, the Captain talking as high as ever he did, and more because of the fall of his brother Thurlow.[3] Hence I went to Captain Stone, who told me how Squib had been with him, and that he could do nothing with him, so I returned to Mr. Carter and with him to Will's, where I spent upon him and Monsieur L' Impertinent, alias Mr. Butler, who I took thither with me, and thence to the Rhenish wine house, and in our way met with Mr. Hoole, where I paid for my cozen Roger Pepys his wine, and after drinking we parted. So I home, in my way delivering a letter which among the rest I had from my Lord to-day to Sir N. Wheeler. At home my wife's brother[4] brought her a

---

[1] College Entry Book, Junij 27, 1651: "Thomas ffossan, filius Thomæ ffossan, civis Londinensis, annum agens decimū Septimū e schola de St. Mary Axe apud Londinenses, admissus est Pensionarius, tutore Dno. Moreland."—M. B.

[2] The Rev. Charles Carter, a minister in Huntingdonshire; see December 23rd, 1660.

[3] John Thurloe, born 1616; Secretary of State to Cromwell; M.P. for Ely, 1656, and for the University of Cambridge in Richard Cromwell's Parliament of December, 1658. He was never employed after the Restoration, although the King solicited his services. He died February 21st, 1668. Pepys spells the name Thurlow, which was a common spelling at the time.

[4] Balthasar St. Michel. Pepys seems to have done well for his brother-in-law in later life, although, from the entries in the Diary, he does not appear to

pretty black dog which I liked very well, and went away again.
Hence sending a porter with the hamper of bottles to the Temple
I called in my way upon Mrs. Jem, who was much frighted till
I came to tell her that her mother was well. So to the Temple,
where I delivered the wine and received the money of my cos.
Roger that I laid out, and thence to my father's, where he shewed
me a base angry letter that he had newly received from my uncle
Robert about my brother John, at which my father was very sad,
but I comforted him and wrote an answer. My brother John
has an exhibition granted him from the school. My father and
I went down to his kitchen, and there we eat and drank, and
about 9 o'clock I went away homewards, and in Fleet Street,
received a great jostle from a man that had a mind to take the
wall, which I could not help.[1] I came home and to bed. Went to
bed with my head not well by my too much drinking to-day,
and I had a boil under my chin which troubled me cruelly.

[9th]. Soon as out of my bed I wrote letters into the country
to go by carrier to-day. Before I was out of my bed, I heard the
soldiers very busy in the morning, getting their horses ready
where they lay at Hilton's, but I knew not then their meaning
in so doing. After I had wrote my letters I went to Westminster
up and down the Hall, and with Mr. Swan walked a good [deal]
talking about Mr. Downing's business. I went with him to Mr.
Phelps's house where he had some business to solicit, where we
met Mr. Rogers my neighbour, who did solicit against him and
talked very high, saying that he would not for a £1,000 appear
in a business that Swan did, at which Swan was very angry,
but I believe he might be guilty enough. In the Hall I understand how Monk is this morning gone into London with his
army; and met with Mr. Fage, who told me that he do be-

have had a high opinion of him. St. Michel was Muster Master at Deal in
1674, Storekeeper at Tangier in 1681, and Naval Commissioner at Deptford
in 1685.

[1] This was a constant trouble to the pedestrian until the rule of passing to the
right of the person met was generally accepted. Gay commences his "Trivia"
with an allusion to this—

"When to assert the wall, and when resign"—

and the epigram on the haughty courtier and the scholar is well known.

lieve that Monk is gone to secure some of the Common-council
of the City, who were very high yesterday there, and did vote
that they would not pay any taxes till the House was filled up.
I went to my office, where I wrote to my Lord after I had been
at the Upper Bench,[1] where Sir Robert Pye[2] this morning came
to desire his discharge from the Tower; but it could not be
granted. After that I went to Mrs. Jem, who I had promised to
go along with to her Aunt Wright's, but she was gone, so I went
thither, and after drinking a glass of sack I went back to Westminster Hall, and meeting with Mr. Pierce the surgeon, who
would needs take me home, where Mr. Lucy, Burrell, and others
dined, and after dinner I went home and to Westminster Hall,
where meeting Swan I went with him by water to the Temple
to our Counsel, and did give him a fee to make a motion to-
morrow in the Exchequer for Mr. Downing. Thence to Westminster Hall, where I heard an action very finely pleaded between my Lord Dorset[3] and some other noble persons, his lady
and other ladies of quality being here, and it was about £330
per annum, that was to be paid to a poor Spittal,[4] which was given
by some of his predecessors; and given on his side. Then Swan
and I to a drinking-house near Temple Bar, where while he
wrote I played on my flageolet till a dish of poached eggs was
got ready for us, which we eat, and so by coach home. I called

---

[1] The King's Bench was called the Upper Bench at the time of the Commonwealth, when the word King was abolished universally.

[2] Sir Robert Pye, the elder, was auditor of the Exchequer, and a staunch
Royalist. He garrisoned his house at Faringdon, which was besieged by his
son, of the same names, a decided Republican, son-in-law to Hampden, and
colonel of horse under Fairfax. The son, here spoken of, was subsequently
committed to the Tower for presenting a petition to the House of Commons
from the county of Berks, which he represented in Parliament, complaining
of the want of a settled form of government. He had, however, the courage
to move for an habeas corpus, but Judge Newdigate decided that the courts
of law had not the power to discharge him. Upon Monk's coming to London,
the secluded members passed a vote to liberate Pye, and at the Restoration he
was appointed equerry to the King. He died in 1701.—B.

[3] Richard, fifth Earl of Dorset, died 1677.

[4] This was the Sackville College for the poor, at East Grinstead, founded by
Robert Sackville, second Earl of Dorset, who died in 1608. There is a good
account of Sackville College in the "Gentleman's Magazine" for December,
1848.—B.

at Mr. Harper's, who told me how Monk had this day clapt up many of the Common-council, and that the Parliament had voted that he should pull down their gates and portcullisses, their posts and their chains, which he do intend to do, and do lie in the City all night. I went home and got some allum to my mouth, where I have the beginnings of a cancer, and had also a plaster to my boil underneath my chin.

[10th]. In the morning I went to Mr. Swan, who took me to the Court of Wards,[1] where I saw the three Lords Commissioners sitting upon some cause where Mr. Scobell was concerned, and my Lord Fountaine[2] took him up very roughly about some things that he said. After that we went to the Exchequer, where the Barons were hearing of causes, and there I made affidavit that Mr. Downing was gone into Holland by order of the Council of State, and this affidavit I gave to Mr. Stevens our lawyer.

[1] The Court of Wards and Liveries was first erected in the reign of Henry VIII. for the administration of the estates of the king's wards during their minority, and for delivery of seizin upon coming of age. The court was practically put an end to by the Long Parliament (by resolution of both houses), and was abolished 12 Car. II.

[2] Sir Thomas Widdrington and Sergeants Thomas Tyrrell and John Fountaine had just been appointed Lords Commissioners of the Great Seal.

Thence to my office, where I got money of Mr. Hawly to pay the lawyer, and there found Mr. Lenard, one of the Clerks of the Council, and took him to the Swan and gave him his morning draft. Then home to dinner, and after that to the Exchequer, where I heard all the afternoon a great many causes before the Barons; in the end came ours, and Squib proved clearly by his patent that the house and office did now belong to him. Our lawyer made some kind of opposition, but to no purpose, and so the cause was found against us, and the foreman of the Jury brought in £10 damages, which the whole Court cried shame of, and so he cried 12d. Thence I went home, vexed about this business, and there I found Mr. Moore, and with him went into London to Mr. Fage about the cancer in my mouth, which begins to grow dangerous, who gave me something for it, and also told me what Monk had done in the City, how he had pulled down the most part of the gates and chains that they could break down, and that he was now gone back to White Hall. The City look mighty blank, and cannot tell what in the world to do; the Parliament having this day ordered that the Common-council sit no more, but that new ones be chosen according to what qualifications they shall give them. Thence I went and drank with Mr. Moore at the Sugar Loaf[1] by Temple Bar, where Swan and I were last night, and so we parted. At home I found Mr. Hunt, who sat talking with me awhile, and so to bed.

[11th]. This morning I lay long abed, and then to my office, where I read all the morning my Spanish book of Rome. At noon I walked in the Hall, where I heard the news of a letter from Monk, who was now gone into the City again, and did resolve to stand for the sudden filling up of the House, and it was very strange how the countenance of men in the Hall was all changed with joy in half an hour's time. So I went up to the lobby, where I saw the Speaker reading of the letter; and after it was read, Sir A. Haselrigge came out very angry, and Billing[2] standing at the door, took him by the arm, and cried,

[1] There are tokens of George Bryan at the Sugar Loaf without Temple Bar (see "Boyne's Trade Tokens," ed. Williamson, vol. i., 1889, p. 761).

[2] The quaker mentioned before on the 7th of this month.

"Thou man, will thy beast carry thee no longer? thou must fall!" The House presently after rose, and appointed to meet again at three o'clock. I went then down into the Hall, where I met with Chetwind, who had not dined no more than myself, and so we went toward London, in our way calling at two or three shops, but could have no dinner. At last, within Temple Bar, we found a pullet ready roasted, and there we dined. After that he went to his office in Chancery Lane, calling at the Rolls, where I saw the lawyers pleading. Then to his office, where I sat in his study singing, while he was with his man (Mr. Powell's son) looking after his business. Thence we took coach for the City to Guildhall, where the Hall was full of people expecting Monk and Lord Mayor[1] to come thither, and all very joyfull. Here we stayed a great while, and at last meeting with a friend of his we went to the 3 Tun tavern and drank half a pint of wine, and not liking the wine we went to an alehouse, where we met with company of this third man's acquaintance, and there we drank a little. Hence I went alone to Guildhall to see whether Monk was come again or no, and met with him coming out of the chamber where he had been with the Mayor and Aldermen, but such a shout I never heard in all my life, crying out, "God bless your Excellence." Here I met with Mr. Lock,[2] and took him to an alehouse, and left him there to fetch Chetwind; when we were come together, Lock told us the substance of the letter that went from Monk to the Parliament; wherein, after complaints that he and his officers were put upon such offices against the City as they could not do with any content or honour, that there are many members now in the House that were of the late tyrannical Committee of Safety.[3]

---

[1] Thomas Allen, afterwards created a baronet.

[2] Matthew Lock, the famous composer, was a native of Exeter and a chorister in the cathedral of that city. He was employed to write some triumphal music for performance during the King's progress from the Tower to Whitehall. After which he was appointed composer in ordinary to the King. The music to "Macbeth," associated with his name, is by many attributed to Purcell. Lock became a Roman Catholic, and resigning his appointment at the Chapel Royal was made organist to the Queen at Somerset House. He died in August, 1677.

[3] The Committee of Public Safety consisted of the following members: Fleetwood, Lambert, Desborough, Steel, Whitelocke, Vane, Ludlow, Sydenham,

That Lambert and Vane are now in town, contrary to the vote
of Parliament. That there were many in the House that do press
for new oaths to be put upon men; whereas we have more cause
to be sorry for the many oaths that we have already taken and
broken. That the late petition of the fanatique people presented
by Barebone,[1] for the imposing of an oath upon all sorts of people,
was received by the House with thanks. That therefore he
[Monk] do desire that all writs for filling up of the House be
issued by Friday next, and that in the mean time, he would retire into the City and only leave them guards for the security
of the House and Council. The occasion of this was the order
that he had last night to go into the City and disarm them,
and take away their charter; whereby he and his officers say
that the House had a mind to put them upon things that should
make them odious; and so it would be in their power to do
what they would with them. He told us that they [the Parlia-
ment] had sent Scott[2] and Robinson to him [Monk] this afternoon, but he would not hear them. And that the Mayor and
Aldermen had offered him their own houses for himself and
his officers; and that his soldiers would lack for nothing. And indeed I saw many people give the soldiers drink and money, and
all along in the streets cried, "God bless them!" and extraordinary good words. Hence we went to a merchant's house hard
by, where Lock wrote a note and left, where I saw Sir Nich.
Crisp,[3] and so we went to the Star Tavern (Monk being then

Salloway, Strickland, Berry, Lawrence, Sir James Harrington, Johnston of
Warriston, Henry Brandreth, Cornelius Holland, Colonels Hewson, Clarke,
Bennet, and Lilburn.

[1] Praise God Barebone (or Barbon), an active member of the Parliament called
by his name. About this period he had appeared at the head of a band of
fanatics, and alarmed Monk, who well knew his influence. He was a leather
seller in Fleet Street. He died January, 1679-80, and was buried at St. Andrew's, Holborn.

[2] Thomas Scott, referred to on January 10th of this year, and Luke Robinson.
Both were members of Parliament and of the Council of State. They were
selected, as firm adherents of the Rump, to watch Monk's proceedings.

[3] An eminent merchant actively engaged in the African trade, and one of the
farmers of the Customs. He had advanced large sums to assist Charles I., who
knighted him, January 1st, 1641. He was elected member of Parliament for
Winchelsea in the Long Parliament, but expelled February 2nd, 1641. He
was one of the Commission sent to Charles II. at Breda, and created a baronet

at Benson's), where we dined and wrote a letter to my Lord from thence. In Cheapside there was a great many bonfires, and Bow bells and all the bells in all the churches as we went home were a-ringing. Hence we went homewards, it being about ten o'clock. But the common joy that was every where to be seen! The number of bonfires, there being fourteen between St. Dunstan's and Temple Bar, and at Strand Bridge[1] I could at one view tell thirty-one fires. In King-street seven or eight; and all along burning, and roasting, and drinking for rumps. There being rumps tied upon sticks and carried up and down. The butchers at the May Pole at the Strand[2] rang a peal with their knives when they were going to sacrifice their rump. On Ludgate Hill there was one turning of the spit that had a rump tied upon it, and another basting of it. Indeed it was past imagination, both the greatness and the suddenness of it. At one end of the street you would think there was a whole lane of fire, and so hot that we were fain to keep still on the further side merely for heat. We came to the Chequers at Charing Cross, where Chetwind wrote a letter and I gave him an account of what I had wrote for him to write. Thence home and sent my letters to the post-house in London, and my wife and I (after Mr. Hunt was gone, whom I found waiting at my house) went out again to show her the fires, and after walking as far as the Exchange we returned and to bed.

[12th]. In the morning, it being Lord's day, Mr. Pierce came to me to enquire how things go. We drank our morning draft together and thence to White Hall, where Dr. Holmes[3] preached;

April 16th, 1665. He died February 26th, 1665-6, and was buried in the church of St. Mildred, Bread Street. His mansion at Hammersmith stood on the site of Brandenburgh House.

[1] Described in Maitland's "History of London" as a handsome bridge crossing the Strand, near the east end of Catherine Street, under which a small stream glided from the fields into the Thames, near Somerset House.

[2] Where stands the church of St. Mary-le-Strand.

[3] Nathaniel Holmes, D.D., of Exeter College, Oxford. He was the intruding incumbent of St. Mary Staining, London, and ejected by the Act of Uniformity, and died in 1676. He was a very learned, but voluminous and fanciful writer. A list of his works is given in Wood's "Athenæ" (ed. Bliss), vol. iii., 1160. See also Kennett's "Register," p. 827.

but I staid not to hear, but walking in the court, I heard that Sir Arth. Haselrigge was newly gone into the City to Monk, and that Monk's wife[1] removed from White Hall last night. Home again, where at noon came according to my invitation my cos. Thos. Pepys and his partner and dined with me, but before dinner we went and took a walk round the park, it being a most pleasant day as ever I saw. After dinner we three went into London together, where I heard that Monk had been at Paul's in the morning, and the people had shouted much at his coming out of the church. In the afternoon he was at a church in Broad-street,[2] whereabout he do lodge. But not knowing how to see him we went and walked half a hour in Moorfields, which were full of people, it being so fine a day. Here I took leave of them, and so to Paul's, where I met with Mr. Kirton's[3] apprentice (the crooked fellow) and walked up and down with him two hours, sometimes in the street looking for a tavern to drink in, but not finding any open, we durst not knock; other times in the church-yard, where one told me that he had seen the letter printed. Thence to Mr. Turner's, where I found my wife, Mr. Edw. Pepys,[4] and Roger[5] and Mr. Armiger being there, to whom I gave as good an account of things as I could, and so to my father's, where Charles Glascocke[6] was overjoyed to see how

---

[1] Anne Clarges, said to be the daughter of a blacksmith, but a more distinguished parentage has been given to her brother. She was bred a milliner, and became first mistress of General Monk and afterwards (1654) his wife. It was said that when she married Monk she had a husband named Radford living.

[2] Monk lodged at the Glasshouse in Broad Street. "Feb. 12, 1659-60, Monk drew up his forces in Finsbury, dined with the Lord Mayor, had conference with him and the Court of Aldermen, retired to the Bull Head in Cheapside, and quartered at the Glass-House in Broad Street."—Whitelocke.

[3] Joseph Kirton was a bookseller in St. Paul's Churchyard, at the sign of "The King's Arms," ruined by the Fire of London. His death, in October, 1667, is recorded in Smith's "Obituary," printed for the Camden Society. He was buried in St. Faith's.

[4] Edward Pepys of Broomsthorpe, co. Norfolk, and of the Middle Temple, born 1617; married Elizabeth, daughter and co-heiress of John Walpole of Broomsthorpe. He was brother of Mrs. Turner, and died December 22nd, 1663.

[5] Roger Pepys.

[6] Pepys calls Charles Glasscock cousin under July 29th, 1661, but he was really no relation. He was brother-in-law of his first cousin's wife (Judith Pepys, née Cutter). Glasscock lived in Fleet Street (see April 22nd, 1661).

things are now; who told me the boys had last night broke Bare-bone's windows. Hence home, and being near home we missed our maid, and were at a great loss and went back a great way to find her, but when we could not see her we went homewards and found her there, got before us which we wondered at greatly. So to bed, where my wife and I had some high words upon my telling her that I would fling the dog which her brother gave her out of window if he [dirtied] the house any more.

[13th]. To my office till noon, thence home to dinner, my mouth being very bad of the cancer and my left leg beginning to be sore again. After dinner to see Mrs. Jem, and in the way met with Catan on foot in the street and talked with her a little, so home and took my wife to my father's. In my way I went to Play-ford's,[1] and for two books that I had and 6s. 6d. to boot I had my great book of songs which he sells always for 14s. At my father's I staid a while, while my mother sent her maid Bess to Cheapside for some herbs to make a water for my mouth. Then I went to see Mr. Cumberland, and after a little stay with him I returned, and took my wife home, where after supper to bed. This day Monk was invited to White Hall to dinner by my Lords; not seeming willing, he would not come. I went to Mr. Fage from my father's, who had been this afternoon with Monk, who do promise to live and die with the City, and for the honour of the City; and indeed the City is very open-handed to the sol-diers, that they are most of them drunk all day, and have money given them. He did give me something for my mouth which I did use this night.

[14th]. Called out in the morning by Mr. Moore, whose voice my wife hearing in my dressing-chamber with me, got herself ready, and came down and challenged him for her valentine, this being the day.[2] To Westminster Hall, there being many

---

[1] John Playford (1623-1693), the music-seller, whose shop was in the Temple. His "Introduction to the Skill of Musick," first published in 1655, went through many editions. He was known as "Honest John Playford," and was succeeded in his business by his son Henry.

[2] The practice of choosing valentines was very general at this time, but some of the best examples of the custom are found in this Diary.

new remonstrances and declarations from many counties to Monk and the City, and one coming from the North from Sir Thomas Fairfax.[1] Hence I took him to the Swan and gave him his morning draft. So to my office, where Mr. Hill of Worcestershire came to see me and my partner in our office, with whom we went to Will's to drink. At noon I went home and so to Mr. Crew's, but they had dined, and so I went to see Mrs. Jem where I stayed a while, and home again where I stayed an hour or two at my lute, and so forth to Westminster Hall, where I heard that the Parliament hath now changed the oath so much talked of to a promise; and that among other qualifications for the members that are to be chosen, one is, that no man, nor the son of any man that hath been in arms during the life of the father, shall be capable of being chosen to sit in Parliament. To Will's, where like a fool I staid and lost 6d. at cards. So home, and wrote a letter to my Lord by the post. So after supper to bed. This day, by an order of the House, Sir H. Vane[2] was sent out of town to his house in Lincolnshire.

[15th]. Called up in the morning by Captain Holland and Captain Cuttance,[3] and with them to Harper's, thence to my office, thence with Mr. Hill of Worcestershire to Will's, where I gave him a letter to Nan Pepys,[4] and some merry pamphlets against the Rump to carry to her into the country. So to Mr. Crew's, where the dining room being full, Mr. Walgrave[5] and I dined below in the buttery by ourselves upon a good dish of buttered

[1] Thomas Lord Fairfax, mentioned before. He had succeeded to the Scotch barony of Fairfax of Cameron, on the death of his father in 1647; even after his accession to the title he is frequently styled "Sir Thomas" in the pamphlets and papers of the day.

[2] Sir H. Vane the younger had married Frances, daughter of Sir Christopher Wray of Ashby, Lincolnshire, Bart.

[3] Roger Cuttance, a native of Weymouth, appointed captain of the "Peace" frigate in 1651, and to the "Naseby" in 1657. He was knighted, July 1st, 1665, after having in the battle of June 3rd mainly contributed to the defeat of the Dutch. He afterwards fell into disgrace.

[4] Anne Pepys, of Worcestershire, married Mr. Fisher for her second husband. (See June 12th, 1662.)

[5] Edward Walgrave (or Waldegrave) was the father of Jemima wife of John Crew, afterwards Lord Crew.

salmon. Thence to Hering[1] the merchant about my Lord's
Worcester money and back to Paul's Churchyard, where I staid
reading in Fuller's History of the Church of England[2] an hour
or two, and so to my father's, where Mr. Hill came to me and I
gave him direction what to do at Worcester about the money.
Thence to my Lady Wright's and gave her a letter from my
Lord privily. So to Mrs. Jem and sat with her, who dined at Mr.
Crew's to-day, and told me that there was at her coming away
at least forty gentlemen (I suppose members that were secluded,
for Mr. Walgrave told me that there were about thirty met there
the last night) came dropping in one after another thither.
Thence home and wrote into the country against to-morrow by
the carrier and so to bed. At my father's I heard how my cousin
Kate Joyce[3] had a fall yesterday from her horse and had some
hurt thereby. No news to-day, but all quiet to see what the
Parliament will do about the issuing of the writs to-morrow for
filling up of the House, according to Monk's desire.

[16th]. In the morning at my lute. Then came Shaw and Hawly,
and I gave them their morning draft at my house. So to my
office, where I wrote by the carrier to my Lord and sealed my
letter at Will's, and gave it old East to carry it to the carrier's,
and to take up a box of china oranges and two little barrels of
scallops at my house, which Captain Cuttance sent to me for my
Lord. Here I met with Osborne[4] and with Shaw and Spicer,
and we went to the Sun Tavern in expectation of a dinner, where
we had sent us only two trenchers full of meat, at which we
were very merry, while in came Mr. Wade and his friend Capt.
Moyse (who told us of his hopes to get an estate merely for his
name's sake), and here we staid till seven at night, I winning
a quart of sack of Shaw that one trencherfull that was sent us
was all lamb and he that it was veal. I by having but 3d. in
my pocket made shift to spend no more, whereas if I had had

---

[1] Mr. Herring was a merchant in Colman Street.
[2] Thomas Fuller's "Church History of Britain," London, 1656, folio, is in the
Pepysian Library.
[3] Kate, wife of Anthony Joyce, who kept the Three Stags at Holborn Conduit.
[4] Nicholas Osborne, Mr. Gauden's clerk.

more I had spent more as the rest did, so that I see it is an advantage to a man to carry little in his pocket. Home, and after supper, and a little at my flute, I went to bed.

[17th]. In the morning Tom that was my Lord's footboy came to see me and had 10s. of me of the money which I have to keep of his. So that now I have but 35s. more of his. Then came Mr. Hills the instrument maker, and I consulted with him about the altering my lute and my viall. After that I went into my study and did up my accounts, and found that I am about £40 beforehand in the world, and that is all. So to my office and from thence brought Mr. Hawly home with me to dinner, and after dinner wrote a letter to Mr. Downing about his business and gave it Hawly, and so went to Mr. Gunning's to his weekly fast, and after sermon, meeting there with Monsieur L'Impertinent, we went and walked in the park till it was dark. I played on my pipe at the Echo, and then drank a cup of ale at Jacob's. So to Westminster Hall, and he with me, where I heard that some of the members of the House were gone to meet with some of the secluded members and General Monk in the City. Hence we went to White Hall, thinking to hear more news, where I met with Mr. Hunt, who told me how Monk had sent for all his goods that he had here into the City; and yet again he told me, that some of the members of the House had this day laid in firing into their lodgings at White Hall for a good while, so that we are at a great stand to think what will become of things, whether Monk will stand to the Parliament or no. Hence Mons. L' Impertinent and I to Harper's, and there drank a cup or two to the King, and to his fair sister Frances'[1] good health, of whom we had much discourse of her not being much the worse for the small pox, which she had this last summer. So home and to bed. This day we are invited to my uncle Fenner's wedding feast, but went not, this being the 27th year.

[18th]. A great while at my vial and voice, learning to sing "Fly boy, fly boy," without book. So to my office, where little to do. In the Hall I met with Mr. Eglin and one Looker, a famous

___

[1] Frances Butler, the great beauty, who is sometimes styled *la belle Boteler*.

gardener, servant to my Lord Salsbury, and among other things the gardener told a strange passage in good earnest. . . . Home to dinner, and then went to my Lord's lodgings to my turret there and took away most of my books, and sent them home by my maid. Thither came Capt. Holland to me who took me to the Half Moon tavern and Mr. Southorne, Blackburne's clerk. Thence he took me to the Mitre in Fleet Street, where we heard (in a room over the music room) very plainly through the ceiling. Here we parted and I to Mr. Wotton's, and with him to an alehouse and drank while he told me a great many stories of comedies that he had formerly seen acted, and the names of the principal actors, and gave me a very good account of it. Thence to Whitehall, where I met with Luellin and in the clerk's chamber wrote a letter to my Lord. So home and to bed. This day two soldiers were hanged in the Strand for their late mutiny at Somerset-house.[1]

[19th] (Lord's day). Early in the morning I set my books that I brought home yesterday up in order in my study. Thence forth to Mr. Harper's to drink a draft of purle,[2] whither by appointment Monsieur L'Impertinent, who did intend too upon my desire to go along with me to St. Bartholomew's, to hear one Mr. Sparks, but it raining very hard we went to Mr. Gunning's and heard an excellent sermon, and speaking of the character that the Scripture gives of Ann the mother of the blessed Virgin, he did there speak largely in commendation of widowhood, and not as we do to marry two or three wives or husbands, one after another. Here I met with Mr. Moore, and went home with him to dinner, where he told me the discourse that happened between the secluded members and the members of the House, before Monk last Friday. How the secluded said, that they did not intend by coming in to express revenge upon these men, but only to meet and dissolve themselves, and only

---

[1] "They were brought to the place of execution, which was at Charing Cross, and over against Somerset House in the Strand, where were two gibbets erected. These men were the grand actors in the mutinies at Gravesend, at Somerset House, and in St. James' Fields."—Rugge's *Diurnal.*—B.

[2] Purl is hot beer flavoured with wormwood or other aromatic herbs. The name is also given to hot beer flavoured with gin, sugar, and ginger.

to issue writs for a free Parliament. He told me how Haselrigge was afraid to have the candle carried before him, for fear that the people seeing him, would do him hurt; and that he is afraid to appear in the City. That there is great likelihood that the secluded members will come in, and so Mr. Crew and my Lord are likely to be great men, at which I was very glad. After dinner there was many secluded members come in to Mr. Crew, which, it being the Lord's day, did make Mr. Moore believe that there was something extraordinary in the business. Hence home and brought my wife to Mr. Mossum's to hear him, and indeed he made a very good sermon, but only too eloquent for a pulpit. Here Mr. L'Impertinent helped me to a seat. After sermon to my father's, and fell in discourse concerning our going to Cambridge the next week with my brother John. To Mrs. Turner where her brother, Mr. Edward Pepys, was there, and I sat a great while talking of public business of the times with him. So to supper to my Father's, all supper talking of John's going to Cambridge. So home, and it raining my wife got my mother's French mantle and my brother John's hat, and so we went all along home and to bed.

[20th]. In the morning at my lute. Then to my office, where my partner and I made even our balance. Took him home to dinner with me, where my brother John came to dine with me. After dinner I took him to my study at home and at my Lord's, and gave him some books and other things against his going to Cambridge. After he was gone I went forth to Westminster Hall, where I met with Chetwind, Simons, and Gregory.[1] And with them to Marsh's at Whitehall to drink, and staid there a pretty while reading a pamphlet well writ and directed to General Monk, in praise of the form of monarchy which was settled here before the wars.[2] They told me how the Speaker Lenthall

---

[1] Thomas Gregory was, in 1672, Clerk of the Cheque at Chatham.

[2] This pamphlet is among the Thomason Collection of Civil War Tracts (British Museum), and dated in MS. this same day, February 20th—"A Plea for Limited Monarchy as it was established in this Nation before the late War. In an Humble Address to his Excellency General Monck. By a Zealot for the good old Laws of his Country, before any Faction or Caprice, with additions." "An Eccho to the Plea for Limited Monarchy, &c.," was published soon afterwards.

do refuse to sign the writs for choice of new members in the place of the excluded; and by that means the writs could not go out to-day. In the evening Simons and I to the Coffee Club, where nothing to do only I heard Mr. Harrington, and my Lord of Dorset and another Lord, talking of getting another place as the Cockpit, and they did believe it would come to something. After a small debate upon the question whether learned or unlearned subjects are the best the Club broke up very poorly, and I do not think they will meet any more. Hence with Vines, &c. to Will's, and after a pot or two home, and so to bed.

[21st]. In the morning going out I saw many soldiers going towards Westminster, and was told that they were going to admit the secluded members again. So I to Westminster Hall, and in Chancery Row[1] I saw about twenty of them who had been at White Hall with General Monk, who came thither this morning, and made a speech to them, and recommended to them a Commonwealth, and against Charles Stuart.[2] They came to the House and went in one after another, and at last the Speaker came. But it is very strange that this could be carried so private, that the other members of the House heard nothing of all this, till they found them in the House, insomuch that the soldiers that stood there to let in the secluded members, they took for such as they had ordered to stand there to hinder their coming in. Mr. Prin[3] came with an old basket hilt sword on, and had a great many great shouts upon his going into the Hall. They sat till noon, and at their coming out Mr. Crew saw me, and bid me come to his house, which I did, and he would have me dine with him, which I did; and he very joyful told me that the House

[1] Chancery Row must have been near the end of the hall where the Court of Chancery was situated.

[2] This remarkable speech is given at length by Rugge, who adds that about fourscore of the secluded members attended the first meeting of the House. It is highly probable that Monk had ascertained that they were ready to support him, before he committed himself to the Parliament.—B.

[3] William Prynne, born 1600, well known by his voluminous publications, and the persecution which he endured. He was M.P. for Bath, 1660, and died October 24th, 1669. Appointed Keeper of Tower Records, 1660.

had made General Monk, General of all the Forces in England, Scotland, and Ireland; and that upon Monk's desire, for the service that Lawson had lately done in pulling down the Committee of Safety, he had the command of the Sea for the time being. He advised me to send for my Lord forthwith, and told

GENERAL MONK

me that there is no question that, if he will, he may now be employed again; and that the House do intend to do nothing more than to issue writs, and to settle a foundation for a free Parliament. After dinner I back to Westminster Hall with him in his coach. Here I met with Mr. Lock and Pursell,[1] Masters of Music, and with them to the Coffee House, into a room next the

---

[1] Matthew Lock, see *ante*, February 11th, 1659-60. Henry Purcell, father of the celebrated composer, was gentleman of the Chapel Royal, member of the Royal Band, singing-man at Westminster Abbey, master of the boys there, and music copyist. He died 1664.

water, by ourselves, where we spent an hour or two till Captain Taylor came to us, who told us, that the House had voted the gates of the City to be made up again, and the members of the City[1] that are in prison to be set at liberty; and that Sir G. Booth's[2] case be brought into the House to-morrow. Here we had variety of brave Italian and Spanish songs, and a canon for eight voices, which Mr. Lock had lately made on these words: "Domine salvum fac Regem," an admirable thing. Here also Capt. Taylor began a discourse of something that he had lately writ about Gavelkind[3] in answer to one that had wrote a piece upon the same subject; and indeed discovered a great deal of study in antiquity in his discourse. Here out of the window it was a most pleasant sight to see the City from one end to the other with a glory about it, so high was the light of the bonfires, and so thick round the City, and the bells rang everywhere. Hence home and wrote to my Lord, afterwards came down and found Mr. Hunt (troubled at this change) and Mr. Spong, who staid late with me singing of a song or two, and so parted. My wife not very well, went to bed before. This morning I met in the Hall with Mr. Fuller, of Christ's, and told him of my design to go to Cambridge, and whither. He told me very freely the temper of Mr. Widdrington, how he did oppose all the fellows in the College, and that there was a great distance between him and the rest, at which I was very sorry, for that he told me he feared it would be little to my brother's advantage to be his pupil.

[22nd]. In the morning intended to have gone to Mr. Crew's to borrow some money, but it raining I forbore, and went to my Lord's lodging and look that all things were well there. Then home and sang a song to my viall, so to my office and to Will's, where Mr. Pierce found me out, and told me that he would go with me to Cambridge, where Colonel Ayre's regiment, to which

---

[1] Richard Brown, William Wilde, John Robinson, and William Vincent.
[2] Sir George Booth of Dunham Massey, Bart., created Baron de la Mere, 1661, for his services in behalf of the King. At this time he was a prisoner in the Tower, from which he was released the next day. Died 1684.
[3] Silas Taylor published "The History of Gavel-kind" in 1663.

he was surgeon, lieth. Walking in the Hall, I saw Major-General Brown,[1] who had a long time been banished by the Rump, but now with his beard overgrown, he comes abroad and sat in the House. To my father's to dinner, where nothing but a small dish of powdered beef[2] and dish of carrots; they being all busy to get things ready for my brother John to go to-morrow. After dinner, my wife staying there, I went to Mr. Crew's, and got £5 of Mr. Andrews, and so to Mrs. Jemimah, who now hath her instrument about her neck, and indeed is infinitely altered, and holds her head upright.[3] I paid her 40s. of the money that I have received of Mr. Andrews. Hence home to my study, where I only wrote thus much of this day's passages to this* and so out again. To White Hall, where I met with Will. Simons and Mr. Mabbot at Marsh's, who told me how the House had this day voted that the gates of the City should be set up at the cost of the State. And that Major-General Brown's being proclaimed a traitor be made void, and several other things of that nature. Home for my lanthorn and so to my father's, where I directed John what books to put for Cambridge. After that to supper, where my Uncle Fenner and my Aunt, The. Turner, and Joyce, at a brave leg of veal roasted, and were very merry against John's going to Cambridge. I observed this day how abominably Barebone's windows are broke again last night. At past 9 o'clock my wife and I went home.

[23rd]. Thursday, my birthday, now twenty-seven years. A pretty fair morning, I rose and after writing a while in my study I went forth. To my office, where I told Mr. Hawly of my thoughts to go out of town to-morrow. Hither Mr. Fuller comes

---

[1] Richard Brown, a major-general of the Parliament forces, citizen of London and a woodmonger; Sheriff of London, 1647. He was imprisoned for five years, but in Richard Cromwell's Parliament he was one of the members for London. He was one of the deputation from the City of London to Charles II. at Breda, and he and his eldest son were knighted. Lord Mayor, 1660; he was created a baronet for his prompt action during Venner's insurrection, and the City rewarded him with a pension of £500. He died September 24th, 1669.

[2] Boiled salt beef. To powder was to sprinkle with salt, and the powdering tub a vessel in which meat was salted.

[3] This support for the neck is mentioned on the previous February 1st, where Mrs. Scott and her husband are said to have promised to get it made.

to me and my Uncle Thomas too, thence I took them to drink, and so put off my uncle. So with Mr. Fuller home to my house, where he dined with me, and he told my wife and me a great many stories of his adversities, since these troubles, in being forced to travel in the Catholic countries, &c. He shewed me his bills, but I had not money to pay him. We parted, and I to Whitehall, where I was to see my horse which Mr. Garthwayt lends me to-morrow. So home, where Mr. Pierce comes to me about appointing time and place where and when to meet to-morrow. So to Westminster Hall, where, after the House rose, I met with Mr. Crew, who told me that my Lord was chosen by 73 voices, to be one of the Council of State. Mr. Pierpoint[1] had the most, 101, and himself the next, 100. He brought me in the coach home. He and Mr. Anslow being in it. I back to the Hall, and at Mrs. Michell's shop staid talking a great while with her and my Chaplain, Mr. Mumford, and drank a pot or two of ale on a wager that Mr. Prin is not of the Council. Home and wrote to my Lord the news of the choice of the Council by the post, and so to bed.

[24th]. I rose very early, and taking horse at Scotland Yard, at Mr. Garthwayt's stable, I rode to Mr. Pierce's, who rose, and in a quarter of an hour, leaving his wife in bed (with whom Mr. Lucy methought was very free as she lay in bed), we both mounted, and so set forth about seven of the clock, the day and the way very foul. About Ware we overtook Mr. Blayton, brother-in-law to Dick Vines, who went thenceforwards with us, and at Puckeridge we baited, where we had a loin of mutton fried, and were very merry, but the way exceeding bad from Ware thither. Then up again and as far as Foulmer, within six miles of Cambridge, my mare being almost tired: here we lay at the Chequer, playing at cards till supper, which was a breast of veal roasted. I lay with Mr. Pierce, who we left here the next morning upon his going to Hinchingbroke to speak with my Lord before his going to London, and we two come to Cambridge by eight o'clock in the morning.

---

[1] William Pierrepont, M.P. of Thoresby, second son to Robert, first Earl of Kingston, and known as "Wise" Pierrepont. He died 1678, aged 71.

[25th]. To the Falcon,[1] in the Petty Cury,[2] where we found my father and brother very well. After dressing myself, about ten o'clock, my father, brother, and I to Mr. Widdrington, at Christ's College, who received us very civilly, and caused my brother to be admitted,[3] while my father, he, and I, sat talking. After that done, we take leave. My father and brother went to visit some friends, Pepys's, scholars in Cambridge,[4] while I went to Magdalene College, to Mr. Hill,[5] with whom I found Mr. Zanchy,[6] Burton,[7] and

---

[1] The old Falcon Inn is on the south side of Petty Cury. It is now divided into three houses, one of which is the present Falcon Inn, the other two being houses with shops. The Falcon yard is but little changed. From the size of the whole building it must have been the principal inn of the town. The room said to have been used by Queen Elizabeth for receptions retains its original form.—M. B.

[2] The Petty Cury. The derivation of the name of this street, so well known to all Cambridge men, is a matter of much dispute among antiquaries. (See "Notes and Queries.") The most probable meaning of it is the *Parva Cokeria*, or *little cury*, where the cooks of the town lived, just as "The Poultry," where the Poulters (now Poulterers) had their shops. *"The Forme of Cury,"* a Roll of Antient English Cookery, was compiled by the principal cooks of that "best and royalest viander of all Christian Kings," Richard the Second, and edited with a copious Index and Glossary by Dr. Samuel Pegge, 1780.—M. B.

[3] Extract from admission-book of Christ's College, Cambridge:

"Febr. 25º. 1660.

"Johannes a Johanne Pepys Londini natus literas edoctus a Dno Crumble-holm Scholæ Paulinæ Moderatore annos natus 18 admissus est Sizator sub Mro. Widdrington.

"Hic cum prius admissus est in Collegium Magdalense Maii 26to. ut ex literis testimonialibus constat ejusdem etiam anni apud nos habendus est."—M. B.

[4] This might read "Pepys's scholars," but there do not appear to have been any such scholars.

[5] Joseph Hill, a native of Yorkshire, chosen in 1649 Fellow of Magdalene College, and in 1659 University Proctor: he afterwards retired to London, and, according to Calamy, was offered a bishopric by Charles II., which he declined, disliking the terms of conformity; and accepting a call to the English Church at Rotterdam in 1678, died there in 1707, aged 83.—*Nonconformists' Memorial.*—B.

[6] Clement Zanchy, admitted at Magdalene College, Cambridge, 1648, and Foundation Fellow, 1654. At the College meetings he spelt his name "Zanchy," at first, but in 1656 he changed it to "Sankey," and it is sometimes spelt "Sanchy."—M. B.

[7] Hezekiah Burton, of Lound, Nottinghamshire, pensioner of Magdalene College, 1647. His admission to a Wray Fellowship is curious:

Hollins, and was exceeding civilly received by them. I took leave on promise to sup with them, and to my Inn again, where I dined with some others that were there at an ordinary. After dinner my brother to the College, and my father and I to my Cozen Angier's,[1] to see them, where Mr. Fairbrother[2] came to us. Here we sat a while talking. My father he went to look after his things at the carrier's, and my brother's chamber, while Mr. Fairbrother, my Cozen Angier, and Mr. Zanchy, whom I met at Mr. Merton's shop (where I bought *Elenchus Motuum*,[3] having given my former to Mr. Downing when he was here), to the Three Tuns, where we drank pretty hard and many healths to the King, &c., till it began to be darkish: then we broke up and I and Mr. Zanchy went to Magdalene College, where a very handsome supper at Mr. Hill's chambers, I suppose upon a club among them, where in their discourse I could find that there was nothing at all left of the old preciseness in their discourse, specially on Saturday nights. And Mr. Zanchy told me that there was no such thing now-a-days among them at any time. After supper and some discourse then to my Inn, where I found my father in his chamber, and after some discourse, and he well satisfied with this day's

---

"Mar. 8. 1650.

"Hezekias Burton in Artibus Baccalaureus hujus Collij, authoritate ordinationis Parliamentariæ, admissus est in sodalitium M[ri]. Johannis David, eadem authoritate vacant." The last word is not quite clear.—M. B.

[1] Percival Angier. His affairs appear to have got into disorder at the end of 1663, and he became a bankrupt. He died in January, 1664-65, and was buried on the 19th of that month.

[2] William Fairbrother, Fellow of King's College, Cambridge, was made D.D. of Cambridge, *per Regias litteras*, in 1661. He was taken prisoner at the battle of Naseby while fighting on the King's side, and sent to London.

[3] A pamphlet by George Bate, M.D., first published anonymously in 1649, and frequently reprinted. It was translated into Italian and published at Venice in 1652. After the Restoration it was reprinted and a second part added. The following is the title: "Elenchus Motuum nuperorum in Anglia; simul ac juris Regii et Parlamentarii brevis enarratio. A. 2455 Lutetiæ Parisiorum pro R. R. An. Dom. 1649." 12⁰. Address to the reader signed "Theodorus Veridicus." "Elenchi Motuum Nuperorum in Anglia pars prima; simul ac Juris Regii & Parlamentarii brevis enarratio, ab autore Geor. Batio, M.D. Regiæ Majestatis Protomedico recognita & aucta Ære Christianæ Anno 1660. Londini typis J. Flesher & prostant apud R. Royston in Ivy Lane, 1661." 8vo. "Pars Secunda. Simul ac Regis Effugii mirabilis è Prætio Wigornia enarratio. Londini, 1663."

work, we went to bed, my brother lying with me, his things not being come by the carrier that he could not lie in the College.

[26th] (Sunday). My brother went to the College to Chapel. My father and I went out in the morning, and walked out in the fields behind King's College, and in King's College Chapel Yard, where we met with Mr. Fairbrother, who took us to Botolph's Church, where we heard Mr. Nicholas, of Queen's College, who I knew in my time to be Tripos,[1] with great applause, upon this text, "For thy commandments are broad." Thence my father and I to Mr. Widdrington's chamber to dinner, where he used us very courteously again, and had two Fellow Commoners at table with him, and Mr. Pepper, a Fellow of the College. After dinner, while we sat talking by the fire, Mr. Pierce's man [came] to tell me that his master was come to town, so my father and I took leave, and found Mr. Pierce at our Inn, who told us that he had lost his journey, for my Lord was gone from Hinchingbroke to London on Thursday last, at which I was a little put to a stand. So after a cup of drink I went to Magdalene College to get the certificate of the College for my brother's entrance there, that he might save his year. I met with Mr. Burton in the Court, who took me to Mr. Pechell's chamber,[2] where he was and Mr. Zanchy. By and by,

---

[1] The Tripos or Bachelor of the Stool, who made the speech on Ash Wednesday, when the senior Proctor called him up and exhorted him to be witty but modest withal. Their speeches, especially after the Restoration, tended to be boisterous, and even scurrilous. "26 Martii 1669. Dˢ Hollis, fellow of Clare Hall is to make a publick Recantation in the Bac. Schools for his Tripos speeche." The Tripos verses still come out, and are circulated on Ash Wednesday. The list of successful candidates for honours is printed on the same paper, hence the term "Tripos" applied to it.

[2] John Peachell, Vicar of Stanwick and Prebendary of Carlisle, made Master of Magdalene College, 1679, suspended from that office and deprived of the Vice-Chancellorship, May 7th, 1687, for refusing to admit Alban Francis, a Benedictine monk, to the degree of Master of Arts without his taking the oaths. He was restored by James II.'s letter to the Mastership, October, 1688, and died 1690.

A copy of Dr. Peachell's sentence as it was fixed on the publick School Doors and Magdalene College Gates:

"By His Majesties Commissioners for Ecclesiastical Causes and for the Visitation of the University and of every Collegiate and Cathedral Churches, Colledges, Grammar Schools, Hospitals and other the like Incorporations or Foundations or Societies.

"Whereas John Peachell Dʳ. of Divinity, Vice Chancellour of Cambridge,

Mr. Pechell and Sanchy and I went out, Pechell to Church, Sanchy and I to the Rose Tavern,[1] where we sat and drank till sermon done, and then Mr. Pechell came to us, and we three sat drinking the King's and his whole family's health till it began to be dark. Then we parted; Sanchy and I went to my lodging, where we found my father and Mr. Pierce at the door, and I took them both and Mr. Blayton to the Rose Tavern, and there gave them a quart or two of wine, not telling them that we had been there before. After this we broke up, and my father, Mr. Zanchy, and I to my Cosen Angier to supper, where I caused two bottles of wine to be carried from the Rose Tavern; that was drunk up, and I had not the wit to let them know at table that it was I that paid for them, and so I lost my thanks for them. After supper Mr. Fairbrother, who supped there with us, took me into a room by himself, and shewed me a pitiful copy of verses upon Mr. Prinn

Master of Magdalen Colledge, in the said University, has been conveñd before us for his disobedience to his Majesties Royal Letters mandatory and other his contempts: and the said Dr. John Peachell having been fully heard thereupon, we have thought fit after mature consideration of the matter to declare, decree and pronounce that the said Dr. John Peachell, shall for the said disobedience and contempt, be deprived from being Vice Chancellour of the said University, and from all power of acting in the same: and also that he be suspended ab officio et beneficio of his Mastership of the said Colledge, during his Majesties pleasure: and accordingly we do by these presents deprive him the said Dr. John Peachell from being Vice Chancellour of the said University and from all power of acting in the same. And we also suspend him ab officio et beneficio of his Mastership of the said Colledge, peremptorily admonishing and requiring him hereby to abstain from the function of Master of the said Colledge, during the said suspension under pain of deprivation from his said Mastership. And we also further order and decree, that the profit and perquisites belonging to his said Mastership, shall during the same suspension be applied to the use and benefit of the said Colledge.

"Given under our Seal, the 7th day of May 1687.

"Finis."

"I find in the first Lord Dartmouth's manuscript notes on Bishop Burnet's History, that Dr. Peachell afterwards starved himself to death, Archbishop Sancroft having rebuked him for setting an ill example in the University by drunkenness and other loose behaviour. He did penance by four days' abstinence, after which he would have eaten but could not."—From the Master of Magdalene's "private" book. For his *red nose*, which made Pepys ashamed to be seen with him, see Diary, May 3rd, 1667.—M. B.

[1] The Rose tavern opened on the Market Hill at the end of Rose Crescent.— M. B.

which he esteemed very good, and desired that I would get them given to Mr. Prinn, in hopes that he would get him some place for it, which I said I would do, but did laugh in my sleeve to think of his folly, though indeed a man that has always expressed great civility to me. After that we sat down and talked; I took leave of all my friends, and so to my Inn, where after I had wrote a note and enclosed the certificate to Mr. Widdrington, I bade good night to my father, and John went to bed, but I staid up a little while, playing the fool with the lass of the house at the door of the chamber, and so to bed.

[27th]. Up by four o'clock, and after I was ready, took my leave of my father, whom I left in bed, and the same of my brother John, to whom I gave 10s. Mr. Blayton and I took horse and straight to Saffron Walden, where at the White Hart, we set up our horses, and took the master of the house to shew us Audley End House,[1] who took us on foot through the park, and so to the house, where the housekeeper shewed us all the house, in which the stateliness of the ceilings, chimney-pieces, and form of the whole was exceedingly worth seeing. He took us into the cellar, where we drank most admirable drink, a health to the King. Here I played on my flageolette, there being an excellent echo. He shewed us excellent pictures; two especially, those of the four Evangelists and Henry VIII. After that I gave the man 2s. for his trouble, and went back again. In our going, my landlord carried us through a very old hospital or almshouse, where forty poor people was maintained; a very old foundation; and over the chimney in the mantelpiece was an inscription in brass: "Orate pro animâ Thomæ Bird," &c.;[2] and the poor box also was on the same chimney-piece, with an iron door and locks to it, into which I put 6d. They brought me a draft of their drink in a brown bowl, tipt

---

[1] Then the residence of James Howard, third Earl of Suffolk. It was built by Thomas, the first earl, at the commencement of the seventeenth century, and called after his maternal ancestor, Lord Chancellor Audley, to whom the monastery of Walden, the site of which is occupied by the present house, had been granted at the Dissolution.—B.

[2] The inscription and the bowl are still to be seen at King Edward VI.'s almshouses, Saffron Walden. There is an engraving and description of this bowl in Mr. W. H. St. John Hope's paper, "On the English mediæval drinking bowls called Mazers," in "Archæologia," vol. l. (p. 163 and plate xiii.).

with silver, which I drank off, and at the bottom was a picture of the Virgin and the child in her arms, done in silver. So we went to our Inn, and after eating of something, and kissed the daughter of the house, she being very pretty, we took leave, and so that night, the road pretty good, but the weather rainy to Ep[p]ing, where we sat and played a game at cards, and after supper, and some merry talk with a plain bold maid of the house, we went to bed.

[28th]. Up in the morning, and had some red herrings to our breakfast, while my boot-heel was a-mending, by the same token the boy left the hole as big as it was before. Then to horse, and for

London through the forest, where we found the way good, but only in one path, which we kept as if we had rode through a canal all the way. We found the shops all shut, and the militia of the red regiment in arms at the Old Exchange,[1] among whom I found and spoke to Nich. Osborne, who told me that it was a thanksgiv-

[1] Royal Exchange.

ing-day through the City for the return of the Parliament. At Paul's I light, Mr. Blayton holding my horse, where I found Dr. Reynolds[1] in the pulpit, and General Monk there, who was to have a great entertainment at Grocers' Hall.[2] So home, where my wife and all well. Shifted myself,[3] and so to Mr. Crew's, and then to Sir Harry Wright's, where I found my Lord at dinner, who called for me in, and was glad to see me. There was at dinner also Mr. John Wright and his lady, a very pretty lady, Alderman Allen's daughter. I dined there with Will Howe,[4] and after dinner went out with him to buy a hat (calling in my way and saw my mother), which we did at the Plough in Fleet Street by my Lord's direction, but not as for him. Here we met with Mr. Pierce a little before, and he took us to the Greyhound Tavern,[5] and gave us a pint of wine, and as the rest of the seamen do, talked very high again of my Lord. After we had done about the hat we went homewards, he to Mr. Crew's and I to Mrs. Jem, and sat with her a little. Then home, where I found Mr. Sheply, almost drunk, come to see me, afterwards Mr. Spong comes, with whom I went up and played with him a Duo or two, and so good night. I was indeed a little vexed with Mr. Sheply, but said nothing, about his breaking open of my study at my house, merely to give him the key of the stair door at my Lord's, which lock he might better have broke than mine.

[1] Edward Reynolds, D.D., Preacher of Lincoln's Inn; Dean of Christ Church, 1648-50; Bishop of Norwich, 1660-1676. He died July 28th, 1676, aged 76. The sermon which Pepys heard was printed, and has the following title: "The Wall and Glory of Jerusalem, in a Sermon preached in St. Paul's Church, London, before the Right Honourable the Lord Mayor, Lord General, Aldermen, Common Council and Companies of the Honourable City of London, February 28, 1659, being a day of solemn Thanksgiving unto God for restoring the Parliament and Common Council and for preserving the City. By Edward Reynolds, D.D. London, 1660."
[2] Grocers' Hall was the scene of many important occurrences during the period of the Great Rebellion. This was the first hall on the present site between the Poultry and Princes Street, which was built in 1427. The second hall was built after the Great Fire, and the present one was opened in 1802.
[3] Changed his dress.
[4] William Howe is frequently mentioned in the Diary, and he appears more than once to have got into trouble. He is mentioned as Deputy Treasurer of the Navy, under date September 18th, 1665.
[5] As the Greyhound is mentioned so soon after the Plough it also may have been in Fleet Street. See November 12th, 1661.

[29th]. To my office, and drank at Will's with Mr. Moore, who told me how my Lord is chosen General at Sea by the Council, and that it is thought that Monk will be joined with him therein. Home and dined, after dinner my wife and I by water to London, and thence to Herring's, the merchant in Coleman Street, about £50 which he promises I shall have on Saturday next. So to my mother's, and then to Mrs. Turner's, of whom I took leave, and her company, because she was to go out of town to-morrow with Mr. Pepys into Norfolk. Here my cosen Norton[1] gave me a brave cup of metheglin,[2] the first I ever drank. To my mother's and supped there. She shewed me a letter to my father from my uncle inviting him to come to Brampton while he is in the country. So home and to bed. This day my Lord came to the House, the first time since he came to town; but he had been at the Council before.

[March 1st]. In the morning went to my Lord's lodgings, thinking to have spoke with Mr. Sheply, having not been to visit him since my coming to town. But he being not within I went up, and out of the box where my Lord's pamphlets lay, I chose as many as I had a mind to have for my own use and left the rest. Then to my office, where little to do, but Mr. Sheply comes to me, so at dinner time he and I went to Mr. Crew's, whither Mr. Thomas[3] was newly come to town, being sent with Sir H. Yelverton,[4] my old school-fellow at Paul's School, to bring the thanks of the county to General Monk for the return of the Parliament. But old Mr. Crew and my Lord not coming home to dinner, we tarried late before we went to dinner, it being the day

---

[1] Probably Joyce Norton, see *ante*, January 7th, 1659-60.

[2] A liquor made of honey and water, boiled and fermenting. By 12 Charles II. cap. 23, a grant of certain impositions upon beer, ale, and other liquors, a duty of 1/2d. per gallon was laid upon "all metheglin or mead."

[3] Thomas Crew, eldest son of John, afterwards first Lord Crew.

[4] Son of Sir Christopher Yelverton, the first baronet, grandson of Sir Henry Yelverton, Judge C. P., author of the "Reports." He married Susan, Baroness Grey de Ruthyn, which title descended to his issue. His son was afterwards advanced to the dignity of Viscount Longueville, and his grandson to the earldom of Sussex. The Yelverton Collection of MSS. belongs to Lord Calthorpe, whose ancestor married a daughter of the first Viscount Longueville.—B.

that John, Mr. John Crew's coachman, was to be buried in the afternoon, he being a day or two before killed with a blow of one of his horses that struck his skull into his brain. From thence Mr. Sheply and I went into London to Mr. Laxton's, my Lord's apothecary, and so by water to Westminster, where at the Sun[1] he and I spent two or three hours in a pint or two of wine, discoursing of matters in the country, among other things telling me that my uncle did to him make a very kind mention of me, and what he would do for me. Thence I went home, and went to bed betimes. This day the Parliament did vote that they would not sit longer than the 15th day of this month.

[2nd]. This morning I went early to my Lord at Mr. Crew's where I spoke to him. Here were a great many come to see him, as Secretary Thurlow who is now by this Parliament chosen again Secretary of State. There were also General Monk's trumpeters to give my Lord a sound of their trumpets this morning. Thence I went to my office, and wrote a letter to Mr. Downing about the business of his house. Then going home, I met with Mr. Eglin, Chetwind, and Thomas, who took me to the Leg in King's street,[2] where we had two brave dishes of meat, one of fish, a carp and some other fishes, as well done as ever I ate any. After that to the Swan tavern, where we drank a quart or two of wine, and so parted. So I to Mrs. Jem and took Mr. Moore with me (who I met in the street), and there I met W. Howe and Sheply. After that to Westminster Hall, where I saw Sir G. Booth at liberty. This day I hear the City militia is put into good posture, and it is thought that Monk will not be able to do any great matter against them now, if he have a mind. I understand that my Lord Lambert did yesterday send a letter to the Council, and that to-night he is to come and appear to the Council in person. Sir

---

[1] Probably the Sun tavern in King Street, Westminster (see August 3rd, 1668). There is a token of this house described in "Boyne's Trade Tokens," ed. Williamson, vol. i., 1889, p. 649.

[2] The Leg tavern in King Street appears to have been a house of good resort. It is mentioned in Burton's Diary as the scene of a dinner of the Clothworkers' Company, December 18th, 1656, who had then a cause before the House of Commons. Pepys frequently visited it.

Arthur Haselrigge do not yet appear in the House. Great is the talk of a single person, and that it would now be Charles, George, or Richard again.[1] For the last of which, my Lord St. John is said to speak high. Great also is the dispute now in the House, in whose name the writs shall run for the next Parliament; and it is said that Mr. Prin, in open House, said, "In King Charles's."[2] From Westminster Hall home. Spent the evening in my study, and so after some talk with my wife, then to bed.

[3rd]. To Westminster Hall, where I found that my Lord was last night voted one of the Generals at Sea, and Monk the other. I met my Lord in the Hall, who bid me come to him at noon. I met with Mr. Pierce the purser, Lieut. Lambert, Mr. Creed,[3] and Will. Howe, and went with them to the Swan tavern. Up to my office, but did nothing. At noon home to dinner to a sheep's head. My brother Tom came and dined with me, and told me that my mother was not very well, and that my Aunt Fenner was very ill too. After dinner I to Warwick House,[4] in Holborn,

---

[1] Charles II., or George Monk, or Richard Cromwell.

[2] Compare a letter of Mr. Luttrell to Ormond, March 9th, 1660, in Carte's "Letters," vol. ii. p. 312: "Yesterday there was a debate about the form of the dissolution, when Mr. Prynne asserted the King's right in such bold language that I think he may be styled the Cato of this age."—*Notes and Queries*, vol. x. p. 2.—M. B.

[3] John Creed of Oundle, Esq. From the way in which Pepys speaks of his friend, he was probably of humble origin, and nothing is known of his history previously to the Restoration, when he seems to have been a retainer in the service of Sir Edward Montagu. In 1662 he was made Secretary to the Commissioners for Tangier, and in 1668 he married Elizabeth Pickering, the niece of his original patron, by whom he had eleven children. Major Richard Creed, the eldest son, who was killed at the battle of Blenheim, lies buried in Tichmarsh Church, in Northamptonshire, where there is also a monument erected to his father, describing him as "of Oundle," and as having served King Charles II. in divers honourable employments at home and abroad, lived with honour, and died lamented, A.D. 1701. What these employments were cannot now be ascertained. There exists still a cenotaph to the memory of the major in Westminster Abbey. Mrs. Creed, wife of John Creed of Oundle, Esq., was the only daughter of Sir Gilbert Pickering, Bart., by Elizabeth, only daughter of Sir Edward Montagu, and sister of Edward Montagu, first Earl of Sandwich. See Malone's "Life of Dryden," p. 339.—B.

[4] Warwick House, on the north side of Holborn, a little to the west of Gray's Inn Gate. It had given place to Warwick Court in 1708.

to my Lord, where he dined with my Lord of Manchester,[1] Sir Dudley North,[2] my Lord Fiennes,[3] and my Lord Barkly.[4] I staid in the great hall, talking with some gentlemen there, till they all came out. Then I, by coach with my Lord, to Mr. Crew's, in our way talking of publick things, and how I should look after getting of his Commissioner's despatch. He told me he feared there was new design hatching, as if Monk had a mind to get into the saddle. Here I left him, and went by appointment to Hering, the merchant, but missed of my money, at which I was much troubled, but could not help myself. Returning, met Mr. Gifford, who took me and gave me half a pint of wine, and told me, as I hear this day from many, that things are in a very doubtful posture, some of the Parliament being willing to keep the power in their hands. After I had left him, I met with Tom Harper, who took me into a place in Drury Lane, where we drank a great deal of strong water,[5] more than ever I did in my life at one time before. He talked huge high that my Lord Protector would come in place again, which indeed is much discoursed of again, though I do not see it possible. Hence home and

[1] Edward Montagu, second Earl of Manchester, the Parliamentary General, afterwards particularly instrumental in the King's Restoration, became Chamberlain of the Household, K. G., a Privy Councillor, and Chancellor of the University of Cambridge. He died in 1671, having been five times married.

[2] Sir Dudley North, K.B., became the fourth Lord North on the death of his father in 1666. He died 1677.

[3] John, third son of William, first Viscount Say and Sele, and one of Oliver's Lords.

[4] George, fourteenth Lord Berkeley of Berkeley, created Viscount Dursley and Earl of Berkeley, 1679. There were at this time two Lord Berkeleys, each possessing a town house called after his name, which misled Pennant. George, fourteenth Lord Berkeley of Berkeley, advanced to an earldom in 1679, the peer here spoken of, lived at Berkeley House, in the parish of St. John's, Clerkenwell, which had been in his family for three generations, and he had a country-seat at Durdans, near Epsom, mentioned by Evelyn and Pepys. He presented the library of his uncle, Sir Robert Coke, to Sion College, and that institution possesses a painted portrait of the earl in his robes. He died October 14th, 1698. The other nobleman, originally known as Sir John Berkeley, and in the service of Charles I., created in 1658 Baron Berkeley of Stratton, subsequently filled many high offices in the State. See *post*, July 12th, 1660.

[5] There is a token of "Edmund Browne at the Pall Mall," on which he describes himself as "Strong water man" (see "Boyne's Trade Tokens," ed. Williamson, vol. i., 1889, p. 694).

wrote to my father at Brampton by the post. So to bed. This day I was told that my Lord General Fleetwood told my Lord that he feared the King of Sweden[1] is dead of a fever at Gottenburg.

[4th] (Lord's day). Before I went to church I sang Orpheus' Hymn[2] to my viall. After that to Mr. Gunning's, an excellent sermon upon charity. Then to mother to dinner, where my wife and the maid were come. After dinner we three to Mr. Messum's where we met Mons. L'Impertinent, who got us a seat and told me a ridiculous story how that last week he had caused a simple citizen to spend £80 in entertainments of him and some friends of his upon pretence of some service that he would do him in his suit after a widow. Then to my mother again, and after supper she and I talked very high about religion, I in defence of the religion I was born in. Then home.

[5th]. Early in the morning Mr. Hill comes to string my theorbo,[3] which we were about till past ten o'clock, with a great deal of pleasure. Then to Westminster, where I met with Mr. Sheply and Mr. Pinkney at Will's, who took me by water to Billingsgate, at the Salutation Tavern,[4] whither by-and-by, Mr. Talbot and Adams came, and bring a great [deal of] good meat, a ham of bacon, &c. Here we staid and drank till Mr. Adams began to be overcome. Then we parted, and so to Westminster by water,

---

[1] Charles X., Gustavus, King of Sweden, died on February 3rd, 1659-60 (see March 8th).

[2] Orpheus' hymn, "King of Heaven and Hell and Sea and Earth," by Henry Lawes, is printed in "The Second Book of Ayres and Dialogues. London (Playford), 1655."

[3] The theorbo was a bass lute. Having gut strings it was played with the fingers. There is a humorous comparison of the long waists of ladies, which came into fashion about 1621, with the theorbo, by Bishop Corbet:

> "She was barr'd up in whale-bones, that did leese
> None of the whale's length, for they reached her knees:
> Off with her head, and then she hath a middle
> As her waste stands, just like the new found fiddle,
> The favourite *Theorbo*, truth to tell ye,
> Whose neck and throat are deeper than the belly."
>
> Corbet, *Iter Boreale*.

[4] There is a token of the Salutation at Billingsgate (see "Boyne's Trade Tokens," ed. Williamson, vol. i., 1889, p. 531).

only seeing Mr. Pinkney at his own house, where he shewed me how he had alway kept the Lion and Unicorn, in the back of his chimney, bright, in expectation of the King's coming again. At home I found Mr. Hunt, who told me how the Parliament had voted that the Covenant be printed and hung in churches again. Great hopes of the King's coming again. To bed.

[6th] (Shrove Tuesday). I called Mr. Sheply and we both went up to my Lord's lodgings at Mr. Crew's, where he bade us to go home again, and get a fire against an hour after. Which we did at White Hall, whither he came, and after talking with him and me about his going to sea, he called me by myself to go along with him into the garden, where he asked me how things were with me, and what he had endeavoured to do with my uncle to get him to do something for me but he would say nothing too. He likewise bade me look out now at this turn some good place, and he would use all his own, and all the interest of his friends that he had in England, to do me good. And asked me whether I could, without too much inconvenience, go to sea as his secretary, and bid me think of it. He also began to talk of things of State, and told me that he should want one in that capacity at sea, that he might trust in, and therefore he would have me to go. He told me also, that he did believe the King would come in, and did discourse with me about it, and about the affection of the people and City, at which I was full glad. After he was gone, I waiting upon him through the garden till he came to the Hall, where I left him and went up to my office, where Mr. Hawly brought one to me, a seaman, that had promised £10 to him if he get him a purser's place, which I think to endeavour to do. Here comes my uncle Tom, whom I took to Will's and drank with, poor man, he comes to inquire about the knights of Windsor,[1] of which he desires to get to be one. While we were

[1] The body of Poor Knights of Windsor was founded by Edward III. The intention of the king with regard to the poor knights was to provide relief and comfortable subsistence for such valiant soldiers as happened in their old age to fall into poverty and decay. On September 20th, 1659, a Report having been read respecting the Poor Knights of Windsor, the House "ordered that it be referred to a Committee, to look into the revenue for maintenance of the Poor Knights of Windsor," &c. (See Tighe and Davis's "Annals of Windsor.")

drinking, in comes Mr. Day, a carpenter in Westminster, to tell me that it was Shrove Tuesday, and that I must go with him to their yearly Club upon this day, which I confess I had quite forgot. So I went to the Bell, where were Mr. Eglin, Veezy, Vincent a butcher, one more, and Mr. Tanner, with whom I played upon a viall, and he a viallin, after dinner, and were very merry, with a special good dinner, a leg of veal and bacon, two capons and sausages and fritters, with abundance of wine. After that I went home, where I found Kate Sterpin who hath not been here a great while before. She gone I went to see Mrs. Jem, at whose chamber door I found a couple of ladies, but she not being there, we hunted her out, and found that she and another had hid themselves behind a door. Well, they all went down into the dining-room, where it was full of tag, rag, and bobtail, dancing, singing, and drinking, of which I was ashamed, and after I had staid a dance or two I went away. Going home, called at my Lord's for Mr. Sheply, but found him at the Lion with a pewterer, that he had bought pewter to-day of. With them I drank, and so home and wrote by the post, by my Lord's command, for J. Goods[1] to come up presently. For my Lord intends to go forthwith into the Swiftsure[2] till the Nazeby[3] be ready. This day I hear that the Lords do intend to sit, and great store of them are now in town, and I see in the Hall to-day. Overton[4] at Hull do stand out, but can, it is thought, do nothing; and Lawson, it is said, is gone with some ships thither, but all that is nothing. My Lord told me, that there was great endeavours to bring in the Protector again; but he told me, too, that he did believe it would not last long if he were brought in; no, nor the King neither (though he seems to think that he will come in), unless he carry himself very soberly and well. Every body now

---

[1] John Goods. He went to sea with Sir Edward Montagu.

[2] The "Swiftsure" was a second-rate of sixty guns, built at Woolwich in 1654 by Christopher Pett.

[3] The "Nazeby" was commanded by Captain, afterwards Sir Richard Stayner. It was a first-rate of eighty guns, built at Woolwich in 1655 by Christopher Pett.

[4] Major-General Overton was committed to the Tower in 1649, 1655, and in December, 1660.

drinks the King's health without any fear, whereas before it was very private that a man dare do it. Monk this day is feasted at Mercers' Hall, and is invited one after another to all the twelve Halls in London.[1] Many think that he is honest yet, and some or more think him to be a fool that would raise himself, but think that he will undo himself by endeavouring it. My mind, I must needs remember, has been very much eased and joyed at my Lord's great expressions of kindness this day, and in discourse thereupon my wife and I lay awake an hour or two in our bed.

[7th] (Ash Wednesday). In the morning I went to my Lord at Mr. Crew's, in my way Washington overtook me and told me upon my question whether he knew of any place now void that I might have, by power over friends, that this day Mr. G. Montagu was to be made Custos Rotulorum for Westminster, and that by friends I might get to be named by him Clerk of the Peace, with which I was, as I am at all new things, very much joyed, so when I came to Mr. Crew's, I spoke to my Lord about it, who told me he believed Mr. Montagu had already promised it, and that it was given him only that he might gratify one person with the place I look for. Here, among many that were here, I met with Mr. Lynes, the surgeon, who promised me some seeds of the sensitive plant.[2] I spoke too with Mr. Pierce the surgeon, who gave me great encouragement to go to sea with my Lord. Thence going homewards, my Lord overtook me in his coach, and called me in, and so I went with him to St. James's, and G. Montagu being gone to White Hall, we walked over the Park thither, all the way he discoursing of the times, and of the change of things since the last year, and wondering how he could bear with so great disappointment as he did. He did give me the best advice that he could what was best for me, whether to stay or go with him, and offered all the ways that could be, how he might do me good, with the greatest liberty and love that could

[1] See note, April 11th, 1660, where it is stated that Monk had dined at nine of the halls.

[2] Evelyn, about the same date (August 9th, 1661), "tried several experiments on the sensitive plant and humilis, which contracted with the least touch of the sun through a burning glass, though it rises and opens only when it shines on it."

be. I left him at Whitehall, and myself went to Westminster to my office, whither nothing to do, but I did discourse with Mr. Falconbridge about Le Squire's place, and had his consent to get it if I could. I afterwards in the Hall met with W. Simons, who put me in the best way how to get it done. Thence by appointment to the Angel[1] in King Street, where Chetwind, Mr. Thomas and Doling were at oysters, and beginning Lent this day with a fish dinner. After dinner Mr. Thomas and I by water to London, where I went to Herring's and received the £50 of my Lord's upon Frank's bill from Worcester. I gave in the bill and set my hand to his bill. Thence I went to the Pope's Head Alley and called on Adam Chard, and bought a catcall there, it cost me two groats. Thence went and gave him a cup of ale. After that to the Sun behind the Exchange,[2] where meeting my uncle Wight by the way, took him with me thither, and after drinking a health or two round at the Cock[3] (Mr. Thomas being gone thither), we parted, he and I homewards, parted at Fleet Street, where I found my father newly come home from Brampton[4] very well. He left my uncle with his leg very dangerous, and do believe he cannot continue in that condition long. He tells me that my uncle did acquaint him very largely what he did intend to do with his estate, to make me his heir and give my brother Tom something, and that my father and mother should have likewise something, to raise portions for John and Pall.[5] I pray God he may be as good as his word. Here I staid and supped and so home, there being Joyce Norton there and Ch. Glascock. Going home

---

[1] The Angel tavern in King Street, Westminster. A token of this house, kept by Will. Carter, is described in "Boyne's Trade Tokens," by Williamson, vol. i., 1889, p. 647.

[2] The Sun tavern behind the Royal Exchange was a famous house in its day. A token of it is described in "Boyne's Trade Tokens," by Williamson, vol. i., 1889, p. 591. It was rebuilt by John Wadlow after the Great Fire.

[3] The Cock alehouse at Temple Bar was originally called the Cock and Bottle, and dates back to the reign of James I. It was pulled down in 1882. There is a very scarce token of the house, dated 1665 (see "Boyne's Trade Tokens," ed. Williamson, vol. i., 1889, p. 762).

[4] Brampton in Huntingdonshire, where Pepys was probably born, and where his father afterwards retired.

[5] John Pepys, younger brother of Samuel; Paulina, sister of Samuel, afterwards Mrs. Jackson.

I called at Wotton's and took home a piece of cheese. At home Mr. Sheply sat with me a little while, and so we all to bed. This news and my Lord's great kindness makes me very cheerful within. I pray God make me thankful. This day, according to order, Sir Arthur [Haselrigge] appeared at the House; what was done I know not, but there was all the Rumpers almost come to the House to-day. My Lord did seem to wonder much why Lambert was so willing to be put into the Tower, and thinks he has some design in it; but I think that he is so poor that he cannot use his liberty for debts, if he were at liberty; and so it is as good and better for him to be there, than any where else.

[8th]. To Whitehall to bespeak some firing for my father at Short's, and likewise to speak to Mr. Blackburne about Batters being gunner in the "Wexford." Then to Westminster Hall, where there was a general damp over men's minds and faces upon some of the Officers of the Army being about making a remonstrance against Charles Stuart or any single person; but at noon it was told, that the General had put a stop to it, so all was well again. Here I met with Jasper, who was to look for me to bring me to my Lord at the lobby; whither sending a note to my Lord, he comes out to me and gives me direction to look after getting some money for him from the Admiralty, seeing that things are so unsafe, that he would not lay out a farthing for the State, till he had received some money of theirs. Home about two o'clock, and took my wife by land to Paternoster Row, to buy some Paragon for a petticoat and so home again. In my way meeting Mr. Moore, who went home with me while I ate a bit and so back to Whitehall again, both of us. He waited at the Council for Mr. Crew. I to the Admiralty, where I got the order for the money, and have taken care for the getting of it assigned upon Mr. Hutchinson,[1] Treasurer for the Navy, against to-morrow. Hence going home I met with Mr. King that belonged to the Treasurers at War and took him to Harper's, who told me that he and the rest of his fellows are cast out of office by the new

---

[1] Richard Hutchinson was Deputy Treasurer to Sir Henry Vane, whom he succeeded as Treasurer of the Navy in 1651. He continued to hold the office until the Restoration.

Treasurers. This afternoon, some of the Officers of the Army, and some of the Parliament, had a conference at White Hall to make all right again, but I know not what is done. This noon I met at the Dog tavern[1] Captain Philip Holland, with whom I advised how to make some advantage of my Lord's going to sea, which he told me might be by having of five or six servants entered on board, and I to give them what wages I pleased, and so their pay to be mine; he was also very urgent to have me take the Secretary's place, that my Lord did proffer me. At the same time in comes Mr. Wade and Mr. Sterry, secretary to the plenipotentiary in Denmark, who brought the news of the death of the King of Sweden[2] at Gottenburgh the 3rd of the last month, and he told me what a great change he found when he came here, the secluded members being restored. He also spoke very freely of Mr. Wade's profit, which he made while he was in Zeeland, how he did believe that he cheated Mr. Powell, and that he made above £500 on the voyage, which Mr. Wade did very angrily deny, though I believe he was guilty enough.

[9th]. To my Lord at his lodging, and came to Westminster with him in the coach, with Mr. Dudley with him, and he in the Painted Chamber[3] walked a good while; and I telling him that I was willing and ready to go with him to sea, he agreed that I should, and advised me what to write to Mr. Downing about it, which I did at my office, that by my Lord's desire I offered that my place might for a while be supplied by Mr. Moore, and that I and my security should be bound by the same bond for him. I went and dined at Mr. Crew's, where Mr. Hawly comes to me, and I told him the business and shewed him the letter promising him £20 a year, which he liked very well of. I did the same to

---

[1] There were several Dog taverns in London, but the one at Westminster mentioned by Pepys was the famous tavern in King Street, which was frequented previously by Ben Jonson. It was chiefly resorted to by Cavaliers. There is a token of the "Black Dogg" (see "Boyne's Trade Tokens," ed. Williamson, vol. i., 1889, p. 649).

[2] Charles X., Gustavus, son of John Casimir, Count Palatine of the Rhine. He succeeded his cousin Christina, who resigned the crown in 1654.

[3] The Painted Chamber, or St. Edward's Chamber, in the old Palace at Westminster. The first name was given to it from the curious paintings on the walls, and the second from the tradition that Edward the Confessor died in it.

Mr. Moore, which he also took for a courtesy. In the afternoon by coach, taking Mr. Butler with me to the Navy Office,[1] about the £500 for my Lord, which I am promised to have to-morrow morning. Then by coach back again, and at White Hall at the Council Chamber spoke with my Lord and got him to sign the acquittance for the £500, and he also told me that he had spoke to Mr. Blackburne to put off Mr. Creed and that I should come to him for direction in the employment. After this Mr. Butler and I to Harper's, where we sat and drank for two hours till ten at night; the old woman she was drunk and began to talk foolishly in commendation of her son James. Home and to bed. All night troubled in my thoughts how to order my business upon this great change with me that I could not sleep, and being over-heated with drink I made a promise the next morning to drink no strong drink this week, for I find that it makes me sweat and puts me quite out of order. This day it was resolved that the writs do go out in the name of the Keepers of the Liberty, and I hear that it is resolved privately that a treaty be offered with the King. And that Monk did check his soldiers highly for what they did yesterday.

[10th]. In the morning went to my father's, whom I took in his cutting house,[2] and there I told him my resolution to go to sea with my Lord, and consulted with him how to dispose of my wife, and we resolve of letting her be at Mr. Bowyer's.[3] Thence to the Treasurer of the Navy, where I received £500 for my Lord, and having left £200 of it with Mr. Rawlinson[4] at his house for Sheply, I went with the rest to the Sun tavern on Fish Street Hill, where Mr. Hill, Stevens and Mr. Hater[5] of the Navy Office

---

[1] This is the first notice in the Diary of the Navy Office in Crutched Friars.

[2] His father was a tailor, and this was his cutting-out room.

[3] Mr. Bowyer, of Huntsmore, Bucks, was an old friend of Pepys, and, according to a habit of the time, he sometimes styled him father (see November 7th, 1660). This misled Lord Braybrooke into supposing that he was Mrs. Pepys's stepfather.

[4] Daniel Rawlinson, the Royalist host of the Mitre in Fenchurch Street.

[5] Thomas Hater appears to have been a clerk at the Navy Office before Pepys went there. In July, 1660, he became Pepys's clerk; in 1674 he was appointed Clerk of the Acts, and in 1679 Secretary of the Admiralty.

had invited me, where we had good discourse and a fine breakfast of Mr. Hater. Then by coach home, where I took occasion
to tell my wife of my going to sea, who was much troubled at it,
and was with some dispute at last willing to continue at Mr.
Bowyer's in my absence. After this to see Mrs. Jem and paid
her maid £7, and then to Mr. Blackburne, who told me what
Mr. Creed did say upon the news of my coming into his place,
and that he did propose to my Lord that there should be two
Secretaries, which made me go to Sir H. Wright's where my
Lord dined and spoke with him about it, but he seemed not to
agree to the motion. Hither W. Howe comes to me and so to
Westminster. In the way he told me, what I was to provide and
so forth against my going. He went with me to my office, whither
also Mr. Madge comes half foxed and played the fool upon the
violin that made me weary. Then to Whitehall and so home and
set many of my things in order against my going. My wife was
late making of caps for me, and the wench making an end of a
pair of stockings that she was knitting of. So to bed.

[11th] (Sunday). All the day busy without my band on, putting
up my books and things, in order to my going to sea. At night my
wife and I went to my father's to supper, where J. Norton and
Chas. Glascocke supt with us, and after supper home, where the
wench had provided all things against to-morrow to wash, and
so to bed, where I much troubled with my cold and coughing.

[12th]. This day the wench rose at two in the morning to wash,
and my wife and I lay talking a great while. I by reason of my
cold could not tell how to sleep. My wife and I to the Exchange,
where we bought a great many things, where I left her and went
into London, and at Bedells the bookseller's at the Temple gate
I paid £12 10s. 6d. for Mr. Fuller by his direction. So came
back and at Wilkinson's found Mr. Shenly and some sea people,
as the cook of the Nazeby and others, at dinner. Then to the
White Horse in King Street, where I got Mr. Buddle's horse to
ride to Huntsmore[1] to Mr. Bowyer's, where I found him and all

---

[1] Huntsmore, a hamlet belonging to Iver, in which parish Robert Bowyer
founded a free school about 1750.—Lyson's *Hist. of Bucks*, p. 587.

well, and willing to have my wife come and board with them
while I was at sea, which was the business I went about. Here I
lay and took a thing for my cold, namely a spoonful of honey
and a nutmeg scraped into it, by Mr. Bowyer's direction, and so
took it into my mouth, which I found did do me much good.

[13th]. It rained hard and I got up early, and got to London by
8 o'clock at my Lord's lodgings, who told me that I was to be
secretary, and Creed to be deputy treasurer to the Fleet, at which
I was troubled, but I could not help it. After that to my father's
to look after things, and so at my shoemaker's and others. At
night to Whitehall, where I met with Simons and Luellin at
drink with them at Roberts at Whitehall. Then to the Admiralty,
where I talked with Mr. Creed till the Brothers, and they were
very seemingly willing and glad that I have the place since my
Lord would dispose of it otherwise than to them. Home and to
bed. This day the Parliament voted all that had been done by
the former Rump against the House of Lords be void, and to-
night that the writs go out without any qualification. Things
seem very doubtful what will be the end of all; for the Parliament seems to be strong for the King, while the soldiers do all
talk against.

[14th]. To my Lord, where infinity of applications to him and
to me. To my great trouble, my Lord gives me all the papers that
was given to him, to put in order and give him an account of
them. Here I got half-a-piece of a person of Mr. Wright's rec-
ommending to my Lord to be Preacher of the Speaker frigate.[1]
I went hence to St. James's and Mr. Pierce the surgeon with me,
to speak with Mr. Clerke,[2] Monk's secretary, about getting some
soldiers removed out of Huntingdon to Oundle, which my Lord
told me he did to do a courtesy to the town, that he might have
the greater interest in them, in the choice of the next Parliament;
not that he intends to be chosen himself, but that he might have

---

[1] The "Speaker" was renamed the "Mary" after the Restoration. It was built
at Woolwich by Christopher Pett in 1649. It was a third-rate of fifty-four guns
and 395 tonnage.
[2] Clement Clerke of Lawnde Abbey, co. Leicester, created a baronet in 1661.

Mr. G. Montagu and my Lord Mandeville[1] chose there in spite of the Bernards.[2] This done (where I saw General Monk and methought he seemed a dull heavy man), he and I to Whitehall, where with Luellin we dined at Marsh's. Coming home telling my wife what we had to dinner, she had a mind to some cabbage, and I sent for some and she had it. Went to the Admiralty, where a strange thing how I am already courted by the people. This morning among others that came to me I hired a boy of Jenkins of Westminster and Burr[3] to be my clerk. This night I went to Mr. Creed's chamber where he gave me the former book of the proceedings in the fleet and the Seal. Then to Harper's where old Beard was and I took him by coach to my Lord's, but he was not at home, but afterwards I found him out at Sir H. Wright's. Thence by coach, it raining hard, to Mrs. Jem, where I staid a while, and so home, and late in the night put up my things in a sea-chest that Mr. Sheply lent me, and so to bed.

[15th]. Early packing up my things to be sent by cart with the rest of my Lord's. So to Will's, where I took leave of some of my friends. Here I met Tom Alcock, one that went to school with me at Huntingdon, but I had not seen him these sixteen years. So in the Hall paid and made even with Mrs. Michell; afterwards met with old Beale, and at the Axe paid him this quarter to Ladyday next. In the afternoon Dick Mathews comes to dine, and I went and drank with him at Harper's. So into London by water, and in Fish Street my wife and I bought a bit of salmon for 8d. and went to the Sun Tavern and ate it, where I did promise to give her all that I have in the world but my books, in case I should die at sea. From thence homewards; in the way

---

[1] Robert Montagu, Viscount Mandeville, eldest son of the Earl of Manchester, whom he succeeded in 1671.

[2] Robert Bernard, created a baronet in 1662, served in Parliament for Huntingdon, before and after the Restoration, and died in 1666. His son and successor, Sir John Bernard, the second baronet, at the time of his death, in 1669, was one of the knights of the shire for the county of Huntingdon. The inscription upon his monument in Brampton Church is given in the "Topographer and Genealogist," vol. i. p. 113. Sir Nicholas Pedley, who was also burgess for Huntingdon, married a daughter of Sir Robert Bernard.—B.

[3] John Burr, the clerk who accompanied Pepys to sea.

my wife bought linen for three smocks and other things. I went
to my Lord's and spoke with him. So home with Mrs. Jem by
coach and then home to my own house. From thence to the Fox
in King-street to supper on a brave turkey of Mr. Hawly's, with
some friends of his there, Will Bowyer, &c. After supper I went
to Westminster Hall, and the Parliament sat till ten at night,
thinking and being expected to dissolve themselves to-day, but
they did not. Great talk to-night that the discontented officers
did think this night to make a stir, but prevented. To the Fox
again. Home with my wife, and to bed extraordinary sleepy.

[16th]. No sooner out of bed but troubled with abundance of
clients, seamen. My landlord Vanly's man came to me by my
direction yesterday, for I was there at his house as I was going
to London by water, and I paid him rent for my house for this
quarter ending at Lady day, and took an acquittance that he
wrote me from his master. Then to Mr. Sheply, to the Rhenish
Tavern House, where Mr. Pim, the tailor, was, and gave us a
morning draft and a neat's tongue. Home and with my wife to
London, we dined at my father's, where Joyce Norton and
Mr. Armiger dined also. After dinner my wife took leave of them
in order to her going to-morrow to Huntsmore. In my way home
I went to the Chapel[1] in Chancery Lane to bespeak papers of
all sorts and other things belonging to writing against my voyage. So home, where I spent an hour or two about my business
in my study. Thence to the Admiralty, and staid a while, so home
again, where Will Bowyer came to tell us that he would bear my
wife company in the coach to-morrow. Then to Westminster
Hall, where I heard how the Parliament had this day dissolved
themselves, and did pass very cheerfully through the Hall, and
the Speaker without his mace. The whole Hall was joyful there-
at, as well as themselves, and now they begin to talk loud of the
King. To-night I am told, that yesterday, about five o'clock in
the afternoon, one came with a ladder to the Great Exchange,[2]

---

[1] The Rolls Chapel, where were kept the rolls and records of the Court of
Chancery until the erection of the Record Office in Fetter Lane in 1856.
[2] On February 28th Pepys styles the Royal Exchange the Old Exchange; now
it is the Great Exchange.

and wiped with a brush the inscription that was upon King Charles, and that there was a great bonfire made in the Exchange, and people called out "God bless King Charles the Second!"[1] From the Hall I went home to bed, very sad in mind to part with my wife, but God's will be done.

[17th]. This morning bade adieu in bed to the company of my wife. We rose and I gave my wife some money to serve her for a time, and what papers of consequence I had. Then I left her to

---

[1] "Then the writing in golden letters, that was engraven under the statue of Charles I., in the Royal Exchange (*Exit tyrannus, Regum ultimus, anno libertatis Angliæ, anno Domini* 1648, *Januarie* xxx.) was washed out by a painter, who in the day time raised a ladder, and with a pot and brush washed the writing quite out, threw down his pot and brush, and said it should never do him any more service, in regard that it had the honour to put out rebels' hand-writing. He then came down, took away his ladder, not a misword said to him, and by whose order it was done was not then known. The merchants

get her ready and went to my Lord's with my boy Eliezer to my
Lord's lodging at Mr. Crew's. Here I had much business with my
Lord, and papers, great store, given me by my Lord to dispose of
as of the rest. After that, with Mr. Moore home to my house and
took my wife by coach to the Chequer in Holborn, where, after
we had drank, &c., she took coach and so farewell. I staid behind
with Tom Alcock and Mr. Anderson, my old chamber fellow
at Cambridge his brother, and drank with them there, who were
come to me thither about one that would have a place at sea.
Thence with Mr. Hawly to dinner at Mr. Crew's. After dinner
to my own house, where all things were put up into the dining-
room and locked up, and my wife took the keys along with her.
This day, in the presence of Mr. Moore (who made it) and Mr.
Hawly, I did before I went out with my wife, seal my will to her,
whereby I did give her all that I have in the world, but my books
which I give to my brother John, excepting only French books,
which my wife is to have. In the evening at the Admiralty, I
met my Lord there and got a commission for Williamson to be
captain of the Harp frigate,[1] and afterwards went by coach taking Mr. Crips with me to my Lord and got him to sign it at table
as he was at supper. And so to Westminster back again with him
with me, who had a great desire to go to sea and my Lord told
me that he would do him any favour. So I went home with
him to his mother's house by me in Axe Yard, where I found
Dr. Clodius's wife and sat there talking and hearing of old Mrs.
Crisp playing of her old lessons upon the harpsichon till it was
time to go to bed. After that to bed, and Laud, her son,[2] lay with
me in the best chamber in her house, which indeed was finely
furnished.

were glad and joyful, many people were gathered together, and against the
Exchange made a bonfire."—Rugge's *Diurnal*. In the Thomason Collection of
Civil War Tracts at the British Museum is a pamphlet which is dated in MS.
March 21st, 1659-60, where this act is said to be by order of Monk: "The
Loyal Subjects Teares for the Sufferings and Absence of their Sovereign
Charles II., King of England, Scotland, and Ireland, with an Observation upon
the expunging of *Exit Tyrannus, Regum ultimus,* by order of General Monk,
and some Advice to the Independents, Anabaptists, Phanatiques, &c. London,
1660."
[1] The "Harp" was a sixth-rate of eight guns, built at Dublin in 1656.
[2] Laud Crisp was afterwards page to Lady Sandwich.

[18th]. I rose early and went to the barber's (Jervas) in Palace Yard and I was trimmed by him, and afterwards drank with him a cup or two of ale, and did begin to hire his man to go with me to sea. Then to my Lord's lodging where I found Captain Williamson and gave him his commission to be Captain of the Harp, and he gave me a piece of gold and 20s. in silver. So to my own house, where I staid a while and then to dinner with Mr. Shepley at my Lord's lodgings. After that to Mr. Mossum's, where he made a very gallant sermon upon "Pray for the life of the King and the King's son." (Ezra vi. 10.) From thence to Mr. Crew's, but my Lord not being within I did not stay, but went away and met with Mr. Woodfine, who took me to an alehouse in Drury Lane, and we sat and drank together, and ate toasted cakes which were very good, and we had a great deal of mirth with the mistress of the house about them. From thence homewards, and called at Mr. Blagrave's,[1] where I took up my note that he had of mine for 40s., which he two years ago did give me as a pawn while he had my lute. So that all things are even between him and I. So to Mrs. Crisp, where she and her daughter and son and I sat talking till ten o'clock at night, I giving them the best advice that I could concerning their son, how he should go to sea, and so to bed.

[19th]. Early to my Lord, where infinity of business to do, which makes my head full; and indeed, for these two or three days, I have not been without a great many cares and thoughts concerning them. After that to the Admiralty, where a good while with Mr. Blackburne, who told me that it was much to be feared that the King would come in, for all good men and good things were now discouraged. Thence to Wilkinson's, where Mr. Sheply and I dined; and while we were at dinner, my Lord Monk's lifeguard come by with the Serjeant at Arms before them, with two Proclamations, that all Cavaliers do depart the town; but the other that all officers that were lately disbanded should do the same. The last of which Mr. R. Creed,[2] I remem-

---

[1] Thomas Blagrave was one of the Gentlemen of the Royal Chapel and a cornet-player of repute.

[2] Major Richard Creed, who commanded a troop under Lambert when that

ber, said, that he looked upon it as if they had said, that all God's people should depart the town. Thence with some sea officers to the Swan, where we drank wine till one comes to me to pay me some money from Worcester, viz., £25. His name is Wilday. I sat in another room and took my money and drank with him till the rest of my company were gone and so we parted. Going home the water was high, and so I got Crockford to carry me over it. So home, and left my money there. All the discourse now-a-day is, that the King will come again; and for all I see, it is the wishes of all; and all do believe that it will be so. My mind is still much troubled for my poor wife, but I hope that this undertaking will be worth my pains. To Whitehall and staid about business at the Admiralty late, then to Tony Robins's, where Capt. Stokes, Mr. Luddington and others were, and I did solicit the Captain for Laud Crisp, who gave me a promise that he would entertain him. After that to Mrs. Crisp's where Dr. Clodius and his wife were. He very merry with drink. We played at cards late and so to bed. This day my Lord dined at my Lord Mayor's [Allen], and Jasper was made drunk, which my Lord was very angry at.

[20th]. This morning I rose early and went to my house to put things in a little order against my going, which I conceive will be to-morrow (the weather still very rainy). After that to my Lord, where I found very great deal of business, he giving me all letters and papers that come to him about business, for me to give him account of when we come on shipboard. Hence with Capt. Isham by coach to Whitehall to the Admiralty. He and I and Chetwind, Doling and Luellin dined together at Marsh's at Whitehall. So to the Bull Head whither W. Simons comes to us and I gave them my foy[1] against my going to sea; and so we took leave one of another, they promising me to write to me to

---

general surrendered to Ingoldsby: see April 24th following. He was imprisoned with the rest of the officers, but his name does not recur in the Diary, nor is it known whether he was related to John Creed, so frequently mentioned hereafter.

[1] Foy. A feast given by one who is about to leave a place. In Kent, according to Grose, a treat to friends, either at going abroad or coming home. See Diary, November 25th, 1661.

sea. Hither comes Pim's boy, by my direction, with two mon-teeres[1] for me to take my choice of, and I chose the saddest colour and left the other for Mr. Sheply. Hence by coach to London, and took a short melancholy leave of my father and mother, with-out having them to drink, or say anything of business one to an-other. And indeed I had a fear upon me I should scarce ever see my mother again, she having a great cold then upon her.[2] Then to Westminster, where by reason of rain and an easterly wind, the water was so high that there was boats rowed in King Street and all our yard was drowned, that one could not go to my house, so as no man has seen the like almost, most houses full of water.[3] Then back by coach to my Lord's, where I met Mr. Sheply, who staid with me waiting for my Lord's coming in till very late. Then he and I, and William Howe went with our swords to bring my Lord home from Sir H. Wright's. He re-solved to go to-morrow if the wind ceased. Sheply and I home by coach. I to Mrs. Crisp's, who had sat over a good supper long looking for me. So we sat talking and laughing till it was very late, and so Laud and I to bed.

[21st]. To my Lord's, but the wind very high against us, and the weather bad we could not go to-day; here I did very much business, and then to my Lord Widdrington's from my Lord, with his desire that he might have the disposal of the writs of the Cinque Ports. My Lord was very civil to me, and called for wine, and writ a long letter in answer. Thence I went to a tavern over against Mr. Pierce's with Judge Advocate Fowler and Mr. Burr, and sat and drank with them two or three pints of wine. After that to Mr. Crew's again and gave my Lord an account of

---

[1] Monteeres, montero (Spanish), a kind of huntsman's cap.

[2] In the MS. there is the following note appended to this: "In an error here, for I did not take leave of them till the next day."

[3] "In this month the wind was very high, and caused great tides, so that great hurt was done to the inhabitants of Westminster, King Street being quite drowned. The Maidenhead boat was cast away, and twelve persons with her. Also, about Dover the waters brake in upon the mainland; and in Kent was very much damage done; so that report said, there was £20,000 worth of harm done."—Rugge's *Diurnal.*—B.

what I had done, and so about my business to take leave of my father and mother, which by a mistake I have put down yesterday. Thence to Westminster to Crisp's, where we were very merry; the old woman sent for a supper for me, and gave me a handkercher with strawberry buttons on it, and so to bed.

[22nd]. Up very early and set things in order at my house, and so took leave of Mrs. Crispe and her daughter (who was in bed) and of Mrs. Hunt. Then to my Lord's lodging at the gate and did so there, where Mr. Hawly came to me and I gave him the key of my house to keep, and he went with me to Mr. Crew's, and there I took my last leave of him. But the weather continuing very bad my Lord would not go to-day. My Lord spent this morning private in sealing of his last will and testament with Mr. W. Montagu.[1] After that I went forth about my own business to buy a pair of riding grey serge stockings and sword and belt and hose, and after that took Wotton and Brigden to the Pope's Head Tavern[2] in Chancery Lane, where Gilb. Holland and Shelston were, and we dined and drank a great deal of wine, and they paid all. Strange how these people do now promise me anything; one a rapier, the other a vessel of wine or a gun, and one offered me his silver hatband to do him a courtesy. I pray God to keep me from being proud or too much lifted up hereby. After that to Westminster, and took leave of Kate Sterpin who was very sorry to part with me, and after that of Mr. George Mountagu, and received my warrant of Mr. Blackburne, to be Secretary to the two Generals of the Fleet. Then to take my leave of the Clerks of the Council, and thence Doling and Luellin would have me go with them to Mount's chamber, where we sat and talked and then I went away. So to my Lord (in my way meeting Chetwind and Swan and bade them farewell) where I lay all night with Mr. Andrews. This day Mr. Sheply went away on board and I sent my boy with him. This

---

[1] William, second son of Edward, first Lord Montagu of Boughton, and first cousin to Sir Edward Montagu. He was appointed Lord Chief Baron 1676. Died 1707, aged 89.

[2] There is a token of the Pope's Head tavern in Chancery Lane described in "Boyne's Trade Tokens," by Williamson, 1889, vol. i. p. 554.

96

day also Mrs. Jemimah went to Marrowbone,[1] so I could not
see her. Mr. Moore being out of town to-night I could not take
leave of him nor speak to him about business which troubled me
much. I left my small case therefore with Mr. Andrews for him.

[23rd]. Up early, carried my Lord's will in a black box to Mr.
William Montagu for him to keep for him. Then to the barber's
and put on my cravat there. So to my Lord again, who was almost ready to be gone and had staid for me. Hither came Gilb.
Holland, and brought me a stick rapier and Shelston a sugar-loaf,
and had brought his wife who he said was a very pretty woman to
the Ship tavern hard by for me to see but I could not go. Young
Reeve also brought me a little perspective glass which I bought for
my Lord, it cost me 8s. So after that my Lord in Sir H. Wright's
coach with Captain Isham,[2] Mr. Thomas, John Crew, W. Howe,
and I in a Hackney to the Tower, where the barges staid for us;
my Lord and the Captain in one, and W. Howe and I, &c., in the
other, to the Long Reach,[3] where the Swiftsure lay at anchor;
(in our way we saw the great breach which the late high water
had made, to the loss of many £1000 to the people about Lime-
house). Soon as my Lord on board, the guns went off bravely
from the ships. And a little while after comes the Vice-Admiral
Lawson,[4] and seemed very respectful to my Lord, and so did the
rest of the Commanders of the frigates that were thereabouts. I
to the cabin allotted for me, which was the best that any had that
belonged to my Lord. I got out some things out of my chest for
writing and to work presently, Mr. Burr and I both. I supped at
the deck table with Mr. Sheply. We were late writing of orders
for the getting of ships ready, &c.; and also making of others
to all the seaports between Hastings and Yarmouth, to stop all
dangerous persons that are going or coming between Flanders

---

[1] The name Mary-le-bone has been corrupted from St. Mary-le-bourne, but
this is a still further corruption, and an amazing instance of popular ety-
mology.

[2] Sir Sidney Montagu, brother of the first Earl of Manchester, and the father
of "my Lord," had married for his second wife one of the Isham family, of
Lamport.

[3] Long Reach, between Erith and Gravesend.

[4] Vice-Admiral John Lawson, knighted by Charles II. in September, 1660.

and there. After that to bed in my cabin, which was but short; however I made shift with it and slept very well, and the weather being good I was not sick at all yet, I know not what I shall be.

[24th]. At work hard all the day writing letters to the Council, &c. This day Mr. Creed came on board and dined very boldly with my Lord, but he could not get a bed there. At night Capt. Isham who had been at Gravesend all last night and to-day came and brought Mr. Lucy (one acquainted with Mrs. Pierce, with whom I had been at her house), I drank with him in the Captain's cabin, but my business could not stay with him. I despatch many letters to-day abroad and it was late before we could get to bed. Mr. Sheply and Howe supped with me in my cabin. The boy Eliezer flung down a can of beer upon my papers which made me give him a box of the ear, it having all spoiled my papers and cost me a great deal of work. So to bed.

[25th] (Lord's day). About two o'clock in the morning, letters came from London by our coxon, so they waked me, but I would not rise but bid him stay till morning, which he did, and then I rose and carried them in to my Lord, who read them a-bed. Among the rest, there was the writ and mandate for him to dispose to the Cinque Ports for choice of Parliament-men. There was also one for me from Mr. Blackburne, who with his own hand superscribes it to S. P. Esq., of which God knows I was not a little proud. After that I wrote a letter to the Clerk of Dover Castle, to come to my Lord about issuing of those writs. About ten o'clock Mr. Ibbott,[1] at the end of the long table, begun to pray and preach and indeed made a very good sermon, upon the duty of all Christians to be stedfast in faith. After that Captain Cuttance[2] and I had oysters, my Lord being in his cabin not intending to stir out to-day. After that up into the great cabin above to dinner with the Captain, where was Captain Isham and all the officers of the ship. I took place of all but the Captains; after dinner I wrote a great many letters to my friends at London. After

---

[1] Edmund Ibbott, S.T.B., chaplain of the ship, in 1662 made rector of Deal. Died 1677.

[2] Captain Roger Cuttance, commander of the "Naseby," afterwards the "Charles."

that, sermon again, at which I slept, God forgive me! After that, it being a fair day, I walked with the Captain upon the deck talking. At night I supped with him and after that had orders from my Lord about some business to be done against to-morrow, which I sat up late and did and then to bed.

[26th]. This day it is two years since it pleased God that I was cut of the stone at Mrs. Turner's in Salisbury Court. And did resolve while I live to keep it a festival, as I did the last year at my house, and for ever to have Mrs. Turner and her company with me. But now it pleases God that I am where I am and so prevented to do it openly; only within my soul I can and do rejoice, and bless God, being at this time, blessed be his holy name, in as good health as ever I was in my life. This morning I rose early, and went about making of an establishment of the whole Fleet, and a list of all the ships, with the number of men and guns. About an hour after that, we had a meeting of the principal commanders and seamen, to proportion out the number of these things. After that to dinner, there being very many commanders on board. All the afternoon very many orders were made, till I was very weary. At night Mr. Sheply and W. Howe came and brought some bottles of wine and some things to eat in my cabin, where we were very merry, remembering the day of being cut for the stone. Captain Cuttance came afterwards and sat drinking a bottle of wine till eleven, a kindness he do not usually do the greatest officer in the ship. After that to bed.

[27th]. Early in the morning at making a fair new establishment of the Fleet to send to the Council. This morning, the wind came about, and we fell into the Hope,[1] and in our passing by the Vice-Admiral, he and the rest of the frigates with him, did give us abundance of guns and we them, so much that the report of them broke all the windows in my cabin and broke off the iron bar that was upon it to keep anybody from creeping in at the Scuttle.[2] This noon I sat the first time with my Lord at table since my

---

[1] A reach of the Thames near Tilbury.

[2] "A small hole or port cut either in the deck or side of a ship, generally for ventilation. That in the deck is a small hatch-way."—Smyth's *Sailor's Word-Book.*

coming to sea. All the afternoon exceeding busy in writing of letters and orders. In the afternoon, Sir Harry Wright came on board us, about his business of being chosen Parliament-man. My Lord brought him to see my cabin, when I was hard a-writing. At night supped with my Lord too, with the Captain, and after that to work again till it be very late. So to bed.

[28th]. This morning and the whole day busy, and that the more because Mr. Burr was about his own business all the day at Gravesend. At night there was a gentleman very well bred, his name was Banes, going for Flushing, who spoke French and Latin very well, brought by direction from Captain Clerke[1] hither, as a prisoner, because he called out of the vessel that he went in, "Where is your King, we have done our business, Vive le Roi." He confessed himself a Cavalier in his heart, and that he and his whole family had fought for the King; but that he was then drunk, having been all night taking his leave at Gravesend the night before, and so could not remember what it was that he said; but in his words and carriage showed much of a gentleman. My Lord had a great kindness for him, but did not think it safe to release him, but commanded him to be used civilly, so he was taken to the Master's Cabin and had supper there. In the meantime I wrote a letter to the Council about him, and an order for the vessel to be sent for back that he was taken out of. But a while after, he sent a letter down to my Lord, which my Lord did like very well, and did advise with me what was best to be done. So I put in something to my Lord and then to the Captain that the gentleman was to be released and the letter stopped, which was done. So I went up and sat and talked with him in Latin and French, and drank a bottle or two with him; and about eleven at night he took boat again, and so God bless him. Thence I to my cabin and to bed. This day we had news of the election at Huntingdon for Bernard and Pedly,[2] at which my Lord was much troubled for his friends' missing of it.

---

[1] Robin Clerke, Captain of the "Speaker," afterwards the "Mary."

[2] John Bernard and Nicholas Pedley, re-elected in the next Parliament. The latter had been a Commissioner of the Wine Office. Sir Edward Montagu had set up Lord Mandeville, the Earl of Manchester's eldest son, and Mr. G. Montagu, as candidates. See *ante*, March 14th.

[29th]. We lie still a little below Gravesend. At night Mr. Sheply returned from London, and told us of several elections for the next Parliament. That the King's effigies was new making to be set up in the Exchange again. This evening was a great whispering of some of the Vice-Admiral's captains that they

were dissatisfied, and did intend to fight themselves, to oppose the General. But it was soon hushed, and the Vice-Admiral did wholly deny any such thing, and protested to stand by the General. At night Mr. Sheply, W. Howe, and I supped in my cabin. So up to the Master's cabin, where we sat talking, and then to bed.

[30th]. I was saluted in the morning with two letters, from some that I had done a favour to, which brought me in each a piece of gold. This day, while my Lord and we were at dinner, the Nazeby

came in sight towards us, and at last came to anchor close by us. After dinner my Lord and many others went on board her, where every thing was out of order, and a new chimney made for my Lord in his bed-chamber, which he was much pleased with. My Lord, in his discourse, discovered a great deal of love to this ship.[1]

[31st]. This morning Captain Jowles of the "Wexford" came on board, for whom I got commission from my Lord to be commander of the ship. Upon the doing thereof he was to make the 20s. piece that he sent me yesterday, up £5; wherefore he sent me a bill that he did owe me £4, which I sent my boy to Gravesend with him, and he did give the boy £4 for me, and the boy gave him the bill under his hand. This morning, Mr. Hill[2] that lives in Axe-yard was here on board with the Vice-Admiral. I did give him a bottle of wine, and was exceedingly satisfied of the power that I have to make my friends welcome. Many orders to make all the afternoon. At night Mr. Sheply, Howe, Ibbott, and I supped in my cabin together.

[April 1st] (Lord's day). Mr. Ibbott preached very well. After dinner my Lord did give me a private list of all the ships that were to be set out this summer, wherein I do discern that he hath made it his care to put by as much of the Anabaptists as he can. By reason of my Lord and my being busy to send away the packet by Mr. Cooke of the Nazeby, it was four o'clock before we could begin sermon again. This day Captain Guy come on board from Dunkirk, who tells me that the King will come in, and that the soldiers at Dunkirk do drink the King's health in the streets. At night the Captain, Sir R. Stayner, Mr. Sheply, and I did sup together in the Captain's cabin. I made a commission for Captain Wilgness, of the Bear, to-night, which got me 30s. So after writing a while I went to bed.

---

[1] Sir E. Montagu's flag was on board the "Naseby" when he went to the Sound in 1658.

[2] Mr. Hill, who was a neighbour of Pepys's in Axe Yard, is mentioned again under date August 5th, 1660, when Pepys sat in his pew at St. Margaret's, Westminster.

[2nd]. Up very early, and to get all my things and my boy's packed up. Great concourse of commanders here this morning to take leave of my Lord upon his going into the Nazeby, so that the table was full, so there dined below many commanders, and Mr. Creed, who was much troubled to hear that he could not go along with my Lord, for he had already got all his things thither, thinking to stay there, but W. Howe was very high against it, and he indeed did put him out, though everybody was glad of it. After dinner I went in one of the boats with my boy before my Lord, and made shift before night to get my cabin in pretty good order. It is but little, but very convenient, having one window to the sea and another to the deck, and a good bed. This morning comes Mr. Ed. Pickering,[1] like a coxcomb as he always was. He tells me that the King will come in, but that Monk did resolve to have the doing of it himself, or else to hinder it.

[3rd]. Late to bed. About three in the morning there was great knocking at my cabin, which with much difficulty (so they say) waked me, and I rose, but it was only for a packet, so went to my bed again, and in the morning gave it my Lord. This morning Capt. Isham comes on board to see my Lord and drunk his wine before he went into the Downs, there likewise come many merchants to get convoy to the Baltique, which a course was taken for. They dined with my Lord, and one of them by name Alderman Wood talked much to my Lord of the hopes that we have now to be settled, (under the King he meant); but my Lord

---

[1] Younger brother of Sir Gilbert Pickering, Bart., born 1618, and bred to the law; and in 1681 a resident in Lincoln's Inn. He married Dorothy, one of the daughters of Sir John Weld of Arnolds, in Edmonton, Middlesex, and died in 1698, s. p. s.; his widow survived till December, 1707. Roger North ("Life of Lord Keeper Guildford," 1742, p. 58) has drawn a very unfavourable picture of Edward Pickering, calling him a subtle fellow, a money-hunter, a great trifler, and avaricious, but withal a great pretender to puritanism, frequenting the Rolls' Chapel, and most busily writing the sermon in his hat, *that he might not be seen.* We learn from the same authority that Sir John Cutts of Childerley, having left his aunt, Mrs. Edward Pickering, an estate worth £300 per annum, for ninety-nine years, *if she should so long live,* her husband, who was the executor, erased from the will the words of reference to her life, with intention to possess himself of the property for the term, absolutely, which fraud being suspected, the question was tried in a court of law, and the jury without hesitation found Pickering the author of the erasure, before the publication of the will.—B.

took no notice of it. After dinner which was late my Lord went on shore, and after him I and Capt. Sparling went in his boat, but the water being almost at low water we could not stay for fear of not getting into our boat again. So back again. This day come the Lieutenant of the Swiftsure, who was sent by my Lord to Hastings, one of the Cinque Ports, to have got Mr. Edward Montagu[1] to have been one of their burgesses, but could not, for they were all promised before. After he had done his message, I took him and Mr. Pierce, the surgeon (who this day came on board, and not before), to my cabin, where we drank a bottle of wine. At night, busy a-writing, and so to bed. My heart exceeding heavy for not hearing of my dear wife, and indeed I do not remember that ever my heart was so apprehensive of her absence as at this very time.

[4th]. This morning I dispatch many letters of my own private business to London. There come Colonel Thomson with the wooden leg, and General Pen,[2] and dined with my Lord and Mr. Blackburne, who told me that it was certain now that the King must of necessity come in, and that one of the Council told him there is something doing in order to a treaty already among them. And it was strange to hear how Mr. Blackburne did already begin to commend him for a sober man, and how quiet he would be under his government, &c. I dined all alone to pre-

---

[1] Edward Montagu, eldest son of Edward, second Lord Montagu of Boughton, killed in the action in Bergen, 1665.

[2] This is the first mention in the Diary of Admiral (afterwards Sir William) Penn, with whom Pepys was subsequently so particularly intimate. At this time admirals were sometimes styled generals. William Penn was born at Bristol in 1621, of the ancient family of the Penns of Penn Lodge, Wilts. He was Captain at the age of twenty-one; Rear-Admiral of Ireland at twenty-three; Vice-Admiral of England and General in the first Dutch war, at thirty-two. He was subsequently M.P. for Weymouth, Governor of Kingsale, and Vice-Admiral of Munster. He was a highly successful commander, and in 1654 he obtained possession of Jamaica. He was appointed a Commissioner of the Navy in 1660, in which year he was knighted. After the Dutch fight in 1665, where he distinguished himself as second in command under the Duke of York, he took leave of the sea, but continued to act as a Commissioner for the Navy till 1669, when he retired to Wanstead, on account of his bodily infirmities, and dying there, September 16th, 1670, aged forty-nine, was buried in the church of St. Mary Redcliffe, in Bristol, where a monument to his memory was erected.

vent company, which was exceeding great to-day, in my cabin. After these two were gone Sir W. Wheeler and Sir John Petters came on board and staid about two or three hours, and so went away. The Commissioners came to-day, only to consult about a further reducement of the Fleet, and to pay them as fast as they can. I did give Davis, their servant, £5 10s. to give to Mr. Moore from me, in part of the £7 that I borrowed of him, and he is to discount the rest out of the 36s. that he do owe me. At night, my Lord resolved to send the Captain of our ship to Waymouth and promote his being chosen there, which he did put himself into a readiness to do the next morning.

[5th]. Infinity of business all the morning of orders to make, that I was very much perplexed that Mr. Burr had failed me of coming back last night, and we ready to set sail, which we did about noon, and came in the evening to Lee roads and anchored. At night Mr. Sheply overtook us who had been at Gray's Market[1] this morning. I spent all the afternoon upon the deck, it being very pleasant weather. This afternoon Sir Rich. Stayner and Mr. Creed, after we were come to anchor, did come on board, and Creed brought me £30, which my Lord had ordered him to pay me upon account, and Captain Clerke brought me a noted caudle. At night very sleepy to bed.

[6th]. This morning came my brother-in-law Balty[2] to see me, and to desire to be here with me as Reformado,[3] which did much trouble me. But after dinner (my Lord using him very civilly, at table), I spoke to my Lord, and he presented me a letter to Captain Stokes[4] for him that he should be there. All the day with him walking and talking, we under sail as far as the Spitts. In the afternoon, W. Howe and I to our viallins, the first time since we came on board. This afternoon I made even with my Lord to this day, and did give him all the money remaining in my hands.

---

[1] Gray's Thurrock, a market town on the Thames, in the county of Essex.

[2] Balthasar St. Michel, Mrs. Pepys's brother.

[3] Reformado, "a broken or disbanded officer." Boyer translates "Officier reformé, a reformado." See Diary, October 1st, 1660.

[4] John Stokes, or Stoakes, was captain of the "Royal James." He died at Portsmouth, February, 1664-65.

In the evening, it being fine moonshine, I staid late walking upon the quarter-deck with Mr. Cuttance, learning of some sea terms; and so down to supper and to bed, having an hour before put Balty into Burr's cabin, he being out of the ship.

[7th]. This day, about nine o'clock in the morning, the wind grew high, and we being among the sands lay at anchor; I began to be dizzy and squeamish. Before dinner my Lord sent for me down to eat some oysters, the best my Lord said that ever he ate in his life, though I have ate as good at Bardsey.[1] After dinner, and all the afternoon I walked upon the deck to keep myself from being sick, and at last about five o'clock, went to bed and got a caudle made me, and sleep upon it very well. This day Mr. Sheply went to Sheppy.

[8th] (Lord's day). Very calm again, and I pretty well, but my head aked all day. About noon set sail; in our way I see many vessels and masts, which are now the greatest guides for ships. We had a brave wind all the afternoon, and overtook two good merchantmen that overtook us yesterday, going to the East Indies. The lieutenant and I lay out of his window with his glass, looking at the women that were on board them, being pretty handsome. This evening Major Willoughby, who had been here three or four days on board with Mr. Pickering,[2] went on board a catch[3] for Dunkirk. We continued sailing when I went to bed, being somewhat ill again, and Will Howe, the surgeon, parson, and Balty supped in the Lieutenant's cabin and afterwards sat disputing, the parson for and I against extempory prayers, very hot.

[9th]. We having sailed all night, were come in sight of the Nore and South Forelands in the morning, and so sailed all day. In the afternoon we had a very fresh gale, which I brooked better than I thought I should be able to do. This afternoon I first saw

---

[1] Perhaps Bawdsey, north of Felixstowe in Suffolk.

[2] Probably Edward Pickering, see *ante* April 2nd (note).

[3] "A vessel of the galliot order, equipped with two masts, viz., the main and mizen masts, usually from 100 to 250 tons burden. Ketches were principally used as yachts for conveying great personages from one place to another." —Smyth's *Sailor's Word-Book*, 1867.

France and Calais, with which I was much pleased, though it was at a distance. About five o'clock we came to the Goodwin, so to the Castles about Deal,[1] where our Fleet lay, among whom we anchored. Great was the shout of guns from the castles and ships, and our answers, that I never heard yet so great rattling of guns. Nor could we see one another on board for the smoke that was among us, nor one ship from another. Soon as we came to anchor, the captains came from on board their ships all to us on board. This afternoon I wrote letters for my Lord to the Council, &c., which Mr. Pickering was to carry, who took his leave this night of my Lord, and Balty after I had wrote two or three letters by him to my wife and Mr. Bowyer, and had drank a bottle of wine with him in my cabin which J. Goods and W. Howe brought on purpose, he took leave of me too to go away to-morrow morning with Mr. Pickering. I lent Balty 15s. which he was to pay to my wife. It was one in the morning before we parted. This evening Mr. Sheply came on board, having escaped a very great danger upon a sand coming from Chatham.

[10th]. This morning many or most of the commanders in the Fleet came on board and dined here, so that some of them and I dined together in the Round-house, where we were very merry. Hither came the Vice-Admiral to us, and sat and talked and seemed a very good-natured man. At night as I was all alone in my cabin, in a melancholy fit playing on my viallin, my Lord and Sir R. Stayner came into the coach[2] and supped there, and called me out to supper with them. After that up to the Lieutenant's cabin, where he and I and Sir Richard sat till 11 o'clock talking, and so to bed. This day my Lord Goring[3] returned from France, and landed at Dover.

---

[1] The castles were Walmer, Sandgate, Sandwich, Deal, and Dover.

[2] "A sort of chamber or apartment in a large ship of war, just before the great cabin. The floor of it is formed by the aftmost part of the quarter deck, and the roof of it by the poop: it is generally the habitation of the flag-captain."— Smyth's *Sailor's Word-Book*.

[3] Charles, who succeeded his father as second Earl of Norwich. He had been banished eleven years before by the Parliament for heading an army, and keeping the town of Colchester for the use of the King. At his first coming he went to the Council of State, and had leave to remain in London, provided he did not disturb the peace of the nation.—Rugge's *Diurnal*.—B.

[11th]. A Gentleman came this morning from my Lord of Manchester to my Lord for a pass for Mr. Boyle,[1] which was made him. I ate a good breakfast by my Lord's orders with him in the great cabin below. The wind all this day was very high, so that a gentleman that was at dinner with my Lord that came along with Sir John Bloys[2] (who seemed a fine man) was forced to rise from table. This afternoon came a great packet of letters from London directed to me, among the rest two from my wife, the first that I have since coming away from London. All the news from London is that things go on further towards a King. That the Skinners' Company the other day at their entertaining of General Monk[3] had took down the Parliament Arms in their Hall, and set up the King's. In the evening my Lord and I had a great deal of discourse about the several Captains of the Fleet and his interest among them, and had his mind clear to bring in the King. He confessed to me that he was not sure of his own Captain [Cuttance] to be true to him, and that he did not like Captain Stokes. At night W. Howe and I at our viallins in my cabin, where Mr. Ibbott and the lieutenant were late. I staid the lieutenant late, shewing him my manner of keeping a journal. After that to bed. It comes now into my mind to observe that I am sensible that I have been a little too free to make mirth with the minister of our ship, he being a very sober and an upright man.

[12th]. This day, the weather being very bad, we had no strangers on board. In the afternoon came the Vice-Admiral on board, with whom my Lord consulted, and I sent a packet to London at night with several letters to my friends, as to my wife about my getting of money for her when she should need it, to

---

[1] The Hon. Robert Boyle, youngest son of Richard, first Earl of Cork.

[2] Probably a miswriting for Sir John Boys, the celebrated Royalist commander, who was released from Dover Castle on February 23rd, 1659-60, having been imprisoned for petitioning for a free parliament. See *post* April 21st (note).

[3] "His Excellency had now dined at nine of the chief Halls; at every Hall there was after dinner a kind of stage-play, and many pretty conceits, and dancing and singing and many shapes and ghosts, and the like, and all to please Lord Monk." Rugge's *Diurnal.*—B.

Mr. Bowyer that he tell me when the Messieurs of the offices be paid, to Mr. Moore about the business of my office, and making even with him as to matter of money. At night after I had despatched my letters, to bed.

[13th]. This day very foul all day for rain and wind. In the afternoon set my own things in my cabin and chests in better order than hitherto, and set my papers in order. At night sent another packet to London by the post, and after that was done I went up to the lieutenant's cabin and there we broached a vessel of ale that we had sent for among us from Deal to-day. There was the minister and doctor with us. After that till one o'clock in the morning writing letters to Mr. Downing about my business of continuing my office to myself, only Mr. Moore to execute it for me. I had also a very serious and effectual letter from my Lord to him to that purpose. After that done then to bed, and it being very rainy, and the rain coming upon my bed, I went and lay with John Goods in the great cabin below, the wind being so high that we were fain to lower some of the masts. I to bed, and what with the goodness of the bed and the rocking of the ship I slept till almost ten o'clock, and then—

[14th]. Rose and drank a good morning draught there with Mr. Sheply, which occasioned my thinking upon the happy life that I live now, had I nothing to care for but myself. The sea was this morning very high, and looking out of the window I saw our boat come with Mr. Pierce, the surgeon, in it in great danger, who endeavouring to come on board us, had like to have been drowned had it not been for a rope. This day I was informed that my Lord Lambert is got out of the Tower[1] and that there is £100 proffered

[1] The manner of the escape of John Lambert, out of the Tower, on the 11th inst., as related by Rugge:—"That about eight of the clock at night he escaped by a rope tied fast to his window, by which he slid down, and in each hand he had a handkerchief; and six men were ready to receive him, who had a barge to hasten him away. She who made the bed, being privy to his escape, that night, to blind the warder when he came to lock the chamber-door, went to bed, and possessed Colonel Lambert's place, and put on his night-cap. So, when the said warder came to lock the door, according to his usual manner, he found the curtains drawn, and conceiving it to be Colonel John Lambert, he said, 'Good night, my Lord.' To which a seeming voice replied, and prevented all further jealousies. The next morning, on coming to unlock the door, and

to whoever shall bring him forth to the Council of State. My Lord is chosen at Waymouth this morning; my Lord had his freedom brought him by Captain Tiddiman[1] of the port of Dover, by which he is capable of being elected for them. This day I heard that the Army had in general declared to stand by what the next Parliament shall do. At night supped with my Lord.

[15th] (Lord's day). Up early and was trimmed by the barber in the great cabin below. After that to put my clothes on and then to sermon, and then to dinner, where my Lord told us that the University of Cambridge had a mind to choose him for their burgess, which he pleased himself with, to think that they do look upon him as a thriving man, and said so openly at table. At dinner-time Mr. Cook came back from London with a packet which caused my Lord to be full of thoughts all day, and at night he bid me privately to get two commissions ready, one for Capt. Robert Blake to be captain of the Worcester,[2] in the room of Capt. Dekings, an anabaptist, and one that had witnessed a great deal of discontent with the present proceedings. The other for Capt. Coppin[3] to come out of that into the Newbury in the room of Blake, whereby I perceive that General Monk do resolve to make a thorough change, to make way for the King. From London I hear that since Lambert got out of the Tower, the Fanatiques had held up their heads high, but I hope all that will come to nothing. Late a writing of letters to London to get ready for Mr. Cook. Then to bed.

[16th]. And about 4 o'clock in the morning Mr. Cook waked me where I lay in the great cabin below, and I did give him his packet and directions for London. So to sleep again. All the

---

espying her face, he cried out, 'In the name of God, Joan, what makes you here? Where is my Lord Lambert?' She said, 'He is gone; but I cannot tell whither.' Whereupon he caused her to rise, and carried her before the officer in the Tower and [she] was committed to custody. Some said that a lady knit for him a ladder of silk, by which he was conveyed down, and that she received £100 for her pains."—B.

[1] Captain, afterwards Admiral Sir Thomas Teddiman.

[2] The "Worcester" (formerly the "Dunkirk") was a third-rate of forty-eight guns, built at Woolwich in 1651 by Mr. Russell.

[3] John Coppin was captain of the "Lambert," afterwards the "Henrietta."

morning giving out orders and tickets to the Commanders of the Fleet to discharge all supernumeraries that they had above the number that the Council had set in their last establishment. After dinner busy all the afternoon writing, and so till night, then to bed.

[17th]. All the morning getting ready commissions for the Vice-Admiral[1] and the Rear-Admiral,[2] wherein my Lord was very careful to express the utmost of his own power, commanding them to obey what orders they should receive from the Parliament, &c., or both or either of the Generals.[3] The Vice-Admiral dined with us, and in the afternoon my Lord called me to give him the commission for him, which I did, and he gave it him himself. A very pleasant afternoon, and I upon the deck

---

[1] Sir John Lawson (see *ante*, January 1st, note).

[2] Sir Richard Stayner, knighted and made a Vice-Admiral by Cromwell, 1657, and after the Restoration sent to command at Tangier till the Governor arrived.

[3] Sir Edward Montagu afterwards recommended the Duke of York as High

all the day, it was so clear that my Lord's glass shewed us Calais very plain, and the cliffs were as plain to be seen as Kent, and my Lord at first made me believe that it was Kent. At night, after supper, my Lord called for the Rear-Admiral's commission, which I brought him, and I sitting in my study heard my Lord discourse with him concerning D. King's and Newberry's being put out of commission. And by the way I did observe that my Lord did speak more openly his mind to me afterwards at night than I can find that he did to the Rear-Admiral, though his great confidant. For I was with him an hour together, when he told me clearly his thoughts that the King would carry it, and that he did think himself very happy that he was now at sea, as well as for his own sake, as that he thought he might do his country some service in keeping things quiet. To bed, and shifting myself from top to toe, there being J. Goods and W. Howe sat late by my bedside talking. So to sleep, every day bringing me a fresh sense of the pleasure of my present life.

[18th]. This morning very early came Mr. Edward Montagu on board, but what was the business of his coming again or before without any servant and making no stay at all I cannot guess. This day Sir R. Stayner, Mr. Sheply, and as many of my Lord's people as could be spared went to Dover to get things ready against to-morrow for the election there. I all the afternoon dictating in my cabin (my own head being troubled with multiplicity of business) to Burr, who wrote for me above a dozen letters, by which I have made my mind more light and clear than I have had it yet since I came on board. At night sent a packet to London, and Mr. Cook returned hence bringing me this news, that the Sectaries do talk high what they will do, but I believe all to no purpose, but the Cavaliers are something unwise to talk so high on the other side as they do. That the Lords do meet every day at my Lord of Manchester's, and resolve to sit the first day of the Parliament. That it is evident now that the General and the Council do resolve to make way for the King's coming. And

Admiral, to give regular and lawful commissions to the Commanders of the Fleet, instead of those which they had received from Sir Edward himself, or from the Rump Parliament.—Kennett's *Register*, p. 163.

it is now clear that either the Fanatiques must now be undone, or the gentry and citizens throughout England, and clergy must fall, in spite of their militia and army, which is not at all possible I think. At night I supped with W. Howe and Mr. Luellin (being the first time that I had been so long with him) in the great cabin below. After that to bed, and W. Howe sat by my bedside, and he and I sang a psalm or two and so I to sleep.

[19th]. A great deal of business all this day, and Burr being gone to shore without my leave did vex me much. At dinner news was brought us that my Lord was chosen at Dover. This afternoon came one Mr. Mansell on board as a Reformado, to whom my Lord did shew exceeding great respect, but upon what account I do not yet know. This day it has rained much, so that when I came to go to bed I found it wet through, so I was fain to wrap myself up in a dry sheet, and so lay all night.

[20th]. All the morning I was busy to get my window altered, and to have my table set as I would have it, which after it was done I was infinitely pleased with it, and also to see what a command I have to have every one ready to come and go at my command. This evening came Mr. Boyle on board, for whom I writ an order for a ship to transport him to Flushing. He supped with my Lord, my Lord using him as a person of honour. This evening too came Mr. John Pickering on board us. This evening my head ached exceedingly, which I impute to my sitting backwards in my cabin, otherwise than I am used to do. To-night Mr. Sheply told me that he heard for certain at Dover that Mr. Edw. Montagu did go beyond sea when he was here first the other day, and I am at to believe that he went to speak with the King. This day one told me how that at the election at Cambridge for knights of the shire, Wendby[1] and Thornton[2] by declaring to stand for the Parliament and a King and the settlement of the Church, did carry it against all expectation against Sir Dudley North and Sir Thomas Willis.[3] I supped to-

[1] Thomas Wendy of Haselingfield.
[2] Isaac Thornton of Smallwell.
[3] He had represented Cambridgeshire in the preceding Parliament.

night with Mr. Sheply below at the half-deck table, and after
that I saw Mr. Pickering whom my Lord brought down to his
cabin, and so to bed.

[21st]. This day dined Sir John Boys[1] and some other gentlemen
formerly great Cavaliers, and among the rest one Mr. Norwood,[2]
for whom my Lord gave a convoy to carry him to the Brill,[3] but
he is certainly going to the King. For my Lord commanded me
that I should not enter his name in my book. My Lord do show
them and that sort of people great civility. All their discourse
and others are of the King's coming, and we begin to speak of it
very freely. And heard how in many churches in London, and
upon many signs there, and upon merchants' ships in the river
they had set up the King's arms. In the afternoon the Captain
would by all means have me up to his cabin, and there treated
me huge nobly, giving me a barrel of pickled oysters, and opened
another for me, and a bottle of wine, which was a very great
favour. At night late singing with W. Howe, and under the
barber's hands in the coach. This night there came one with a
letter from Mr. Edw. Montagu to my Lord, with command to deliver it to his own hands. I do believe that he do carry some close
business on for the King.[4] This day I had a large letter from Mr.
Moore, giving me an account of the present dispute at London
that is like to be at the beginning of the Parliament, about the
House of Lords, who do resolve to sit with the Commons, as not
thinking themselves dissolved yet. Which, whether it be granted
or no, or whether they will sit or no, it will bring a great many

[1] Of Bonnington and Sandwich, Gentleman of the Privy-Chamber to Charles I.
He defended Donnington Castle, Berkshire, for the King against Jeremiah
Horton, 1644, and received an augmentation to his arms in consequence. See
ante, April 11th (note).

[2] A Major Norwood had been Governor of Dunkirk: and a person of the same
name occurs as one of the esquires of the body at the Coronation of Charles II.
Richard Norwood of Danes Court, in the Isle of Thanet, see December 1st,
1662.—B.

[3] Brielle, or Den Briel, a seaport town in the province of South Holland.

[4] Pepys's guess at E. Montagu's business is confirmed by Clarendon's account
of his employment of him to negotiate with Lord Sandwich on behalf of the
King. ("History of the Rebellion," book xvi.)—*Notes and Queries*, vol. x. p. 3.—
M. B.

inconveniences. His letter I keep, it being a very well writ one.

[22nd] (Easter Sunday). Several Londoners, strangers, friends of the Captains, dined here, who, among other things told us, how the King's Arms are every day set up in houses and churches, particularly in Allhallows Church in Thames-street,[1] John Simpson's church, which being privately done was a great eye-sore to his people when they came to church and saw it. Also they told us for certain, that the King's statue is making by the Mercers' Company (who are bound to do it)[2] to set up in the Exchange. After sermon in the afternoon I fell to writing letters against to-morrow to send to London. After supper to bed.

[23rd]. All the morning very busy getting my packet ready for London, only for an hour or two had the Captain and Mr. Sheply in my cabin at the barrel of pickled oysters that the Captain did give me on Saturday last. After dinner I sent Mr. Dunn to London with the packet. This afternoon I had 40s. given me by Captain Cowes of the Paradox.[3] In the evening the first time that we had any sport among the seamen, and indeed there was extraordinary good sport after my Lord had done playing at ninepins. After that W. Howe and I went to play two trebles in the great cabin below, which my Lord hearing, after supper he called for our instruments, and played a set of Lock's, two trebles, and a base, and that being done, he fell to singing of a song made upon the Rump, with which he played himself well, to the tune of "The Blacksmith."[4] After all that done, then to bed.

[24th]. This morning I had Mr. Luellin and Mr. Sheply to the remainder of my oysters that were left yesterday. After that very busy all the morning. While I was at dinner with my Lord,

---

[1] Allhallows the Great, a church in Upper Thames Street. The old church destroyed in the Great Fire was also known as "Allhallows in the Ropery."

[2] As trustees for Sir Thomas Gresham, the founder of the Royal Exchange.

[3] The "Paradox" was a sixth-rate of twelve guns.

[4] "The Blacksmith" was the same tune as "Green Sleeves." The earliest known copy of "The Praise of the Blacksmith" is in "An Antidote against Melancholy," 1661. See "Roxburghe Ballads," ed. W. Chappell, 1872, vol. ii. p. 126. (Ballad Society.)

the Coxon of the Vice-Admiral came for me to the Vice-Admiral to dinner. So I told my Lord and he gave me leave to go. I rose therefore from table and went, where there was very many commanders, and very pleasant we were on board the London,[1] which hath a state-room much bigger than the Nazeby, but not so rich. After that, with the Captain on board our own ship, where we were saluted with the news of Lambert's being taken, which news was brought to London on Sunday last. He was taken in Northamptonshire by Colonel Ingoldsby,[2] at the head of a party, by which means their whole design is broke, and things now very open and safe. And every man begins to be merry and full of hopes. In the afternoon my Lord gave a great large character to write out, so I spent all the day about it, and after supper my Lord and we had some more very good musique and singing of "Turne Amaryllis," as it is printed in the song book, with which my Lord was very much pleased. After that to bed.

[25th]. All the morning about my Lord's character. Dined to-day with Captain Clerke on board the Speaker (a very brave ship) where was the Vice-Admiral, Rear-Admiral, and many other commanders. After dinner home, not a little contented to see how I am treated, and with what respect made a fellow to the best commanders in the Fleet. All the afternoon finishing of the character, which I did and gave it my Lord, it being very handsomely done and a very good one in itself, but that not truly Alphabetical. Supped with Mr. Sheply, W. Howe, &c. in Mr. Pierce, the Purser's cabin, where very merry, and so to bed. Captain Isham came hither to-day.

[26th]. This day came Mr. Donne back from London, who brought letters with him that signify the meeting of the Parlia-

---

[1] The "London" was a second-rate of sixty-four guns, built at Chatham in 1657 by Captain Taylor.

[2] Colonel Richard Ingoldsby had been Governor of Oxford under his kinsman Cromwell. He signed the warrant for the execution of Charles I., but was pardoned for the service here mentioned, and made K.B. at the Coronation of Charles II. He afterwards retired to his seat at Lethenborough, Bucks, and died 1685. He was buried in the church of Hartwell, near Aylesbury.

ment yesterday. And in the afternoon by other letters I hear, that about twelve of the Lords met and had chosen my Lord of Manchester[1] Speaker of the House of Lords (the young lords that never sat yet, do forbear to sit for the present); and Sir Harbottle Grimstone,[2] Speaker for the House of Commons. The House of Lords sent to have a conference with the House of Commons, which, after a little debate, was granted. Dr. Reynolds[3] preached before the Commons before they sat. My Lord told me how Sir H. Yelverton[4] (formerly my school-fellow) was chosen in the first place for Northamptonshire and Mr. Crew in the second. And told me how he did believe that the Cavaliers have now the upper hand clear of the Presbyterians. All the afternoon I was writing of letters, among the rest one to W. Simons, Peter Luellin and Tom Doling, which because it is somewhat merry I keep a copy of. After that done Mr. Sheply, W. Howe and I down with J. Goods into my Lord's storeroom of wine and other drink, where it was very pleasant to observe the massy timbers that the ship is made of. We in the room were wholly under water and yet a deck below that. After that to supper, where Tom Guy supped with us, and we had very good laughing, and after that some musique, where Mr. Pickering beginning to play a bass part upon the viall did it so like a fool that I was ashamed of him. After that to bed.

[27th]. This morning Burr was absent again from on board, which I was troubled at, and spoke to Mr. Pierce, Purser, to speak to him of it, and it is my mind. This morning Pim [the tailor] spent in my cabin, putting a great many ribbons to a suit. After dinner in the afternoon came on board Sir Thomas Hatton[5] and Sir R. Maleverer[6] going for Flushing; but all the world

---

[1] Edward, second Earl of Manchester, whose father, Henry, first earl, had been chosen Speaker of the House of Lords in 1641.

[2] Ancestor of the Earls of Verulam. He was made Master of the Rolls, November following. Born 1594, and died December 31st, 1683.

[3] See *ante*, February 28th, 1659-60.

[4] Of Easton Mauduit, Bart., grandson to the Attorney-General of both his names. Died 1679.

[5] Of Long Stanton, co. Cambridge, Bart.

[6] Of Allerton Maleverer, Yorkshire, Bart.

know that they go where the rest of the many gentlemen go
that every day flock to the King at Breda.[1] They supped here,
and my Lord treated them as he do the rest that go thither, with
a great deal of civility. While we were at supper a packet came,
wherein much news from several friends. The chief is that, that
I had from Mr. Moore, viz. that he fears the Cavaliers in the
House will be so high, that the others will be forced to leave the
House and fall in with General Monk, and so offer things to the
King so high on the Presbyterian account that he may refuse,
and so they will endeavour some more mischief; but when I told
my Lord it, he shook his head and told me, that the Presbyterians
are deceived, for the General is certainly for the King's interest,
and so they will not be able to prevail that way with him. After
supper the two knights went on board the Grantham, that is to
convey them to Flushing. I am informed that the Exchequer is
now so low, that there is not £20 there, to give the messenger
that brought the news of Lambert's being taken; which story is
very strange that he should lose his reputation of being a man
of courage now at one blow, for that he was not able to fight one
stroke, but desired of Colonel Ingoldsby several times for God's
sake to let him escape. Late reading my letters, my mind being
much troubled to think that, after all our hopes, we should have
any cause to fear any more disappointments therein. To bed.
This day I made even with Mr. Creed, by sending him my bill
and he me my money by Burr, whom I sent for it.

[28th]. This morning sending a packet by Mr. Dunne to London. In the afternoon I played at ninepins with Mr. Pickering,
I and Mr. Pett[2] against him and Ned Osgood, and won a crown
apiece of him. He had not money enough to pay me. After supper my Lord exceeding merry, and he and I and W. Howe to
sing, and so to bed.

---

[1] The King arrived at Breda on the 14th April (new style). Sir W. Lower
writes ("Voiage and Residence of Charles II. in Holland," p. 5): "Many con-
siderations obliged him to depart the territories under the obedience of the
King of Spain in this conjuncture of affairs."

[2] As there were several of this name it is impossible to say which Mr. Pett is
meant.

[29th] (Sunday). This day I put on first my fine cloth suit made of a cloak that had like to have been [dirted] a year ago, the very day that I put it on. After sermon in the morning Mr. Cook came from London with a packet, bringing news how all the young lords that were not in arms against the Parliament do now sit. That a letter is come from the King to the House, which is locked up by the Council 'till next Tuesday that it may be read in the open House when they meet again, they having adjourned till then to keep a fast to-morrow. And so the contents is not yet known. £13,000 of the £20,000 given to General Monk is paid out of the Exchequer, he giving £12 among the teller clerks of Exchequer. My Lord called me into the great cabin below, where I opened my letters and he told me that the Presbyterians are quite mastered by the Cavaliers, and that he fears Mr. Crew did go a little too far the other day in keeping out the young lords from sitting. That he do expect that the King should be brought over suddenly, without staying to make any terms at all, saying that the Presbyterians did intend to have brought him in with such conditions as if he had been in chains. But he shook his shoulders when he told me how Monk had betrayed him, for it was he that did put them upon standing to put out the lords and other members that came not within the qualifications, which he [Montagu] did not like, but however he [Monk] had done his business, though it be with some kind of baseness. After dinner I walked a great while upon the deck with the chyrurgeon and purser, and other officers of the ship, and they all pray for the King's coming, which I pray God send.

[30th]. All the morning getting instructions ready for the Squadron of ships that are going to-day to the Streights, among others Captain Teddiman, Curtis, and Captain Robert Blake to be commander of the whole Squadron. After dinner to ninepins, W. Howe and I against Mr. Creed and the Captain. We lost 5s. apiece to them. After that W. Howe, Mr. Sheply and I got my Lord's leave to go to see Captain Sparling.[1] So we took boat and first went on shore, it being very pleasant in the fields; but a very pitiful town Deal is. We went to Fuller's (the famous place for

---

[1] Captain Thomas Sparling, of the "Assistance."

ale), but they have none but what was in the vat. After that to Poole's, a tavern in the town, where we drank, and so to boat again, and went to the Assistance, where we were treated very civilly by the Captain, and he did give us such music upon the harp by a fellow that he keeps on board that I never expect to hear the like again, yet he is a drunken simple fellow to look on as any I ever saw. After that on board the Nazeby, where we found my Lord at supper, so I sat down and very pleasant my Lord was with Mr. Creed and Sheply, who he puzzled about finding out the meaning of the three notes which my Lord had cut over the chrystal of his watch. After supper some musique. Then Mr. Sheply, W. Howe and I up to the Lieutenant's cabin, where we drank, and I and W. Howe were very merry, and among other frolics he pulls out the spigot of the little vessel of ale that was therein the cabin and drew some into his mounteere, and after he had drank, I endeavouring to dash it in his face, he got my velvet studying cap and drew some into mine too, that we made ourselves a great deal of mirth, but spoiled my clothes with the ale that we dashed up and down. After that to bed very late with drink enough in my head.

[May 1st]. This morning, I was told how the people of Deal have set up two or three Maypoles, and have hung up their flags upon the top of them, and do resolve to be very merry to-day. It being a very pleasant day, I wished myself in Hide Park.[1] This day I do count myself to have had full two years of perfect cure for the stone, for which God of heaven be blessed. This day Captain Parker came on board, and without his expectation I had a commission for him for the Nonsuch[2] frigate (he being now in the Cheriton), for which he gave me a French pistole. Captain H. Cuttance[3] has commission for the Cheriton. After dinner to nine-

[1] In 1656 was published "The Yellow Book, or a serious letter sent by a private Christian to the Lady Consideration the first of May 1656, which she is desired to communicate in Hide Park to the Gallants of the Times a little after sunset. Also a brief account of the names of some vain persons that intend to be there."

[2] The "Nonsuch" was a fourth-rate of thirty-two guns, built at Deptford in 1646 by Peter Pett, jun. The captain was John Parker.

[3] Captain Henry Cuttance, of the "Cheriton," afterwards the "Speedwell."

pins, and won something. The rest of the afternoon in my cabin writing and piping. While we were at supper we heard a great noise upon the Quarter Deck, so we all rose instantly, and found it was to save the coxon of the Cheriton, who, dropping overboard, could not be saved, but was drowned. To-day I put on my suit that was altered from the great skirts to little ones. To-day I hear they were very merry at Deal, setting up the King's flag upon one of their maypoles, and drinking his health upon their knees in the streets, and firing the guns, which the soldiers of the Castle threatened, but durst not oppose.

[2nd]. In the morning at a breakfast of radishes at the Purser's cabin. After that to writing till dinner. At which time comes Dunne from London, with letters that tell us the welcome news of the Parliament's votes yesterday, which will be remembered for the happiest May-day that hath been many a year to England. The King's letter was read in the House, wherein he submits himself and all things to them, as to an Act of Oblivion[1] to all, unless they shall please to except any, as to the confirming of the sales of the King's and Church lands, if they see good. The house upon reading the letter, ordered £50,000 to be forthwith provided to send to His Majesty for his present supply; and a committee chosen to return an answer of thanks to His Majesty for his gracious letter; and that the letter be kept among the records of the Parliament; and in all this not so much as one No. So that Luke Robinson[2] himself stood up and made a recantation for what he had done, and promises to be a loyal subject to his Prince for the time to come. The City of London have put out a Declaration, wherein they do disclaim their owing any other government but

---

[1] "His Majesty added thereunto an excellent Declaration for the safety and repose of those, who tortured in their consciences, for having partaken in the rebellion, might fear the punishment of it, and in that fear might oppose the tranquillity of the Estate, and the calling in of their lawful Prince. It is printed and published as well as the letter, but that shall not hinder me to say, that there was never seen a more perfect assemblage of all the most excellent natural qualities, and of all the vertues, as well Royal as Christian, wherewith a great Prince may be endowed, than was found in those two wonderful productions."—Sir William Lower's *Relation . . . of the Voiage and Residence which . . . Charles the II. hath made in Holland*, Hague, 1660, folio, p. 3.

[2] Of Pickering Lyth, in Yorkshire, M.P. for Scarborough; discharged from sitting in the House of Commons, July 21st, 1660.

that of a King, Lords, and Commons. Thanks was given by the
House to Sir John Greenville,[1] one of the bedchamber to the King,
who brought the letter, and they continued bare all the time it
was reading. Upon notice made from the Lords to the Commons,
of their desire that the Commons would join with them in their
vote for the King, Lords, and Commons; the Commons did con-
cur and voted that all books whatever that are out against the
Government of King, Lords, and Commons, should be brought
into the House and burned. Great joy all yesterday at London,
and at night more bonfires than ever, and ringing of bells, and
drinking of the King's health upon their knees in the streets,
which methinks is a little too much. But every body seems to be
very joyfull in the business, insomuch that our sea-commanders
now begin to say so too, which a week ago they would not do.[2]
And our seamen, as many as had money or credit for drink, did
do nothing else this evening. This day came Mr. North[3] (Sir
Dudley North's son) on board, to spend a little time here, which
my Lord was a little troubled at, but he seems to be a fine gentleman, and at night did play his part exceeding well at first sight.
After musique I went up to the Captain's Cabin with him and
Lieutenant Ferrers, who came hither to-day from London to
bring this news to my Lord, and after a bottle of wine we all
to bed.

[3rd]. This morning my Lord showed me the King's declaration
and his letter to the two Generals to be communicated to the
fleet.[4] The contents of the letter are his offer of grace to all that

[1] Created Earl of Bath, 1661; son of Sir Bevil Grenville, killed at the battle of
Lansdowne; he was, when a boy, left for dead on the field at the second battle
of Newbury, and said to have been the only person entrusted by Charles II.
and Monk in bringing about the Restoration.

[2] "The picture of King Charles II. was often set up in houses, without the least
molestation, whereas a little while ago, it was almost a hanging matter so to
do; but now the Rump Parliament was so hated and jeered at, that the butchers' boys would say, 'Will you buy any Parliament rumps and kidneys?' And
it was a very ordinary thing to see little children make a fire in the streets,
and burn rumps."—Rugge's *Diurnal.*—B.

[3] Charles, eldest son of Dudley, afterwards fourth Lord North. On the death
of his father in 1677 he became fifth Lord North.

[4] "King Charles II. his Declaration to all his loving Subjects of the Kingdome
of England, dated from his Court at Breda in Holland 4/14 of April, 1660, and

will come in within forty days, only excepting them that the
Parliament shall hereafter except. That the sales of lands during these troubles, and all other things, shall be left to the Parliament, by which he will stand. The later dated at Breda, April
4/14 1660, in the 12th year of his reign. Upon the receipt of it
this morning by an express, Mr. Phillips, one of the messengers
of the Council from General Monk, my Lord summoned a council of war, and in the mean time did dictate to me how he would
have the vote ordered which he would have pass this council.
Which done, the Commanders all came on board, and the council sat in the coach (the first council of war that had been in my
time), where I read the letter and declaration; and while they

were discoursing upon it, I seemed to draw up a vote, which being offered, they passed. Not one man seemed to say no to it,
though I am confident many in their hearts were against it. After

read in Parliament with his Majesties Letter of the same date to his Excellence
the Ld. Gen. Monck to be communicated to the Ld. President of the Council
of State and to the Officers of the Army under his Command. London, Printed
by W. Godbid for John Playford in the Temple, 1660." 4to, pp. 8.

this was done, I went up to the quarter-deck with my Lord and the Commanders, and there read both the papers and the vote; which done, and demanding their opinion, the seamen did all of them cry out, "God bless King Charles!" with the greatest joy imaginable. That being done, Sir R. Stayner, who had invited us yesterday, took all the Commanders and myself on board him to dinner, which not being ready, I went with Captain Hayward to the Plimouth and Essex,[1] and did what I had to do there and returned, where very merry at dinner. After dinner, to the rest of the ships (staid at the Assistance to hear the harper a good while) quite through the fleet. Which was a very brave sight to visit all the ships, and to be received with the respect and honour that I was on board them all; and much more to see the great joy that I brought to all men; not one through the whole fleet showing the least dislike of the business. In the evening as I was going on board the Vice-Admiral, the General began to fire his guns, which he did all that he had in the ship, and so did all the rest of the Commanders, which was very gallant, and to hear the bullets go hissing over our heads as we were in the boat. This done and finished my Proclamation, I returned to the Nazeby, where my Lord was much pleased to hear how all the fleet took it in a transport of joy, showed me a private letter of the King's to him, and another from the Duke of York in such familiar style as to their common friend, with all kindness imaginable. And I found by the letters, and so my Lord told me too, that there had been many letters passed between them for a great while, and I perceive unknown to Monk. And among the rest that had carried these letters Sir John Boys is one, and that Mr. Norwood, which had a ship to carry him over the other day, when my Lord would not have me put down his name in the book. The King speaks of his being courted to come to the Hague, but do desire my Lord's advice whither to come to take ship. And the Duke offers to learn the seaman's trade of him, in such familiar words as if Jack Cole and I had writ them. This was very strange to me, that my Lord should carry all things so wisely and prudently as he do, and I

---

[1] John Hayward was captain of the "Plymouth." Thomas Binns commanded the "Essex."

was over joyful to see him in so good condition, and he did not a little please himself to tell me how he had provided for himself so great a hold on the King.

After this to supper, and then to writing of letters till twelve at night, and so up again at three in the morning. My Lord seemed to put great confidence in me, and would take my advice in many things. I perceive his being willing to do all the honour in the world to Monk, and to let him have all the honour of doing the business, though he will many times express his thoughts of him to be but a thick-sculled fool. So that I do believe there is some agreement more than ordinary between the King and my Lord to let Monk carry on the business, for it is he that must do the business, or at least that can hinder it, if he be not flattered and observed. This, my Lord will hint himself sometimes. My Lord, I perceive by the King's letter, had writ to him about his father, Crew,[1] and the King did speak well of him; but my Lord tells me, that he is afeard that he hath too much concerned himself with the Presbyterians against the House of Lords, which will do him a great discourtesy.

[4th]. I wrote this morning many letters, and to all the copies of the vote of the council of war I put my name, that if it should come in print my name may be at it. I sent a copy of the vote to Doling, inclosed in this letter: —

> "SIR,
> "He that can fancy a fleet (like ours) in her pride, with pendants loose, guns roaring, caps flying, and the loud 'Vive le Roys,' echoed from one ship's company to another, he, and he only, can apprehend the joy this inclosed vote was received with, or the blessing he thought himself possessed of that bore it, and is
>
> "Your humble servant."

About nine o'clock I got all my letters done, and sent them by the messenger that came yesterday. This morning came Captain Isham on board with a gentleman going to the King, by whom very cunningly, my Lord tells me, he intends to send an

---

[1] When only seventeen years old, Montagu had married Jemima, daughter of John Crew, created afterwards Baron Crew of Stene.

account of this day's and yesterday's actions here, notwith-standing he had writ to the Parliament to have leave of them to send the King the answer of the fleet. Since my writing of the last paragraph, my Lord called me to him to read his letter to the King, to see whether I could find any slips in it or no. And as much of the letter[1] as I can remember, is thus: —

"May it please your Most Excellent Majesty," and so begins.

"That he yesterday received from General Monk his Majes-ty's letter and direction; and that General Monk had desired him to write to the Parliament to have leave to send the vote of the seamen before he did send it to him, which he had done by writing to both Speakers; but for his private satisfaction he had sent it thus privately (and so the copy of the proceedings yester-day was sent him), and that this come by a gentleman that came this day on board, intending to wait upon his Majesty, that he is my Lord's countryman, and one whose friends have suffered much on his Majesty's behalf. That my Lords Pembroke[2] and Salisbury[3] are put out of the House of Lords. That my Lord is very joyful that other countries do pay him the civility and re-spect due to him; and that he do much rejoice to see that the King do resolve to receive none of their assistance (or some such words), from them, he having strength enough in the love and loyalty of his own subjects to support him. That his Majesty had chosen the best place, Sheveling,[4] for his embarking, and that there is nothing in the world of which he is more ambitious, than to have the honour of attending his Majesty, which he hoped would be speedy. That he had commanded the vessel to attend at Helversluce[5] till this gentleman returns, that so if his Majesty do not think it fit to command the fleet himself, yet that he may be there to receive his commands and bring them to his Lordship.

[1] See the letter printed in Lister's "Life of Lord Clarendon," vol. iii. p. 404. It is dated 4th May.

[2] Philip, fifth Earl of Pembroke, and second Earl of Montgomery, died 1669. Clarendon says, "This young earl's affections were entire for his Majesty."

[3] William, second Earl of Salisbury. After Cromwell had put down the House of Peers, he was chosen a member of the House of Commons, and sat with them. Died 1668.

[4] Scheveningen, the port of the Hague.

[5] Hellevoetsluis, in South Holland.

He ends his letter, that he is confounded with the thoughts of the high expressions of love to him in the King's letter, and concludes,

"Your most loyall, dutifull, faithfull and obedient subject and servant,

"E. M."

The rest of the afternoon at ninepins. In the evening came a packet from London, among the rest a letter from my wife, which tells me that she has not been well, which did exceedingly trouble me, but my Lord sending Mr. Cook at night, I wrote to her and sent a piece of gold enclosed to her, and wrote also to Mrs. Bowyer, and enclosed a half piece to her for a token. After supper at the table in coach, my Lord talking concerning the uncertainty of the places of the Exchequer to them that had them now; he did at last think of an office which do belong to him in case the King do restore every man to his places that ever had been patent, which is to be one of the clerks of the signet, which will be a fine employment for one of his sons. After all this discourse we broke up and to bed.

In the afternoon came a minister on board, one Mr. Sharpe, who is going to the King; who tells me that Commissioners are chosen both of Lords and Commons to go to the King; and that Dr. Clarges[1] is going to him from the Army, and that he will be here to-morrow. My letters at night tell me, that the House did deliver their letters to Sir John Greenville, in answer to the King's sending, and that they give him £500 for his pains, to buy him a jewel, and that besides the £50,000 ordered to be borrowed of the City for the present use of the King, the twelve companies of the City do give every one of them to his Majesty, as a present, £1,000.

---

[1] Thomas Clarges, physician to the army, created a baronet, 1674, died 1695. He had been previously knighted; his sister Anne married General Monk. "The Parliament also permitted General Monk to send Mr. Clarges, his brother-in-law, accompanied with some officers of the army, to assure his Majesty of the fidelity and obedience of the army, which had made publick and solemn protestations thereof, after the Letter and Declaration was communicated unto them by the General."—Sir William Lower's *Relation . . . of the Voiage and Residence which . . . Charles the II. hath made in Holland*, Hague, 1660, folio.

[5th]. All the morning very busy writing letters to London, and a packet to Mr. Downing, to acquaint him with what had been done lately in the fleet. And this I did by my Lord's command, who, I thank him, did of himself think of doing it, to do me a kindness, for he writ a letter himself to him, thanking him for his kindness to me. All the afternoon at ninepins, at night after supper good musique, my Lord, Mr. North, I and W. Howe. After that to bed. This evening came Dr. Clarges to Deal, going to the King; where the towns-people strewed the streets with herbes against his coming, for joy of his going. Never was there so general a content as there is now. I cannot but remember that our parson did, in his prayer to-night, pray for the long life and happiness of our King and dread Soveraign, that may last as long as the sun and moon endureth.

[6th] (Lord's day). This morning while we were at sermon comes in Dr. Clarges and a dozen gentlemen to see my Lord, who, after sermon, dined with him; I remember that last night upon discourse concerning Clarges my Lord told me that he was a man of small *entendimiento*.[1] This afternoon there was a gentleman with me, an officer of Dunkirk going over, who came to me for an order and told me he was lately with my uncle and Aunt Fenner and that Kate's[2] fits of the convulsions did hold her still. It fell very well to-day, a stranger preached here for Mr. Ibbot, one Mr. Stanley, who prayed for King Charles, by the Grace of God, &c., which gave great contentment to the gentlemen that were on board here, and they said they would talk of it, when they come to Breda, as not having it done yet in London so publickly. After they were gone from on board, my Lord writ a letter to the King and give it to me to carry privately to Sir William Compton[3] on board the Assistance, which I did, and

---

[1] Entendimiento, *Spanish:* the understanding.

[2] Kate Fenner married Anthony Joyce.

[3] Third son of Spencer, Earl of Northampton, a Privy Councillor and Master of the Ordnance, ob. 1663, aged 39. When only eighteen years of age, he had charged with his gallant father at the battle of Edgehill. His mother was first cousin to George Villiers, Duke of Buckingham, and to John Ashburnham; and his great uncle, Sir Thomas Compton, had been the third husband of the Duke's mother, Mary, Countess of Buckingham.—B.

after a health to his Majesty on board there, I left them under sail for Breda. Back again and found them at sermon. I went up to my cabin and looked over my accounts, and find that, all my debts paid and my preparations to sea paid for, I have £40 clear in my purse. After supper to bed.

[7th]. This morning Captain Cuttance sent me 12 bottles of Margate ale. Three of them I drank presently with some friends in the Coach. My Lord went this morning about the flag-ships in a boat, to see what alterations there must be, as to the arms and flags. He did give me order also to write for silk flags and scarlett waistcloathes.[1] For a rich barge; for a noise of trumpets,[2] and a set of fidlers. Very great deal of company come to-day, among others Mr. Bellasses,[3] Sir Thomas Lenthropp,[4] Sir Henry Chichley, Colonel Philip Honiwood,[5] and Captain Titus,[6] the last of whom my Lord showed all our cabins, and I suppose he is to take notice what room there will be for the King's entertainment. Here were also all the Jurates of the town of Dover[7] come to give my Lord a visit, and after dinner all went away. I could not but observe that the Vice-Admiral after dinner came into the great cabin below, where the Jurates and I and the commanders for want of room dined, and there told us we must drink a health to the King, and himself called for a bottle of wine, and begun his and the Duke of York's. In the afternoon I lost 5s. at ninepins. After supper musique, and to bed. Having also among us at the Coach table wrote a letter to the French ambassador, in French, about the release of a ship we had taken.

---

[1] Waist-cloths are the painted canvas coverings of the hammocks which are stowed in the waist-nettings.

[2] A set or company of musicians, an expression constantly used by old writers without any disparaging meaning. It is sometimes applied to voices as well as to instruments.

[3] Henry, eldest son of Lord Bellasis, made K.B. at Charles II.'s coronation.

[4] Sir Thomas Leventhorpe, Bart., married Mary, daughter of Sir Capell Bedell, Bart. Died 1671.

[5] Colonel, afterwards Sir Philip Honywood, son of Robert Honywood of Charing, Kent.

[6] Colonel Silas Titus, Gentleman of the Bedchamber to Charles II., author of "Killing no Murder."

[7] The jurats of the Cinque Ports answered to the aldermen of other towns.

After I was in bed Mr. Sheply and W. Howe came and sat in my cabin, where I gave them three bottles of Margate ale, and sat laughing and very merry, till almost one o'clock in the morning, and so good night.

[8th]. All the morning busy. After dinner come several persons of honour, as my Lord St. John and others, for convoy to Flushing, and great giving of them salutes. My Lord and we at ninepins: I lost 9s. While we were at play Mr. Cook brings me word of my wife. He went to Huntsmore to see her, and brought her and my father Bowyer to London, where he left her at my father's, very well, and speaks very well of her love to me. My letters to-day tell me how it was intended that the King should be proclaimed to-day in London, with a great deal of pomp. I had also news who they are that are chosen of the Lords and Commons to attend the King. And also the whole story of what we did the other day in the fleet, at reading of the King's declaration, and my name at the bottom of it. After supper some musique and to bed. I resolving to rise betimes to-morrow to write letters to London.

[9th]. Up very early, writing a letter to the King, as from the two Generals of the fleet, in answer to his letter to them, wherein my Lord do give most humble thanks for his gracious letter and declaration; and promises all duty and obedience to him. This letter was carried this morning to Sir Peter Killigrew,[1] who came hither this morning early to bring an order from the Lords' House to my Lord, giving him power to write an answer to the King. This morning my Lord St. John and other persons of honour were here to see my Lord and so away to Flushing. After they were gone my Lord and I to write letters to London, which we sent by Mr. Cook, who was very desirous to go because of seeing my wife before she went out of town. As we were sitting down to dinner, in comes Noble with a letter from the House of

---

[1] Sir Peter Killigrew, Knight, of Arwenack, Cornwall, was known as "Peter the Post," from the alacrity with which he despatched "like wild fire" all the messages and other commissions entrusted to him in the King's cause. His son Peter, who succeeded his uncle as second baronet in 1665, was M.P. for Camelford in 1660.

Lords to my Lord, to desire him to provide ships to transport the Commissioners to the King, which are expected here this week. He brought us certain news that the King was proclaimed yesterday with great pomp, and brought down one of the Proclamations, with great joy to us all; for which God be praised. After dinner to ninepins and lost 5s. This morning came Mr. Saunderson,[1] that writ the story of the King, hither, who is going over to the King. He calls me cozen and seems a very knowing man. After supper to bed betimes, leaving my Lord talking in the Coach with the Captain.

[10th]. This morning came on board Mr. Pinkney and his son, going to the King with a petition finely writ by Mr. Whore, for to be the King's embroiderer; for whom and Mr. Saunderson I got a ship. This morning come my Lord Winchelsea[2] and a great deal of company, and dined here. In the afternoon, while my Lord and we were at musique in the great cabin below, comes in a messenger to tell us that Mr. Edward Montagu,[3] my Lord's son, was come to Deal, who afterwards came on board with Mr. Pickering with him. The child was sick in the evening. At night, while my Lord was at supper, in comes my Lord Lauderdale[4] and Sir John Greenville, who supped here, and so went away. After they were gone, my Lord called me into his cabin, and told me how he was commanded to set sail presently for the King,[5] and was very glad thereof, and so put me to writ-

---

[1] Afterwards Sir William Sanderson, gentleman of the chamber, author of the "History of Mary Queen of Scots, James I., and Charles I." His wife, Dame Bridget, was mother of the maids.

[2] Heneage Finch, second Earl of Winchelsea, constituted by General Monk Governor of Dover Castle, July, 1660; made Lord Lieutenant of Kent, and afterwards ambassador to Turkey. Died 1689.

[3] Sir Edward Montagu's eldest son, afterwards second Earl of Sandwich, called by Pepys "The Child."

[4] John Maitland, second Earl, and afterwards created Marquis of March, Duke of Lauderdale, and Earl of Guilford (in England), and K.G. He became sole Secretary of State for Scotland in 1661, and was a Gentleman of his Majesty's Bedchamber, and died in 1682, s.p.—B.

[5] "Ordered that General Montagu do observe the command of His Majesty for the disposing of the fleet, in order to His Majesty's returning home to England to his kingly government: and that all proceedings in law be in His Majesty's name."—Rugge's *Diurnal.*—B.

ing of letters and other work that night till it was very late, he going to bed. I got him afterwards to sign things in bed. After I had done some more work I to bed also.

[11th]. Up very early in the morning, and so about a great deal of business in order to our going hence to-day. Burr going on shore last night made me very angry. So that I sent for Mr. Pitts[1] to come to me from the Vice-Admiral's, intending not to have employed Burr any more. But Burr by and by coming and desiring humbly that I would forgive him and Pitts not coming I did set him to work. This morning we began to pull down all the State's arms in the fleet, having first sent to Dover for paint-ers and others to come to set up the King's.[2] The rest of the morn-ing writing of letters to London which I afterwards sent by Dunne. I had this morning my first opportunity of discoursing with Dr. Clarke,[3] whom I found to be a very pretty man and very knowing. He is now going in this ship to the King. There dined here my Lord Crafford[4] and my Lord Cavendish,[5] and other Scotchmen whom I afterwards ordered to be received on board the Plymouth, and to go along with us. After dinner we set sail from the Downs, I leaving my boy to go to Deal for my linen. In the afternoon overtook us three or four gentlemen; two of the Berties,[6] and one Mr. Dormerhoy,[7] a Scotch gentleman, whom

---

[1] Mr. Pitts was secretary to Sir J. Lawson, Vice-Admiral.

[2] "Die Mercurii 9 Maii 1660. Ordered by the Lords and Commons in Parlia-ment assembled that the armes of this Common-wealth wherever they are standing be forthwith taken down, and that the Kings Majesties armes be set up in stead thereof."

[3] Timothy Clarke, M.D., one of the original Fellows of the Royal Society. He was appointed one of the physicians in ordinary to Charles II. on the death of Dr. Quartermaine in 1667.

[4] John, fourteenth Earl of Crauford, restored in 1661 to the office of High Treasurer of Scotland, which he had held eight years under Charles I.—B.

[5] William, Lord Cavendish, afterwards fourth Earl and first Duke of Devon-shire.

[6] Robert and Edward Bertie, two of the surviving sons of Robert, first Earl of Lindsay, killed at Edgehill. Their mother was Elizabeth, only child of Ed-ward, first Lord Montagu of Boughton; they were, therefore, nearly connected with Sir E. Montagu, and with Pepys in some degree.—B.

[7] Probably Thomas Dalmahoy, who had married the Duchess Dowager of Hamilton: see (infra) Speaker Onslow's note to Burnet. The husband of the

I afterwards found to be a very fine man, who, telling my Lord
that they heard the Commissioners were come out of London to-
day, my Lord dropt anchor over against Dover Castle (which give
us about thirty guns in passing), and upon a high debate with
the Vice and Rear-Admiral whether it were safe to go and not
stay for the Commissioners, he did resolve to send Sir R. Stayner
to Dover, to enquire of my Lord Winchelsea, whether or no they
are come out of London, and then to resolve to-morrow morning of going or not; which was done. It blew very hard all this
night that I was afeard of my boy. About 11 at night came the
boats from Deal, with great store of provisions, by the same
token John Goods told me that above 20 of the fowls are smothered, but my boy was put on board the Northwich. To bed.

[12th]. This morning I inquired for my boy, whether he was
come well or no, and it was told me that he was well in bed.
My Lord called me to his chamber, he being in bed, and gave me
many orders to make for direction for the ships that are left in
the Downs, giving them the greatest charge in the world to bring
no passengers with them, when they come after us to Scheveling
Bay, excepting Mr. Edward Montagu, Mr. Thomas Crew, and
Sir H. Wright. Sir R. Stayner hath been here early in the morning and told my Lord, that my Lord Winchelsea understands by
letters, that the Commissioners are only to come to Dover to
attend the coming over of the King. So my Lord did give order for
weighing anchor, which we did, and sailed all day. In our way
in the morning, coming in the midway between Dover and Calais, we could see both places very easily, and very pleasant it

loyal Duchess would be naturally one of the first to welcome the King; and
Onslow says he was in the interest of the Duke of York:—"Lord Middleton
retired, after his disgrace, to the Friary, near Guildford, to one Dalmahoy
there, a genteel, generous man, who was of Scotland: had been Gentleman of
the Horse to William Duke of Hamilton (killed at the battle of Worcester);
married that Duke's widow; and by her had this house, &c. This man, Dalmahoy, being much in the interest of the Duke of York, and a man to be relied
upon, and long a candidate for the town of Guildford, at the election of the
Parliament after the Long one, in 1678, and being opposed, I think, by the
famous Algernon Sidney, the Duke of York came from Windsor to Dalmahoy's house, to countenance his election, and appeared for him in the open
court, when the election was taken."—Note to Burnet's *O. T.*, vol. i. p. 350.

was to me that the further we went the more we lost sight of
both lands. In the afternoon at cards with Mr. North and the
Doctor.[1] There by us, in the Lark frigate,[2] Sir R. Freeman and
some others, going from the King to England, come to see my
Lord and so onward on their voyage. In the afternoon upon the
quarter-deck the Doctor told Mr. North and me an admirable
story called "The Fruitless Precaution," an exceeding pretty
story and worthy my getting without book when I can get the
book. This evening came Mr. Sheply on board, whom we had left
at Deal and Dover getting of provision and borrowing of money.
In the evening late, after discoursing with the Doctor, &c., to bed.

[13th] (Lord's day). Trimmed in the morning, after that to the
cook's room with Mr. Sheply, the first time that I was there this
voyage. Then to the quarter-deck, upon which the tailors and
painters were at work, cutting out some pieces of yellow cloth
into the fashion of a crown and C. R. and put it upon a fine sheet,
and that into the flag instead of the State's arms, which after
dinner was finished and set up after it had been shewn to my
Lord, who took physic to-day and was in his chamber, and liked
it so well as to bid me give the tailors 20s. among them for doing of it. This morn Sir J. Boys and Capt. Isham met us in
the Nonsuch, the first of whom, after a word or two with my
Lord, went forward, the other staid. I heard by them how Mr.
Downing had never made any address to the King, and for that
was hated exceedingly by the Court, and that he was in a Dutch
ship which sailed by us, then going to England with disgrace.
Also how Mr. Morland[3] was knighted by the King this week, and

---

[1] Dr. Timothy Clarke; see note on the previous day.

[2] The "Lark" carried ten guns and forty men. Its captain was Thomas Levidge.

[3] Samuel Morland, son of the Rev. Thomas Morland, of Sulhamstead Banister,
near Reading, Berks, was born about 1625. He was educated at Winchester
School, whence he removed to Magdalene College, Cambridge; admitted to a
scholarship, July 8th, 1645; to a quinquennial fellowship, November 30th,
1649; and to a foundation fellowship, September 24th, 1651. One of the fellows who signed Pepys's admission entry, October 1st, 1650. He became afterwards one of Thurloe's under-secretaries, and was employed in several em-
bassies, particularly to the Vaudois, by Cromwell, whose interests he betrayed,
by secretly communicating with Charles II. He published in 1658, in a folio
volume, his "History of the Evangelical Churches of the Valleys of Piemont."

that the King did give the reason of it openly, that it was for his giving him intelligence all the time he was clerk to Secretary Thurloe. In the afternoon a council of war, only to acquaint them that the Harp must be taken out of all their flags,[1] it being very offensive to the King. Mr. Cook, who came after us in the Yarmouth, bringing me a letter from my wife and a Latin letter from my brother John, with both of which I was exceedingly pleased. No sermon all day, we being under sail, only at night prayers, wherein Mr. Ibbott prayed for all that were related to us in a spiritual and fleshly way. We came within sight of Middle's shore. Late at night we writ letters to the King of the news of our coming, and Mr. Edward Pickering carried them. Capt. Isham went on shore, nobody showing of him any respect; so the old man very fairly took leave of my Lord, and my Lord very coldly bid him "God be with you," which was very strange, but that I hear that he keeps a great deal of prating and talking on shore, on board, at the King's Courts, what command he had with my Lord, &c. After letters were gone then to bed.

He was knighted at Breda, and afterwards created a baronet. He was an ingenious mechanic, and made some improvements in the steam engine. At the Restoration he was made Master of Mechanics to Charles II., who presented him with a medal as an "honourable badge of his signal loyalty." He subsequently received a pension of £400, but he sold it for ready money. He died December 30th, 1695, and was buried in Hammersmith church on the 6th of the following January. His MSS. are at Cambridge, in the Public Library.

"We think to relate here, as a thing most remarkable that the same day Mr. Moorland, Chief Commissioner under Mr. Thurlo, who was Secretary of Estate under Oliver Cromwell, his chief and most confident minister of his tyranny, arrived at Breda, where he brought divers letters and notes of most great importance, forasmuch as the King discovered there a part of the intricate plots of the interreign, and likewise the perfidiousness of some of those who owed him, without doubt, the greatest fidelity of the world. The King received him perfectly well, made him knight, and rendered him this publick testimony, that he had received most considerable services from him for some years past."—Sir William Lower's *Relation . . . of the Voiage and Residence which . . . Charles the II. hath made in Holland*, Hague, 1660, folio.

[1] In May, 1658, the old Union Jack (being the crosses of St. George and St. Andrew combined) was revived, with the Irish harp over the centre of the flag. This harp was taken off at the Restoration. (See "The National Flags of the Commonwealth," by H. W. Henfrey, "Journ. Brit. Arch. Assoc.," vol. xxxi. p. 54.) The sign of the "Commonwealth Arms" was an uncommon one, but a token of one exists—"Francis Wood at ye Commonwealth arms in Mary Maudlens" [St. Mary Magdalen, Old Fish Street].

[14th]. In the morning when I woke and rose, I saw myself out of the scuttle close by the shore; which afterwards I was told to be the Dutch shore; the Hague was clearly to be seen by us. My Lord went up in his nightgown into the cuddy,[1] to see how to dispose thereof for himself and us that belong to him, to give order for our removal to-day. Some nasty Dutchmen came on board to proffer their boats to carry things from us on shore, &c., to get money by us. Before noon some gentlemen came on board from the shore to kiss my Lord's hands. And by and by Mr. North and Dr. Clerke went to kiss the Queen of Bohemia's[2] hands, from my Lord, with twelve attendants from on board to wait on them, among which I sent my boy, who, like myself, is with child to see any strange thing. After noon they came back again after having kissed the Queen of Bohemia's hand, and were sent again by my Lord to do the same to the Prince of Orange.[3] So I got the Captain to ask leave for me to go, which my Lord did give, and I taking my boy and Judge Advocate[4] with me, went in company with them. The weather bad; we were sadly washed when we came near the shore, it being very hard to land there. The shore is, as all the country between that and the Hague, all sand. The rest of the company got a coach by themselves; Mr. Creed and I went in the fore part of a coach wherein were two very pretty ladies, very fashionable and with black patches, who very merrily sang all the way and that very well, and were very free to kiss the two blades that were with them. I took out my flageolette and piped, but in piping I dropped my rapier-stick, but when I came to the Hague, and I sent my boy back again for it and he found it, for which I did give him 6d., but some horses had gone over it and broke the scabbard. The Hague is a most neat place in all respects. The houses so neat in all places

---

[1] "A sort of cabin or cook-room, generally in the fore-part, but sometimes near the stern of lighters and barges of burden."—Smyth's *Sailor's Word-Book*.

[2] Elizabeth, daughter of James I. and widow of Frederick, Elector Palatine and titular King of Bohemia. She was known as the "Queen of Hearts" and the "White Queen." She is supposed to have married Lord Craven, and died February 12th, 1661-63.

[3] Son of the Prince of Orange and Mary, eldest daughter of Charles I., afterwards William III. He was then in his tenth year, having been born in 1650.

[4] Fowler, see *ante*, March 21st.

and things as is possible. Here we walked up and down a great
while, the town being now very full of Englishmen, for that the
Londoners were come on shore to-day. But going to see the
Prince,[1] he was gone forth with his governor, and so we walked
up and down the town and court to see the place; and by the
help of a stranger, an Englishman, we saw a great many places,
and were made to understand many things, as the intention of
may-poles, which we saw there standing at every great man's
door, of different greatness according to the quality of the person. About 10 at night the Prince comes home, and we found an
easy admission. His attendance very inconsiderable as for a
prince; but yet handsome, and his tutor a fine man, and himself
a very pretty boy. It was bright moonshine to-night. This done
we went to a place we had taken to sup in, where a sallet and
two or three bones of mutton were provided for a matter of ten
of us which was very strange. After supper the Judge and I to
another house, leaving them there, and he and I lay in one press
bed, there being two more in the same room, but all very neat
and handsome, my boy sleeping upon a bench by me.

[15th]. We lay till past three o'clock, then up and down the
town, to see it by daylight, where we saw the soldiers of the
Prince's guard, all very fine, and the burghers of the town with
their arms and muskets as bright as silver. And meeting this
morning a schoolmaster that spoke good English and French, he
went along with us and shewed us the whole town, and indeed
I cannot speak enough of the gallantry of the town. Every body
of fashion speaks French or Latin, or both. The women many
of them very pretty and in good habits, fashionable and black
spots. He went with me to buy a couple of baskets, one of them
for Mrs. Pierce, the other for my wife. After he was gone, we
having first drank with him at our lodging, the Judge and I to
the Grande Salle where we were shewed the place where the
States General sit in council. The hall is a great place, where the
flags that they take from their enemies are all hung up; and
things to be sold, as in Westminster Hall, and not much unlike
it, but that not so big, but much neater. After that to a book-

---

[1] Prince of Orange, afterwards William III.

seller's and bought for the love of the binding three books: the French Psalms in four parts, Bacon's Organon, and Farnab. Rhetor.[1] After that the Judge, I and my boy by coach to Scheveling again, where we went into a house of entertainment and

drank there, the wind being very high, and we saw two boats overset and the gallant forced to be pulled on shore by the heels, while their trunks, portmanteaus, hats, and feathers, were swimming in the sea. Among others I saw the ministers that come along with the Commissioners (Mr. Case[2] among the rest) sadly dipped. So they came in where we were, and I being in haste left my Copenhagen knife, and so lost it. Having staid here

[1] "Index Rhetoricus" of Thomas Farnaby was a book which went through several editions. The first was published at London by R. Allot in 1633.

[2] Thomas Case, born 1598, was a famous preacher and a zealous advocate for the Solemn League and Covenant, a member of the assembly of divines, and rector of St. Giles's-in-the-Fields. He was one of the deputation to Charles II. at Breda, and appointed a royal chaplain. He was ejected by the Act of Uniformity, but remained in London after his ejection. Died May 30th, 1682.

a great while a gentleman that was going to kiss my Lord's hand, from the Queen of Bohemia, and I hired a Dutch boat for four rixdollars to carry us on board. We were fain to wait a great while before we could get off from the shore, the sea being very rough. The Dutchman would fain have made all pay that came into our boat besides us two and our company, there being many of our ship's company got in who were on shore, but some of them had no money, having spent all on shore. Coming on board we found all the Commissioners of the House of Lords at dinner with my Lord, who after dinner went away for shore. Mr. Morland, now Sir Samuel, was here on board, but I do not find that my Lord or any body did give him any respect, he being looked upon by him and all men as a knave. Among others he betrayed Sir Rich. Willis[1] that married Dr. F. Jones's daughter, that he had paid him £1000 at one time by the Protector's and Secretary Thurloe's order, for intelligence that he sent concerning the King. In the afternoon my Lord called me on purpose to show me his fine cloathes which are now come hither, and indeed are very rich as gold and silver can make them, only his sword he and I do not like. In the afternoon my Lord and I walked together in the coach two hours, talking together upon all sorts of discourse: as religion, wherein he is, I perceive, wholly sceptical, as well as I, saying, that indeed the Protestants as to the Church of Rome are wholly fanatiques: he likes uniformity and form of prayer; about State-business, among other things he told me that his conversion to the King's cause (for so I was saying that I wondered from what time the King could look upon him to become his friend), commenced from his being in the Sound, when he found what usage he was likely to have from a Com-

---

[1] This is somewhat different to the usual account of Morland's connection with Sir Richard Willis. In the beginning of 1659 Cromwell, Thurloe, and Willis formed a plot to inveigle Charles II. into England and into the hands of his enemies. The plot was discussed in Thurloe's office, and Morland, who pretended to be asleep, heard it and discovered it. Willis sent for Morland, and received him in a cellar. He said that one of them must have discovered the plot. He laid his hand upon the Bible and swore that he had not been the discoverer, calling upon Morland to do the same. Morland, with presence of mind, said he was ready to do so if Willis would give him a reason why he should suspect him. By this ready answer he is said to have escaped the ordeal (see Birch's "Life of Thurloe").

monwealth. My Lord, the Captain, and I supped in my Lord's
chamber, where I did perceive that he did begin to show me much
more respect than ever he did yet. After supper, my Lord sent
for me, intending to have me play at cards with him, but I not
knowing cribbage, we fell into discourse of many things, till it
was so rough sea and the ship rolled so much that I was not able
to stand, and so he bid me go to bed.

[16th]. Soon as I was up I went down to be trimmed below in
the great cabin, but then come in some with visits, among the
rest one from Admiral Opdam,[1] who spoke Latin well, but not
French nor English, to whom my Lord made me to give his answer and to entertain; he brought my Lord a tierce of wine and a
barrel of butter, as a present from the Admiral. After that to
finish my trimming, and while I was doing of it in comes Mr.
North very sea-sick from shore, and to bed he goes. After that
to dinner, where Commissioner Pett[2] was come to take care to
get all things ready for the King on board. My Lord in his best
suit, this the first day, in expectation to wait upon the King. But
Mr. Edw. Pickering coming from the King brought word that
the King would not put my Lord to the trouble of coming to him;
but that he would come to the shore to look upon the fleet to-day,
which we expected, and had our guns ready for fire, and our
scarlet waistcloathes out and silk pendants, but he did not come.

---

[1] The admiral celebrated in Lord Dorset's ballad, "To all you ladies now at
land."

> "Should foggy Opdam chance to know
>   Our sad and dismal story;
> The Dutch would scorn so weak a foe,
>   And quit their fort at Goree:
> For what resistance can they find
> From men who've left their hearts behind?"—B.

[2] Peter Pett succeeded his father, Phineas Pett, as Commissioner of the Navy
at Chatham, in 1647; he was continued in his office after the Restoration, but
in 1667, in consequence of the Dutch attack upon Chatham, he was superseded, sent to the Tower, and threatened with impeachment. The threat was
not carried out, but he was never restored to office. Fuller observes that the
mystery of shipwrights for some descents hath been preserved successively in
families, "of which the Pettes of Chatham are of singular regard."—*Worthies
of England.* There is an interesting autobiographical memoir of Phineas Pett,
in his own handwriting, in the British Museum (Harl. MS. 6279). Extracts
from a copy of this MS. were printed in the "Archæologia" (vol. xii.).

My Lord and we at ninepins this afternoon upon the Quarter-deck, which was very pretty sport. This evening came Mr. John Pickering[1] on board, like an ass, with his feathers and new suit that he had made at the Hague. My Lord very angry for his staying on shore, bidding me a little before to send to him, telling me that he was afraid that for his father's sake he might have some mischief done him, unless he used the General's name. To supper, and after supper to cards. I stood by and looked on till 11 at night and so to bed. This afternoon Mr. Edwd. Pickering told me in what a sad, poor condition for clothes and money the king was, and all his attendants, when he came to him first from my Lord, their clothes not being worth forty shillings the best of them.[2] And how overjoyed the King was when Sir J. Greenville brought him some money; so joyful, that he called the Princess Royal[3] and Duke of York to look upon it as it lay in the portmanteau before it was taken out. My Lord told me, too, that the Duke of York is made High Admiral of England.[4]

[17th]. Up early to write down my last two days' observations. Dr. Clerke came to me to tell me that he heard this morning, by some Dutch that are come on board already to see the ship, that there was a Portuguese taken yesterday at the Hague, that had a design to kill the King. But this I heard afterwards was only the mistake upon one being observed to walk with his sword naked, he having lost his scabbard. Before dinner Mr. Edw.

---

[1] Eldest son of Sir Gilbert Pickering, whom he succeeded in his titles and estates in 1668. His father had been an active Commonwealth man, and was one of the knights of the shire for the county of Northampton in 1656; he was also of Cromwell's council, chamberlain of the court, and high steward of Westminster. Sir Gilbert Pickering's petition being read, he was ordered to be excepted as to the penalties to be inflicted not reaching to life, by an act provided for that purpose.—*Commons' Journals;* see June 19th, 1660.—B.

[2] Andrew Marvell alludes to the poor condition, for clothes and money, in which the King was at this time, in "A Historical Poem":—

"At length, by wonderful impulse of fate,
The people call him back to help the State;
And what is more, they send him money, too,
And clothe him all from head to foot anew."

[3] Mary, Princess of Orange.

[4] James's patent was dated June 6th, 1660.

141

Pickering and I, W. Howe, Pim, and my boy,[1] to Scheveling, where we took coach, and so to the Hague, where walking, intending to find one that might show us the King incognito, I met with Captain Whittington (that had formerly brought a letter to my Lord from the Mayor of London) and he did promise me to do it, but first we went and dined at a French house, but paid 16s. for our part of the club. At dinner in came Dr. Cade, a merry mad parson of the King's. And they two after dinner got the child and me (the others not being able to crowd in) to see the King, who kissed the child very affectionately. Then we kissed his, and the Duke of York's, and the Princess Royal's hands. The King seems to be a very sober man; and a very splendid Court he hath in the number of persons of quality that are about him, English very rich in habit. From the King to the Lord Chancellor,[2] who did lie bed-rid of the gout: he spoke very merrily to the child and me. After that, going to see the Queen of Bohemia, I met with Dr. Fuller,[3] whom I sent to a tavern with Mr. Edw. Pickering, while I and the rest went to see the Queen,[4] who used us very respectfully; her hand we all kissed. She seems a very debonaire, but plain lady. After that to the Dr.'s, where we drank a while or so. In a coach of a friend's of Dr. Cade we went to see a house of the Princess Dowager's in a park about half-a-mile or a mile from the Hague, where there is one, the most beautiful room for pictures in the whole world.[5] She had here one picture upon the top, with these words, dedicating it to the memory of her husband: — "Incomparibili marito inconsola-

[1] Edward Montagu, afterwards Lord Hinchinbroke.

[2] On January 29th, 1658, Charles II. entrusted the Great Seal to Sir Edward Hyde, with the title of Lord Chancellor, and in that character Sir Edward accompanied the King to England.

[3] Thomas Fuller, born June, 1608; D.D. 1660; one of the most delightful writers in the English language; Chaplain to the King, Lecturer at the Savoy, Prebendary of Salisbury and Rector of Cranford. He died at his lodgings in Covent Garden, August 16th, 1661, and was buried at Cranford.

[4] Henrietta Maria.

[5] The House in the Wood (Huis ten Bosch) at the Hague is still a show place, and the picture described by Pepys can still be seen in the Oranje Zaal (Orange Hall). The hall was built by a Princess of Solms, grandmother of our William III., and decorated with paintings in honour of her husband, Prince Frederick Henry of Orange.

bilis vidua." [1] Here I met with Mr. Woodcock of Cambridge, Mr. Hardy and another, and Mr. Woodcock beginning we had two or three fine songs, he and I, and W. Howe to the Echo, which was very pleasant, and the more because in a heaven of pleasure and in a strange country, that I never was taken up more with a sense of pleasure in my life. After that we parted and back to the Hague and took a tour or two about the Forehault,[2] where the ladies in the evening do as our ladies do in Hide Park. But for my life I could not find one handsome, but their coaches very rich and themselves so too. From thence, taking leave of the Doctor, we took wagon to Scheveling, where we had a fray with the Boatswain of the Richmond, who would not freely carry us on board, but at last he was willing to it, but then it was so late we durst not go. So we returned between 10 and 11 at night in the dark with a wagon with one horse to the Hague, where being come we went to bed as well as we could be accommodated, and so to sleep.

[18th]. Very early up, and, hearing that the Duke of York, our Lord High Admiral, would go on board to-day, Mr. Pickering and I took waggon for Sheveling, leaving the child in Mr. Pierce's hands, with directions to keep him within doors all day till he heard from me. But the wind being very high that no boats could get off from shore, we returned to the Hague (having breakfasted with a gentleman of the Duke's and Commissioner Pett, sent on purpose to give notice to my Lord of his coming), where I hear that the child is gone to Delfe[3] to see the town. So we all and Mr. Ibbott, the Minister, took a schuit[4] and very much pleased with the manner and conversation of the passengers, where most speak French; went after them, but met them by the way. But however we went forward making no stop. Where

---

[1] Mary, Princess Royal, eldest daughter of Charles I., and widow of William of Nassau, Prince of Orange. She was not supposed to be inconsolable, and scandal followed her at the court of Charles II., where she died of small-pox, December 24th, 1660.

[2] The Voorhout is the principal street of the Hague, and it is lined with handsome trees.

[3] Delft is about five miles from the Hague.

[4] The trekschuit (drag-boat) along the canal is still described as an agreeable conveyance from Leyden to Delft.

when we were come we got a smith's boy of the town to go along with us, but could speak nothing but Dutch, and he showed us the church where Van Trump lies entombed with a very fine monument. His epitaph concluded thus:— "Tandem Bello Anglico tantum non victor, certe invictus, vivere et vincere desiit." There is a sea-fight cut in marble, with the smoke, the best expressed that ever I saw in my life.[1] From thence to the great church, that stands in a fine great market-place, over against the Stadthouse, and there I saw a stately tomb of the old Prince of Orange,[2] of marble and brass; wherein among other rarities there are the angels with their trumpets expressed as it were crying. Here were very fine organs in both the churches. It is a most sweet town, with bridges, and a river in every street. Observing that in every house of entertainment there hangs in every room a poor-man's box, and desiring to know the reason thereof, it was told me that it is their custom to confirm all bargains by putting something into the poor people's box, and that that binds as fast as any thing. We also saw the Guesthouse, where it was very pleasant to see what neat preparation there is for the poor. We saw one poor man a-dying there. After we had seen all, we light by chance of an English house to drink in, where we were very merry, discoursing of the town and the thing that hangs up in the Stadthouse[3] like a bushel, which I was told is a sort of punishment for some sort of offenders to carry through the streets of the town over his head, which is a great weight. Back by water, where a pretty sober Dutch lass sat reading all the way, and I could not fasten any discourse upon her. At our landing we met with Commissioner Pett going down to the water-side with Major Harly,[4] who is going upon a dispatch into England. They

---

[1] Admiral Martin van Tromp's monument here described is in the Oude Kerk (*Old Church*) at Delft.

[2] The costly but clumsy monument erected by the United Provinces to the memory of William I., Prince of Orange (who was assassinated at Delft, 10th July, 1584), is in the so-called *New Church* at Delft.

[3] The Stadhuis is a fine building situated in the market-place.

[4] Afterwards Colonel Edward Harley, M.P. for Hereford, and Governor of Dunkirk; ancestor of the Earls of Oxford of that race, now extinct in the male line. He was afterwards made a Knight of the Bath at the Coronation of Charles II.

having a coach I left the Parson[1] and my boy and went along with Commissioner Pett, Mr. Ackworth[2] and Mr. Dawes his friends, to the Princess Dowager's house again. Thither also my Lord Fairfax and some other English Lords did come to see it, and my pleasure was increased by seeing of it again. Besides we went into the garden, wherein are gallant nuts better than ever I saw, and a fine Echo under the house in a vault made on purpose with pillars, where I played on my flageolette to great advantage. Back to the Hague, where not finding Mr. Edward, I was much troubled, but went with the Parson to supper to Commissioner Pett, where we sat late. And among other mirth Mr. Ackworth vyed wives, each endeavouring to set his own wife out to the best advantage, he having as they said an extraordinary handsome wife. But Mr. Dawes could not be got to say anything of his. After that to our lodging where W. Howe and I exceeding troubled not to know what is become of our young gentleman. So to bed.

[19th]. Up early, hearing nothing of the child, and went to Scheveling, where I found no getting on board, though the Duke of York sent every day to see whether he could do it or no. Here I met with Mr. Pinkney and his sons, and with them went back to the Hague, in our way lighting and going to see a woman that makes pretty rock-work in shells, &c., which could I have carried safe I would have bought some of. At the Hague we went to buy some pictures, where I saw a sort of painting done upon woollen cloth, drawn as if there was a curtain over it, which was very pleasant, but dear. Another pretty piece of painting I saw, on which there was a great wager laid by young Pinkney and me whether it was a principal or a copy. But not knowing how to decide, it was broken off, and I got the old man to lay out as much as my piece of gold come to, and so saved my money, which had been 24s. lost, I fear. While we were here buying of pictures, we saw Mr. Edward and his company land. Who told me that they had been at Leyden all night, at which I was very angry

---

[1] Edmond Ibbott, made rector of Deal in 1662. See *ante*, March 25th.

[2] Mr. Ackworth seems to have held some office in Deptford Yard, see January 14th, 1660-61.

with Mr. Pierce, and shall not be friends I believe a good while.
To our lodging to dinner. After that out to buy some linen to
wear against to-morrow, and so to the barber's. After that by
waggon to Lausdune, where the 365 children were born. We saw
the hill where they say the house stood and sunk wherein the
children were born. The basins wherein the male and female
children were baptized do stand over a large table that hangs
upon a wall, with the whole story of the thing in Dutch and
Latin, beginning, "Margarita Herman Comitissa," &c. The thing
was done about 200 years ago.

The town is a little small village which answers much to one of
our small villages, such a one as Chesterton in all respects, and
one could have thought it in England but for the language of the
people. We went into a little drinking house where there were a
great many Dutch boors eating of fish in a boorish manner, but
very merry in their way. But the houses here as neat as in the
great places. From thence to the Hague again playing at crambo[1]
in the waggon, Mr. Edward, Mr. Ibbott, W. Howe, Mr. Pinkney,
and I. When we were come thither W. Howe, and Mr. Ibbott,
and Mr. Pinckney went away for Scheveling, while I and the
child to walk up and down the town, where I met my old cham-
ber-fellow, Mr. Ch. Anderson, and a friend of his (both Physicians), Mr. Wright, who took me to a Dutch house, where there
was an exceeding pretty lass, and right for the sport, but it being
Saturday we could not have much of her company, but however I staid with them (having left the child with my uncle Pickering,[2] whom I met in the street) till 12 at night. By that time
Charles was almost drunk, and then broke up, he resolving to go
thither again, after he had seen me at my lodging, and lie with
the girl, which he told me he had done in the morning. Going to
my lodging we met with the bellman, who struck upon a clapper, which I took in my hand, and it is just like the clapper that
our boys frighten the birds away from the corn with in summer
time in England. To bed.

---

[1] Crambo is described as "a play at short verses in which a word is given, and
the parties contend who can find most rhymes to it."
[2] There were several Pickerings, and it is not easy to say which of them Pepys
would style "uncle."

[20th]. Up early, and with Mr. Pickering and the child by waggon to Scheveling, where it not being yet fit to go off, I went to lie down in a chamber in the house, where in another bed there was a pretty Dutch woman in bed alone, but though I had a month's-mind[1] I had not the boldness to go to her. So there I slept an hour or two. At last she rose, and then I rose and walked up and down the chamber, and saw her dress herself after the Dutch dress, and talked to her as much as I could, and took occasion, from her ring which she wore on her first finger, to kiss her hand, but had not the face to offer anything more. So at last I left her there and went to my company. About 8 o'clock I went into the church at Scheveling, which was pretty handsome, and in the chancel a very great upper part of the mouth of a whale, which indeed was of a prodigious bigness, bigger than one of our long boats that belong to one of our ships. Commissioner Pett at last came to our lodging, and caused the boats to go off; so some in one boat and some in another we all bid adieu to the shore. But through badness of weather we were in great danger, and a great while before we could get to the ship, so that of all the company not one but myself that was not sick. I keeping myself in the open air, though I was soundly wet for it. This hath not been known four days together such weather at this time of year, a great while. Indeed our fleet was thought to be in great danger, but we found all well, and Mr. Thos. Crew came on board. I having spoke a word or two with my Lord, being not very well settled, partly through last night's drinking and want of sleep, I lay down in my gown upon my bed and slept till the 4 o'clock gun the next morning waked me, which I took for 8 at night, and rising . . . mistook the sun rising for the sun setting on Sunday night.

[21st]. So into my naked bed[2] and slept till 9 o'clock, and then

---

[1] Month's mind. An earnest desire or longing, explained as alluding to "a woman's longing." See Shakespeare, "Two Gentlemen of Verona," act i. sc. 2:

"I see you have a *month's mind* to them."—M. B.

[2] This is a somewhat late use of an expression which was once universal. It was formerly the custom for both sexes to sleep in bed without any night-linen.

"Who sees his true love in her *naked bed*,
Teaching the sheets a whiter hue than white."
Shakespeare, *Venus and Adonis*.

John Goods waked me, [by] and by the captain's boy brought me
four barrels of Mallows oysters, which Captain Tatnell had sent
me from Murlace.[1] The weather foul all this day also. After dinner, about writing one thing or other all day, and setting my
papers in order, having been so long absent. At night Mr. Pierce,
Purser (the other Pierce and I having not spoken to one another
since we fell out about Mr. Edward), and Mr. Cook sat with me
in my cabin and supped with me, and then I went to bed. By
letters that came hither in my absence, I understand that the
Parliament had ordered all persons to be secured, in order to a
trial, that did sit as judges in the late King's death, and all the
officers too attending the Court. Sir John Lenthall[2] moving in the
House, that all that had borne arms against the King should be
exempted from pardon, he was called to the bar of the House,
and after a severe reproof he was degraded his knighthood. At
Court I find that all things grow high. The old clergy talk as
being sure of their lands again, and laugh at the Presbytery; and
it is believed that the sales of the King's and Bishops' lands will
never be confirmed by Parliament, there being nothing now in
any man's power to hinder them and the King from doing what
they have a mind, but every body willing to submit to any thing.
We expect every day to have the King and Duke on board as soon
as it is fair. My Lord do nothing now, but offers all things to the
pleasure of the Duke as Lord High Admiral. So that I am at a loss
what to do.

Nares ("Glossary") notes the expression so late as in the very odd novel by
T. Amory, called "John Buncle," where a young lady declares, after an alarm,
"that she would never go into *naked bed* on board ship again." Octavo edition,
vol. i. p. 90.

[1] Apparently Mallows stands for St. Malo and Murlace for Morlaise.

[2] Sir John Lenthall, who survived till 1681, was the only son of Speaker
Lenthall, and Cromwell's Governor of Windsor Castle. He had been knighted
by the Protector in 1657; but is styled "Mr. Lenthall" in the "Commons' Journals of the House," May 12th, 1660, where the proceedings alluded to by
Pepys are fully detailed. Mrs. Hutchinson also gives an account of them, in
her "Memoirs of Colonel Hutchinson," p. 367, 4to edit. On the 22nd of May
following, Lenthall lost his seat for Abingdon, the double return for that
borough have been decided in favour of Sir John Stonehouse; probably the
then recent offence which Lenthall had given to the House of Commons had
more influence in the adverse issue of the petition than the actual merits of

[22nd]. Up very early, and now beginning to be settled in my wits again, I went about setting down my last four days' observations this morning. After that, was trimmed by a barber that has not trimmed me yet, my Spaniard being on shore. News brought that the two Dukes are coming on board, which, by and by, they did, in a Dutch boat, the Duke of York in yellow trimmings, the Duke of Gloucester[1] in grey and red. My Lord went in a boat to meet them, the Captain, myself, and others, standing at the entering port. So soon as they were entered we shot the guns off round the fleet. After that they went to view the ship all over, and were most exceedingly pleased with it. They seem to be both very fine gentlemen. After that done, upon the quarter-deck table, under the awning, the Duke of York and my Lord, Mr. Coventry,[2] and I, spent an hour at allotting to every ship their service, in their return to England; which having done, they went to dinner, where the table was very full: the two Dukes at the upper end, my Lord Opdam next on one side, and my Lord on the other. Two guns given to every man while he was drinking the King's health, and so likewise to the Duke's health. I took

the case. Sir John Lenthall, of whom Pepys speaks, August 10th, 1663, was the brother to the Speaker. See that passage.—B.

[1] Henry, Duke of Gloucester, the youngest child of Charles I., born July 6th, 1640, who, with his sister Elizabeth, was allowed a meeting with his father on the night before the King's execution. Burnet says: "He was active, and loved business; was apt to have particular friendships, and had an insinuating temper which was generally very acceptable. The King loved him much better than the Duke of York." He died of small-pox at Whitehall, September 13th, 1660, and was buried in Henry VII.'s Chapel.

[2] William Coventry, to whom Pepys became so warmly attached afterwards, was the fourth son of Thomas, first Lord Coventry, the Lord Keeper. He was born in 1628, and entered at Queen's College, Oxford, in 1642; after the Restoration he became private secretary to the Duke of York, his commission as Secretary to the Lord High Admiral not being conferred until 1664; elected M.P. for Great Yarmouth in 1661. In 1662 he was appointed an extra Commissioner of the Navy, an office he held until 1667; in 1665, knighted and sworn a Privy Councillor, and, in 1667, constituted a Commissioner of the Treasury; but, having been forbid the court on account of his challenging the Duke of Buckingham, he retired into the country, nor could he subsequently be prevailed upon to accept of any official employment. Burnet calls Sir William Coventry the best speaker in the House of Commons, and "a man of the finest and best temper that belonged to the court," and Pepys never omits an opportunity of paying a tribute to his public and private worth. He died, 1686, of gout in the stomach.

down Monsieur d'Esquier to the great cabin below, and dined
with him in state alone with only one or two friends of his. All
dinner the harper belonging to Captain Sparling played to the
Dukes. After dinner, the Dukes and my Lord to see the Vice and
Rear-Admirals, and I in a boat after them. After that done, they
made to the shore in the Dutch boat that brought them, and I got
into the boat with them; but the shore was so full of people to expect their coming, as that it was as black (which otherwise is
white sand), as every one could stand by another. When we came
near the shore, my Lord left them and came into his own boat,
and General Pen[1] and I with him; my Lord being very well
pleased with this day's work. By the time we came on board
again, news is sent us that the King is on shore; so my Lord fired
all his guns round twice, and all the fleet after him, which in the
end fell into disorder, which seemed very handsome. The gun
over against my cabin I fired myself to the King, which was the
first time that he had been saluted by his own ships since this
change; but holding my head too much over the gun, I had almost
spoiled my right eye. Nothing in the world but going of guns
almost all this day. In the evening we began to remove cabins; I
to the carpenter's cabin, and Dr. Clerke with me, who came on
board this afternoon, having been twice ducked in the sea to-day
coming from shore, and Mr. North and John Pickering the like.
Many of the King's servants came on board to-night; and so
many Dutch of all sorts came to see the ship till it was quite dark,
that we could not pass by one another, which was a great trouble
to us all. This afternoon Mr. Downing (who was knighted yesterday by the King[2]) was here on board, and had a ship for his

---

[1] Admiral Sir William Penn (see *ante*, April 4th).

[2] "About midnight arrived there Mr. Downing, who did the affairs of England
to the Lords the Estates, in quality of Resident under Oliver Cromwell, and
afterward under the pretended Parliament, which having changed the form
of the government, after having cast forth the last Protector, had continued
him in his imploiment, under the quality of Extraordinary Envoy. He began
to have respect for the King's person, when he knew that all England declared
for a free parliament, and departed from Holland without order, as soon as he
understood that there was nothing that could longer oppose the re-establish-
ment of monarchal government, with a design to crave letters of recommendation to General Monk. This lord considered him, as well because of the birth
of his wife, which is illustrious, as because Downing had expressed some re-

passage into England, with his lady and servants. By the same
token he called me to him when I was going to write the order, to
tell me that I must write him Sir G. Downing. My Lord lay in
the round-house to-night. This evening I was late writing a
French letter myself by my Lord's order to Monsieur Kragh,[1]
Embassador de Denmarke à la Haye, which my Lord signed in
bed. After that I to bed, and the Doctor, and sleep well.

[23rd]. The Doctor and I waked very merry, only my eye was
very red and ill in the morning from yesterday's hurt. In the
morning came infinity of people on board from the King to go
along with him. My Lord, Mr. Crew, and others, go on shore to
meet the King as he comes off from shore, where Sir R. Stayner
bringing His Majesty into the boat, I hear that His Majesty did
with a great deal of affection kiss my Lord upon his first meeting.
The King, with the two Dukes and Queen of Bohemia, Princess
Royal, and Prince of Orange, came on board, where I in their
coming in kissed the King's, Queen's, and Princess's hands, having done the other before. Infinite shooting off of the guns, and
that in a disorder on purpose, which was better than if it had
been otherwise. All day nothing but Lords and persons of honour
on board, that we were exceeding full. Dined in a great deal of
state, the Royall company by themselves in the coach, which was
a blessed sight to see. I dined with Dr. Clerke, Dr. Quarterman,[2]

spect for him in a time when that eminent person could not yet discover his
intentions. He had his letters when he arrived at midnight at the house of the
Spanish Embassador, as we have said. He presented them forthwith to the
King, who arose from table a while after, read the letters, receiv'd the sub-
missions of Downing, and granted him the pardon and grace which he asked
for him to whom he could deny nothing. Some daies after the King knighted
him, and would it should be believed, that the strong aversions which this
minister of the Protector had made appear against him on all occasions, and
with all sorts of persons indifferently, even a few daies before the publick and
general declaration of all England, proceeded not from any evil intention,
but only from a deep dissimulation, wherewith he was constrained to cover
his true sentiments, for fear to prejudice the affairs of his Majesty."—Sir William Lower's *Relation . . . of the Voiage and Residence which . . . Charles the
II. hath made in Holland*, Hague, 1660, folio, pp. 72-73.

[1] Otte Krag was one of the two extraordinary ambassadors from the King of
Denmark to Charles II. at the Hague. See Lower's "Voiage and Residence of
Charles II. in Holland," 1660, p. 41.

[2] William Quartermain, M.D., matriculated as member of Brasenose College,

and Mr. Darcy[1] in my cabin. This morning Mr. Lucy came on board, to whom and his company of the King's Guard in another ship my Lord did give three dozen bottles of wine. He made friends between Mr. Pierce and me. After dinner the King and Duke altered the name of some of the ships, viz. the Nazeby into Charles;[2] the Richard, James;[3] the Speaker,[4] Mary; the Dunbar (which was not in company with us), the Henry;[5] Winsly, Happy Return;[6] Wakefield, Richmond;[7] Lambert, the Henrietta;[8] Cheriton, the Speedwell;[9] Bradford, the Success.[10] That done, the Queen, Princess Royal, and Prince of Orange, took leave of the King, and the Duke of York went on board the London, and the Duke of Gloucester, the Swiftsure. Which done, we weighed

---

Oxford, and afterwards removed to Pembroke College. He was appointed one of the physicians in ordinary to Charles II., and died in June, 1667.

[1] Marmaduke, fifth son of Conyers, Lord Darcy, one of the companions of Charles's exile, whom the King was wont to call " 'Duke Darcey," and he is so styled in Charles's narrative of his escape, as given to Pepys. On the pavement in the south aisle of St. George's Chapel, Windsor, is the following inscription:—"Here lyeth the body of the Honourable Marmaduke Darcy, Esq., brother to the Earl of Holderness, first gentleman usher of the privy-chamber to his Majesty, who died in this castle on Sunday, the 3d of July, in the seventy-third year of his age, A.D. 1687."—Pote's *History of Windsor*, p. 365.—B.

[2]
> "The Naseby now no longer England's shame,
> But better to be lost in Charles his name."
>   Dryden, *Astræa Redux*.

Another "Charles" was built at Deptford in 1667 by Jo. Shish.

[3] The "Richard" was a second-rate of seventy guns, built at Woolwich in 1658 by Christopher Pett.

[4] The "Speaker" was a third-rate of fifty-two guns, built at Woolwich in 1649 by Christopher Pett.

[5] The "Henry," then "Dunbar," was a second-rate of sixty-four guns, built at Deptford in 1656 by Mr. Callis.

[6] The "Happy Return," then the "Winsley," was built at Yarmouth in 1654 by Edgar; it was a fourth-rate of forty-six guns.

[7] The "Richmond," then the Wakefield," was built at Portsmouth in 1655 by Sir J. Tippets; it was a fifth-rate of twenty-six guns.

[8] The "Henrietta," then the "Lambert," was built at Horslydown in 1653-4 by Bright; it was a third-rate of fifty guns.

[9] The "Speedwell," then the "Cheriton," was a fifth-rate of twenty guns, built at Deptford in 1655 by Mr. Callis.

[10] The "Success," then the "Bradford," was a fifth-rate built at Chatham in 1657 by Captain Taylor.

anchor, and with a fresh gale and most happy weather we set sail for England. All the afternoon the King walked here and there, up and down (quite contrary to what I thought him to have been), very active and stirring. Upon the quarter-deck he fell into discourse of his escape from Worcester,[1] where it made me ready to weep to hear the stories that he told of his difficulties that he had passed through, as his travelling four days and three nights on foot, every step up to his knees in dirt, with nothing but a green coat and a pair of country breeches on, and a pair of country shoes that made him so sore all over his feet, that he could scarce stir. Yet he was forced to run away from a miller and other company, that took them for rogues. His sitting at table at one place, where the master of the house, that had not seen him in eight years, did know him, but kept it private; when at the same table there was one that had been of his own regiment at Worcester, could not know him, but made him drink the King's health, and said that the King was at least four fingers higher than he. At another place he was by some servants of the house made to drink, that they might know him not to be a Roundhead, which they swore he was. In another place at his inn, the master of the house,[2] as the King was standing with his hands upon the back of a chair by the fire-side, kneeled down and kissed his hand, privately, saying, that he would not ask him who he was, but bid God bless him whither he was going. Then the difficulty of getting a boat to get into France, where he was fain to plot with the master thereof to keep his design from the four men and a boy (which was all his ship's company), and so got

---

[1] For the King's own account of his escape dictated to Pepys, see "Boscobel" (Bohn's "Standard Library").

[2] This was at Brighton. The inn was the "George," and the innkeeper was named Smith. Charles related this circumstance again to Pepys in October, 1680. He then said, "And here also I ran into another very great danger, as being confident I was known by the master of the inn; for, as I was standing after supper by the fireside, leaning my hand upon a chair, and all the rest of the company being gone into another room, the master of the inn came in and fell a-talking with me, and just as he was looking about, and saw there was nobody in the room, he upon a sudden kissed my hand that was upon the back of the chair, and said to me, 'God bless you wheresoever you go! I do not doubt before I die, but to be a lord, and my wife a lady.' So I laughed, and went away into the next room."

to Fécamp in France.[1] At Rouen he looked so poorly, that the people went into the rooms before he went away to see whether he had not stole something or other. In the evening I went up to my Lord to write letters for England, which we sent away with word of our coming, by Mr. Edw. Pickering. The King supped alone in the coach; after that I got a dish, and we four supped in my cabin, as at noon. About bed-time my Lord Bartlett[2] (who I had offered my service to before) sent for me to get him a bed, who with much ado I did get to bed to my Lord Middlesex[3] in the great cabin below, but I was cruelly troubled before I could dispose of him, and quit myself of him. So to my cabin again, where the company still was, and were talking more of the King's difficulties; as how he was fain to eat a piece of bread and cheese out of a poor boy's pocket; how, at a Catholique house, he was fain to lie in the priest's hole a good while in the house for his privacy. After that our company broke up, and the Doctor and I to bed. We have all the Lords Commissioners on board us, and many others. Under sail all night, and most glorious weather.

[1] On Saturday, October 11th, 1651, Colonel Gunter made an agreement at Chichester with Nicholas Tettersell, through Francis Mansell (a French merchant), to have Tettersell's vessel ready at an hour's warning. Charles II., in his narrative dictated to Pepys in 1680, said, "We went to a place, four miles off Shoreham, called Brighthelmstone, where we were to meet with the master of the ship, as thinking it more convenient to meet there than just at Shoreham, where the ship was. So when we came to the inn at Brighthelmstone we met with one, the merchant [Francis Mansell] who had hired the vessel, in company with her master [Tettersell], the merchant only knowing me, as having hired her only to carry over a person of quality that was escaped from the battle of Worcester without naming anybody."

The boat was supposed to be bound for Poole, but Charles says in his narrative: "As we were sailing the master came to me, and desired me that I would persuade his men to use their best endeavours with him to get him to set us on shore in France, the better to cover him from any suspicion thereof, upon which I went to the men, which were four and a boy."

After the Restoration Mansell was granted a pension of £200 a year, and Tettersell one of £100 a year. (See "Captain Nicholas Tettersell and the Escape of Charles II.," by F. E. Sawyer, F.S.A., "Sussex Archæological Collections," vol. xxxii. pp. 81-104.)

[2] A mistake for Lord Berkeley of Berkeley, who had been deputed, with Lord Middlesex and four other Peers, by the House of Lords to present an address of congratulation to the King.—B.

[3] Lionel Cranfield, third and last Earl of Middlesex. Died 1674, when the title became extinct.

[24th]. Up, and make myself as fine as I could, with the linning stockings on and wide canons¹ that I bought the other day at Hague. Extraordinary press of noble company, and great mirth all the day. There dined with me in my cabin (that is, the carpenter's) Dr. Earle² and Mr. Hollis,³ the King's Chaplins, Dr. Scarborough,⁴ Dr. Quarterman, and Dr. Clerke, Physicians, Mr. Darcy, and Mr. Fox⁵ (both very fine gentlemen), the King's

---

¹ Canons, canions, or cannions. Thus defined in *Kersey's* Dictionary: "Cannions, boot hose tops; an old-fashioned ornament for the legs." That is to say, a particular addition to breeches. *Coles* says, "Cannions, Perizomata." *Cotgrave*, "Canons de chausses." *Minshew* says, "On les appelle ainsi pourceque, &c., because they are like cannons of artillery, or cans, or pots."—Nares, *Glossary.*—M. B.

² John Earle, born about 1601; appointed in 1643 one of the Westminster Assembly of Divines, but his principles did not allow him to act. He accompanied Charles II. when he was obliged to fly from England. Dean of Westminster at the Restoration, Bishop of Worcester, November 30th, 1662, and translated to Salisbury, September 28th, 1663. He was tender to the Noncomformists, and Baxter wrote of him, "O that they were all such!" Author of "Microcosmography." Died November 17th, 1665, and was buried in the chapel of Merton College, of which he had been a Fellow. Charles II. had the highest esteem for him.

³ Denzil Holles, second son of John, first Earl of Clare, born at Houghton, Notts, in 1597. He was one of the five members charged with high treason by Charles I. in 1641. He was a Presbyterian, and one of the Commissioners sent by Parliament to wait on Charles II. at the Hague. Sir William Lower, in his "Relation," 1660, writes: "All agreed that never person spake with more affection nor expressed himself in better terms than Mr. Denzil Hollis, who was orator for the Deputies of the Lower House, to whom those of London were joined." He was created Baron Holles on April 20th, 1661, on the occasion of the coronation of Charles II.

⁴ Charles Scarburgh, M.D., an eminent physician who suffered for the royal cause during the Civil Wars. He was born in London, and educated at St. Paul's School and Caius College, Cambridge. He was ejected from his fellowship at Caius, and withdrew to Oxford. He entered himself at Merton College, then presided over by Harvey, with whom he formed a lifelong friendship. He was knighted by Charles II. in 1669, and attended the King in his last illness. He was also physician to James II. and to William III., and died February 26th, 1693-4.

⁵ Stephen Fox, born 1627, and said to have been a choir-boy in Salisbury Cathedral. He was the first person to announce the death of Cromwell to Charles II., and at the Restoration he was made Clerk of the Green Cloth, and afterwards Paymaster of the Forces. He was knighted in 1665. He married Elizabeth, daughter of William Whittle of Lancashire. (See June 25th, 1660.) Fox died in 1716. His sons Stephen and Henry were created respectively Earl of Ilchester and Lord Holland.

servants, where we had brave discourse. Walking upon the decks, where persons of honour all the afternoon, among others, Thomas Killigrew[1] (a merry droll, but a gentleman of great esteem with the King), who told us many merry stories: one, how he wrote a letter three or four days ago to the Princess Royal, about a Queen Dowager of Judæa and Palestine, that was at the Hague *incognita*, that made love to the King, &c., which was Mr. Cary (a courtier's) wife that had been a nun, who are all married to Jesus. At supper the three Drs. of Physic again at my cabin; where I put Dr. Scarborough in mind of what I heard him say about the use of the eyes, which he owned, that children do, in every day's experience, look several ways with both their eyes, till custom teaches them otherwise. And that we do now see but with one eye, our eyes looking in parallel lines. After this discourse I was called to write a pass for my Lord Mandeville to take up horses to London, which I wrote in the King's name,[2] and carried it to him to sign, which was the first and only one that ever he signed in the ship Charles.[3] To bed, coming in sight of land a little before night.

[25th]. By the morning we were come close to the land, and every body made ready to get on shore. The King and the two Dukes did eat their breakfast before they went, and there being set some ship's diet before them, not only to show them the manner of the ship's diet, they eat of nothing else but pease and pork, and boiled beef. I had Mr. Darcy in my cabin and Dr. Clerke, who eat with me, told me how the King had given £50 to Mr. Sheply for my Lord's servants, and £500 among the officers and

[1] Thomas Killigrew, fourth son of Sir Robert Killigrew of Hanworth, Middlesex, page of honour to Charles I., and groom of the bedchamber to Charles II., whose fortunes he had followed. He was Resident for the King at Venice, 1650; a great favourite with his master on account of his uncommon vein of humour, and author of several plays. He was born in the parish of St. Margaret, Lothbury, February 7th, 1611-12, and died March, 1682-3, being buried in Westminster Abbey. He married twice: 1, June 29th, 1636, Cicely, daughter of Sir James Crofts of Saxham, co. Suffolk, maid of honour to Queen Henrietta Maria (she died January 1st, 1637-8); 2, January 28th, 1654-5, Charlotte, daughter of John de Hesse (she died at the Hague in 1716).

[2] This right of purveyance was abolished in Charles's reign.

[3] Late the "Naseby."

common men of the ship. I spoke with the Duke of York about business, who called me Pepys by name, and upon my desire did promise me his future favour. Great expectation of the King's making some Knights, but there was none. About noon (though the brigantine that Beale made was there ready to carry him) yet he would go in my Lord's barge with the two Dukes. Our Captain steered, and my Lord went along bare with him. I went, and Mr. Mansell, and one of the King's footmen, with a dog that the King loved,[1] (which [dirted] the boat, which made us laugh, and methink that a King and all that belong to him are but just as others are), in a boat by ourselves, and so got on shore when the King did, who was received by General Monk with all imaginable love and respect at his entrance upon the land of Dover. Infinite the crowd of people and the horsemen, citizens, and noblemen of all sorts. The Mayor of the town came and gave him his white staff, the badge of his place, which the King did give him again. The Mayor also presented him from the town a very rich Bible, which he took and said it was the thing that he loved above all things in the world. A canopy was provided for him to stand under, which he did, and talked awhile with General Monk and others, and so into a stately coach there set for him, and so away through the town towards Canterbury, without making any stay at Dover. The shouting and joy expressed by all is past imagination. Seeing that my Lord did not stir out of his barge, I got into a boat, and so into his barge, whither Mr. John Crew stepped, and spoke a word or two to my Lord, and so returned, we back to the ship, and going did see a man almost drowned that fell out of

---

[1] Charles II.'s love of dogs is well known, but it is not so well known that his dogs were continually being stolen from him. In the "Mercurius Publicus," June 28-July 5, 1660, is the following advertisement, apparently drawn up by the King himself: "We must call upon you again for a Black Dog between a greyhound and a spaniel, no white about him, only a streak on his brest, and his tayl a little bobbed. It is His Majesties own Dog, and doubtless was stoln, for the dog was not born nor bred in England, and would never forsake His master. Whosoever findes him may acquaint any at Whitehal for the Dog was better known at Court, than those who stole him. Will they never leave robbing his Majesty! Must he not keep a Dog? This dog's place (though better than some imagine) is the only place which nobody offers to beg." (Quoted in "Notes and Queries," 7th S., vii. 26, where are printed two other advertisements of Charles's lost dogs.)

his boat into the sea, but with much ado was got out. My Lord almost transported with joy that he had done all this without any the least blur or obstruction in the world, that could give an offence to any, and with the great honour he thought it would be to him. Being overtook by the brigantine, my Lord and we went out of our barge into it, and so went on board with Sir W. Batten[1] and the Vice and Rear-Admirals. At night my Lord supped and Mr. Thomas Crew with Captain Stoakes, I supped with the Captain, who told me what the King had given us. My Lord returned late, and at his coming did give me order to cause the marke to be gilded, and a Crown and C. R. to be made at the head of the coach table, where the King to-day with his own hand did mark his height, which accordingly I caused the painter to do, and is now done as is to be seen.

[26th]. Thanks to God I got to bed in my own poor cabin, and slept well till 9 o'clock this morning. Mr. North and Dr. Clerke and all the great company being gone, I found myself very uncouth all this day for want thereof. My Lord dined with the Vice-Admiral to-day (who is as officious, poor man! as any spaniel can be; but I believe all to no purpose, for I believe he will not hold his place), so I dined commander at the coach table to-day, and all the officers of the ship with me, and Mr. White of Dover. After a game or two at nine-pins, to work all the after-

---

[1] Clarendon describes William Batten as an obscure fellow, and, although unknown to the service, a good seaman, who was in 1642 made Surveyor to the Navy; in which employ he evinced great animosity against the King. The following year, while Vice-Admiral to the Earl of Warwick, he chased a Dutch man-of-war into Burlington Bay, knowing that Queen Henrietta Maria was on board; and then, learning that she had landed and was lodged on the quay, he fired about a hundred shot upon the house, some of which passing through her majesty's chamber, she was obliged, though indisposed, to retire for safety into the open fields. This act, brutal as it was, found favour with the Parliament. But Batten became afterwards discontented; and, when a portion of the fleet revolted, he carried the "Constant Warwick," one of the best ships in the Parliament navy, over into Holland, with several seamen of note. For this act of treachery he was knighted and made a Rear-Admiral by Prince Charles. We hear no more of Batten till the Restoration, when he became a Commissioner of the Navy, and was soon after M.P. for Rochester. See an account of his second wife, in note to November 24th, 1660, and of his illness and death, October 5th, 1667. He had a son, Benjamin, and a daughter, Martha by his first wife.—B.

noon, making above twenty orders. In the evening my Lord
having been a-shore, the first time that he hath been a-shore
since he came out of the Hope (having resolved not to go till he
had brought his Majesty into England), returned on board with
a great deal of pleasure. I supped with the Captain in his cabin
with young Captain Cuttance, and afterwards a messenger from
the King came with a letter, and to go into France, and by that
means we supped again with him at 12 o'clock at night. This
night the Captain told me that my Lord had appointed me £30
out of the 1000 ducats which the King had given to the ship, at
which my heart was very much joyed. To bed.

[27th]. (Lord's day). Called up by John Goods to see the Garter
and Heralds coat, which lay in the coach, brought by Sir Edward
Walker,[1] King at Arms, this morning, for my Lord. My Lord
hath summoned all the Commanders on board him, to see the
ceremony, which was thus: Sir Edward putting on his coat, and
having laid the George and Garter, and the King's letter to my
Lord, upon a crimson cushion (in the coach, all the Commanders
standing by), makes three congees to him, holding the cushion in
his arms. Then laying it down with the things upon it upon a
chair, he takes the letter, and delivers it to my Lord, which my
Lord breaks open and gives him to read. It was directed to our
trusty and well beloved Sir Edward Montagu, Knight, one of our
Generals at sea, and our Companion elect of our Noble Order
of the Garter. The contents of the letter is to show that the Kings
of England have for many years made use of this honour, as a
special mark of favour, to persons of good extraction and virtue
(and that many Emperors, Kings and Princes of other countries
have borne this honour), and that whereas my Lord is of a noble
family, and hath now done the King such service by sea, at this

---

[1] Edward Walker was knighted February 2nd, 1644-5, and on the 24th of the
same month was sworn in as Garter King at Arms. He adhered to the cause of
the king, and published "Iter Carolinum, being a succinct account of the ne-
cessitated marches, retreats, and sufferings of his Majesty King Charles I.,
from Jan. 10, 1641, to the time of his death in 1648, collected by a daily at-
tendant upon his sacred Majesty during all that time." He joined Charles II.
in exile, and received the reward of his loyalty at the Restoration. He died at
Whitehall, February 19th, 1676-7, and was buried at Stratford-on-Avon, his
daughter having married Sir John Clopton of that place.

time, as he hath done; he do send him this George and Garter to wear as Knight of the Order, with a dispensation for the other ceremonies of the habit of the Order, and other things, till hereafter, when it can be done. So the herald putting the ribbon about his neck, and the Garter about his left leg, he salutes him with joy as Knight of the Garter, and that was all. After that was done, and the Captain and I had breakfasted with Sir Edward while my Lord was writing of a letter, he took his leave of my Lord, and so to shore again to the King at Canterbury, where he yesterday gave the like honour to General Monk,[1] who are the only two for many years that have had the Garter given them, before they had other honours of Earldom, or the like, excepting only the Duke of Buckingham, who was only Sir George Villiers when he was made Knight of the Garter.[2] A while after Mr. Thos. Crew and Mr. J. Pickering (who had staid long enough to make all the world see him to be a fool), took ship for London. So there now remain no strangers with my Lord but Mr. Hetley,[3] who had been with us a day before the king went from us. My Lord and the ship's company down to sermon. I staid above to write and look over my new song book, which came last night to me from London in lieu of that that my Lord had of me. The officers being all on board, there was not room for me at table, so I dined in my cabin, where, among other things, Mr. Dunn brought me a lobster and a bottle of oil, instead of a bottle of vinegar, whereby I spoiled my dinner. Many orders in the ordering of ships this afternoon. Late to a sermon. After that up to the Lieutenant's cabin, where Mr. Sheply, I, and the Minister supped, and after that I went down to W. Howe's cabin, and there, with a great deal of pleasure, singing till it was late. After that to bed.

[28th]. Called up at two in the morning for letters for my Lord from the Duke of York, but I went to bed again till 5. Trimmed early this morning. This morning the Captain did call over all the men in the ship (not the boys), and give every one of them a

---

[1] "His Majesty put the George on his Excellency, and the two Dukes put on the Garter. The Princes thus honoured the Lord-General for the restoration of that lawful family."—Rugge's *Diurnal*.

[2] Sir George Villiers received the Garter in 1616.

[3] Mr. Hetley died in the following year, see January 19th, 1660-61.

ducat[1] of the King's money that he gave the ship, and the officers according to their quality. I received in the Captain's cabin, for my share, sixty ducats. The rest of the morning busy writing letters. So was my Lord that he would not come to dinner. After dinner to write again in order to sending to London, but my Lord did not finish his, so we did not send to London to-day. A great part of the afternoon at nine-pins with my Lord and Mr. Hetley. I lost about 4s. Supped with my Lord, and after that to bed. At night I had a strange dream of—myself, which I really did, and having kicked my clothes off, I got cold, and found myself all much wet in the morning, and had a great deal of pain ... which made me very melancholy.

[29th]. The King's birthday. Busy all the morning writing letters to London, among the rest one to Mr. Chetwind to give me an account of the fees due to the Herald for the Order of the Garter, which my Lord desires to know. After dinner got all ready and sent away Mr. Cook to London with a letter and token to my wife. After that abroad to shore with my Lord (which he offered me of himself, saying that I had a great deal of work to do this month, which was very true). On shore we took horses, my Lord and Mr. Edward, Mr. Hetly and I, and three or four servants, and had a great deal of pleasure in riding. Among other things my Lord showed me a house that cost a great deal of money, and is built in so barren and inconvenient a place that my Lord calls it the fool's house. At last we came upon a very high cliff by the sea-side, and rode under it, we having laid great wagers, I and Dr. Mathews, that it was not so high as Paul's; my Lord and Mr. Hetly, that it was. But we riding under it, my Lord made a pretty good measure of it with two sticks, and found it to be not above thirty-five yards high, and Paul's is reckoned to be about ninety.[2] From thence toward the barge again, and in our way found the people at Deal going to make a bonfire for joy of the day, it being the King's birthday, and had some guns which

---

[1] The gold ducat is valued at about 9s. 6d., and the silver at 3s. 4d.

[2] The spire of St. Paul's (which was 208 feet high) was injured by fire in 1561 and taken down soon afterwards. The height of the remaining tower was 285 feet.

they did fire at my Lord's coming by. For which I did give twenty shillings among them to drink. While we were on the top of the cliffe, we saw and heard our guns in the fleet go off for the same joy. And it being a pretty fair day we could see above twenty miles into France. Being returned on board, my Lord called for Mr. Sheply's book of Paul's,[1] by which we were confirmed in our wager. After that to supper and then to musique, and so to bed. The pain that I have got last night by cold is not yet gone, but troubles me at the time of . . . . This day, it is thought, the King do enter the city of London.[2]

[30th]. About eight o'clock in the morning the lieutenant came to me to know whether I would eat a dish of mackerel, newly catched, for my breakfast, which the Captain and we did in the coach. All yesterday and to-day I had a great deal of pain . . . and in my back, which made me afeard. But it proved nothing but cold, which I took yesterday night. All this morning making up my accounts, in which I counted that I had made myself now worth about £80, at which my heart was glad, and blessed God. Many Dover men come and dine with my Lord. My Lord at ninepins in the afternoon. In the afternoon Mr. Sheply told me how my Lord had put me down for 70 guilders among the money which was given to my Lord's servants, which my heart did much rejoice at. My Lord supped alone in his chamber. Sir R. Stayner supped with us, and among other things told us how some of his men did grumble that no more of the Duke's money come to their share and so would not receive any; whereupon he called up those that had taken it, and gives them three shares apiece more, which was very good, and made good sport among the seamen. To bed.

[31st]. This day my Lord took physic, and came not out of his

---

[1] Probably a book on St. Paul's in the possession of Mr. Shepley.

[2] "Divers maidens, in behalf of themselves and others, presented a petition to the Lord Mayor of London, wherein they pray his Lordship to grant them leave and liberty to meet His Majesty on the day of his passing through the city; and if their petition be granted, that they will all be clad in white waistcoats and crimson petticoats, and other ornaments of triumph and rejoicing."—Rugge's *Diurnal*, May, 1660.—B.

chamber. All the morning making orders. After dinner a great
while below in the great cabin trying with W. Howe some of Mr.
Laws' songs,[1] particularly that of "What is a kiss," with which
we had a great deal of pleasure. After that to making of orders
again. Captain Sparling of the Assistance brought me a pair of
silk stockings of a light blue, which I was much pleased with.
The Captain and I to supper, and after that a most pleasant walk
till 10 at night with him upon the deck, it being a fine evening.
My pain was gone again that I had yesterday, blessed be God.
This day the month ends, I in very good health, and all the world
in a merry mood because of the King's coming. This day I began
to teach Mr. Edward,[2] who I find to have a very good foundation
laid for his Latin by Mr. Fuller. I expect every minute to hear
how my poor wife do. I find myself in all things well as to body
and mind, but troubled for the absence of my wife.

[June 1st]. This morning Mr. Sheply disposed of the money
that the Duke of York did give my Lord's servants, 22 ducatoons[3]
came to my share, whereof he told me to give Jaspar something
because my Lord left him out. I did give Mr. Sheply the fine
pair of buckskin gloves that I bought myself about five years ago.
My Lord took physic to-day, and so come not out all day. The
Captain on shore all day. After dinner Captain Jefferys and W.
Howe, and the Lieutenant and I to ninepins, where I lost about
two shillings and so fooled away all the afternoon. At night Mr.
Cooke comes from London with letters, leaving all things there
very gallant and joyful. And brought us word that the Parliament had ordered the 29th of May, the King's birthday,[4] to be
for ever kept as a day of thanksgiving for our redemption from
tyranny, and the King's return to his Government, he entering
London that day. My wife was in London when he came thither,

---

[1] *A Dialogue on a Kisse;* Book 3, Henry Lawes' *Treasury of Musick,* 1669,
p. 29.

[2] Young Edward Montagu.

[3] Foreign coins were in frequent use at this time. A Proclamation, January
29th, 1660-61, declared certain foreign gold and silver coins to be current at
certain rates. The rate of the ducatoon was 5s. 9d.

[4] 12 Car. II. cap. 14, "An Act for a perpetual Anniversary Thanksgiving on
the nine-and-twentieth day of May."

and had been there a week with Mr. Bowyer and his wife. My poor wife has not been well a week before, but thanks be to God is well again. She would fain see me and be at her house again, but we must be content. She writes word how the Joyces grow very rich and very proud, but it is no matter, and that there was a talk that I should be knighted by the King, which they (the Joyces) laugh at; but I think myself happier in my wife and estate than they are in theirs. To bed. The Captain come on board, when I was going to bed, quite fuddled; and himself the next morning told me so too, that the Vice-Admiral, Rear-Admiral, and he had been drinking all day.

[2d]. Being with my Lord in the morning about business in his cabin, I took occasion to give him thanks for his love to me in the share that he had given me of his Majesty's money, and the Duke's. He told me he hoped to do me a more lasting kindness, if all things stand as they are now between him and the King, but, says he, "We must have a little patience and we will rise together; in the mean time I will do you all the good jobs I can." Which was great content for me to hear from my Lord. All the morning with the Captain, computing how much the thirty ships that come with the King from Scheveling their pay comes to for a month (because the King promised to give them all a month's pay), and it comes to £6,538, and the Charles particularly £777. I wish we had the money. All the afternoon with two or three captains in the Captain's cabin, drinking of white wine and sugar, and eating pickled oysters, where Captain Sparling told us the best story that ever I heard, about a gentleman that persuaded a country fool to let him gut his oysters or else they would stink. At night writing letters to London and Weymouth, for my Lord being now to sit in the House of Peers he endeavours to get Mr. Edward Montagu for Weymouth and Mr. George for Dover.[1] Mr. Cooke late with me in my cabin while I wrote to my wife, and drank a bottle of wine and so took leave of me on his journey and I to bed.

[1] One only of these two was elected, for Bullen Reymes became M.P. for Weymouth on June 22nd.

[3d]. Waked in the morning by one who when I asked who it
was, he told me one from Bridewell, which proved Captain Holland. I rose presently to him. He is come to get an order for the
setting out of his ship, and to renew his commission. He tells me
how every man goes to the Lord Mayor to set down their names,
as such as do accept of his Majesty's pardon, and showed me a
certificate under the Lord Mayor's hand that he had done so.

At sermon in the morning; after dinner into my cabin, to cast
my accounts up, and find myself to be worth near £100, for
which I bless Almighty God, it being more than I hoped for so
soon, being I believe not clearly worth £25 when I came to sea
besides my house and goods. Then to set my papers in order,
they being increased much upon my hands through want of time
to put them in order. The ship's company all this while at
sermon. After sermon my Lord did give me instruction to write
to London about business, which done, after supper to bed.

[4th]. Waked in the morning at four o'clock to give some money
to Mr. Hetly, who was to go to London with the letters that I
wrote yesterday night. After he was gone I went and lay down
in my gown upon my bed again an hour or two. At last waked
by a messenger come for a Post Warrant for Mr. Hetly and Mr.
Creed, who stood to give so little for their horses that the men
would not let them have any without a warrant, which I sent
them. All the morning getting Captain Holland's commission
done, which I did, and he at noon went away. I took my leave of
him upon the quarter-deck with a bottle of sack, my Lord being
just set down to dinner. Then he being gone I went to dinner and
after dinner to my cabin to write. This afternoon I showed my
Lord my accounts, which he passed, and so I think myself to be
worth near £100 now. In the evening I made an order for Captain Sparling of the Assistance to go to Middleburgh, to fetch
over some of the King's goods. I took the opportunity to send all
my Dutch money, 70 ducatoons and 29 gold ducats to be changed,
if he can, for English money, which is the first venture that ever
I made, and so I have been since a little afeard of it. After supper
some music and so to bed. This morning the King's Proclamation against drinking, swearing, and debauchery, was read to

our ships' companies in the fleet, and indeed it gives great satisfaction to all.[1]

[5th]. A-bed late. In the morning my Lord went on shore with
the Vice-Admiral a-fishing, and at dinner returned. In the afternoon I played at ninepins with my Lord, and when he went in
again I got him to sign my accounts for £115, and so upon my
private balance I find myself confirmed in my estimation that I
am worth £100. In the evening in my cabin a great while getting
the song without book, "Help, help Divinity, &c."[2] After supper
my Lord called for the lieutenant's cittern,[3] and with two candlesticks with money in them for symballs,[4] we made barber's
music,[5] with which my Lord was well pleased. So to bed.

[6th]. In the morning I had letters come, that told me among
other things, that my Lord's place of Clerk of the Signet was
fallen to him, which he did most lovingly tell me that I should
execute, in case he could not get a better employment for me at
the end of the year. Because he thought that the Duke of York
would command all, but he hoped that the Duke would not remove me but to my advantage.

I had a great deal of talk about my uncle Robert,[6] and he told
me that he could not tell how his mind stood as to his estate, but
he would do all that lay in his power for me. After dinner came

---

[1] The King's "Proclamation against vicious, debauched, and prophane Persons" is dated May 30th. It is printed in "Somers's Tracts," ed. 1812, vol. vii.
p. 423.

[2] "Help, help, O help, Divinity of Love," by Henry Lawes, printed in "The
Second Book of Ayres and Dialogues." London (Playford), 1655. It is entitled
"A Storme."

[3] Cittern (cither), a musical instrument having wire strings, sounded with a
plectrum.

[4] Symballs, i.e. cymbals.

[5] In the "Notices of Popular Histories," printed for the Percy Society, there
is a curious woodcut representing the interior of a barber's shop, in which,
according to the old custom, the person waiting to be shaved is playing on the
"ghittern" till his turn arrives. Decker also mentions a "barber's cittern," for
every serving-man to play upon. This is no doubt "the barber's music" with
which Lord Sandwich entertained himself.—B.

[6] Robert Pepys of Brampton, eldest son of Thomas Pepys the red, and brother
of Samuel's father.

Mr. Cooke from London, who told me that my wife he left well at Huntsmore, though her health not altogether so constant as it used to be, which my heart is troubled for. Mr. Moore's letters tell me that he thinks my Lord will be suddenly sent for up to London, and so I got myself in readiness to go.

My letters tell me, that Mr. Calamy[1] had preached before the King in a surplice (this I heard afterwards to be false); that my Lord, Gen. Monk, and three more Lords, are made Commissioners for the Treasury;[2] that my Lord had some great place conferred on him, and they say Master of the Wardrobe;[3] that the two Dukes[4] do haunt the Park much, and that they were at a play, Madame Epicene,[5] the other day; that Sir Ant. Cooper, Mr. Hollis, and Mr. Annesly,[6] late President of the Council of State, are made Privy Councillors to the King. At night very busy sending Mr. Donne away to London, and wrote to my father for a coat to be made me against I come to London, which I think will not be long. At night Mr. Edward Montagu came on board and

---

[1] Edmund Calamy, D.D., the celebrated Nonconformist divine, born February, 1600, appointed Chaplain to Charles II., 1660. He refused the bishopric of Lichfield which was offered to him. Died October 29th, 1666.

[2] The names of the Commissioners were—Sir Edward Hyde, afterwards Earl of Clarendon, General Monk, Thomas, Earl of Southampton, John, Lord Robartes, Thomas, Lord Colepeper, Sir Edward Montagu, with Sir Edward Nicholas and Sir William Morrice as principal Secretaries of State. The patents are dated June 19th, 1660.

[3] The duty of the Master of the Wardrobe was to provide "proper furniture for coronations, marriages, and funerals" of the sovereign and royal family, "cloaths of state, beds, hangings, and other necessaries for the houses of foreign ambassadors, cloaths of state for Lord Lieutenant of Ireland, Prince of Wales, and ambassadors abroad," as also to provide robes for Ministers of State, Knights of the Garter, &c. The last Master of the Wardrobe was Ralph, Duke of Montague, who died 1709.

[4] Duke of York and Duke of Gloucester.

[5] "Epicene, or the Silent Woman," a comedy, by Ben Jonson.

[6] Arthur Annesley, afterwards second Viscount Valentia, born July 10th, 1614. He had been chosen President of the Council of State in February, 1660. He was a Parliamentarian as long as that cause was in the ascendant, but was instrumental in the restoration of Charles II., for which service he was amply rewarded. He was Treasurer of the Navy from 1666 to 1668, and held the office of Lord Privy Seal from 1672 to 1682. Created Earl of Anglesea, 1661. He wrote several books, and died April 26th, 1686.

staid long up with my Lord. I to bed and about one in the morning.

[7th]. W. Howe called me up to give him a letter to carry to my Lord that came to me to-day, which I did and so to sleep again. About three in the morning the people began to wash the deck, and the water came pouring into my mouth, which waked me, and I was fain to rise and get on my gown, and sleep leaning on my table. This morning Mr. Montagu went away again. After dinner come Mr. John Wright and Mr. Moore, with the sight of whom my heart was very glad. They brought an order for my Lord's coming up to London, which my Lord resolved to do to-morrow. All the afternoon getting my things in order to set forth to-morrow. At night walked up and down with Mr. Moore, who did give me an account of all things at London. Among others, how the Presbyterians would be angry if they durst, but they will not be able to do any thing. Most of the Commanders on board and supped with my Lord. Late at night came Mr. Edw. Pickering from London, but I could not see him this night. I went with Mr. Moore to the Master's cabin, and saw him there in order to going to bed. After that to my own cabin to put things in order and so to bed.

[8th]. Out early, took horses at Deale. I troubled much with the King's gittar, and Fairbrother, the rogue that I intrusted with the carrying of it on foot, whom I thought I had lost. Col. Dixwell's horse taken by a soldier and delivered to my Lord, and by him to me to carry to London. Came to Canterbury, dined there. I saw the minster and the remains of Becket's tomb. To Sittingborne and Rochester. At Chatham and Rochester the ships and bridge. Mr. Hetly's mistake about dinner. Come to Gravesend. A good handsome wench I kissed, the first that I have seen a great while. Supped with my Lord, drank late below with Penrose, the Captain. To bed late, having first laid out all my things against to-morrow to put myself in a walking garb. Weary and hot to bed to Mr. Moore.

[9th]. Up betimes, 25s. the reckoning for very bare. Paid the house and by boats to London, six boats. Mr. Moore, W. Howe,

and I, and then the child in the room of W. Howe. Landed at the Temple. To Mr. Crew's. To my father's and put myself into a handsome posture to wait upon my Lord, dined there. To White Hall with my Lord and Mr. Edwd. Montagu. Found the King in the Park. There walked. Gallantly great.

[10th]. (Lord's day.) At my father's found my wife and to walk with her in Lincoln's Inn walks.[1]

[11th]. Betimes to my Lord. Extremely much people and business. So with him to Whitehall to the Duke. Back with him by coach and left him in Covent Garden. I back to Will's and the Hall to see my father. Then to the Leg in King Street with Mr. Moore, and sent for L'Impertinent to dinner with me. After that with Mr. Moore about Privy Seal business. To Mr. Watkins, so to Mr. Crew's. Then towards my father's met my Lord and with him to Dorset House[2] to the Chancellor. So to Mr. Crew's, and saw my Lord at supper, and then home, and went to see Mrs. Turner, and so to bed.

[12th]. Visited by the two Pierces, Mr. Blackburne, Dr. Clerk and Mr. Creed, and did give them a ham of bacon. So to my Lord and with him to the Duke of Gloucester. The two Dukes dined with the Speaker, and I saw there a fine entertainment and dined with the pages. To Mr. Crew's, whither came Mr. Greatorex, and with him to the Faithornes,[3] and so to the Devils tavern. To

---

[1] Lincoln's Inn Gardens were originally known as Coneygarth, from the rabbits which burrowed there. Ben Jonson mentions them:—
 "The walks of Lincoln's Inn
  Under the Elms."—*The Devil is an Ass.*

[2] Dorset House, in Salisbury Court, Fleet Street, at this time occupied by the Chancellor, once the residence of the Bishops of Salisbury, one of whom (Jewel) alienated it to the Sackville family. The house being afterwards pulled down, a theatre was built on its site, in which the Duke of York's troop performed. The name is sill preserved in Dorset Street.

[3] William Faithorne the elder, engraver and portrait painter, born in London in 1616. On the outbreak of the Civil War he took up arms for the King, and was confined for a time in Aldersgate as a prisoner of war. He was banished for refusing to take the oath to Oliver Cromwell, but obtained permission to return to England in 1650, when he settled at the sign of the Drake, outside Temple Bar. About 1680 he went to Printing House Yard, Blackfriars, and died May, 1691.

my Lord's and staid till 12 at night about business. So to my father's, my father and mother in bed, who had been with my uncle Fenner, &c., and my wife all day and expected me. But I found Mr. Cook there, and so to bed.

[13th]. To my Lord's and thence to the Treasurer's of the Navy,[1] with Mr. Creed and Pierce the Purser to Rawlinson's, whither my uncle Wight came, and I spent 12s. upon them. So to Mr. Crew's, where I blotted a new carpet that was hired, but got it out again with fair water.[2] By water with my Lord in a boat to Westminster, and to the Admiralty, now in a new place. After business done there to the Rhenish wine-house with Mr. Blackburne, Creed, and Wivell. So to my Lord's lodging and to my father's, and to bed.

[14th]. Up to my Lord and from him to the Treasurer of the Navy for £500. After that to a tavern with Washington the Purser, very gallant, and ate and drank. To Mr. Crew's and laid my money. To my Lady Pickering[3] with the plate that she did give my Lord the other day. Then to Will's and met William Symons and Doling and Luellin, and with them to the Bullhead,[4] and then to a new alehouse in Brewer's Yard, where Winter that had the fray with Stoakes, and from them to my father's.

[15th]. All the morning at the Commissioners of the Navy about getting out my bill for £50 for the last quarter, which I got done with a great deal of ease, which is not common. After that with Mr. Turner to the Dolphin and drunk, and so by water to W. Symons, where D. Scobell with his wife, a pretty and rich woman. Mrs. Symons, a very fine woman, very merry after dinner with marrying of Luellin and D. Scobell's kinswoman that

---

[1] Sir George Carteret had been appointed Treasurer of the Navy at the Restoration in succession to Richard Hutchinson. See *post*, July 3rd, 1660.

[2] It was customary to use carpets as table cloths.

[3] Elizabeth Montagu, sister to the Earl of Sandwich, who had married Sir Gilbert Pickering, Bart., of Nova Scotia, and of Tichmersh, co. Northampton.

[4] There was another Bull Head at Charing Cross. There were several Brewer's Yards in London, but this was probably the one on the south side of the Strand, near Hungerford Market; and the Bull Head tavern was doubtless the one at Charing Cross.

was there. Then to my Lord who told me how the King has given him the place of the great Wardrobe.[1] My Lord resolves to have Sarah again.[2] I to my father's, and then to see my uncle and aunt Fenner. So home and to bed.

[16th]. Rose betimes and abroad in one shirt, which brought me a great cold and pain. Muford took me to Harvey's by my father's to drink and told me of a business that I hope to get £5 by. To my Lord, and so to White Hall with him about the Clerk of the Privy Seal's place, which he is to have. Then to the Admiralty, where I wrote some letters. Here Coll. Thompson told me, as a great secret, that the Nazeby was on fire when the King was there, but that is not known; when God knows it is quite false. Got a piece of gold from Major Holmes[3] for the horse of Dix-well's I brought to town. Dined at Mr. Crew's, and after dinner with my Lord to Whitehall. Court attendance infinite tedious. Back with my Lord to my Lady-Wright's and staid till it had done raining, which it had not done a great while. After that at night home to my father's and to bed.

[17th]. (Lord's day). Lay long abed. To Mr. Mossum's, a good sermon. This day the organs did begin to play at White Hall before the King.[4] Dined at my father's. After dinner to Mr. Mossum's again, and so in the garden, and heard Chippell's father preach, that was Page to the Protector, and just by the window that I stood at sat Mrs. Butler, the great beauty.[5] After sermon to my Lord. Mr. Edward and I into Gray's Inn walks, and saw many beauties. So to my father's, where Mr. Cook, W. Bowyer, and my coz Roger Wharton supped and to bed.

---

[1] The house attached to the office of the Master of the Wardrobe was near Puddle Wharf, Blackfriars. It was built by Sir John Beauchamp (d. 1359), and his executors sold it to Edward III. When Stow drew up his Survey, Sir John Fortescue was lodged in the house as Master of the Wardrobe.

[2] Mrs. Sarah, Lord Sandwich's housekeeper.

[3] Afterwards Sir Robert Holmes. He is styled "Major," although in the navy. Thus Lord Sandwich and Sir W. Penn were called "Generals"; see also January 6th, 1661-2.

[4] All organs were removed from churches by an ordinance dated 1644.

[5] Frances Butler, sister to Mons. l'Impertinent; see February 17th, 1659-60.

[18th]. To my Lord's, where much business and some hopes of getting some money thereby. With him to the Parliament House, where he did intend to have gone to have made his appearance to-day, but he met Mr. Crew upon the stairs, and would not go in. He went to Mrs. Brown's, and staid till word was brought him what was done in the House. This day they made an end of the twenty men to be excepted from pardon to their estates. By barge to Stepny with my Lord, where at Trinity House we had great entertainment.[1] With my Lord there went Sir W. Pen, Sir H. Wright, Hetly, Pierce, Creed, Hill, I and other servants. Back again to the Admiralty, and so to my Lord's lodgings, where he told me that he did look after the place of the Clerk of the Acts[2] for me. So to Mr. Crew's and my father's and to bed. My wife went this day to Huntsmore for her things, and I was very lonely all night. This evening my wife's brother, Balty, came to me to let me know his bad condition and to get a place for him, but I perceive he stands upon a place for a gentleman, that may not stain his family when, God help him, he wants bread.

[19th]. Called on betimes by Murford, who showed me five pieces to get a business done for him and I am resolved to do it. Much business at my Lord's. This morning my Lord went into the House of Commons, and there had the thanks of the House, in the name of the Parliament and Commons of England, for his late service to his King and Country. A motion was made for a reward for him, but it was quashed by Mr. Annesly, who, above most men, is engaged to my Lord's and Mr. Crew's families. Meeting with Captain Stoakes at Whitehall, I dined with him and Mr. Gullop, a parson (with whom afterwards I was much offended at his importunity and impertinence, such another as Elborough),[3] and Mr. Butler, who complimented much after the same manner as the parson did. After that towards my Lord's

[1] The old hall of the Trinity House was at Deptford. The present building on Tower Hill was erected 1793-95.

[2] The letters patent appointing Pepys to the office of Clerk of the Acts is dated July 13th, 1660.

[3] Thomas Elborough was one of Pepys's schoolfellows, and afterwards parson of St. Lawrence Poultney.

at Mr. Crew's, but was met with by a servant of my Lady Pickering, who took me to her and she told me the story of her husband's case and desired my assistance with my Lord, and did give me, wrapped up in paper, £5 in silver. After that to my Lord's, and with him to Whitehall and my lady Pickering. My Lord went at night with the King to Baynard's Castle[1] to supper, and I home to my father's to bed. My wife and the girl and dog came home to-day. When I came home I found a quantity of chocolate left for me, I know not from whom. We hear of W. Howe being sick to-day, but he was well at night.

[20th]. Up by 4 in the morning to write letters to sea and a commission for him that Murford solicited for. Called on by Captain Sparling, who did give me my Dutch money again, and so much as he had changed into English money, by which my mind was eased of a great deal of trouble. Some other sea captains. I did give them a good morning draught, and so to my Lord (who lay long in bed this day, because he came home late from supper with the King). With my Lord to the Parliament House, and, after that, with him to General Monk's, where he dined at the Cockpit. I home and dined with my wife, now making all things ready there again. Thence to my Lady Pickering, who did give me the best intelligence about the Wardrobe. Afterwards to the Cockpit to my Lord with Mr. Townsend, one formerly and now again to be employed as Deputy of the Wardrobe. Thence to the Admiralty, and despatched away Mr. Cooke to sea; whose business was a letter from my Lord about Mr. G. Montagu to be chosen as a Parliament-man in my Lord's room at Dover;[2] and another to the Vice-Admiral to give my Lord a constant account of all things in the fleet, merely that he may thereby keep up his power there; another letter to Captn. Cuttance to send the barge that brought the King on shore, to Hinchingbroke by Lynne.[3] To my own house, meeting G. Vines, and

---

[1] Baynard's Castle, Thames Street, was garrisoned by the Parliament in 1648. It was destroyed in the Great Fire.

[2] The Hon. George Montagu of Horton, co. Northampton, was elected M.P. for Dover, August 16th, 1660, in place of the Earl of Sandwich.

[3] Whence it would go by water carriage.

drank with him at Charing Cross, now the King's Head Tavern.[1] With my wife to my father's, where met with Swan,[2] an old hypocrite, and with him, his friend and my father, and my cozen Scott to the Bear Tavern. To my father's and to bed.

[21st]. To my Lord, much business. With him to the Council Chamber, where he was sworn; and the charge of his being admitted Privy Counsellor is £26. To the Dog Tavern at Westminster, where Murford with Captain Curle and two friends of theirs went to drink. Captain Curle, late of the Maria, gave me five pieces in gold and a silver can for my wife for the Commission I did give him this day for his ship, dated April 20, 1660 last. Thence to the Parliament door and came to Mr. Crew's to dinner with my Lord, and with my Lord to see the great Wardrobe, where Mr. Townsend brought us to the governor of some poor children in tawny clothes, who had been maintained there these eleven years, which put my Lord to a stand how to dispose of them, that he may have the house for his use. The children did sing finely, and my Lord did bid me give them five pieces in gold at his going away. Thence back to White Hall, where, the King being gone abroad, my Lord and I walked a great while discoursing of the simplicity of the Protector, in his losing all that his father had left him. My Lord told me, that the last words that he parted with the Protector with (when he went to the Sound), were, that he should rejoice more to see him in his grave at his return home, than that he should give way to such things as were then in hatching, and afterwards did ruin him: and the Protector said, that whatever G. Montagu, my Lord Broghill,[3] Jones,[4] and the Secretary, would have him to do, he would do it, be it what it would. Thence to my wife, meeting Mr. Blagrave, who went home with me, and did give me a lesson upon the

[1] At the King's Head there was a half-crown ordinary.

[2] William Swan is called a fanatic and a very rogue in other parts of the Diary.

[3] Roger Boyle, fifth son of Richard, Earl of Cork, born April 25th, 1621, and at the age of seven created Lord Broghill. He was created Earl of Orrery in 1660. Died October 16th, 1679.

[4] Colonel John Jones was M.P. for the City of London in the Parliament summoned to meet May 8th, 1661.

flageolet, and handselled my silver can with my wife and me. To my father's, where Sir Thomas Honeywood and his family were come of a sudden, and so we forced to lie all together in a little chamber, three stories high.

[22d]. To my Lord, where much business. With him to White Hall, where the Duke of York not being up, we walked a good while in the Shield Gallery. Mr. Hill (who for these two or three days hath constantly attended my Lord) told me of an offer of £500 for a Baronet's dignity, which I told my Lord of in the balcone in this gallery, and he said he would think of it. I to my Lord's and gave order for horses to be got to draw my Lord's great coach to Mr. Crew's. Mr. Morrice the upholsterer came himself to-day to take notice what furniture we lack for our lodgings at Whitehall. My dear friend Mr. Fuller of Twickenham[1] and I dined alone at the Sun Tavern, where he told me how he had the grant of being Dean of St. Patrick's, in Ireland; and I

[1] See *ante*, January 17th, 1660.

177

told him my condition, and both rejoiced one for another. Thence to my Lord's, and had the great coach to Brigham's, who went with me to the Half Moon, and gave me a can of good julep,[1] and told me how my Lady Monk[2] deals with him and others for their places, asking him £500, though he was formerly the King's coach-maker, and sworn to it. My Lord abroad, and I to my house and set things in a little order there. So with Mr. Moore to my father's, I staying with Mrs. Turner who stood at her door as I passed. Among other things she told me for certain how my old Lady Middlesex —— herself the other day in the presence of the King, and people took notice of it. Thence called at my father's, and so to Mr. Crew's, where Mr. Hetley had sent a letter for me, and two pair of silk stockings, one for W. Howe, and the other for me. To Sir H. Wright's to my Lord, where he was, and took direction about business, and so by link home about 11 o'clock. To bed, the first time since my coming from sea, in my own house, for which God be praised.

[23d]. By water with Mr. Hill towards my Lord's lodging and so to my Lord. With him to Whitehall, where I left him and went to Mr. Holmes to deliver him the horse of Dixwell's that had staid there fourteen days at the Bell. So to my Lord's lodgings, where Tom Guy came to me, and there staid to see the King touch people for the King's evil.[3] But he did not come at all, it rayned so;

---

[1] A sweet drink which still survives in pharmacy, and the name is used in the United States for a special drink called mint julep.

[2] Anne Clarges, Lady Monk, and Duchess of Albemarle.

[3] This ceremony is usually traced to Edward the Confessor, but there is no direct evidence of the early Norman kings having touched for the evil. Sir John Fortescue, in his defence of the House of Lancaster against that of York, argued that the crown could not descend to a female, because the Queen is not qualified by the form of anointing her, used at the coronation, to cure the disease called the King's evil. Burn asserts, "History of Parish Registers," 1862, p. 179, that "between 1660 and 1682, 92,107 persons were touched for the evil." Everyone coming to the court for that purpose, brought a certificate signed by the minister and church-wardens, that he had not at any time been touched by His Majesty. The practice was supposed to have expired with the Stuarts, but the point being disputed, reference was made to the library of the Duke of Sussex, and four several Oxford editions of the Book of Common Prayer were found, all printed after the accession of the house of Hanover, and all containing, as an integral part of the service, "The Office for the Heal-

and the poor people were forced to stand all the morning in the rain in the garden. Afterward he touched them in the Banquetting-house. With my Lord, to my Lord Frezendorfe's,[1] where he dined to-day. Where he told me that he had obtained a promise of the Clerk of the Acts place for me, at which I was glad. Met with Mr. Chetwind, and dined with him at Hargrave's, the Cornchandler, in St. Martin's Lane, where a good dinner, where he showed me some good pictures, and an instrument he called an Angelique.[2] With him to London, changing all my Dutch money at Backwell's[3] for English, and then to Cardinal's Cap, where he and the City Remembrancer who paid for all. Back to Westminster, where my Lord was, and discoursed with him awhile about his family affairs. So he went away, I home and wrote letters into the country, and to bed.

ing." The Stamp of gold with which the King crossed the sore of the sick person was called an angel, and of the value of ten shillings. It had a hole bored through it, through which a ribbon was drawn, and the angel was hanged about the patient's neck till the cure was perfected. The stamp has the impression of St. Michael the Archangel on one side, and a ship in full sail on the other. "My Lord Anglesey had a daughter cured of the King's evil with three others on Tuesday."—MS. Letter of William Greenhill to Lady Bacon, dated December 31st, 1629, preserved at Audley End. Charles II. "touched" before he came to the throne. "It is certain that the King hath very often touched the sick, as well at Breda, where he touched 260 from Saturday the 17 of April to Sunday the 23 of May, as at Bruges and Bruxels, during the residence he made there; and the English assure . . . it was not without success, since it was the experience that drew thither every day, a great number of those diseased even from the most remote provinces of Germany."—Sir William Lower's *Relation of the Voiage and Residence which Charles the II. hath made in Holland*, Hague, 1660, p. 78. Sir William Lower gives a long account of the touching for the evil by Charles before the Restoration.

[1] John Frederic de Friesendorff, ambassador from Sweden to Charles II., who created him a baronet, 1661.

[2] An angelique is described as a species of guitar in Murray's "New English Dictionary," and this passage from the Diary is given as a quotation. The word appears as *angelot* in Phillips's "English Dictionary" (1678), and is used in Browning's "Sordello," as a "plaything of page or girl."

[3] Alderman Edward Backwell, an eminent banker and goldsmith, who is frequently mentioned in the Diary. His shop was in Lombard Street. He was ruined by the closing of the Exchequer by Charles II. in 1672. The crown then owed him £295,994 16s. 6d., in lieu of which the King gave him an annuity of £17,759 13s. 8d. Backwell retired into Holland after the closing of the Exchequer, and died there in 1679. See Hilton Price's "Handbook of London Bankers," 1876.

[24th]. Sunday. Drank my morning draft at Harper's, and bought a pair of gloves there. So to Mr. G. Montagu, and told him what I had received from Dover, about his business likely to be chosen there. So home and thence with my wife towards my father's. She went thither, I to Mr. Crew's, where I dined and my Lord at my Lord Montagu of Boughton in Little Queen Street. In the afternoon to Mr. Mossum's with Mr. Moore, and we sat in Mr. Butler's pew. Then to Whitehall looking for my Lord but in vain, and back again to Mr. Crew's where I found him and did give him letters. Among others some simple ones from our Lieutenant, Lieut. Lambert to him and myself, which made Mr. Crew and us all laugh. I went to my father's to tell him that I would not come to supper, and so after my business done at Mr. Crew's I went home and my wife within a little while after me, my mind all this while full of thoughts for my place of Clerk of the Acts.

[25th]. With my Lord at White Hall all the morning. I spoke with Mr. Coventry about my business, who promised me all the assistance I could expect. Dined with young Mr. Powell, lately come from the Sound, being amused at our great changes here, and Mr. Southerne, now Clerk to Mr. Coventry, at the Leg in King-street. Thence to the Admiralty, where I met with Mr. Turner,[1] of the Navy-office, who did look after the place of Clerk of the Acts. He was very civil to me, and I to him, and shall be so. There came a letter from my Lady Monk to my Lord about it this evening, but he refused to come to her, but meeting in White Hall, with Sir Thomas Clarges, her brother, my Lord returned answer, that he could not desist in my business; and that he believed that General Monk would take it ill if my Lord should name the officers in his army; and therefore he desired to have the naming of one officer in the fleet. With my Lord by coach to Mr. Crew's, and very merry by the way, discoursing of the late

---

[1] Thomas Turner (or Tourner) was General Clerk at the Navy Office, and on June 30th he offered Pepys £150 to be made joint Clerk of the Acts with him. In a list of the Admiralty officers just before the King came in, preserved in the British Museum, there occur, Richard Hutchinson, Treasury of the Navy, salary £1,500; Thomas Tourner, General Clerk, for himself and clerk, £100.

changes and his good fortune. Thence home, and then with my wife to Dorset House, to deliver a list of the names of the justices of the peace for Huntingdonshire. By coach, taking Mr. Fox part of the way with me, that was with us with the King on board the Nazeby, who I found to have married Mrs. Whittle,[1] that lived at Mr. Geer's so long. A very civil gentleman. At Dorset House I met with Mr. Kipps, my old friend, with whom the world is well changed, he being now sealbearer to the Lord Chancellor, at which my wife and I are well pleased, he being a very good natured man. Home and late writing letters. Then to my Lord's lodging, this being the first night of his coming to Whitehall to lie since his coming from sea.

[26th]. My Lord dined at his lodgings all alone to-day. I went to Secretary Nicholas[2] to carry him my Lord's resolutions about his title, which he had chosen, and that is Portsmouth.[3] I met with Mr. Throgmorton, a merchant, who went with me to the old Three Tuns,[4] at Charing Cross, who did give me five pieces of gold for to do him a small piece of service about a convoy to Bilbo, which I did. In the afternoon, one Mr. Watts came to me, a merchant, to offer me £500 if I would desist from the Clerk of the Acts place. I pray God direct me in what I do herein. Went to my house, where I found my father, and carried him and my wife to Whitefriars, and myself to Puddlewharf,[5] to the Wardrobe, to Mr. Townsend, who went with me to Backwell, the goldsmith's, and there we chose £100 worth of plate for my Lord to give Secretary Nicholas. Back and staid at my father's, and so home to bed.

---

[1] Elizabeth, daughter of William Whittle of Lancashire, married to Mr., afterwards Sir Stephen Fox. See *ante*, May 24th (note).

[2] Sir Edward Nicholas, Secretary of State to Charles I. and II. He was dismissed from his office through the intrigues of Lady Castlemaine in 1663. He died 1669, aged seventy-seven.

[3] Montagu changed his mind, and ultimately took his title from the town of Sandwich, leaving that of Portsmouth for the use of a King's mistress.

[4] There is a token of "Thomas Darling at the Three Tuns neare Charing Cross." See "Boyne's Trade Tokens," vol. i. p. 557.

[5] Puddlewharf was at the foot of St. Andrew's Hill, Upper Thames Street, Blackfriars.

[27th]. With my Lord to the Duke, where he spoke to Mr. Coventry to despatch my business of the Acts, in which place every body gives me joy, as if I were in it, which God send.[1] Dined with my Lord and all the officers of his regiment, who invited my Lord and his friends, as many as he would bring, to dinner, at the Swan,[2] at Dowgate, a poor house and ill dressed, but very good fish and plenty. Here Mr. Symons, the Surgeon, told me how he was likely to lose his estate that he had bought, at which I was not a little pleased. To Westminster, and with Mr. Howe by coach to the Speaker's, where my Lord supped with the King, but I could not get in. So back again, and after a song or two in my chamber in the dark, which do (now that the bed is out) sound very well, I went home and to bed.

[28th]. My brother Tom came to me with patterns to choose for a suit. I paid him all to this day, and did give him £10 upon account. To Mr. Coventry, who told me that he would do me all right in my business. To Sir G. Downing, the first visit I have made him since he came. He is so stingy a fellow I care not to see him; I quite cleared myself of his office, and did give him liberty to take any body in. Hawly and he are parted too, he is going to serve Sir Thos. Ingram.[3] I went also this morning to see Mrs. Pierce, the chirurgeon ['s wife]. I found her in bed in her house in Margaret churchyard. Her husband returned to sea. I did invite her to go to dinner with me and my wife to-day. After all this to my Lord, who lay a-bed till eleven o'clock, it being almost five before he went to bed, they supped so late last night

---

[1] The letters patent, dated July 13th, 12 Charles II., recite and revoke letters patent of February 16th, 14 Charles I., whereby the office of Clerk of the Ships had been given to Dennis Fleming and *Thomas Barlow*, or the survivor. D. F. was then dead, but T. B. living, and Samuel Pepys was appointed in his room, at a salary of £33 6s. 8d. per annum, with 3s. 4d. for each day employed in travelling, and £6 per annum for boat-hire, and all fees due. This salary was only the ancient "fee out of the Exchequer," which had been attached to the office for more than a century. Pepys's salary had been previously fixed at £350 a year.

[2] A token of William Burges, at the Swan at Dowgate Conduit, 1668, is described in "Boyne's Trade Tokens," by Williamson, vol. i., 1889, p. 583.

[3] Sir Thomas Ingram was appointed Commissioner for Tangier.

with the King. This morning I saw poor Bishop Wren[1] going to
Chappel, it being a thanksgiving-day[2] for the King's return.
After my Lord was awake, I went up to him to the Nursery,
where he do lie, and, having talked with him a little, I took leave
and carried my wife and Mrs. Pierce to Clothworkers'-Hall,[3] to
dinner, where Mr. Pierce, the Purser, met us. We were invited
by Mr. Chaplin,[4] the Victualler, where Nich. Osborne was. Our
entertainment very good, a brave hall, good company, and very
good music. Where among other things I was pleased that I could
find out a man by his voice, whom I had never seen before, to be
one that sang behind the curtaine formerly at Sir W. Davenant's[5] opera. Here Dr. Gauden and Mr. Gauden the victualler[6]
dined with us. After dinner to Mr. Rawlinson's,[7] to see him and

[1] Matthew Wren, born 1585, successively Bishop of Hereford, Norwich, and
Ely. At the commencement of the Rebellion he was sent to the Tower, and remained a prisoner there eighteen years. Died April 24th, 1667.

[2] "A Proclamation for setting apart a day of Solemn and Publick Thanksgiving throughout the whole Kingdom," dated June 5th, 1660.

[3] Clothworkers' Hall, in Mincing Lane. The original Hall was burned in the
Great Fire. It will be seen from this entry that Ladies were admitted to the
dinners.

[4] Mr., afterwards Sir Francis Chaplin, from Bury St. Edmund's, Alderman of
Vintry Ward and Clothworker. He was Sheriff in 1668, and Lord Mayor in
1677.

[5] This must either have been in Davenant's "Siege of Rhodes," acted at Rut-
land House in 1656, or in the same author's "Cruelty of the Spaniards in
Peru," acted at the Cockpit in 1658. It is unfortunate that the Diarist does not
tell us who it was that sang behind the scenes.

[6] Dennis Gauden, Victualler to the Navy, subsequently knighted while sheriff
of London: the large house at Clapham, in which Pepys died, was built by
him, and intended as a palace for the Bishops of Winchester; his brother, Dr.
John Gauden, then expecting to be translated from Exeter to that See, but he
was promoted to Worcester. Sir Dennis was ultimately ruined, and his villa
purchased by William Hewer.

[7] Daniel Rawlinson kept the Mitre in Fenchurch Street, and there is a farthing token of his extant, "At the Mitetr in Fenchurch Streete, D. M. R." The
initials stand for Daniel and Margaret Rawlinson (See "Boyne's Trade
Tokens," ed. Williamson, vol. i., 1889, p. 595). In "Reliquiæ Hearnianæ" (ed.
Bliss, 1869, vol. ii. p. 39) is the following extract from Thomas Rawlinson's
Note Book R.: "Of Daniel Rawlinson, my grandfather, who kept the Mitre
tavern in Fenchurch Street, and of whose being sequestred in the Rump time I
have heard much, the Whiggs tell this, that upon the king's murder he hung
his signe in mourning. He certainly judged right. The honour of the Mitre was
much eclipsed through the loss of so good a parent of the church of England.

his wife, and would have gone to my Aunt Wight,[1] but that her only child, a daughter, died last night. Home and to my Lord, who supped within, and Mr. E. Montagu, Mr. Thos. Crew, and others with him sat up late. I home and to bed.

[29th]. This day or two my maid Jane[2] has been lame, that we cannot tell what to do for want of her. Up and to White Hall, where I got my warrant from the Duke to be Clerk of the Acts. Also I got my Lord's warrant from the Secretary for his honour of Earle of Portsmouth, and Viscount Montagu of Hinchingbroke. So to my Lord, to give him an account of what I had done. Then to Sir Geffery Palmer,[3] to give them to him to have bills drawn upon them, who told me that my Lord must have some good Latinist to make the preamble to his Patent, which must express his late service in the best terms that he can, and he told me in what high flaunting terms Sir J. Greenville[4] had caused his to be done, which he do not like; but that Sir Richard Fanshawe[5] had done General Monk's very well. Back to Westmin-

These rogues say, this endeared him so much to the churchmen that he soon throve amain and got a good estate." Mrs. Rawlinson died of the plague (see August 9th, 1666), and the house was burnt in the Great Fire. Mr. Rawlinson rebuilt the Mitre, and he had the panels of the great room painted with allegorical figures by Isaac Fuller. Daniel was father of Sir Thomas Rawlinson, of whom Thomas Hearne writes (October 1st, 1705): "Sir Thomas Rawlinson is chosen Lord Mayor of London for yᵉ ensueing notwithstanding the great opposition of yᵉ Whigg party" (Hearne's "Collections," ed. Doble, 1885, vol. i. p. 51). The well-known antiquaries, Thomas and Richard Rawlinson, sons of Sir Thomas, were therefore grandsons of Daniel.

[1] Edith Pepys, daughter of Samuel Pepys of Steeple Bumsted (died 1665), married Thomas Wight of Denston, co. Suffolk.

[2] Jane Wayneman.

[3] Sir Geoffrey Palmer, Attorney-General, and Chief Justice of Chester, 1660; created a baronet, 1661. Died 1670.

[4] Sir John Grenville was a cousin of General Monk, and for his services in the cause of the Restoration was created Lord Grenville of Kilkhampton and Biddeford, Viscount Grenville of Lansdown, and Earl of Bath, April 20th, 1661. Died 1701.

[5] Sir Richard Fanshawe, knight and baronet, born at Ware Park, Herts, 1608, secretary to Charles II. at Breda, and after the Restoration M.P. for Cambridge. He negotiated the marriage with Catherine of Braganza. He was a good linguist, and "gave our language," says Campbell, "some of its earliest and most important translations from modern literature." He was appointed ambassador to Spain in 1664, and died at Madrid, 1666.

ster, and meeting Mr. Townsend in the Palace, he and I and another or two went and dined at the Leg there. Then to White Hall, where I was told by Mr. Hutchinson at the Admiralty, that Mr. Barlow,[1] my predecessor, Clerk of the Acts, is yet alive, and coming up to town to look after his place, which made my heart sad a little. At night told my Lord thereof, and he bade me get possession of my Patent; and he would do all that could be done to keep him out. This night my Lord and I looked over the list of the Captains, and marked some that my Lord had a mind to have put out. Home and to bed. Our wench very lame, abed these two days.

[30th]. By times to Sir R. Fanshawe to draw up the preamble to my Lord's Patent. So to my Lord, and with him to White Hall, where I saw a great many fine antique heads of marble, that my Lord Northumberland[2] had given the King. Here meeting with Mr. De Cretz,[3] he looked over many of the pieces in the gallery with me and told me [by] whose hands they were, with great pleasure. Dined at home and Mr. Hawly with me upon six of my pigeons, which my wife has resolved to kill here. This day came Will,[4] my boy, to me; the wench continuing lame, so that my wife could not be longer without somebody to help her. In the afternoon with Sir Edward Walker, at his lodgings by St. Giles Church, for my Lord's pedigree, and carried it to Sir R. Fanshawe. To Mr. Crew's, and there took money and paid Mrs. Anne, Mrs. Jemima's maid, off quite, and so she went away and another came to her. To White Hall with Mr. Moore, where I met with a letter from Mr. Turner, offering me £150 to be joined with me in my patent, and to advise me how to improve the ad-

[1] Thomas Barlow was originally in the service of Algernon, Earl of Northumberland, and was appointed by him Muster Master of the Fleet under his command in 1636. He was appointed in 1638 joint Clerk of the Acts (with Dennis Fleming).

[2] Algernon Percy, tenth Earl of Northumberland, Lord High Admiral to Charles I.

[3] Thomas De Critz was Serjeant Painter to Charles I., and some account of him is given in Walpole's "Anecdotes of Painting." This Mr. De Cretz, who was probably his son, was a copier of pictures.

[4] William Wayneman was constantly getting into trouble, and Pepys had to cane him. He was dismissed on July 7th, 1663.

vantage of my place, and to keep off Barlow. To my Lord's till late at night, and so home.

[July 1st]. This morning came home my fine Camlett cloak,[1] with gold buttons, and a silk suit, which cost me much money, and I pray God to make me able to pay for it. I went to the cook's and got a good joint of meat, and my wife and I dined at home alone. In the afternoon to the Abbey, where a good sermon by a stranger, but no Common Prayer yet. After sermon called in at Mrs. Crisp's, where I saw Mynheer Roder,[2] that is to marry Sam Hartlib's sister,[3] a great fortune for her to light on, she being worth nothing in the world. Here I also saw Mrs. Greenlife, who is come again to live in Axe Yard with her new husband Mr. Adams. Then to my Lord's, where I staid a while. So to see for Mr. Creed to speak about getting a copy of Barlow's patent. To my Lord's, where late at night comes Mr. Morland, whom I left prating with my Lord, and so home.

[2nd]. Infinite of business that my heart and head and all were full. Met with purser Washington, with whom and a lady, a friend of his, I dined at the Bell Tavern[4] in King Street, but the rogue had no more manners than to invite me and to let me pay my club. All the afternoon with my Lord, going up and down the town; at seven at night he went home, and there the principal Officers of the Navy,[5] among the rest myself was reckoned one.

---

[1] Camlet was a mixed stuff of wool and silk. It was very expensive, and later Pepys gave £24 for a suit. (See June 1st, 1664.)

[2] John Roder, knighted August 5th, 1660. Le Neve calls him Roth, and says he was of Utrecht.

[3] Nan Hartlib.

[4] The Bell Tavern in King Street, Westminster, was of some antiquity. It is mentioned in 1466 among Sir John Howard's expenses, and was famous in the reign of Queen Anne. Here the October Club met.

[5] A list of the Officers of the Admiralty, May 31st, 1660.

From a MS. in the Pepysian Library in Pepys's own handwriting.

His Royal Highness James, Duke of York, Lord High Admiral.
Sir George Carteret, Treasurer.
Sir Robert Slingsby, (soon after) Comptroller.
Sir William Batten, Surveyor.
Samuel Pepys, Esq., Clerk of the Acts.
John, Lord Berkeley [of Stratton], ⎫
Sir William Penn,   ⎬ Commissioners.
Peter Pett, Esq.   ⎭   —B.

We had order to meet to-morrow, to draw up such an order of the Council as would put us into action before our patents were passed. At which my heart was glad. At night supped with my Lord, he and I together, in the great dining-room alone by ourselves, the first time I ever did it in London. Home to bed, my maid pretty well again.

[3d]. All the morning the Officers and Commissioners of the Navy, we met at Sir G. Carteret's[1] chamber, and agreed upon orders for the Council to supersede the old ones, and empower us to act. Dined with Mr. Stephens, the Treasurer's man of the Navy, and Mr. Turner, to whom I offered £50 out of my own purse for one year, and the benefit of a Clerk's allowance beside, which he thanked me for; but I find he hath some design yet in his head, which I could not think of. In the afternoon my heart was quite pulled down, by being told that Mr. Barlow was to enquire to-day for Mr. Coventry; but at night I met with my Lord, who told me that I need not fear, for he would get me the place against the world. And when I came to W. Howe, he told me that Dr. Petty had been with my Lord, and did tell him that Barlow was a sickly man, and did not intend to execute the place himself, which put me in great comfort again. Till 2 in the morning writing letters and things for my Lord to send to sea. So home to my wife to bed.

[4th]. Up very early in the morning and landing my wife at White Friars stairs, I went to the Bridge and so to the Treasurer's of the Navy, with whom I spake about the business of my office, who put me into very good hopes of my business. At his house comes Commissioner Pett, and he and I went to view the house in

---

[1] Sir George Carteret, born 1599, had originally been bred to the sea service, and became Comptroller of the Navy to Charles I., and Governor of Jersey, where he obtained considerable reputation by his gallant defence of that island against the Parliament forces. At the Restoration he was made Vice-Chamberlain to the King, Treasurer of the Navy, and a Privy Councillor, and in 1661 he was elected M.P. for Portsmouth. In 1666 he exchanged the Treasurership of the Navy with the Earl of Anglesea for the Vice-Treasurership of Ireland. He became a Commissioner of the Admiralty in 1673. He continued in favour with Charles II. till his death, January 14th, 1679, in his eightieth year. He married his cousin Elizabeth, daughter of Sir Philip Carteret, Knight of St. Ouen, and had issue three sons and five daughters.

Seething Lane, belonging to the Navy,[1] where I find the worst
very good, and had great fears in my mind that they will shuffle
me out of them, which troubles me. From thence to the Excise
Office[2] in Broad Street, where I received £500 for my Lord, by
appointment of the Treasurer, and went afterwards down with
Mr. Luddyard and drank my morning draft with him and other
officers. Thence to Mr. Backewell's, the goldsmith, where I took
my Lord's £100 in plate for Mr. Secretary Nicholas, and my
own piece of plate, being a state dish and cup in chased work for
Mr. Coventry, cost me above £19. Carried these and the money
by coach to my Lord's at White Hall, and from thence carried
Nicholas's plate to his house and left it there, intending to speak
with him anon. So to Westminster Hall, where meeting with
Mons. L'Impertinent and W. Bowyer, I took them to the Sun
Tavern, and gave them a lobster and some wine, and sat talking
like a fool till 4 o'clock. So to my Lord's, and walking all the afternoon in White Hall Court, in expectation of what shall be done
in the Council as to our business. It was strange to see how all the
people flocked together bare, to see the King looking out of the
Council window. At night my Lord told me how my orders that
I drew last night about giving us power to act, are granted by the
Council. At which he and I were very glad. Home and to bed, my
boy lying in my house this night the first time.

[5th]. This morning my brother Tom brought me my jack-
anapes coat with silver buttons. It rained this morning, which
makes us fear that the glory of this great day will be lost; the
King and Parliament being to be entertained by the City to-day[3]

---

[1] The Navy Office was erected on the site of Lumley House, formerly belonging to the Fratres Sanctæ Crucis (or Crutched Friars), and all business connected with naval concerns was transacted there till its removal to Somerset
House. The ground was afterwards occupied by the East India Company's
warehouses. The civil business of the Admiralty was removed from Somerset
House to Spring Gardens in 1869.

[2] The first Excise Office was in Smithfield, and it was frequently removed to
different parts of London.

[3] "July 5th. His Majesty, the two Dukes, the House of Lords, and the House
of Commons, and the Privy Council, dined at the Guildhall. Every Hall appeared with their colours and streamers to attend His Majesty; the Masters in
gold chains. Twelve pageants in the streets between Temple Bar and Guild-

with great pomp. Mr. Hater[1] was with me to-day, and I agreed with him to be my clerk. Being at White Hall, I saw the King, the Dukes, and all their attendants go forth in the rain to the City, and it bedraggled many a fine suit of clothes. I was forced to walk all the morning in White Hall, not knowing how to get out because of the rain. Met with Mr. Cooling,[2] my Lord Chamberlain's secretary, who took me to dinner among the gentlemen waiters, and after dinner into the wine-cellar. He told me how he had a project for all us Secretaries to join together, and get money by bringing all business into our hands. Thence to the Admiralty, where Mr. Blackburne and I (it beginning to hold up) went and walked an hour or two in the Park, he giving of me light in many things in my way in this office that I go about. And in the evening I got my present of plate carried to Mr. Coventry's. At my Lord's at night comes Dr. Petty to me, to tell me that Barlow had come to town, and other things, which put me into a despair, and I went to bed very sad.

[6th]. In the morning with my Lord at Whitehall, got the order of the Council for us to act. From thence to Westminster Hall, and there met with the Doctor that shewed us so much kindness at the Hague, and took him to the Sun tavern, and drank with him. So to my Lord's and dined with W. Howe and Sarah, thinking it might be the last time that I might dine with them together. In the afternoon my Lord and I, and Mr. Coventry and Sir G. Carteret, went and took possession of the Navy Office, whereby my mind was a little cheered, but my hopes not great. From thence Sir G. Carteret and I to the Treasurer's Office, where he set some things in order. And so home, calling upon Sir Geoffry Palmer, who did give me advice about my patent, which put me

---

hall. Forty brace of bucks were that day spent in the City of London."—Rugge's *Diurnal.*—B.

[1] Thomas Hayter. He remained with Pepys for some time; and by his assistance was made Petty Purveyor of Petty Missions. He succeeded Pepys as Clerk of the Acts in 1673, and in 1679 he was Secretary of the Admiralty, and Comptroller of the Navy from 1680 to 1682. See *ante,* March 10th (note).

[2] Richard Cooling or Coling, A.M., of All Souls College, Secretary to the Earls of Manchester and Arlington when they filled the office of Lord Chamberlain, and a Clerk of the Privy Council in ordinary. There is a mezzotinto print of him in the Pepysian Collection.—B.

to some doubt to know what to do, Barlow being alive. Afterwards called at Mr. Pim's, about getting me a coat of velvet, and he took me to the Half Moon, and the house so full that we staid above half an hour before we could get anything. So to my Lord's, where in the dark W. Howe and I did sing extemporys, and I find by use that we are able to sing a bass and a treble pretty well. So home, and to bed.

[7th]. To my Lord, one with me to buy a Clerk's place, and I did demand £100. To the Council Chamber, where I took an order for the advance of the salaries of the officers of the Navy, and I find mine to be raised to £350 per annum.[1] Thence to the Change, where I bought two fine prints of Ragotti from Rubens, and afterwards dined with my Uncle and Aunt Wight, where her sister Cox and her husband were. After that to Mr. Rawlinson's with my uncle, and thence to the Navy Office, where I began to take an inventory of the papers, and goods, and books of the office. To my Lord's, late writing letters. So home to bed.

[8th]. (Lord's day). To White Hall chapel, where I got in with ease by going before the Lord Chancellor with Mr. Kipps. Here I heard very good music, the first time that ever I remember to have heard the organs and singing-men in surplices in my life.[2]

---

[1] This salary was in place of the ancient fee out of the Exchequer of £33 6s. 8d.

[2] During the Commonwealth organs were destroyed all over the country, and the following is the title of the Ordinances under which this destruction took place: "Two Ordinances of the Lords and Commons assembled in Parliament, for the speedy demolishing of all organs, images, and all matters of superstitious monuments in all Cathedrals and Collegiate or Parish Churches and Chapels throughout the Kingdom of England and the dominion of Wales; the better to accomplish the blessed reformation so happily begun, and to remove all offences and things illegal in the worship of God. Dated May 9th, 1644." When at the period of the Restoration music again obtained its proper place in the services of the Church, there was much work for the organ builders. According to Dr. Rimbault ("Hopkins on the Organ," 1855, p. 74), it was more than fifty years after the Restoration when our parish churches began commonly to be supplied with organs. Drake says, in his "Eboracum" (published in 1733), that at that date only one parish church in the city of York possessed an organ. Bernard Schmidt, better known as "Father Smith," came to England from Germany at the time of the Restoration, and he it was who built the organ at the Chapel Royal. He was in high favour with Charles II., who allowed him apartments in Whitehall Palace.

The Bishop of Chichester[1] preached before the King, and made a great flattering sermon, which I did not like that Clergy should meddle with matters of state. Dined with Mr. Luellin and Salisbury[2] at a cook's shop. Home, and staid all the afternoon with my wife till after sermon. There till Mr. Fairebrother came to call us out to my father's to supper. He told me how he had perfectly procured me to be made Master in Arts by proxy,[3] which did somewhat please me, though I remember my cousin Roger Pepys was the other day persuading me from it. While we were at supper came Wm. Howe to supper to us, and after supper went home to bed.

[9th]. All the morning at Sir G. Palmer's advising about getting my bill drawn. From thence to the Navy office, where in the afternoon we met and sat, and there I begun to sign bills in the Office the first time. From thence Captain Holland and Mr. Browne of Harwich took me to a tavern and did give me a collation. From thence to the Temple to further my bills being done, and so home to my Lord, and thence to bed.

[10th]. This day I put on first my new silk suit, the first that ever I wore in my life. This morning came Nan Pepys' husband Mr. Hall to see me being lately come to town. I had never seen him before. I took him to the Swan tavern with Mr. Eglin and there drank our morning draft. Home, and called my wife, and took her to Dr. Clodius's to a great wedding of Nan Hartlib to Mynheer Roder, which was kept at Goring House[4] with very great

---

[1] Henry King, Dean of Rochester, advanced to the See of Chichester, February, 1641-42. Died September 30th, 1669, in the seventy-seventh year of his age.

[2] Salisbury, portrait painter, not mentioned by Walpole.

[3] The Grace which passed the University, on this occasion, is preserved in Kennett's Chronicle, and commenced as follows:—"Cum Sam. Pepys, Coll. Magd. Inceptor in Artibus in Regiâ Classe existat e Secretis, exindeq. apud mare adeo occupatissimus ut Comitiis proximè futuris interesse non possit; placet vobis ut dictus S. P. admissionem suam necnon creationem recipiat ad gradum Magistri in Artibus sub personâ Timothei Wellfit, Inceptoris, &c. &c. —June 26, 1660." See post, August 14th, 1660.—B.

[4] Goring House in St. James's Park, the town residence of George, Lord Goring, Earl of Norwich. It occupied the site of Buckingham House, afterwards Buckingham Palace. Goring House was burnt in 1674, at which time the Earl of Arlington was living there.

state, cost, and noble company. But, among all the beauties there, my wife was thought the greatest. After dinner I left the company, and carried my wife to Mrs. Turner's. I went to the Attorney-General's, and had my bill which cost me seven pieces.[1] I called my wife, and set her home. And finding my Lord in White Hall garden, I got him to go to the Secretary's, which he did, and desired the dispatch of his and my bills to be signed by the King. His bill is to be Earl of Sandwich, Viscount Hinchingbroke, and Baron of St. Neot's.[2] Home, with my mind pretty quiet: not returning, as I said I would, to see the bride put to bed.

[11th]. With Sir W. Pen by water to the Navy office, where we met, and dispatched business. And that being done, we went all to dinner to the Dolphin,[3] upon Major Brown's invitation. After that to the office again, where I was vexed, and so was Commissioner Pett, to see a busy fellow come to look out the best lodgings for my Lord Barkley,[4] and the combining between him and Sir W. Pen; and, indeed, was troubled much at it. Home to White

[1] That would be £1 13s. 3d. The rate at which the Mexico or Seville piece of eight was to be received was 4s. 9d.

[2] The motive for Sir Edward Montagu's so suddenly altering his intended title is not explained; probably, the change was adopted as a compliment to the town of Sandwich, off which the Fleet was lying before it sailed to bring Charles from Scheveling. Montagu had also received marked attentions from Sir John Boys and other principal men at Sandwich; and it may be recollected, as an additional reason, that one or both of the seats for that borough have usually been placed at the disposal of the Admiralty. The title of Portsmouth was given, in 1673, *for her life,* to the celebrated Louise de Querouaille, and becoming extinct with her, was, in 1743, conferred upon John Wallop, Viscount Lymington, the ancestor of the present Earl of Portsmouth.—B.

[3] Pepys was a frequent visitor to the Dolphin, which was conveniently situated in Tower Street. There is a farthing token of this tavern which is dated 1650 (see "Boyne's Trade Tokens," ed. Williamson, vol. i., 1889, p. 779).

[4] Sir John Berkeley, son of Sir Maurice Berkeley of Bruton, co. Somerset, knighted at Berwick in 1637-8. He was distinguished as a royalist officer in the Civil Wars, and created Baron Berkeley of Stratton in 1658 by letters patent dated at Brussels. At the Restoration he was appointed an Extra Commissioner of the Navy, which office he held until December, 1664; sworn in the Privy Council in 1663, and appointed Lord Lieutenant of Ireland in 1670. He went as ambassador to France in 1674. He built, in 1665, a mansion in Piccadilly, at a cost of £30,000, called Berkeley House, which was destroyed by fire in 1733, when in the possession of the Duke of Devonshire, and Devonshire House now occupies its site. He died in 1678.

THE EARL OF SANDWICH

Hall, and took out my bill signed by the King, and carried it to Mr. Watkins of the Privy Seal to be despatched there, and going home to take a cap, I borrowed a pair of sheets of Mr. Howe, and by coach went to the Navy office, and lay (Mr. Hater, my clerk, with me) at Commissioner Willoughby's[1] house, where I was received by him very civilly and slept well.

[12th]. Up early and by coach to White Hall with Commissioner Pett, where, after we had talked with my Lord, I went to the Privy Seal and got my bill perfected there, and at the Signet: and then to the House of Lords, and met with Mr. Kipps, who directed me to Mr. Beale to get my patent engrossed; but he not having time to get it done in Chancery-hand, I was forced to run all up and down Chancery-lane, and the Six Clerks' Office,[2] but could find none that could write the hand, that were at leisure. And so in a despair went to the Admiralty, where we met the first time there, my Lord Montagu,[3] my Lord Barkley, Mr. Coventry, and all the rest of the principal Officers and Commissioners, [except] only the Controller, who is not yet chosen. At night to Mr. Kipps's lodgings, but not finding him, I went to Mr. Spong's and there I found him and got him to come to me to my Lord's lodgings at 11 o'clock of night, when I got him to take my bill to write it himself (which was a great providence that he could do it) against to-morrow morning. I late writing letters to

---

[1] Willoughby's name does not occur in the list of "Naval Commissioners, 1660-1760, by Sir George Jackson," privately printed by Sir G. F. Duckett in 1889.

[2] The Six Clerks' Office was in Chancery Lane, near the Holborn end. The business of the office was to enroll commissions, pardons, patents, warrants, &c., that had passed the Great Seal; also other business in Chancery. "In the early history of the Court of Chancery, the Six Clerks and their under-clerks appear to have acted as the attorneys of the suitors. As business increased, these under-clerks became a distinct body, and were recognized by the court under the denomination of 'sworn clerks,' or 'clerks in court.' The advance of commerce, with its consequent accession of wealth, so multiplied the subjects requiring the judgment of a Court of Equity, that the limits of a public office were found wholly inadequate to supply a sufficient number of officers to conduct the business of the suitors. Hence originated the 'Solicitors' of the Court of Chancery." See Smith's "Chancery Practice," p. 62, 3rd edit. The "Six Clerks" were abolished by act of Parliament, 5 Vict. c. 5.

[3] Edward, second Lord Montagu of Boughton. He died 1683.

sea by the post, and so home to bed. In great trouble because I heard at Mr. Beale's to-day that Barlow had been there and said that he would make a stop in the business.

[13th]. Up early, the first day that I put on my black camlett coat with silver buttons. To Mr. Spong, whom I found in his night-gown writing of my patent, and he had done as far as he could "for that &c." by 8 o'clock. It being done, we carried it to Worcester House[1] to the Chancellor, where Mr. Kipps (a strange providence that he should now be in a condition to do me a kindness, which I never thought him capable of doing for me), got me the Chancellor's recepi to my bill; and so carried it to Mr. Beale for a dockett; but he was very angry, and unwilling to do it, because he said it was ill writ (because I had got it writ by another hand, and not by him); but by much importunity I got Mr. Spong to go to his office and make an end of my patent; and in the mean time Mr. Beale to be preparing my dockett, which being done, I did give him two pieces, after which it was strange how civil and tractable he was to me. From thence I went to the Navy office, where we despatched much business, and resolved of the houses for the Officers and Commissioners, which I was glad of, and I got leave to have a door made me into the leads. From thence, much troubled in mind about my patent, I went to Mr. Beale again, who had now finished my patent and made it ready for the Seal, about an hour after I went to meet him at the Chancellor's. So I went away towards Westminster, and in my way met with Mr. Spong, and went with him to Mr. Lilly and ate some bread and cheese, and drank with him, who still would be giving me council of getting my patent out, for fear of another change, and my Lord Montagu's fall. After that to Worcester House, where by Mr. Kipps's means, and my pressing in General Montagu's name to the Chancellor, I did, beyond all expectation, get my seal passed; and while it was doing in one room, I was forced to keep Sir G. Carteret (who by chance met me there, ignorant of my business) in talk, while it was a doing. Went

---

[1] The Earls of Worcester had a large house in the Strand between Durham Place and the Savoy, the site of which is now marked by Beaufort Buildings, which Lord Clarendon rented while his own mansion was building.

home and brought my wife with me into London, and some
money, with which I paid Mr. Beale £9 in all, and took my
patent of him and went to my wife again, whom I had left in a
coach at the door of Hinde Court, and presented her with my
patent at which she was overjoyed; so to the Navy office, and
showed her my house, and were both mightily pleased at all
things there, and so to my business. So home with her, leaving
her at her mother's door. I to my Lord's, where I dispatched an
order for a ship to fetch Sir R. Honywood home, for which I got
two pieces of my Lady Honywood by young Mr. Powell. Late
writing letters; and great doings of music at the next house,
which was Whally's; the King and Dukes there with Madame
Palmer,[1] a pretty woman that they have a fancy to, to make her
husband a cuckold. Here at the old door that did go into his lodgings, my Lord, I, and W. Howe, did stand listening a great while
to the music. After that home to bed. This day I should have been
at Guildhall to have borne witness for my brother Hawly against
Black Collar, but I could not, at which I was troubled. To bed
with the greatest quiet of mind that I have had a great while,
having ate nothing but a bit of bread and cheese at Lilly's to-
day, and a bit of bread and butter after I was a-bed.

[14th]. Up early and advised with my wife for the putting of
all our things in a readiness to be sent to our new house. To my
Lord's, where he was in bed very late. So with Major Tollhurst[2]
and others to Harper's, and I sent for my barrel of pickled oysters
and there ate them; while we were doing so, comes in Mr. Pagan

[1] Barbara Villiers, only child of William, second Viscount Grandison, born
November, 1640, married April 14th, 1659, to Roger Palmer, created Earl of
Castlemaine, 1661. She became the King's mistress soon after the Restoration,
and was in 1670 made Baroness Nonsuch, Countess of Southampton, and
Duchess of Cleveland. She had six children by the King, one of them being
created Duke of Grafton, and the eldest son succeeding her as Duke of Cleveland. She subsequently married Beau Fielding, who she prosecuted for big-
amy. She died October 9th, 1709, aged sixty-nine. Her life was written by
G. Steinman Steinman, and privately printed 1871, with addenda 1874, and
second addenda 1878.

[2] Major Tollhurst was an old friend of Pepys's, and is mentioned again on
January 9th, 1662-63.

Fisher,[1] the poet, and promises me what he had long ago done, a book in praise of the King of France, with my armes, and a dedication to me very handsome. After him comes Mr. Sheply come from sea yesterday, whom I was glad to see that he may ease me of the trouble of my Lord's business. So to my Lord's, where I staid doing his business and taking his commands. After that to Westminster Hall, where I paid all my debts in order to my going away from hence. Here I met with Mr. Eglin, who would needs take me to the Leg in King Street and gave me a dish of meat to dinner; and so I sent for Mons. L'Impertinent, where we sat long and were merry. After that parted, and I took Mr. Butler [Mons. L'Impertinent] with me into London by coach and shewed him my house at the Navy Office, and did give order for the laying in coals. So into Fenchurch Street, and did give him a glass of wine at Rawlinson's, and was trimmed in the street. So to my Lord's late writing letters, and so home, where I found my wife had packed up all her goods in the house fit for a removal. So to bed.

[15th]. Lay long in bed to recover my rest. Going forth met with Mr. Sheply, and went and drank my morning draft with him at Wilkinson's, and my brother Spicer.[2] After that to Westminster Abbey, and in Henry the Seventh's Chappell heard part of a sermon, the first that ever I heard there. To my Lord's and dined all alone at the table with him. After dinner he and I alone fell to discourse, and I find him plainly to be a sceptic in all things of

---

[1] Payne Fisher, who styled himself Paganus Piscator, was born in 1616, in Dorsetshire, and removed from Hart Hall, Oxford, of which he had been a commoner, to Magdalene College, Cambridge, in 1634, and there took a degree of B.A., and first discovered a turn for poetry. He was afterwards a captain in the King's service at Marston Moor fight; but, leaving his command, employed his pen against the cause which he had supported with his sword, and became a favourite of Cromwell's. After the King's return, he obtained a scanty subsistence by flattering men in power, and was frequently imprisoned for debt. He borrowed from Pepys, see *post*, 28th of this same month. He died, 1693, in the Fleet Prison (Harl. MS. 1460). He published several poems, chiefly in Latin, and, in 1682, printed a book of Heraldry, with the arms of such of the gentry as he had waited upon with presentation copies. He was a man of talents, but vain, unsteady, and conceited, and a great time-server.—B.

[2] Jack Spicer, brother clerk of the Privy Seal.

religion, and to make no great matter of anything therein, but
to be a perfect Stoic. In the afternoon to Henry the Seventh's
Chappell, where I heard service and a sermon there, and after
that meeting W. Bowyer there, he and I to the Park, and walked
a good while till night. So to Harper's and drank together, and
Captain Stokes came to us and so I fell into discourse of buying
paper at the first hand in my office, and the Captain promised me
to buy it for me in France. After that to my Lord's lodgings,
where I wrote some business and so home. My wife at home all
the day, she having no clothes out, all being packed up yesterday.
For this month I have wholly neglected anything of news, and so
have beyond belief been ignorant how things go, but now by my
patent my mind is in some quiet, which God keep. I was not at
my father's to-day, I being afraid to go for fear he should still
solicit me to speak to my Lord for a place in the Wardrobe, which
I dare not do, because of my own business yet. My wife and I
mightily pleased with our new house that we hope to have. My
patent has cost me a great deal of money, about £40, which is
the only thing at present which do trouble me much. In the afternoon to Henry the Seventh's chapel, where I heard a sermon and
spent (God forgive me) most of my time in looking upon Mrs.
Butler. After that with W. Bowyer to walk in the Park. Afterwards to my Lord's lodgings, and so home to bed, having not been
at my father's to-day.

[16th]. This morning it proved very rainy weather so that I
could not remove my goods to my house. I to my office and did
business there, and so home, it being then sunrise, but by the
time that I got to my house it began to rain again, so that I could
not carry my goods by cart as I would have done. After that to
my Lord's and so home and to bed.

[17th]. This morning (as indeed all the mornings now-a-days)
much business at my Lord's. There came to my house before I
went out Mr. Barlow, an old consumptive man, and fair condi-
tioned, with whom I did discourse a great while, and after much
talk I did grant him what he asked, viz., £50 per annum, if my
salary be not increased, and £100 per annum, in case it be to

£350, at which he was very well pleased to be paid as I received my money and not otherwise. Going to my Lord's I found my Lord had got a great cold and kept his bed, and so I brought him to my Lord's bedside, and he and I did agree together to this purpose what I should allow him. That done and the day proving fair I went home and got all my goods packed up and sent away, and my wife and I and Mrs. Hunt went by coach, overtaking the carts a-drinking in the Strand. Being come to my house and set in the goods, and at night sent my wife and Mrs. Hunt to buy something for supper; they bought a Quarter of Lamb, and so we ate it, but it was not half roasted. Will,[1] Mr. Blackburne's nephew, is so obedient, that I am greatly glad of him. At night he and I and Mrs. Hunt home by water to Westminster. I to my Lord, and after having done some business with him in his chamber in the Nursery, which has been now his chamber since he came from sea, I went on foot with a link-boy to my home, where I found my wife in bed and Jane washing the house, and Will the boy sleeping, and a great deal of sport I had before I could wake him. I to bed the first night that I ever lay here with my wife.

[18th]. This morning the carpenter made an end of my door out of my chamber upon the leads. This morning we met at the office: I dined at my house in Seething Lane, and after that, going about 4 o'clock to Westminster, I met with Mr. Carter and Mr. Cooke coming to see me in a coach, and so I returned home. I did also meet with Mr. Pierce, the surgeon, with a porter with him, with a barrel of Lemons, which my man Burr sends me from sea. I took all these people home to my house and did give them some drink, and after them comes Mr. Sheply, and after a little stay we all went by water to Westminster as far as the New

---

[1] William Hewer, of whose family little more is known than that his father died of the plague, September 14th, 1665. He was first the clerk, and afterwards the faithful friend of Pepys, who died in his house at Clapham, previously the residence of Sir Dennis Gauden. He was appointed Deputy Judge Advocate of the Fleet in 1677, and Commissioner of the Navy in 1685, and elected M.P. for Yarmouth, Isle of Wight, in 1685. He was also Treasurer for Tangier. Mr. Hewer was buried in the old church at Clapham, where a large monument of marble, with his bust in alto-relievo, erected to his memory, was, on the rebuilding of the church, placed outside.

Exchange.[1] Thence to my Lord about business, and being in talk
in comes one with half a buck from Hinchinbroke, and it smell-
ing a little strong my Lord did give it me (though it was as good
as any could be). I did carry it to my mother, where I had not
been a great while, and indeed had no great mind to go, because
my father did lay upon me continually to do him a kindness at
the Wardrobe, which I could not do because of my own business
being so fresh with my Lord. But my father was not at home, and
so I did leave the venison with her to dispose of as she pleased.
After that home, where W. Hewer now was, and did lie this
night with us, the first night. My mind very quiet, only a little
trouble I have for the great debts which I have still upon me to
the Secretary, Mr. Kipps, and Mr. Spong for my patent.

[19th]. I did lie late a-bed. I and my wife by water, landed her
at Whitefriars with her boy with an iron of our new range which
is already broke and my wife will have changed, and many other
things she has to buy with the help of my father to-day. I to my
Lord and found him in bed. This day I received my commission
to swear people the oath of allegiance and supremacy delivered
me by my Lord.[2] After talk with my Lord I went to Westminster
Hall, where I took Mr. Michell and his wife, and Mrs. Murford
we sent for afterwards, to the Dog Tavern, where I did give them
a dish of anchovies and olives and paid for all, and did talk of our
old discourse when we did use to talk of the King, in the time of
the Rump, privately; after that to the Admiralty Office, in White
Hall, where I staid and writ my last observations for these four
days last past. Great talk of the difference between the Episcopal
and Presbyterian Clergy, but I believe it will come to nothing.
So home and to bed.

[20th]. We sat at the office this morning, Sir W. Batten and Mr.

---

[1] The New Exchange on the south side of the Strand, built on the site of the
stables of Durham House. The first stone was laid June 10th, 1608, and the
new building was named by James I. "Britain's Burse." It was a much
frequented place after the Restoration, and the destruction of the Royal
Exchange in the Great Fire caused it much prosperity for a time. It was taken
down in 1737.
[2] The oath of allegiance was printed on July 2nd.

Pett being upon a survey to Chatham. This morning I sent my wife to my father's and he is to give me £5 worth of pewter. After we rose at the office, I went to my father's, where my Uncle Fenner and all his crew and Captain Holland and his wife and my wife were at dinner at a venison pasty of the venison that I did give my mother the other day. I did this time show so much coldness to W. Joyce that I believe all the table took notice of it. After that to Westminster about my Lord's business and so home, my Lord having not been well these two or three days, and I hear that Mr. Barnwell[1] at Hinchinbroke is fallen sick again. Home and to bed.

[21st]. This morning Mr. Barlow had appointed for me to bring him what form I would have the agreement between him and me to pass, which I did to his lodgings at the Golden Eagle in the new street[2] between Fetter Lane and Shoe Lane, where he liked it very well, and I from him went to get Mr. Spong to engross it in duplicates. To my Lord and spoke to him about the business of the Privy Seal for me to be sworn, though I got nothing by it, but to do Mr. Moore a kindness, which he did give me a good answer to. Went to the Six Clerks' office to Mr. Spong for the writings, and dined with him at a club at the next door, where we had three voices to sing catches. So to my house to write letters and so to Whitehall about business of my Lord's concerning his creation,[3] and so home and to bed.

[22nd]. Lord's day. All this last night it had rained hard. My brother Tom came this morning the first time to see me, and I paid him all that I owe my father to this day. Afterwards I went out and looked into several churches, and so to my uncle Fenner's, whither my wife was got before me, and we, my father and mother, and all the Joyces, and my aunt Bell, whom I had not seen many a year before. After dinner to White Hall (my wife to church with K. Joyce), where I find my Lord at home, and walked in the garden with him, he showing me all the respect

---

[1] Robert Barnwell. He died in 1662. See *post*, June 4th, 1662.
[2] Still retains the name New Street.
[3] As Earl of Sandwich.

that can be. I left him and went to walk in the Park, where great endeavouring to get into the inward Park,[1] but could not get in; one man was basted by the keeper, for carrying some people over on his back through the water. Afterwards to my Lord's, where I staid and drank with Mr. Sheply, having first sent to get a pair of oars. It was the first time that ever I went by water on the Lord's day. Home, and at night and a chapter read; and I read prayers out of the Common Prayer Book, the first time that ever I read prayers in this house. So to bed.

[23rd]. This morning Mr. Barlow comes to me, and he and I went forth to a scrivener in Fenchurch Street, whom we found sick of the gout in bed, and signed and sealed our agreement before him. He urged to have these words (in consideration whereof) to be interlined, which I granted, though against my will. Met this morning at the office, and afterwards Mr. Barlow by appointment came and dined with me, and both of us very pleasant and pleased. After dinner to my Lord, who took me to Secretary Nicholas, and there before him and Secretary Morris,[2] my Lord and I upon our knees together took our oaths of Allegiance and Supremacy; and the Oath of the Privy Seal, of which I was much glad, though I am not likely to get anything by it at present; but I do desire it, for fear of a turn-out of our office. That done and my Lord gone from me, I went with Mr. Cooling and his brother, and Sam Hartlibb, little Jennings and some others to the King's Head Tavern at Charing Cross, where after drinking I took boat and so home, where we supped merrily among ourselves (our little boy proving a droll) and so after prayers to bed. This day my Lord had heard that Mr. Barnwell was dead, but it is not so yet, though he be very ill. I was troubled all this day with Mr. Cooke, being willing to do him good, but my mind is so taken up with my own business that I cannot.

[24th]. To White Hall, where I did acquaint Mr. Watkins with my being sworn into the Privy Seal, at which he was much

---

[1] This is still railed off from St. James's Park, and called the Enclosure.
[2] Sir William Morrice, born November 6th, 1602, at Exeter, Secretary of State from 1660 to 1668. He died December 12th, 1676. He was kinsman to General Monk.

troubled, but put it up and did offer me a kinsman of his to be my clerk, which I did give him some hope of, though I never intend it. In the afternoon I spent much time in walking in White Hall Court with Mr. Bickerstaffe,[1] who was very glad of my Lord's being sworn, because of his business with his brother Baron,[1] which is referred to my Lord Chancellor, and to be ended to-morrow. Baron had got a grant beyond sea, to come in before the reversionary of the Privy Seal. This afternoon Mr. Mathews came to me, to get a certificate of my Lord's and my being sworn, which I put in some forwardness, and so home and to bed.

[25th]. In the morning at the office, and after that down to Whitehall, where I met with Mr. Creed, and with him and a Welsh schoolmaster, a good scholar but a very pedagogue, to the ordinary at the Leg in King Street.[2] I got my certificate of my Lord's and my being sworn. This morning my Lord took leave of the House of Commons, and had the thanks of the House for his great services to his country.[3] In the afternoon (but this is a mistake, for it was yesterday in the afternoon) Monsieur L'Im-pertinent and I met and I took him to the Sun and drank with him, and in the evening going away we met his mother and sisters and father coming from the Gatehouse,[4] where they lodge, where I did the first time salute them all, and very pretty Ma-dame Frances[5] is indeed. After that very late home and called in Tower Street, and there at a barber's was trimmed the first time. Home and to bed.

[26th]. Early to White Hall, thinking to have a meeting of my Lord and the principal officers, but my Lord could not, it being the day that he was to go and be admitted in the House of Lords, his patent being done, which he presented upon his knees to the

[1] They were both clerks of the Privy Seal.
[2] My dining with Mr. Creed and seeing the Butlers ought to be placed in yesterday's account, it being put here by mistake.—*Pepys.*
[3] In the Journals this is stated to have taken place July 24th.
[4] The Gatehouse at Westminster was a prison. Perhaps they were friends of the keeper.
[5] Frances Butler, the beauty.

Speaker; and so it was read in the House, and he took his place.[1]
I at the Privy Seal Office with Mr. Hooker, who brought me acquainted with Mr. Crofts of the Signet, and I invited them to a
dish of meat at the Leg in King Street, and so we dined there and
I paid for all and had very good light given me as to my employment there. Afterwards to Mr. Pierce's, where I should have
dined but I could not, but found Mr. Sheply and W. Howe there.
After we had drunk hard we parted, and I went away and
met Dr. Castle, who is one of the Clerks of the Privy Seal, and
told him how things were with my Lord and me, which he
received very gladly. I was this day told how Baron against all
expectation and law has got the place of Bickerstaffe, and so I
question whether he will not lay claim to wait the next month,
but my Lord tells me that he will stand for it. In the evening I
met with T. Doling, who carried me to St. James's Fair,[2] and
there meeting with W. Symons and his wife, and Luellin, and D.
Scobell's wife and cousin, we went to Wood's at the Pell Mell[3]
(our old house for clubbing), and there we spent till 10 at night,
at which time I sent to my Lord's for my clerk Will to come to
me, and so by link home to bed. Where I found Commissioner
Willoughby had sent for all his things away out of my bedchamber, which is a little disappointment, but it is better than pay too
dear for them.

[27th]. The last night Sir W. Batten and Sir W. Pen came to
their houses at the office. Met this morning and did business till
noon. Dined at home and from thence to my Lord's where Will,
my clerk, and I were all the afternoon making up my accounts,

---

[1] The Earl of Manchester was chosen Speaker of the House of Lords. See *ante*,
April 26th, 1660.

[2] August, 1661: "This year the Fair, called St. James's Fair, was kept the full
appointed time, being a fortnight; but during that time many lewd and infamous persons were by his Majesty's express command to the Lord Chamberlain, and his Lordship's direction to Robert Nelson, Esq., committed to the
House of Correction."—Rugge's *Diurnal*. St. James's fair was held first in the
open space near St. James's Palace, and afterwards in St. James's Market. It
was prohibited by the Parliament in 1651, but revived at the Restoration. It
was, however, finally suppressed before the close of the reign of Charles II.

[3] This is one of the earliest references to Pall Mall as an inhabited street, and
also one of the earliest uses of the word clubbing.

which we had done by night, and I find myself worth about
£100 after all my expenses. At night I sent to W. Bowyer to
bring me £100, being that he had in his hands of my Lord's in
keeping, out of which I paid Mr. Sheply all that remained due to
my Lord upon my balance, and took the rest home with me late
at night. We got a coach, but the horses were tired and could not
carry us farther than St. Dunstan's. So we 'light and took a link
and so home weary to bed.

[28th]. Early in the morning rose, and a boy brought me a letter from Poet Fisher, who tells me that he is upon a panegyrique
of the King, and desired to borrow a piece of me; and I sent him
half a piece.[1] To Westminster, and there dined with Mr. Sheply
and W. Howe, afterwards meeting with Mr. Henson, who had
formerly had the brave clock that went with bullets (which is
now taken away from him by the King, it being his goods).[2] I
went with him to the Swan Tavern and sent for Mr. Butler, who
was now all full of his high discourse in praise of Ireland, whither
he and his whole family are going by Coll. Dillon's persuasion,
but so many lies I never heard in praise of anything as he told
of Ireland. So home late at night and to bed.

[29th]. Lord's day. I and my boy Will to Whitehall, and I with
my Lord to White Hall Chappell, where I heard a cold sermon
of the Bishop of Salisbury's,[3] and the ceremonies did not please

---

[1] Half a piece was valued at 2s. 4½d., see *ante*, July 10th.

[2] Some clocks are still made with a small ball, or bullet, on an inclined plane,
which turns every minute. The King's clocks probably dropped bullets. Gains-
borough the painter had a brother who was a dissenting minister at Henley-
on-Thames, and possessed a strong genius for mechanics. He invented a clock
of a very peculiar construction, which, after his death, was deposited in the
British Museum. It told the hour by a little bell, and was kept in motion by a
leaden bullet, which dropped from a spiral reservoir at the top of the clock,
into a little ivory bucket. This was so contrived as to discharge it at the bottom, and by means of a counter-weight was carried up to the top of the clock,
where it received another bullet, which was discharged as the former. This
seems to have been an attempt at the perpetual motion.—*Gentleman's Magazine*, 1785, p. 931.—B.

[3] Brian Duppa, born March 10th, 1588-9, tutor to the Prince of Wales, afterwards Charles II., successively Bishop of Chichester, Salisbury, and Winchester. Died March 26th, 1662.

me, they do so overdo them. My Lord went to dinner at Kensington with my Lord Camden.[1] So I dined and took Mr. Birfett, my Lord's chaplain, and his friend along with me, with Mr. Sheply at my Lord's. In the afternoon with Dick Vines and his brother Payton, we walked to Lisson Green and Marybone[2] and back again, and finding my Lord at home I got him to look over my accounts, which he did approve of and signed them, and so we are even to this day. Of this I was glad, and do think myself worth clear money about £120. Home late, calling in at my father's without stay. To bed.

[30th]. Sat at our office to-day, and my father came this day the first time to see us at my new office. And Mrs. Crisp by chance came in and sat with us, looked over our house and advised about the furnishing of it. This afternoon I got my £50, due to me for my first quarter's salary as Secretary to my Lord, paid to Tho. Hater for me, which he received and brought home to me, of which I am full glad. To Westminster and among other things met with Mr. Moore, and took him and his friend, a bookseller of Paul's Churchyard, to the Rhenish Winehouse, and drinking there the sword-bearer of London (Mr. Man) came to ask for us, with whom we sat late, discoursing about the worth of my office of Clerk of the Acts, which he hath a mind to buy, and I asked four years' purchase. We are to speak more of it to-morrow. Home on foot, and seeing him at home at Butler's merry, he lent me a torch, which Will carried, and so home.

[31st]. To White Hall, where my Lord and the principal officers met, and had a great discourse about raising of money for the Navy, which is in very sad condition, and money must be raised for it. Mr. Blackburne, Dr. Clerke, and I to the Quaker's

---

[1] Baptist, third Viscount Campden, Lord Lieutenant of Rutlandshire. Died 1682. Campden House was built about 1612 by Sir Baptist Hicks, first Viscount Campden. The third Earl entertained Charles II. here immediately after the Restoration. The house was burnt down March 23rd, 1862, and rebuilt soon afterwards.

[2] The manor of Lisson Green (Domesday Lilesstone) remained a rural district till the end of the last century, and Dodsley (1761) describes it as "a pleasant village near Paddington." Marylebone was quite a country place in Pepys's day, and long after.

and dined there. I back to the Admiralty, and there was doing things in order to the calculating of the debts of the Navy and other business, all the afternoon. At night I went to the Privy Seal, where I found Mr. Crofts and Mathews making up all their things to leave the office to-morrow, to those that come to wait the next month. I took them to the Sun Tavern and there made them drink, and discoursed concerning the office, and what I was to expect to-morrow about Baron, who pretends to the next month. Late home by coach so far as Ludgate with Mr. Mathews, and thence home on foot with W. Hewer with me, and so to bed.

[August 1st]. Up very early, and by water to Whitehall to my Lord's, and there up to my Lord's lodging (Wm. Howe being now ill of the gout at Mr. Pierce's), and there talked with him about the affairs of the Navy, and how I was now to wait to-day at the Privy Seal. Commissioner Pett went with me, whom I desired to make my excuse at the office for my absence this day. Hence to the Privy Seal Office, where I got (by Mr. Mathews' means) possession of the books and table, but with some expectation of Baron's bringing of a warrant from the King to have this month. Nothing done this morning, Baron having spoke to Mr. Woodson and Groome (clerks to Mr. Trumbull of the Signet) to keep all work in their hands till the afternoon, at which time he expected to have his warrant from the King for this month.[1] I took at noon Mr. Harper to the Leg in King Street, and did give him his dinner, who did still advise me much to act wholly myself at the Privy Seal, but I told him that I could not, because I had other business to take up my time. In the afternoon at the office again, where we had many things to sign; and I went to the Council Chamber, and there got my Lord to sign the first bill, and the rest all myself; but received no money to-day. After I had signed all, I went with Dick Scobell and Luellin to drink at a bottle beer house in the Strand, and after staying there a while (had sent W. Hewer home before), I took boat and homewards went, and in Fish Street bought a Lobster, and as I had bought it I met with Winter and Mr. Delabarr, and there with a piece of

[1] The clerks of the Privy Seal took the duty of attendance for a month by turns.

sturgeon of theirs we went to the Sun Tavern in the street[1] and ate them. Late home and to bed.

[2d]. To Westminster by water with Sir W. Batten and Sir W. Pen (our servants in another boat) to the Admiralty; and from thence I went to my Lord's to fetch him thither, where we stayed in the morning about ordering of money for the victuallers, and advising how to get a sum of money to carry on the business of the Navy. From thence dined with Mr. Blackburne at his house with his friends (his wife being in the country and just upon her return to London), where we were very well treated and merry. From thence W. Hewer and I to the office of Privy Seal, where I stayed all the afternoon, and received about £40 for yesterday and to-day, at which my heart rejoiced for God's blessing to me, to give me this advantage by chance, there being of this £40 about £10 due to me for this day's work. So great is the present profit of this office, above what it was in the King's time; there being the last month about 300 bills, whereas in the late King's time it was much to have 40. With my money home by coach, it being the first time that I could get home before our gates were shut since I came to the Navy office. When I came home I found my wife not very well of her old pain . . . . which she had when we were married first. I went and cast up the expense that I laid out upon my former house (because there are so many that are desirous of it, and I am, in my mind, loth to let it go out of my hands, for fear of a turn). I find my layings-out to come to about £20, which with my fine will come to about £22 to him that shall hire my house of me.[2] To bed.

[3rd]. Up betimes this morning, and after the barber had done with me, then to the office, where I and Sir William Pen only did meet and despatch business. At noon my wife and I by coach to Dr. Clerke's to dinner. I was very much taken with his lady, a comely, proper woman, though not handsome; but a woman of the best language I ever heard. Here dined Mrs. Pierce and her

---

[1] There is a farthing token of the Sun in New Fish Street (see "Boyne's Trade Tokens," ed. Williamson, vol. i., 1889, p. 681).

[2] Pepys wished to let his house in Axe Yard now that he had apartments at the Navy Office.

husband. After dinner I took leave to go to Westminster, where I was at the Privy Seal Office all day, signing things and taking money, so that I could not do as I had intended, that is to return to them and go to the Red Bull Playhouse,[1] but I took coach and went to see whether it was done so or no, and I found it done. So I returned to Dr. Clerke's, where I found them and my wife, and by and by took leave and went away home.

[4th]. To White Hall, where I found my Lord gone with the King by water to dine at the Tower with Sir J. Robinson,[2] Lieutenant. I found my Lady Jemimah[3] at my Lord's, with whom I staid and dined, all alone; after dinner to the Privy Seal Office, where I did business. So to a Committee of Parliament (Sir Hen[eage] Finch,[4] Chairman), to give them an answer to an order of theirs, "that we could not give them any account of the Accounts of the Navy in the years 36, 37, 38, 39, 40, as they desire." After that I went and bespoke some linen of Betty Lane in

---

[1] This well-known theatre was situated in St. John's Street on the site of Red Bull Yard. Pepys went there on March 23rd, 1661, when he expressed a very poor opinion of the place. T. Carew, in some commendatory lines on Sir William Davenant's play, "The Just Italian," 1630, abuses both audiences and actors:—

> "There are the men in crowded heaps that throng
> To that adulterate stage, where not a tongue
> Of th' untun'd kennel can a line repeat
> Of serious sense."

There is a token of this house (see "Boyne's Trade Tokens," ed. Williamson, vol. i., 1889, p. 725).

[2] Sir John Robinson, clothworker, son of Archdeacon Robinson of Nottingham. He was one of the Commissioners sent to Breda to desire Charles II. to return to England immediately, and was created a baronet for his services to the King, 1660, and had an augmentation to his arms. He was alderman of Dowgate, afterwards of Cripplegate; Lord Mayor, 1662. He retained the Lieutenancy of the Tower till 1678. A portrait of him is at Clothworkers' Hall.

[3] Lady Jemima Montagu, daughter of Lord Sandwich, previously described as Mrs. Jem.

[4] Heneage Finch, son of Sir Heneage Finch, Recorder of London, was born December 23rd, 1621. He was called to the bar in 1645, and soon obtained considerable fame as a counsel. He was styled "the silver-tongued lawyer," "the English Cicero," and "the English Roscius." A week after the King's return in 1660 he was appointed Solicitor-General and created a baronet; Attorney-General, 1670; Lord Keeper, and created Baron Finch, 1673; Lord Chancellor, 1675; Earl of Nottingham, 1681. Died December 18th, 1682.

the Hall, and after that to the Trumpet, where I sat and talked
with her, &c. At night, it being very rainy, and it thundering
and lightning exceedingly, I took coach at the Trumpet door,
taking Monsieur L'Impertinent along with me as far as the
Savoy, where he said he went to lie with Cary Dillon,[1] and is
still upon the mind of going (he and his whole family) to Ireland.
Having set him down I made haste home, and in the courtyard, it
being very dark, I heard a man inquire for my house, and having
asked his business, he told me that my man William (who went
this morning out of town to meet his aunt Blackburne) was come
home not very well to his mother, and so could not come home
to-night. At which I was very sorry. I found my wife still in pain.
To bed, having not time to write letters, and indeed having so
many to write to all places that I have no heart to go about them.
Mrs. Shaw did die yesterday and her husband so sick that he is
not like to live.

[5th]. Lord's day. My wife being much in pain, I went this
morning to Dr. Williams (who had cured her once before of this
business), in Holborn, and he did give me an ointment which I
sent home by my boy, and a plaister which I took with me to
Westminster (having called and seen my mother in the morning
as I went to the doctor), where I dined with Mr. Sheply (my Lord
dining at Kensington). After dinner to St. Margaret's, where the
first time I ever heard Common Prayer in that Church. I sat with
Mr. Hill in his pew; Mr. Hill that married in Axe Yard and that
was aboard us in the Hope. Church done I went and Mr. Sheply
to see W. Howe at Mr. Pierce's, where I staid singing of songs
and psalms an hour or two, and were very pleasant with Mrs.
Pierce and him. Thence to my Lord's, where I staid and talked
and drank with Mr. Sheply. After that to Westminster stairs,
where I saw a fray between Mynheer Clinke, a Dutchman, that
was at Hartlibb's wedding, and a waterman, which made good
sport. After that I got a Gravesend boat, that was come up to
fetch some bread on this side the bridge, and got them to carry
me to the bridge, and so home, where I found my wife. After

---

[1] Colonel Cary Dillon, a friend of the Butlers, who courted the fair Frances;
but the engagement was subsequently broken off, see December 31st, 1662.

prayers I to bed to her, she having had a very bad night of it. This morning before I was up Will came home pretty well again, he having been only weary with riding, which he is not used to.

[6th]. This morning at the office, and, that being done, home to dinner all alone, my wife being ill in pain a-bed, which I was troubled at, and not a little impatient. After dinner to Whitehall at the Privy Seal all the afternoon, and at night with Mr. Man to Mr. Rawlinson's in Fenchurch Street, where we staid till eleven o'clock at night. So home and to bed, my wife being all this day in great pain. This night Mr. Man offered me £1,000 for my office of Clerk of the Acts, which made my mouth water; but yet I dared not take it till I speak with my Lord to have his consent.

[7th]. This morning to Whitehall to the Privy Seal, and took Mr. Moore and myself and dined at my Lord's with Mr. Sheply. While I was at dinner in come Sam. Hartlibb[1] and his brother-in-law,[2] now knighted by the King, to request my promise of a ship for them to Holland, which I had promised to get for them. After dinner to the Privy Seal all the afternoon. At night, meeting Sam. Hartlibb, he took me by coach to Kensington, to my Lord of Holland's;[3] I staid in the coach while he went in about his business. He staying long I left the coach and walked back again before on foot (a very pleasant walk) to Kensington, where I drank and staid very long waiting for him. At last he came, and after drinking at the inn he went towards Westminster. Here I endeavoured to have looked out Jane that formerly lived at Dr. Williams' at Cambridge, whom I had long thought to live at present here, but I found myself in an error, meeting one in the

---

[1] This was Samuel Hartlib the younger, son of the friend of Milton, who was a neighbour of Pepys in Axe Yard. When Pepys refers to the elder Samuel Hartlib he calls him Mr. Hartlib. In Dircks's "Biographical Memoir of Samuel Hartlib" (1865), the mistake is made of supposing that the Samuel Hartlib here referred to was the elder, and Nan Hartlib his sister instead of his daughter.

[2] Sir John Roder or Roth, see *ante*, July 1st and 10th.

[3] Holland House, the fine old mansion still standing at Kensington, was greatly added to and improved by Henry Rich, Earl of Holland, who was beheaded, March 9th, 1649. His house was afterwards successively occupied by Generals Fairfax and Lambert, but subsequently it was restored to the earl's widow; she seems to have let a portion of the house.

place where I expected to have found her, but she proved not she though very like her. We went to the Bullhead, where he and I sat and drank till 11 at night, and so home on foot. Found my wife pretty well again, and so to bed.

[8th]. We met at the office, and after that to dinner at home, and from thence with my wife by water to Catan Sterpin, with whom and her mistress Pye we sat discoursing of Kate's marriage to Mons. Petit,[1] her mistress and I giving the best advice we could for her to suspend her marriage till Mons. Petit had got some place that may be able to maintain her, and not for him to live upon the portion that she shall bring him. From thence to Mr. Butler's to see his daughters, the first time that ever we made a visit to them. We found them very pretty, and Coll. Dillon there, a very merry and witty companion, but methinks they live in a gaudy but very poor condition. From thence, my wife and I intending to see Mrs. Blackburne, who had been a day or two again to see my wife, but my wife was not in condition to be seen, but she not being at home my wife went to her mother's and I to the Privy Seal. At night from the Privy Seal, Mr. Woodson and Mr. Jennings and I to the Sun Tavern till it was late, and from thence to my Lord's, where my wife was come from Mrs. Blackburne's to me, and after I had done some business with my Lord, she and I went to Mrs. Hunt's, who would needs have us to lie at her house to-night, she being with my wife so late at my Lord's with us, and would not let us go home to-night. We lay there all night very pleasantly and at ease. . . .

[9th]. Left my wife at Mrs. Hunt's and I to my Lord's, and from thence with Judge Advocate Fowler, Mr. Creed, and Mr. Sheply to the Rhenish Wine-house, and Captain Hayward of the Plymouth, who is now ordered to carry my Lord Winchelsea, Embassador to Constantinople.[2] We were very merry, and Judge Advocate did give Captain Hayward his Oath of Allegiance and Supremacy. Thence to my office of Privy Seal, and, having signed some things there, with Mr. Moore and Dean Fuller to the Leg

---

[1] Catan did not take the good advice offered her, but married Mons. Petit. See October 23rd, 1660.

[2] Heneage Finch, Earl of Winchelsea. Died 1689.

in King Street, and, sending for my wife, we dined there very merry, and after dinner parted. After dinner with my wife to Mrs. Blackburne to visit her. She being within I left my wife there, and I to the Privy Seal, where I despatch some business, and from thence to Mrs. Blackburne again, who did treat my wife and me with a great deal of civility, and did give us a fine collation of collar of beef, &c. Thence I, having my head full of drink from having drunk so much Rhenish wine in the morning, and more in the afternoon at Mrs. Blackburne's, came home and so to bed, not well, and very ill all night.

[10th]. I had a great deal of pain all night, and a great loosing upon me so that I could not sleep. In the morning I rose with much pain and to the office. I went and dined at home, and after dinner with great pain in my back I went by water to Whitehall to the Privy Seal, and that done with Mr. Moore and Creed to Hide Park by coach, and saw a fine foot-race three times round

the Park[1] between an Irishman and Crow, that was once my Lord Claypoole's[2] footman. (By the way I cannot forget that my Lord Claypoole did the other day make enquiry of Mrs. Hunt, concerning my House in Axe-yard, and did set her on work to get it of me for him, which methinks is a very great change.) Crow beat the other by above two miles. Returned from Hide Park, I went to my Lord's, and took Will (who waited for me there) by coach and went home, taking my lute home with me. It had been all this while since I came from sea at my Lord's for him to play on. To bed in some pain still. For this month or two it is not imaginable how busy my head has been, so that I have neglected to write letters to my uncle Robert in answer to many of his, and to other friends, nor indeed have I done anything as to my own family, and especially this month my waiting at the Privy Seal makes me much more unable to think of anything, because of my constant attendance there after I have done at the Navy Office. But blessed be God for my good chance of the Privy Seal, where I get every day I believe about £3. This place I got by chance, and my Lord did give it me by chance neither he nor I thinking it to be of the worth that he and I find it to be. Never since I was a man in the world was I ever so great a stranger to public affairs as now I am, having not read a new book or anything like it, or enquiring after any news, or what the Parliament do, or in any wise how things go. Many people look after my house in Axe-yard to hire it, so that I am troubled with them, and I have a mind to get the money to buy goods for my house at the Navy Office, and yet I am loth to put it off because that Mr. Man bids me £1,000 for my office, which is

---

[1] Races in Hyde Park were fashionable in the reign of Charles I. They were usually run round the Ring.

[2] John Claypole (born August 21st, 1625) married, on January 13th, 1645-46, Elizabeth, second daughter of Oliver Cromwell, to whom he became Master of the Horse, and a Lord of the Bedchamber: he was also placed in his father-in-law's Upper House. During Richard Cromwell's time he retained all his places at Court; and at the Restoration he was not molested. He was arrested in June, 1678, and imprisoned in the Tower, but speedily released. He died June 26th, 1688. His father had been proceeded against in the Star Chamber, for resisting the payment of Ship Money, and was by Cromwell constituted Clerk of the Hanaper, and created a baronet. Mrs. Claypole died August 6th, 1658.

so great a sum that I am loth to settle myself at my new house, lest I should take Mr. Man's offer in case I found my Lord willing to it.

[11th]. I rose to-day without any pain, which makes me think that my pain yesterday was nothing but from my drinking too much the day before. To my Lord this morning, who did give me order to get some things ready against the afternoon for the Admiralty where he would meet. To the Privy Seal, and from thence going to my own house in Axe-yard, I went in to Mrs. Crisp's, where I met with Mr. Hartlibb, for whom I wrote a letter for my Lord to sign for a ship for his brother and sister, who went away hence this day to Gravesend, and from thence to Holland. I found by discourse with Mrs. Crisp that he is very jealous of her, for that she is yet very kind to her old servant Meade. Hence to my Lord's to dinner with Mr. Sheply, so to the Privy Seal, and at night home, and then sent for the barber, and was trimmed in the kitchen, the first time that ever I was so. I was vexed this night that W. Hewer was out of doors till ten at night, but was pretty well satisfied again when my wife told me that he wept because I was angry, though indeed he did give me a good reason for his being out, but I thought it a good occasion to let him know that I do expect his being at home. So to bed.

[12th]. Lord's day. To my Lord, and with him to White Hall Chappell, where Mr. Calamy preached, and made a good sermon upon these words "To whom much is given, of him much is required." He was very officious with his three reverences to the King, as others do. After sermon a brave anthem of Captain Cooke's,[1] which he himself sung, and the King was well pleased

---

[1] Henry Cooke, chorister of the Chapel Royal, adhered to the royal cause at the breaking out of the Civil Wars, and for his bravery obtained a captain's commission. At the Restoration he received the appointment of Master of the Children of the Chapel Royal; he was an excellent musician, and three of his pupils turned out very distinguished musicians, viz., Pelham Humphrey, John Blow, and Michael Wise. He was one of the original performers in the "Siege of Rhodes." He died July 13th, 1672, and was buried in the cloisters of Westminster Abbey. In another place Pepys says, "a vain coxcomb he is, though he sings so well."

with it. My Lord dined at my Lord Chamberlain's,[1] and I at his
house with Mr. Sheply. After dinner I did give Mr. Donne, who
is going to sea, the key of my cabin and direction for the putting
up of my things. After that I went to walk, and meeting Mrs.
Lane of Westminster Hall, I took her to my Lord's, and did give
her a bottle of wine in the garden, where Mr. Fairbrother, of
Cambridge, did come and found us, and drank with us. After that
I took her to my house, where I was exceeding free in dallying
with her, and she not unfree to take it. At night home and called
at my father's, where I found Mr. Fairbrother, but I did not stay
but went homewards and called in at Mr. Rawlinson's, whither
my uncle Wight was coming and did come, but was exceeding
angry (he being a little fuddled, and I think it was that I should
see him in that case) as I never saw him in my life, which I was
somewhat troubled at. Home and to bed.

[13th]. A sitting day at our office. After dinner to Whitehall, to
the Privy Seal, whither my father came to me, and staid talking
with me a great while, telling me that he had propounded Mr.
John Pickering for Sir Thomas Honywood's daughter,[2] which I
think he do not deserve for his own merit. I know not what he
may do for his estate. My father and Creed and I to the old Rhenish winehouse, and talked and drank till night. Then my father
home, and I to my Lord's, where he told me that he would suddenly go into the country, and so did commend the business of
his sea commission to me in his absence. After that home by
coach, and took my £100 that I had formerly left at Mr. Rawlinson's, home with me, which is the first that ever I was master of
at once. To prayers, and to bed.

[14th]. To the Privy Seal, and thence to my Lord's, where Mr.
Pim, the tailor, and I agreed upon making me a velvet coat.
From thence to the Privy Seal again, where Sir Samuel Morland
came in with a Baronet's grant to pass, which the King had given
him to make money of. Here he staid with me a great while; and

---

[1] Edward Montagu, second Earl of Manchester, K.G., Lord Chamberlain, died
1671.
[2] John Pickering married a fortune of £5,000; see *post*, November 5th, 1666.

told me the whole manner of his serving the King in the time of the Protector; and how Thurloe's bad usage made him to do it; how he discovered Sir R. Willis, and how he hath sunk his fortune for the King; and that now the King hath given him a pension of £500 per annum out of the Post Office for life, and the benefit of two Baronets; all which do make me begin to think that he is not so much a fool as I took him to be. Home by water to the Tower, where my father, Mr. Fairbrother, and Cooke dined with me. After dinner in comes young Captain Cuttance[1] of the Speedwell, who is sent up for the gratuity given the seamen that brought the King over. He brought me a firkin of butter for my wife, which is very welcome. My father, after dinner, takes leave, after I had given him 40s. for the last half year for my brother John at Cambridge. I did also make even with Mr. Fairbrother for my degree of Master of Arts, which cost me about £9 16s.[2] To White Hall, and my wife with me by water, where at the Privy Seal and elsewhere all the afternoon. At night home with her by water, where I made good sport with having the girl and the boy to comb my head, before I went to bed, in the kitchen.

[15th]. To the office, and after dinner by water to White Hall, where I found the King gone this morning by 5 of the clock to see a Dutch pleasure-boat[3] below bridge, where he dines, and my Lord with him. The King do tire all his people that are about him with early rising since he came. To the office, all the afternoon I staid there, and in the evening went to Westminster Hall, where I staid at Mrs. Michell's, and with her and her husband sent for some drink, and drank with them. By the same token she and Mrs. Murford and another old woman of the Hall were going a gossiping to-night. From thence to my Lord's, where I found him within, and he did give me direction about his busi-

---

[1] Captain Henry Cuttance. The "Speedwell" was originally the "Cheriton," see ante, May 1st, 1660.

[2] See ante, July 8th, 1660.

[3] A yacht which was greatly admired, and was imitated and improved by Commissioner Pett, who built a yacht for the King in 1661, which was called the "Jenny." Queen Elizabeth had a yacht, and one was built by Phineas Pett in 1604.

ness in his absence, he intending to go into the country to-morrow morning. Here I lay all night in the old chamber which I had now given up to W. Howe, with whom I did intend to lie, but he and I fell to play with one another, so that I made him to go lie with Mr. Sheply. So I lay alone all night.

[16th]. This morning my Lord (all things being ready) carried me by coach to Mr. Crew's, (in the way talking how good he did hope my place would be to me, and in general speaking that it was not the salary of any place that did make a man rich, but the opportunity of getting money while he is in the place) where he took leave, and went into the coach, and so for Hinchinbroke. My Lady Jemimah and Mr. Thomas Crew in the coach with him. Hence to Whitehall about noon, where I met with Mr. Madge, who took me along with him and Captain Cooke (the famous singer) and other masters of music to dinner at an ordinary about Charing Cross where we dined, all paying their club. Hence to the Privy Seal, where there has been but little work these two days. In the evening home.

[17th]. To the office, and that done home to dinner where Mr. Unthanke, my wife's tailor, dined with us, we having nothing but a dish of sheep's trotters. After dinner by water to Whitehall, where a great deal of business at the Privy Seal. At night I and Creed and the Judge-Advocate went to Mr. Pim, the tailor's, who took us to the Half Moon, and there did give us great store of wine and anchovies, and would pay for them all. This night I saw Mr. Creed show many the strangest emotions to shift off his drink I ever saw in my life. By coach home and to bed.

[18th]. This morning I took my wife towards Westminster by water, and landed her at Whitefriars, with £5 to buy her a petticoat, and I to the Privy Seal. By and by comes my wife to tell me that my father has persuaded her to buy a most fine cloth of 26s. a yard, and a rich lace, that the petticoat will come to £5, at which I was somewhat troubled, but she doing it very innocently, I could not be angry. I did give her more money, and sent her away, and I and Creed and Captain Hayward (who is now unkindly put out of the Plymouth to make way for Captain Allen

to go to Constantinople, and put into his ship the Dover, which I know will trouble my Lord) went and dined at the Leg in King Street, where Captain Ferrers, my Lord's Cornet, comes to us, who after dinner took me and Creed to the Cockpitt play,[1] the first that I have had time to see since my coming from sea, "The Loyall Subject,"[2] where one Kinaston,[3] a boy, acted the Duke's sister, but made the loveliest lady that ever I saw in my life, only her voice not very good. After the play done, we three went to drink, and by Captain Ferrers' means, Kinaston and another that acted Archas, the General, came and drank with us. Hence home by coach, and after being trimmed, leaving my wife to look after her little bitch, which was just now a-whelping, I to bed.

[19th] (Lord's day). In the morning my wife tells me that the bitch has whelped four young ones and is very well after it, my wife having had a great fear that she would die thereof, the dog that got them being very big. This morning Sir W. Batten, Pen, and myself, went to church to the church-wardens, to demand a pew, which at present could not be given us, but we are resolved to have one built. So we staid and heard Mr. Mills,[4] a very good minister. Home to dinner, where my wife had on her new petti-coat that she bought yesterday, which indeed is a very fine cloth and a fine lace; but that being of a light colour, and the lace all

---

[1] The Cockpit Theatre, situated in Drury Lane, was occupied as a playhouse in the reign of James I. It was occupied by Davenant and his company in 1658, and they remained in it until November 15th, 1660, when they removed to Salisbury Court.

[2] A tragi-comedy by Beaumont and Fletcher. Kynaston's part was Olympia.

[3] Edward Kynaston, engaged by Sir W. Davenant, in 1660, to perform the principal female characters; he afterwards assumed the male ones in the first parts of tragedy, and continued on the stage till the end of King William's reign. He died in 1712. We may be sure that Betterton took the character of Archas, as Downes tells us that he was early distinguished for playing in "The Loyal Subject."

[4] Daniel Milles, D.D., thirty-two years rector of St. Olave's, Hart Street, and buried there, October, 1689, aged sixty-three. He was appointed April 17th, 1657. Newcourt ("Repertorium") writes, "Dan Mills was admitted to the church in the late times of usurpation by the Commission for approving Publick Preachers, but at whose presentation I know not." In 1667 Sir Robert Brooks presented him to the rectory of Wanstead, in Essex, which he also held till his death.

silver, it makes no great show. Mr. Creed and my brother Tom
dined with me. After dinner my wife went and fetched the little
puppies to us, which are very pretty ones. After they were gone,
I went up to put my papers in order, and finding my wife's
clothes lie carelessly laid up, I was angry with her, which I was
troubled for. After that my wife and I went and walked in the
garden, and so home to bed.

[20th] (Office day). As Sir W. Pen and I were walking in the
garden, a messenger came to me from the Duke of York to fetch
me to the Lord Chancellor. So (Mrs. Turner with her daughter
The. being come to my house to speak with me about a friend of
hers to send to sea) I went with her in her coach as far as Worcester House, but my Lord Chancellor being gone to the House of
Lords, I went thither, and (there being a law case before them
this day) got in, and there staid all the morning, seeing their
manner of sitting on woolpacks,[1] &c., which I never did before.
After the House was up, I spoke to my Lord, and had order from
him to come to him at night. This morning Mr. Creed did give
me the Papers that concern my Lord's sea commission, which he
left in my hands, and went to sea this day to look after the
gratuity money. This afternoon at the Privy Seal, where reckoning with Mr. Moore, he had got £100 for me together, which
I was glad of, guessing that the profits of this month would come
to £100. In the evening I went all alone to drink at Mr. Harper's,
where I found Mrs. Crisp's daughter, with whom and her friends
I staid and drank, and so with W. Hewer by coach to Worcester
House, where I light, sending him home with the £100 that I received to-day. Here I staid, and saw my Lord Chancellor come
into his Great Hall, where wonderful how much company there
was to expect him at a Seal. Before he would begin any business,
he took my papers of the state of the debts of the Fleet, and there
viewed them before all the people, and did give me his advice
privately how to order things, to get as much money as we can

---

[1] It is said that these woolpacks were placed in the House of Lords for the
judges to sit on, so that the fact that wool was a main source of our national
wealth might be kept in the popular mind. The Lord Chancellor's seat is now
called the Woolsack.

of the Parliament. That being done, I went home, where I found all my things come home from sea (sent by desire by Mr. Dun), of which I was glad, though many of my things are quite spoilt with mould by reason of lying so long a shipboard, and my cabin being not tight. I spent much time to dispose of them to-night, and so to bed.

[21st]. This morning I went to White Hall with Sir W. Pen by water, who in our passage told me how he was bred up under Sir W. Batten. We went to Mr. Coventry's chamber, and consulted of drawing my papers of debts of the Navy against the afternoon for the Committee. So to the Admiralty, where W. Hewer and I did them, and after that he went to his Aunt's Blackburn (who has a kinswoman dead at her house to-day, and was to be buried to-night, by which means he staid very late out). I to Westminster Hall, where I met Mr. Crew and dined with him, where there dined one Mr. Hickeman,[1] an Oxford man, who spoke very much against the height of the now old clergy, for putting out many of the religious fellows of Colleges, and inveighing against them for their being drunk, which, if true, I am sorry to hear. After that towards Westminster, where I called on Mr. Pim, and there found my velvet coat (the first that ever I had) done, and a velvet mantle, which I took to the Privy Seal Office, and there locked them up, and went to the Queen's Court, and there, after much waiting, spoke with Colonel Birch,[2] who read my papers, and desired some addition, which done I returned to the Privy Seal, where little to do, and with Mr. Moore towards London, and in our way meeting Monsieur Eschar (Mr. Montagu's man), about the Savoy, he took us to the Brazennose Tavern, and there drank and so parted, and I home by coach, and there, it being post-

---

[1] Henry Hickman, a native of Worcestershire, took the degree of B.A. at St. Catherine's Hall, Cambridge, and, migrating to Oxford, obtained a fellowship at Magdalen College, from the usurping powers, which he lost in 1660, to make room for the rightful owner. He then retired to Holland and passed most of his time abroad, dying at Leyden in 1692. He wrote several theological tracts, and was considered a severe enemy to the ceremonies of the Church of England.—B.

[2] Colonel John Birch, elected M.P. for Leominster in 1646, and continued until 1660. He represented Penrhyn in the parliament of 1661.

night, I wrote to my Lord to give him notice that all things are well; that General Monk[1] is made Lieutenant of Ireland, which my Lord Roberts[2] (made Deputy) do not like of, to be Deputy to any man but the King himself. After that to bed.

[22nd]. Office, which done, Sir W. Pen took me into the garden, and there told me how Mr. Turner do intend to petition the Duke for an allowance extra as one of the Clerks of the Navy, which he desired me to join with him in the furthering of, which I promised to do so that it did not reflect upon me or to my damage to have any other added, as if I was not able to perform my place; which he did wholly disown to be any of his intention, but far from it. I took Mr. Hater home with me to dinner, with whom I did advise, who did give me the same counsel. After dinner he and I to the office about doing something more as to the debts of the Navy than I had done yesterday, and so to Whitehall to the Privy Seal, and having done there, with my father (who came to see me) to Westminster Hall and the Parliament House to look for Col. Birch, but found him not. In the House, after the Committee was up, I met with Mr. G. Montagu, and joyed him in his entrance (this being his 3d day) for Dover. Here he made me sit all alone in the House, none but he and I, half an hour, discoursing how things stand, and in short he told me how there was like to be many factions at Court between Marquis Ormond,[3] General Monk, and the Lord Roberts, about the business of Ireland; as there is already between the two Houses about the Act of Indemnity; and in the House of Commons, between the Episcopalian and Presbyterian men. Hence to my father's (walking with Mr. Herring, the minister of St. Bride's), and took them to the Sun Tavern, where I found George, my old drawer, come again. From thence by water, landed them at Blackfriars, and so home and to bed.

---

[1] Monk, Duke of Albemarle, was appointed Lord Lieutenant of Ireland with the understanding that he should perform the duties by deputy.

[2] John Robartes, second Lord Robartes, afterwards (1661) Lord Privy Seal, advanced to the Earldom of Radnor, 1679. Lord Robartes went again to Ireland as Lord Lieutenant in 1669. Died 1685.

[3] James Butler, afterwards created Duke of Ormond, and K.G., and twice Lord Lieutenant of Ireland.

[23rd]. By water to Doctors' Commons to Dr. Walker,[1] to give him my Lord's papers to view over concerning his being empowered to be Vice-Admiral under the Duke of York. There meeting with Mr. Pinkney, he and I to a morning draft, and thence by water to White Hall, to the Parliament House, where I spoke with Colonel Birch, and so to the Admiralty chamber, where we and Mr. Coventry had a meeting about several businesses. Amongst others, it was moved that Phineas Pett[2] (kinsman to the Commissioner) of Chatham, should be suspended his employment till he had answered some articles put in against him, as that he should formerly say that the King was a bastard and his mother a whore. Hence to Westminster Hall, where I met with my father Bowyer, and Mr. Spicer, and them I took to the Leg in King Street, and did give them a dish or two of meat, and so away to the Privy Seal, where, the King being out of town, we have had nothing to do these two days. To Westminster Hall, where I met with W. Symons, T. Doling, and Mr. Booth, and with them to the Dogg, where we eat a musk melon[3] (the first that I have eat this year), and were very merry with W. Symons, calling him Mr. Dean, because of the Dean's lands that his uncle had left him, which are like to be lost all. Hence home by water, and very late at night writing letters to my Lord to Hinchinbroke, and also to the Vice-Admiral in the Downs, and so to bed.

[24th]. Office, and thence with Sir William Batten and Sir William Pen to the parish church to find out a place where to build a seat or a gallery to sit in, and did find one which is to be done speedily.[4] Hence with them to dinner at a tavern in Thames Street, where they were invited to a roasted haunch of venison

---

[1] Dr. (afterwards Sir William) Walker was one of the Judges of the Admiralty.

[2] Phineas Pett, Assistant Master Shipwright at Chatham, was suspended on this frivolous charge, and dismissed in October.

[3] "Melons were hardly known in England till Sir George Gardiner brought one from Spain, when they became in general estimation. The ordinary price was five or six shillings."—*Quarterly Review*, vol. xix. p. 20.

[4] The gallery built for the officers of the Navy House remained until the restoration of the church in 1870-71 under the direction of Mr. (now Sir Arthur) Blomfield, A.R.A. The memorial to Pepys, erected in 1884, was placed on the wall where the gallery was situated.

and other very good victuals and company. Hence to Whitehall to the Privy Seal, but nothing to do. At night by land to my father's, where I found my mother not very well. I did give her a pint of sack. My father came in, and Dr. T. Pepys,[1] who talked with me in French about looking out for a place for him. But I found him a weak man, and speaks the worst French that ever I heard of one that had been so long beyond sea. Hence into Paul's Churchyard and bought Barkley's Argenis[2] in Latin, and so home and to bed. I found at home that Captain Burr had sent me 4 dozen bottles of wine to-day. The King came back to Whitehall to-night.

[25th]. This morning Mr. Turner and I by coach from our office to Whitehall (in our way I calling on Dr. Walker for the papers I did give him the other day, which he had perused and found that the Duke's counsel had abated something of the former draught which Dr. Walker drew for my Lord) to Sir G. Carteret, where we there made up an estimate of the debts of the Navy for the Council. At noon I took Mr. Turner and Mr. Moore to the Leg in King Street, and did give them a dinner, and afterward to the Sun Tavern, and did give Mr. Turner a glass of wine, there coming to us Mr. Fowler the apothecary (the Judge's son) with a book of lute lessons which his father had left there for me, such as he formerly did use to play when a young man, and had the use of his hand. To the Privy Seal, and found some business now again to do there. To Westminster Hall for a new half-shirt of Mrs. Lane, and so home by water. Wrote letters by the post to my Lord and to sea. This night W. Hewer brought me home from Mr. Pim's my velvet coat and cap, the first that ever I had. So to bed.

[26th] (Lord's day). With Sir W. Pen to the parish church, where we are placed in the highest pew of all, where a stranger preached a dry and tedious long sermon. Dined at home. To

---

[1] Thomas Pepys, M.A., M.D., son of Talbot Pepys of Middle Temple and Impington, born at Norwich, June 5th, 1621, Fellow of Trinity Hall, Cambridge. He died unmarried at Impington.

[2] "Jo. Barclaii Argenis. Lugd. Bat. 1659" is in the Pepysian Library, as also the second and third parts published in 1689.

church again in the afternoon with my wife; in the garden and on the leads at night, and so to supper and to bed.

[27th]. This morning comes one with a vessel of Northdown ale from Mr. Pierce, the purser, to me, and after him another with a brave Turkey carpet and a jar of olives from Captain Cuttance, and a pair of fine turtle-doves from John Burr to my wife. These things came up to-day in our smack, and my boy Ely came along with them, and came after office was done to see me. I did give him half a crown because I saw that he was ready to cry to see that he could not be entertained by me here. In the afternoon to the Privy Seal, where good store of work now toward the end of the month. From thence with Mr. Mount, Luellin, and others to the Bull head till late, and so home, where about 10 o'clock Major Hart came to me, whom I did receive with wine and anchovies, which made me so dry that I was ill with them all night, and was fain to have the girle rise and fetch me some drink.

[28th]. At home looking over my papers and books and house as to the fitting of it to my mind till two in the afternoon. Some time I spent this morning beginning to teach my wife some scale in music, and found her apt beyond imagination. To the Privy Seal, where great store of work to-day. Colonel Scroope[1] is this day excepted out of the Act of Indemnity, which has been now long in coming out, but it is expected to-morrow. I carried home £80 from the Privy Seal, by coach, and at night spent a little more time with my wife about her music with great content. This day I heard my poor mother had then two days been very ill, and I fear she will not last long. To bed, a little troubled that I fear my boy Will[2] is a thief and has stole some money of mine, particularly a letter that Mr. Jenkins did leave the last week with me with half a crown in it to send to his son.

[29th] (Office day). Before I went to the office my wife and I examined my boy Will about his stealing of things, but he denied

---

[1] Colonel Adrian Scroope, one of the persons who sat in judgment upon Charles I.

[2] Pepys refers to two Wills. This was Will Wayneman; the other was William Hewer.

all with the greatest subtlety and confidence in the world. To the
office, and after office then to the Church, where we took another
view of the place where we had resolved to build a gallery, and
have set men about doing it. Home to dinner, and there I found
my wife had discovered my boy Will's theft and a great deal
more than we imagined, at which I was vexed and intend to put
him away. To my office at the Privy Seal in the afternoon, and
from thence at night to the Bull Head, with Mount, Luellin, and
others, and hence to my father's, and he being at my uncle Fenner's, I went thither to him, and there sent for my boy's father
and talked with him about his son, and had his promise that if I
will send home his boy, he will take him notwithstanding his indenture. Home at night, and find that my wife had found out
more of the boy's stealing 6s. out of W. Hewer's closet, and hid
it in the house of office, at which my heart was troubled. To bed,
and caused the boy's clothes to be brought up to my chamber. But
after we were all a-bed, the wench (which lies in our chamber)
called us to listen of a sudden, which put my wife into such a
fright that she shook every joint of her, and a long time that I
could not get her out of it. The noise was the boy, we did believe,
got in a desperate mood out of his bed to do himself or William
[Hewer] some mischief. But the wench went down and got a
candle lighted, and finding the boy in bed, and locking the doors
fast, with a candle burning all night, we slept well, but with a
great deal of fear.

[30th]. We found all well in the morning below stairs, but the
boy in a sad plight of seeming sorrow; but he is the most cunning rogue that ever I met with of his age. To White Hall, where
I met with the Act of Indemnity[1] (so long talked of and hoped
for), with the Act of Rate for Pole-money, and for judicial proceedings. At Westminster Hall I met with Mr. Paget the lawyer,
and dined with him at Heaven. This afternoon my wife went to
Mr. Pierce's wife's child's christening, and was urged to be godmother, but I advised her beforehand not to do it, so she did not,
but as proxy for my Lady Jemimah. This the first day that ever I

---

[1] 12 Car. II. cap. 11, an act of free and general pardon, indemnity, and
oblivion.

saw my wife wear black patches since we were married.[1] My
Lord came to town to-day, but coming not home till very late I
staid till 10 at night, and so home on foot. Mr. Sheply and Mr.
Childe[2] this night at the tavern.

[31st]. Early to wait upon my Lord at White Hall, and with him
to the Duke's chamber. So to my office in Seething Lane. Dined
at home, and after dinner to my Lord again, who told me that he
is ordered to go suddenly to sea, and did give me some orders to
be drawing up against his going. This afternoon I agreed to let
my house quite out of my hands to Mr. Dalton (one of the wine
sellers to the King, with whom I had drunk in the old wine cellar
two or three times) for £41. At night made even at Privy Seal
for this month against to-morrow to give up possession, but we
know not to whom, though we most favour Mr. Bickerstaffe, with
whom and Mr. Matthews we drank late after office was done at
the Sun, discoursing what to do about it to-morrow against Baron,
and so home and to bed. Blessed be God all things continue well
with and for me. I pray God fit me for a change of my fortune.

[September 1st]. This morning I took care to get a vessel to carry
my Lord's things to the Downs on Monday next, and so to White
Hall to my Lord, where he and I did look over the Commission
drawn for him by the Duke's Council, which I do not find my
Lord displeased with, though short of what Dr. Walker did formerly draw for him. Thence to the Privy Seal to see how things
went there, and I find that Mr. Baron had by a severe warrant
from the King got possession of the office from his brother Bickerstaffe, which is very strange, and much to our admiration, it being against all open justice. Mr. Moore and I and several others
being invited to-day by Mr. Goodman, a friend of his, we dined
at the Bullhead upon the best venison pasty that ever I eat of in

---

[1] The fashion of placing black patches on the face was introduced towards the
close of the reign of Charles I., and the practice is ridiculed in the "Spectator."

[2] Probably Josiah Child (born 1630), Deputy Treasurer of the Fleet, Mayor
of Portsmouth, Director, and afterwards Chairman of the East India Company, which he ruled despotically. He wrote "Brief Observations on Trade,"
1668, a second edition of which appeared in 1690 as "A new Discourse of
Trade," and which went through many subsequent editions. He was created
a baronet in 1678, and died June 22nd, 1699.

my life, and with one dish more, it was the best dinner I ever was at. Here rose in discourse at table a dispute between Mr. Moore and Dr. Clerke, the former affirming that it was essential to a tragedy to have the argument of it true, which the Doctor denied, and left it to me to be judge, and the cause to be determined next Tuesday morning at the same place, upon the eating of the remains of the pasty, and the loser to spend 10s. All this afternoon sending express to the fleet, to order things against my Lord's coming: and taking direction of my Lord about some rich furniture to take along with him for the Princess.[1] And talking of this, I hear by Mr. Townsend, that there is the greatest preparation against the Prince de Ligne's[2] coming over from the King of Spain, that ever was in England for their Embassador. Late home, and what with business and my boy's roguery my mind being unquiet, I went to bed.

[2nd] (Sunday). To Westminster, my Lord being gone before my coming to chapel. I and Mr. Sheply told out my money, and made even for my Privy Seal fees and gratuity money, &c., to this day between my Lord and me. After that to chappell, where Dr. Fern,[3] a good honest sermon upon "The Lord is my shield." After sermon a dull anthem, and so to my Lord's (he dining abroad) and dined with Mr. Sheply. So to St. Margarett's, and heard a good sermon upon the text "Teach us the old way," or something like it, wherein he ran over all the new tenets in policy and religion, which have brought us into all our late divisions. From church to Mrs. Crisp's (having sent Wm. Hewer home to tell my wife that I could not come home to-night because of my

---

[1] Mary, Princess Royal and Princess of Orange, who died in December of this year.

[2] Claude Lamoral, Prince de Ligne, had commanded the cavalry in the Low Countries, was afterwards Viceroy of Sicily and Governor of Milan. He died at Madrid in 1679. He had married, by dispensation, his cousin Maria Clara of Nassau, widow of his brother Albert Henry, who had died without issue. In our own time his descendant, the Prince de Ligne, was Ambassador Extraordinary from Belgium at the coronation of Queen Victoria.—B.

[3] Henry Ferne, born at York in 1602, D.D. 1643, Chaplain Extraordinary to Charles I., Master of Trinity College, Cambridge, Dean of Ely, 1662, Bishop of Chester, February, 1661-62, and died five weeks after his consecration on the 16th March. He wrote many controversial pamphlets.

Lord's going out early to-morrow morning), where I sat late, and did give them a great deal of wine, it being a farewell cup to Laud Crisp. I drank till the daughter began to be very loving to me and kind, and I fear is not so good as she should be. To my Lord's, and to bed with Mr. Sheply.

[3rd]. Up and to Mr. ——, the goldsmith near the new Exchange, where I bought my wedding ring, and there, with much ado, got him to put a gold ring to the jewell, which the King of Sweden[1] did give my Lord: out of which my Lord had now taken the King's picture, and intends to make a George of it. This morning at my Lord's I had an opportunity to speak with Sir George Downing, who has promised me to give me up my bond, and to pay me for my last quarter while I was at sea, that so I may pay Mr. Moore and Hawly. About noon my Lord, having taken leave of the King in the Shield Gallery (where I saw with what kindness the King did hug my Lord at his parting), I went over with him and saw him in his coach at Lambeth, and there took leave of him, he going to the Downs, which put me in mind of his first voyage that ever he made, which he did begin like this from Lambeth. In the afternoon with Mr. Moore to my house to cast up our Privy Seal accounts, where I found that my Lord's comes to 400 and odd pounds, and mine to £132, out of which I do give him as good as £25 for his pains, with which I doubt he is not satisfied, but my heart is full glad. Thence with him to Mr. Crew's, and did fetch as much money as did make even our accounts between him and me. Home, and there found Mr. Cooke come back from my Lord for me to get him some things bought for him to be brought after them, a toilet cap and comb case of silk, to make use of in Holland, for he goes to the Hague, which I can do to-morrow morning. This day my father and my uncle Fenner, and both his sons, have been at my house to see it, and my wife did treat them nobly with wine and anchovies. By reason of my Lord's going to-day I could not get the office to meet to-day.

[4th]. I did many things this morning at home before I went out,

[1] Gustavus XI., King of Sweden.

229

as looking over the joiners, who are flooring my dining-room, and doing business with Sir Williams[1] both at the office, and so to Whitehall, and so to the Bullhead, where we had the remains of our pasty, where I did give my verdict against Mr. Moore upon last Saturday's wager, where Dr. Fuller coming in do confirm me in my verdict. From thence to my Lord's and despatched Mr. Cooke away with the things to my Lord. From thence to Axe Yard to my house, where standing at the door Mrs. Diana comes by, whom I took into my house upstairs, and there did dally with her a great while, and found that in Latin "Nulla puella negat." So home by water, and there sat up late setting my papers in order, and my money also, and teaching my wife her music lesson, in which I take great pleasure. So to bed.

[5th]. To the office. From thence by coach upon the desire of the principal officers to Master of Chancery to give Mr. Stowell his oath, whereby he do answer that he did hear Phineas Pett say very high words against the King a great while ago. Coming back our coach broke, and so Stowell and I to Mr. Rawlinson's, and after a glass of wine parted, and I to the office, home to dinner, where (having put away my boy in the morning) his father brought him again, but I did so clear up my boy's roguery to his father, that he could not speak against my putting him away, and so I did give him 10s. for the boy's clothes that I made him, and so parted and tore his indenture. All the afternoon with the principal officers at Sir W. Batten's about Pett's business (where I first saw Col. Slingsby,[2] who has now his appointment for Comptroller), but did bring it to no issue. This day I saw our Dedimus to be sworn in the peace by, which will be shortly. In the evening my wife being a little impatient I went along with her to buy her a necklace of pearl, which will cost £4 10s., which I am willing to comply with her in for her encouragement, and because I have lately got money, having now above £200 in cash beforehand in the world. Home, and having in our way bought a

---

[1] "Both Sir Williams" is a favourite expression with Pepys, meaning Sir William Batten and Sir William Penn.

[2] Colonel, afterwards Sir Robert Slingsby, Bart., appointed Comptroller of the Navy in 1660. He died October 28th, 1661, and Pepys grieved for his loss.

rabbit and two little lobsters, my wife and I did sup late, and so to bed. Great news now-a-day of the Duke d'Anjou's[1] desire to marry the Princess Henrietta. Hugh Peters[2] is said to be taken, and the Duke of Gloucester is ill, and it is said it will prove the small-pox.

[6th]. To Whitehall by water with Sir W. Batten, and in our passage told me how Commissioner Pett did pay himself for the entertainment that he did give the King at Chatham at his coming in, and 20s. a day all the time he was in Holland, which I wonder at, and so I see there is a great deal of envy between the two. At Whitehall I met with Commissioner Pett, who told me how Mr. Coventry and Fairbank his solicitor are falling out, one complaining of the other for taking too great fees, which is too true. I find that Commissioner Pett is under great discontent, and is loth to give too much money for his place, and so do greatly desire me to go along with him in what we shall agree to give Mr. Coventry, which I have promised him, but am unwilling to mix my fortune with him that is going down the wind. We all met this morning and afterwards at the Admiralty, where our business is to ask provision of victuals ready for the ships in the Downs, which we did, Mr. Gauden promising to go himself thither and see it done. Dined Will and I at my Lord's upon a joint of meat that I sent Mrs. Sarah for. Afterwards to my office and sent all my books to my Lord's, in order to send them to my house that I now dwell in. Home and to bed.

[7th]. Not office day, and in the afternoon at home all the day, it

---

[1] Philip, Duke of Anjou, afterwards Duke of Orleans, brother of Louis XIV. (born 1640, died 1701), married the Princess Henrietta, youngest daughter of Charles I., who was born June 16th, 1644, at Exeter. She was known as "La belle Henriette." In May, 1670, she came to Dover on a political mission from Louis XIV. to her brother Charles II., but the visit was undertaken much against the wish of her husband. Her death occurred on her return to France, and was attributed to poison. It was the occasion of one of the finest of Bossuet's "Oraisons Funèbres."

[2] Hugh Peters, born at Fowey, Cornwall, and educated at Trinity College, Cambridge, where he graduated M.A. 1622. He was tried as one of the regicides, and executed. A broadside, entitled "The Welsh Hubub, or the Unkennelling and earthing of Hugh Peters that crafty Fox," was printed October 3rd, 1660.

being the first that I have been at home all day since I came hither. Putting my papers, books and other things in order, and writing of letters. This day my Lord set sail from the Downs for Holland.

[8th]. All day also at home. At night sent for by Sir W. Pen, with whom I sat late drinking a glass of wine and discoursing, and I find him to be a very sociable man, and an able man, and very cunning.

[9th] (Sunday). In the morning with Sir W. Pen to church, and a very good sermon of Mr. Mills. Home to dinner, and Sir W. Pen with me to such as I had, and it was very handsome, it being the first time that he ever saw my wife or house since we came hither. Afternoon to church with my wife, and after that home, and there walked with Major Hart,[1] who came to see me, in the garden, who tells me that we are all like to be speedily disbanded,[2] and then I lose the benefit of a muster. After supper to bed.

[10th] (Office day). News of the Duke's intention to go to-morrow to the fleet for a day or two to meet his sister. Col. Slingsby and I to Whitehall, thinking to proffer our service to the Duke to wait upon him, but meeting with Sir G. Carteret he sent us in all haste back again to hire two Catches for the present use of the Duke. So we returned and landed at the Bear at the Bridge foot,[3] where we saw Southwark Fair[4] (I having not at all seen Bartholomew Fair), and so to the Tower wharf, where we did hire two catches. So to the office and found Sir W. Batten at dinner

---

[1] Major Hart; he lived in Cannon Street; see *post*, September 20th.

[2] The Trained Bands were abolished in 1663; but those of the City of London were specially excepted. The officers of the Trained Bands were supplied by the Hon. Artillery Company.

[3] The Bear at the Bridge foot was a famous tavern at the Southwark end of old London Bridge, on the west side of High Street. It was pulled down in December, 1761.

[4] Liberty to hold an annual fair in Southwark on September 7th, 8th, and 9th, was granted to the City of London by the charter of 2 Edward IV. (November 2nd, 1462). Though the allowed time for its continuance by charter was only three days, it generally continued, like other fairs, for fourteen days.

with some friends upon a good chine of beef, on which I ate heartily, I being very hungry. Home, where Mr. Snow (whom afterwards we called one another cozen) came to me to see me, and with him and one Shelston, a simple fellow that looks after an employment (that was with me just upon my going to sea last), to a tavern, where till late with them. So home, having drunk too much, and so to bed.

[11th]. At Sir W. Batten's with Sir W. Pen we drank our morning draft, and from thence for an hour in the office and dispatch a little business. Dined at Sir W. Batten's, and by this time I see that we are like to have a very good correspondence and neighbourhood, but chargeable. All the afternoon at home looking over my carpenters. At night I called Thos. Hater out of the office to my house to sit and talk with me. After he was gone I caused the girl to wash the wainscot of our parlour, which she did very well, which caused my wife and I good sport. Up to my chamber to read a little, and wrote my Diary for three or four days past. The Duke of York did go to-day by break of day to the Downs. The Duke of Gloucester ill. The House of Parliament was to adjourn to-day. I know not yet whether it be done or no. To bed.

[12th] (Office day). This noon I expected to have had my cousin Snow and my father come to dine with me, but it being very rainy they did not come. My brother Tom came to my house with a letter from my brother John, wherein he desires some books: Barthol. Anatom., Rosin. Rom. Antiq., and Gassend. Astronom.,[1] the last of which I did give him, and an angel[2] against my father buying of the others. At home all the afternoon looking after my workmen, whose laziness do much trouble me. This day the Parliament adjourned.

[13th]. Old East comes to me in the morning with letters, and I did give him a bottle of Northdown ale, which made the poor

---

[1] "Thomæ Bartholini Anatomia," Hagæ Comitis, 1660, "Joannis Rosini Antiquitatum Romanarum Corpus," Amstelodami, 1685, "Petri Gassendi Institutio Astronomica," 1683, are in Pepys's library.

[2] A gold coin varying in value at different times from 6s. 8d. to 10s.

man almost drunk. In the afternoon my wife went to the burial of a child of my cozen Scott's, and it is observable that within this month my Aunt Wight was brought to bed of two girls, my cozen Stradwick[1] of a girl and a boy, and my cozen Scott of a boy, and all died. In the afternoon to Westminster, where Mr. Dalton was ready with his money to pay me for my house, but our writings

THE DUKE OF GLOUCESTER

not being drawn it could not be done to-day. I met with Mr. Hawly, who was removing his things from Mr. Bowyer's, where he has lodged a great while, and I took him and W. Bowyer to the Swan and drank, and Mr. Hawly did give me a little black rattoon,[2] painted and gilt. Home by water. This day the Duke of

[1] Elizabeth Stradwick, sister of Richard Pepys, and wife of Thomas Stradwick.

[2] Probably an Indian rattan cane.

Gloucester died of the small-pox, by the great negligence of the doctors.[1]

[14th] (Office day). I got £42 15s. appointed me by bill for my employment of Secretary to the 4th of this month, it being the last money I shall receive upon that score. My wife went this afternoon to see my mother, who I hear is very ill, at which my heart is very sad. In the afternoon Luellin comes to my house, and takes me out to the Mitre in Wood Street,[2] where Mr. Samford, W. Symons and his wife, and Mr. Scobell, Mr. Mount and Chetwind, where they were very merry, Luellin being drunk, and I being to defend the ladies from his kissing them, I kissed them myself very often with a great deal of mirth. Parted very late, they by coach to Westminster, and I on foot.

[15th]. Met very early at our office this morning to pick out the twenty-five ships which are to be first paid off. After that to Westminster and dined with Mr. Dalton at his office, where we had one great court dish, but our papers not being done we could [not] make an end of our business till Monday next. Mr. Dalton and I over the water to our landlord Vanly, with whom we agree as to Dalton becoming a tenant. Back to Westminster, where I met with Dr. Castles, who chidd me for some errors in our Privy-Seal business; among the rest, for letting the fees of the six judges pass unpaid, which I know not what to say to, till I speak to Mr. Moore. I was much troubled, for fear of being forced to pay the money myself. Called at my father's going home, and bespoke mourning for myself, for the death of the Duke of Gloucester. I found my mother pretty well. So home and to bed.

[16th] (Sunday). To Dr. Hardy's church,[3] and sat with Mr.

---

[1] Elegies on the Duke of Gloucester's death were printed. One of these was entitled, "Some Teares dropt on the Herse of the incomparable Prince Henry, Duke of Gloucester."

[2] The Mitre in Wood Street was kept by William Proctor, who died insolvent of the plague, 1665 (see July 31st, 1665). The tavern was destroyed in the Great Fire (see "Boyne's Trade Tokens," ed. Williamson, vol. i., 1889, p. 800).

[3] Nathaniel Hardy, D.D., was for many years preacher at the church of St. Dionis Backchurch, and on August 10th, 1660, he was appointed rector of that parish. He was son of Anthony Hardy, and born in the Old Bailey,

Rawlinson and heard a good sermon upon the occasion of the Duke's death. His text was, "And is there any evil in the city and the Lord hath not done it?" Home to dinner, having some sport with Wm. [Hewer], who never had been at Common Prayer before. After dinner I alone to Westminster, where I spent my time walking up and down in Westminster Abbey till sermon time with Ben. Palmer and Fetters the watchmaker, who told me that my Lord of Oxford[1] is also dead of the small-pox; in whom his family dies, after 600 years having that honour in their family and name. From thence to the Park, where I saw how far they had proceeded in the Pell-mell, and in making a river through the Park, which I had never seen before since it was begun.[2] Thence to White Hall garden, where I saw the King in purple mourning[3] for his brother. So home, and in my way met Dinah, who spoke to me and told me she had a desire to speak too about some business when I came to Westminster again. Which she spoke in such a manner that I was afraid she might tell me something that I would not hear of our last meeting at my house at Westminster. Home late, being very dark. A gentleman in the Poultry had a great and dirty fall over a water-pipe that lay along the channel.

[17th]. Office very early about casting up the debts of those twenty-five ships which are to be paid off, which we are to present to the Committee of Parliament. I did give my wife £15 this morning to go to buy mourning things for her and me, which she

September 14th, 1618. He became a prominent Presbyterian minister, but after the Treaty of Uxbridge, 1644, he changed his opinions, and preached a recantation sermon in London. He was appointed Dean of Rochester, December 10th, 1660, and vicar of St. Martin's-in-the-Fields. Died at Croydon, June 1st, 1670, and was buried in the church of St. Martin's.

[1] Aubrey de Vere, then twentieth Earl of Oxford, survived till March 12, 1702-3, when the title became extinct.

[2] This is the Mall in St. James's Park, which was made by Charles II., the former Mall (Pall Mall) having been built upon during the Commonwealth. Charles II. also formed the canal by throwing the several small ponds into one.

[3] "The Queen-mother of France," says Ward, in his Diary, p. 177, "died at Agrippina, 1642, and her son Louis, 1643, for whom King Charles mourned in Oxford, in *purple, which is Prince's mourning*."

did. Dined at home and Mr. Moore with me, and afterwards to Whitehall to Mr. Dalton and drank in the Cellar, where Mr. Vanly according to appointment was. Thence forth to see the Prince de Ligne, Spanish Embassador, come in to his audience, which was done in very great state. That being done, Dalton, Vanly, Scrivener and some friends of theirs and I to the Axe, and signed and sealed our writings, and hence to the Wine cellar again, where I received £41 for my interest in my house, out of which I paid my Landlord to Michaelmas next, and so all is even between him and me, and I freed of my poor little house. Home by link with my money under my arm. So to bed after I had looked over the things my wife had bought to-day, with which being not very well pleased, they costing too much, I went to bed in a discontent. Nothing yet from sea, where my Lord and the Princess are.

[18th]. At home all the morning looking over my workmen in my house. After dinner Sir W. Batten, Pen, and myself by coach to Westminster Hall, where we met Mr. Wayte the lawyer to the Treasurer, and so we went up to the Committee of Parliament, which are to consider of the debts of the Army and Navy, and did give in our account of the twenty-five ships. Col. Birch was very impertinent and troublesome. But at last we did agree to fit the accounts of our ships more perfectly for their view within a few days, that they might see what a trouble it is to do what they desire. From thence Sir Williams both going by water home, I took Mr. Wayte to the Rhenish winehouse, and drank with him and so parted. Thence to Mr. Crew's and spoke with Mr. Moore about the business of paying off Baron our share of the dividend. So on foot home, by the way buying a hat band and other things for my mourning to-morrow. So home and to bed. This day I heard that the Duke of York, upon the news of the death of his brother yesterday, came hither by post last night.

[19th] (Office day). I put on my mourning and went to the office. At noon thinking to have found my wife in hers, I found that the tailor had failed her, at which I was vexed because of an invitation that we have to a dinner this day, but after having waited till

past one o'clock I went, and left her to put on some other clothes and come after me to the Mitre tavern in Wood-street (a house of the greatest note in London), where I met W. Symons, and D. Scobell, and their wives, Mr. Samford, Luellin, Chetwind, one Mr. Vivion, and Mr. White,[1] formerly chaplin to the Lady Protectresse[2] (and still so, and one they say that is likely to get my Lady Francess for his wife). Here we were very merry and had a very good dinner, my wife coming after me hither to us. Among other pleasures some of us fell to handycapp,[3] a sport that I never knew before, which was very good. We staid till it was very late; it rained sadly, but we made shift to get coaches. So home and to bed.

[20th]. At home, and at the office, and in the garden walking with both Sir Williams all the morning. After dinner to White-hall to Mr. Dalton, and with him to my house and took away all my papers that were left in my closet, and so I have now nothing more in the house or to do with it. We called to speak with my Landlord Beale, but he was not within but spoke with the old woman, who takes it very ill that I did not let her have it, but I did give her an answer. From thence to Sir G. Downing and staid late there (he having sent for me to come to him), which was to tell me how my Lord Sandwich had disappointed him of a ship to bring over his child and goods, and made great com-

---

[1] According to Noble, Jeremiah White married Lady Frances Cromwell's waiting-woman, in Oliver's lifetime, and they lived together fifty years. Lady Frances had two husbands, Mr. Robert Rich and Sir John Russell of Chippenham, the last of whom she survived fifty-two years, dying 1721-2. The story is, that Oliver found White on his knees to Frances Cromwell, and that, to save himself, he pretended to have been soliciting her interest with her waiting-woman, whom Oliver compelled him to marry. (Noble's "Life of Cromwell," vol. ii. pp. 151, 152.) White was born in 1629 and died 1707.

[2] Elizabeth, wife of Oliver Cromwell.

[3] "A game at cards not unlike Loo, but with this difference, the winner of one trick has to put in a double stake, the winner of two tricks a triple stake, and so on. Thus, if six persons are playing, and the general stake is 1s., suppose A gains the three tricks, he gains 6s., and has to 'hand i' the cap,' or pool, 4s. for the next deal. Suppose A gains two tricks and B one, then A gains 4s. and B 2s., and A has to stake 3s. and B 2s. for the next deal." Hindley's *Tavern Anecdotes.*—M. B.

plaint thereof; but I got him to write a letter to Lawson,[1] which it may be may do the business for him, I writing another also about it. While he was writing, and his Lady and I had a great deal of discourse in praise of Holland. By water to the bridge, and so to Major Hart's lodgings in Cannon-street, who used me very kindly with wine and good discourse, particularly upon the ill method which Colonel Birch and the Committee use in defending of the army and the navy; promising the Parliament to save them a great deal of money, when we judge that it will cost the King more than if they had nothing to do with it, by reason of their delays and scrupulous enquirys into the account of both. So home and to bed.

[21st] (Office day). There all the morning and afternoon till 4 o'clock. Hence to Whitehall, thinking to have put up my books at my Lord's, but am disappointed from want of a chest which I had at Mr. Bowyer's. Back by water about 8 o'clock, and upon the water saw the corpse of the Duke of Gloucester brought down Somerset House stairs, to go by water to Westminster, to be buried to-night. I landed at the old Swan[2] and went to the Hoop Tavern, and (by a former agreement) sent for Mr. Chaplin, who with Nicholas Osborne and one Daniel came to us and we drank off two or three quarts of wine, which was very good; the drawing of our wine causing a great quarrel in the house between the two drawers which should draw us the best, which caused a great deal of noise and falling out till the master parted them, and came up to us and did give us a large account of the liberty that he gives his servants, all alike, to draw what wine they will to please his customers; and we did eat above 200 walnuts. About 10 o'clock we broke up and so home, and in my way I called in with them at Mr. Chaplin's, where Nicholas Osborne did give me a barrel of samphire,[3] and showed me the keys of Mardyke

[1] The Vice-Admiral.

[2] The Old Swan tavern in Thames Street was a very old house, and mention of it is found as early as 1323. There is a token of Richard Evans dated 1668, which must have been issued from the new building, as the old tavern was destroyed in the Great Fire (see "Boyne's Trade Tokens," ed. Williamson, vol. i., 1889, p. 768).

[3] Samphire was formerly a favourite pickle; hence the "dangerous trade" of

Fort,[1] which he that was commander of the fort sent him as a token when the fort was demolished, which I was mightily pleased to see, and will get them of him if I can. Home, where I found my boy (my maid's brother) come out of the country to-day, but was gone to bed and so I could not see him to-night. To bed.

[22nd]. This morning I called up my boy, and found him a pretty, well-looked boy, and one that I think will please me. I went this morning by land to Westminster along with Luellin, who came to my house this morning to get me to go with him to Capt. Allen to speak with him for his brother to go with him to Constantinople, but could not find him. We walked on to Fleet Street, where at Mr. Standing's in Salsbury Court we drank our morning draft and had a pickled herring. Among other discourse here he told me how the pretty woman that I always loved at the beginning of Cheapside that sells child's coats was served by the Lady Bennett (a famous strumpet), who by counterfeiting to fall into a swoon upon the sight of her in her shop, became acquainted with her, and at last got her ends of her to lie with a gentleman that had hired her to procure this poor soul for him. To Westminster to my Lord's and there in the house of office vomited up all my breakfast, my stomach being ill all this day by reason of the last night's debauch. Here I sent to Mr. Bowyer's for my chest and put up my books and sent them home. I staid here all day in my Lord's chamber and upon the leads gazing upon Diana, who looked out of a window upon me. At last I went out to Mr. Harper's, and she standing over the way at the gate, I went over to her and appointed to meet to-morrow in the afternoon at my Lord's. Here I bought a hanging jack. From thence by coach home (by the way at the New Exchange[2] I bought a

the samphire gatherer ("King Lear," act iv. sc. 6) who supplied the demand. It was sold in the streets, and one of the old London cries was "I ha' Rock Samphier, Rock Samphier!"

[1] A fort four miles east of Dunkirk, probably dismantled when that town was sold to Louis XIV.

[2] In the Strand; built, under the auspices of James I., in 1608, out of the stables of Durham House, the site of the present Adelphi. The New Exchange stood where Coutts's banking-house now is. "It was built somewhat on the model of the Royal Exchange, with cellars beneath, a walk above, and

pair of short black stockings, to wear over a pair of silk ones for mourning; and here I met with The. Turner and Joyce,[1] buying of things to go into mourning too for the Duke, which is now the mode of all the ladies in town), where I wrote some letters by the post to Hinchinbroke to let them know that this day Mr. Edw. Pickering is come from my Lord, and says that he left him well in Holland, and that he will be here within three or four days. To-day not well of my last night's drinking yet. I had the boy up to-night for his sister to teach him to put me to bed, and I heard him read, which he did pretty well.

[23rd] (Lord's day). My wife got up to put on her mourning to-day and to go to Church this morning. I up and set down my journall for these 5 days past. This morning came one from my father's with a black cloth coat, made of my short cloak, to walk up and down in. To church my wife and I, with Sir W. Batten, where we heard of Mr. Mills a very good sermon upon these words, "So run that ye may obtain." After dinner all alone to Westminster. At Whitehall I met with Mr. Pierce and his wife (she newly come forth after child-birth) both in mourning for the Duke of Gloucester. She went with Mr. Child to Whitehall chapel and Mr. Pierce with me to the Abbey, where I expected to hear Mr. Baxter or Mr. Rowe preach their farewell sermon, and in Mr. Symons's pew I sat and heard Mr. Rowe. Before sermon I laughed at the reader, who in his prayer desires of God that He would imprint his word on the thumbs of our right hands and on the right great toes of our right feet.[2] In the midst of the sermon some plaster fell from the top of the Abbey, that made me and

---

rows of shops over that, filled chiefly with milliners, sempstresses, and the like." It was also called "Britain's Burse." "He has a lodging in the Strand . . . to watch when ladies are gone to the china houses, or to the *Exchange*, that he may meet them by chance and give them presents, some two or three hundred pounds worth of toys, to be laughed at."—Ben Jonson, *The Silent Woman*, act i. sc. 1.

[1] Probably Joyce Norton, see *ante*, January 7th (note).

[2] Pepys apparently was ignorant of the instructions in the Levitical law, "Then shalt thou kill the ram, and take of his blood and put it upon the tip of the right ear of Aaron, and upon the tip of the right ear of his sons, and upon the thumb of their right hand, and upon the great toe of their right foot."— *Exodus* xxix. 20. (See also Leviticus viii. 23, xiv. 14.)

all the rest in our pew afeard, and I wished myself out. After sermon with Mr. Pierce to Whitehall, and from thence to my Lord, but Diana did not come according to our agreement. So calling at my father's (where my wife had been this afternoon but was gone home) I went home. This afternoon, the King having news of the Princess being come to Margate, he and the Duke of York went down thither in barges to her.

[24th] (Office day). From thence to dinner by coach with my wife to my Cozen Scott's, and the company not being come, I went over the way to the Barber's. So thither again to dinner, where was my uncle Fenner and my aunt, my father and mother, . and others. Among the rest my Cozen Rich. Pepys,[1] their elder brother, whom I had not seen these fourteen years, ever since he came from New England. It was strange for us to go a gossiping to her, she having newly buried her child that she was brought to bed of. I rose from table and went to the Temple church, where I had appointed Sir W. Batten to meet him; and there at Sir Heneage Finch Sollicitor General's chambers, before him and Sir W. Wilde,[2] Recorder of London (whom we sent for from his chamber) we were sworn justices of peace for Middlesex, Essex, Kent, and Southampton; with which honour I did find myself mightily pleased, though I am wholly ignorant in the duty of a justice of peace. From thence with Sir William to Whitehall by water (old Mr. Smith with us) intending to speak with Secretary Nicholas about the augmentation of our salaries, but being forth we went to the Three Tuns tavern, where we drank awhile, and then came in Col. Slingsby and another gentleman and sat with us. From thence to my Lord's to enquire whether they have had any thing from my Lord or no. Knocking at the door, there

---

[1] Richard Pepys, eldest son of Richard Pepys, Lord Chief Justice of Ireland. He went to Boston, Mass., in 1634, and returned to England about 1646.

[2] William Wilde, elected Recorder on November 3rd, 1659, and appointed one of the commissioners sent to Breda to desire Charles II. to return to England immediately. He was knighted after the King's return, called to the degree of Serjeant, and created a baronet, all in the same year. In 1668 he ceased to be Recorder, and was appointed Judge of the Court of Common Pleas. In 1673 he was removed to the King's Bench. He was turned out of his office in 1679 on account of his action in connection with the Popish Plot, and died November 23rd of the same year.

passed me Mons. L'Impertinent [Mr. Butler] for whom I took a coach and went with him to a dancing meeting in Broad Street,[1] at the house that was formerly the glass-house, Luke Channell[2] Master of the School, where I saw good dancing, but it growing late, and the room very full of people and so very hot, I went home.

[25th]. To the office, where Sir W. Batten, Colonel Slingsby,[3] and I sat awhile, and Sir R. Ford[4] coming to us about some business, we talked together of the interest of this kingdom to have a peace with Spain and a war with France and Holland; where Sir R. Ford talked like a man of great reason and experience. And afterwards I did send for a cup of tee[5] (a China drink) of which I never had drank before, and went away. Then came Col. Birch and Sir R. Browne by a former appointment, and with them from Tower wharf in the barge belonging to our office we went to Deptford to pay off the ship Success, which (Sir G. Carteret and

---

[1] James Howell directed a letter from Middleburg in Zealand, June 6th, 1619, to "Captain Francis Bacon, at the Glass house in Broad Street." Monk was lodged there in February, 1659-60. The place was burned in the Great Fire.

[2] Luke Cheynell, a hop merchant, is mentioned not very respectfully in "Select City Quæries, by Mercurius Philalethes." Part I., London, 1660. This may be the same person.

[3] Colonel, afterwards Sir Robert Slingsby, Comptroller of the Navy, whose father, Sir Guildford Slingsby, held the same office. See *ante*, September 5th.

[4] Sir Richard Ford was one of the commissioners sent to Breda to desire Charles II. to return to England immediately.

[5] The "Mercurius Politicus" of September 30th, 1658, sets forth: "That excellent and by all Physicians, approved, China drink, called by the Chineans Tcha, by other nations Tay alias Tee, is sold at the Sultaness Head Coffee-House, in Sweetings Rents, by the Royal Exchange, London." "Coffee, chocolate, and a kind of drink called *tee*, sold in almost every street in 1659."— Rugge's *Diurnal*. It is stated in "Boyne's Trade Tokens," ed. Williamson, vol. i., 1889, p. 593, "that the word tea occurs on no other tokens than those issued from 'the Great Turk' (Morat yᶜ Great) coffeehouse in Exchange Alley." The Dutch East India Company introduced tea into Europe in 1610, and it is said to have been first imported into England from Holland about 1650. The English "East India Company" purchased and presented 2 lbs. of tea to Charles II. in 1664, and 23 2/3 lbs. in 1666. The first order for its importation by the company was in 1668, and the first consignment of it, amounting to 143 1/2 lbs., was received from Bantam in 1669 (see Sir George Birdwood's "Report on the Old Records at the India Office," 1890, p. 26). By act 12 Car. II., capp. 23, 24, a duty of 8*d.* per gallon was imposed upon the infusion of tea, as well as on chocolate and sherbet.

Sir W. Pen coming afterwards to us) we did, Col. Birch being a mighty busy man and one that is the most indefatigable and forward to make himself work of any man that ever I knew in my life. At the Globe we had a very good dinner, and after that to the pay again, which being finished we returned by water again, and I from our office with Col. Slingsby by coach to Westminster (I setting him down at his lodgings by the way) to inquire for my Lord's coming thither (the King and the Princess[1] coming up the river this afternoon as we were at our pay), and I found him gone to Mr. Crew's, where I found him well, only had got some corns upon his foot which was not well yet. My Lord told me how the ship that brought the Princess and him (The Tredagh[2]) did knock six times upon the Kentish Knock,[3] which put them in great fear for the ship; but got off well. He told me also how the King had knighted Vice-Admiral Lawson and Sir Richard Stayner. From him late and by coach home, where the plasterers being at work in all the rooms in my house, my wife was fain to make a bed upon the ground for her and me, and so there we lay all night.

[26th] (Office day). That done to the church, to consult about our gallery. So home to dinner, where I found Mrs. Hunt, who brought me a letter for me to get my Lord to sign for her husband, which I shall do for her. At home with the workmen all the afternoon, our house being in a most sad pickle. In the evening to the office, where I fell a-reading of Speed's Geography[4] for a while.

---

[1] "The Princess Royall came from Gravesend to Whitehall by water, attended by a noble retinue of about one hundred persons, gentry, and servants, and tradesmen, and tirewomen, and others, that took that opportunity to advance their fortunes, by coming in with so excellent a Princess as without question she is."—Rugge's *Diurnal*. A broadside, entitled "Ourania, the High and Mighty Lady the Princess Royal of Aurange, congratulated on her most happy arrival, September the 25th, 1660," was printed on the 29th.

[2] "The Tredagh," a third-rate of fifty guns, had its name changed to "Resolution."

[3] A shoal in the North Sea, off the Thames mouth, outside the Long Sand, fifteen miles N.N.E. of the North Foreland. It measures seven miles northeastward, and about two miles in breadth. It is partly dry at low water. A revolving light was set up in 1840.

[4] "A Prospect of the most famous Parts of the World . . . by John Speed," London, 1631, is in the Pepysian Library.

So home thinking to have found Will at home, but he not being come home but gone somewhere else I was very angry, and when he came did give him a very great check for it, and so I went to bed.

[27th]. To my Lord at Mr. Crew's, and there took order about some business of his, and from thence home to my workmen all the afternoon. In the evening to my Lord's, and there did read over with him and Dr. Walker my Lord's new commission for sea, and advised thereupon how to have it drawn. So home and to bed.

[28th] (Office day). This morning Sir W. Batten and Col. Slingsby went with Col. Birch and Sir Wm. Doyly[1] to Chatham to pay off a ship there. So only Sir W. Pen and I left here in town. All the afternoon among my workmen till 10 or 11 at night, and did give them drink and very merry with them, it being my luck to meet with a sort of drolling workmen on all occasions. To bed.

[29th]. All day at home to make an end of our dirty work of the plasterers, and indeed my kitchen is now so handsome that I did not repent of all the trouble that I have been put to, to have it done. This day or yesterday, I hear, Prince Rupert[2] is come to Court; but welcome to nobody.

[30th] (Lord's day). To our Parish church both forenoon and afternoon all alone. At night went to bed without prayers, my house being every where foul above stairs.

[October 1st]. Early to my Lord to Whitehall, and there he did give me some work to do for him, and so with all haste to the office. Dined at home, and my father by chance with me. After dinner he and I advised about hangings for my rooms, which are now almost fit to be hung, the painters beginning to do their work to-day. After dinner he and I to the Miter, where with my uncle

---

[1] Sir Wm. Doyly was M.P. for the borough of Great Yarmouth.

[2] This is the first mention in the Diary of this famous prince, third son of Frederick, Prince Palatine of the Rhine, and Elizabeth, daughter of James I., born December 17th, 1619. He died at his house in Spring Gardens, November 29th, 1682.

Wight (whom my father fetched thither), while I drank a glass of wine privately with Mr. Mansell, a poor Reformado of the Charles, who came to see me. Here we staid and drank three or four pints of wine and so parted. I home to look after my workmen, and at night to bed. The Commissioners are very busy disbanding of the army, which they say do cause great robbing. My layings out upon my house in furniture are so great that I fear I shall not be able to go through them without breaking one of my bags of £100, I having but £200 yet in the world.

[2nd]. With Sir Wm. Pen by water to Whitehall, being this morning visited before I went out by my brother Tom, who told me that for his lying out of doors a day and a night my father had forbade him to come any more into his house, at which I was troubled, and did soundly chide him for doing so, and upon confessing his fault I told him I would speak to my father. At Whitehall I met with Captain Clerk, and took him to the Leg in King Street, and did give him a dish or two of meat, and his purser that was with him, for his old kindness to me on board. After dinner I to Whitehall, where I met with Mrs. Hunt, and was forced to wait upon Mr. Scawen at a committee to speak for her husband, which I did. After that met with Luellin, Mr. Fage, and took them both to the Dog, and did give them a glass of wine. After that at Will's I met with Mr. Spicer, and with him to the Abbey to see them at vespers. There I found but a thin congregation already. So I see that religion, be it what it will, is but a humour,[1] and so the esteem of it passeth as other things do. From thence with him to see Robin Shaw, who has been a long time ill, and I have not seen him since I came from sea. He is much changed, but in hopes to be well again. From thence by coach to my father's, and discoursed with him about Tom, and did give my advice to take him home again, which I think he will do in prudence rather than put him upon learning the way of being worse. So home, and from home to Major Hart, who is just going out of town to-morrow,

---

[1] The four humours of the body described by the old physicians were supposed to exert their influence upon the mind, and in course of time the mind as well as the body was credited with its own particular humours. The modern restricted use of the word humour did not become general until the eighteenth century.

and made much of me, and did give me the oaths of supremacy and allegiance, that I may be capable of my arrears. So home again, where my wife tells me what she has bought to-day, namely, a bed and furniture for her chamber, with which very well pleased I went to bed.

[3d]. With Sir W. Batten and Pen by water to White Hall, where a meeting of the Dukes of York and Albemarle, my Lord Sandwich and all the principal officers, about the Winter Guard, but we determined of nothing. To my Lord's, who sent a great iron chest to White Hall; and I saw it carried into the King's closet, where I saw most incomparable pictures. Among the rest a book open upon a desk, which I durst have sworn was a reall book, and back again to my Lord, and dined all alone with him, who do treat me with a great deal of respect; and after dinner did discourse an hour with me, and advise about some way to get himself some money to make up for all his great expenses, saying that he believed that he might have any thing that he would ask of the King. This day Mr. Sheply and all my Lord's goods came from sea, some of them laid at the Wardrobe and some brought to my Lord's house. From thence to our office, where we met and did business, and so home and spent the evening looking upon the painters that are at work in my house. This day I heard the Duke speak of a great design that he and my Lord of Pembroke have, and a great many others, of sending a venture to some parts of Africa to dig for gold ore there. They intend to admit as many as will venture their money, and so make themselves a company. £250 is the lowest share for every man. But I do not find that my Lord do much like it. At night Dr. Fairbrother (for so he is lately made of the Civil Law) brought home my wife by coach, it being rainy weather, she having been abroad to-day to buy more furniture for her house.

[4th]. This morning I was busy looking over papers at the office all alone, and being visited by Lieut. Lambert of the Charles (to whom I was formerly much beholden), I took him along with me to a little alehouse hard by our office, whither my cozen Thomas Pepys the turner had sent for me to show me two gentlemen that

THE DUKE OF YORK

had a great desire to be known to me, one his name is Pepys, of our family, but one that I never heard of before, and the other a younger son of Sir Tho. Bendishes,[1] and so we all called cozens. After sitting awhile and drinking, my two new cozens, myself, and Lieut. Lambert went by water to Whitehall, and from thence I and Lieut. Lambert to Westminster Abbey, where we saw Dr. Frewen[2] translated to the Archbishoprick of York. Here I saw the Bishops of Winchester,[3] Bangor,[4] Rochester,[5] Bath and Wells,[6] and Salisbury,[7] all in their habits, in King Henry Seventh's chappell. But, Lord! at their going out, how people did most of them look upon them as strange creatures, and few with any kind of love or respect. From thence at 2 to my Lord's, where we took Mr. Sheply and Wm. Howe to the Raindeer, and had some oysters, which were very good, the first I have eat this year. So back to my Lord's to dinner, and after dinner Lieut. Lambert and I did look upon my Lord's model, and he told me many things in a ship that I desired to understand. From thence by water I (leaving Lieut. Lambert at Blackfriars) went home, and there by promise met with Robert Shaw and Jack Spicer, who came to see me, and by the way I met upon Tower Hill with Mr. Pierce the surgeon and his wife, and took them home and did give them good wine, ale, and anchovies, and staid them till night, and so adieu. Then to look upon my painters that are now at work in my house. At night to bed.

[5th]. Office day; dined at home, and all the afternoon at home to see my painters make an end of their work, which they did to-day

---

[1] John Pepys of Cottenham (who died 1604) married the daughter of John Bendish of Bower Hall, Steeple Bumsted, co. Essex, so they may have thought there was some relationship. Sir Thomas Bendish was an Essex baronet, and for many years English ambassador at the Porte.

[2] Dr. Accepted Frewen, Bishop of Coventry and Lichfield, died March 28th, 1664.

[3] Brian Duppa, translated from Salisbury, died March 26th, 1662.

[4] William Roberts, elected 1637, died August 12th, 1665.

[5] John Warner, elected 1637, died October 14th, 1666, aged eighty-six.

[6] William Pierce, translated from Peterborough, 1632, died April, 1670.

[7] Humphrey Henchman, elected 1660, translated to London, 1663, died October 7th, 1675, aged eighty-three.

to my content, and I am in great joy to see my house likely once again to be clean. At night to bed.

[6th]. Col. Slingsby and I at the office getting a catch ready for the Prince de Ligne to carry his things away to-day, who is now going home again. About noon comes my cozen H. Alcock, for whom I brought a letter for my Lord to sign to my Lord Broghill for some preferment in Ireland, whither he is now agoing. After him comes Mr. Creed, who brought me some books from Holland with him, well bound and good books, which I thought he did intend to give me, but I found that I must pay him. He dined with me at my house, and from thence to Whitehall together, where I was to give my Lord an account of the stacions and victuals of the fleet in order to the choosing of a fleet fit for him to take to sea, to bring over the Queen, but my Lord not coming in before 9 at night I staid no longer for him, but went back again home and so to bed.

[7th] (Lord's day). To White Hall on foot, calling at my father's to change my long black cloak for a short one (long cloaks being now quite out); but he being gone to church, I could not get one, and therefore I proceeded on and came to my Lord before he went to chapel and so went with him, where I heard Dr. Spurstow[1] preach before the King a poor dry sermon; but a very good anthem of Captn. Cooke's afterwards. Going out of chapel I met with Jack Cole, my old friend (whom I had not seen a great while before), and have promised to renew acquaintance in London together. To my Lord's and dined with him; he all dinner time talking French to me, and telling me the story how the Duke of York hath got my Lord Chancellor's daughter with child,[2] and that she do lay it to him, and that for certain he did promise her marriage, and had signed it with his blood, but that he by stealth had got the paper out of her cabinet. And that the King would

---

[1] William Spurstow, D.D., Vicar of Hackney and Master of Catherine Hall, Cambridge, both which pieces of preferment he lost for nonconformity, 1662.

[2] Anne Hyde, born March 12th, 1637, daughter of Edward, first Earl of Clarendon. She was attached to the court of the Princess of Orange, daughter of Charles I., 1654, and contracted to James, Duke of York, at Breda, November 24th, 1659. The marriage was avowed in London September 3rd, 1660. She joined the Church of Rome in 1669, and died March 31st, 1671.

have him to marry her, but that he will not.[1] So that the thing is very bad for the Duke, and them all; but my Lord do make light of it, as a thing that he believes is not a new thing for the Duke to do abroad. Discoursing concerning what if the Duke should marry her, my Lord told me that among his father's many old sayings that he had wrote in a book of his, this is one—that he that do get a wench with child and marry her afterwards is as if a man should —— in his hat and then clap it on his head. I perceive my Lord is grown a man very indifferent in all matters of religion, and so makes nothing of these things. After dinner to the Abbey, where I heard them read the church-service, but very ridiculously, that indeed I do not in myself like it at all. A poor cold sermon of Dr. Lamb's,[2] one of the prebends, in his habit, came afterwards, and so all ended, and by my troth a pitiful sorry devotion that these men pay. So walked home by land, and before supper I read part of the Marian persecution in Mr. Fuller.[3] So to supper, prayers, and to bed.

[8th]. Office day, and my wife being gone out to buy some household stuff, I dined all alone, and after dinner to Westminster, in my way meeting Mr. Moore coming to me, who went back again with me calling at several places about business, at my father's about gilded leather for my dining room, at Mr. Crew's about money, at my Lord's about the same, but meeting not Mr. Sheply there I went home by water, and Mr. Moore with me, who staid and supped with me till almost 9 at night. We love one another's discourse so that we cannot part when we do meet. He tells me that the profit of the Privy Seal is much fallen, for which I am very sorry. He gone and I to bed.

[9th]. This morning Sir W. Batten with Colonel Birch to Deptford, to pay off two ships. Sir W. Pen and I staid to do business, and afterwards together to White Hall, where I went to my Lord,

---

[1] The Duke of York married Anne Hyde, and he avowed the marriage September 3rd, so that Pepys was rather behindhand in his information.

[2] James Lamb, D.D., installed prebendary of Westminster July 23rd, 1660, rector of St. Andrew's, Holborn, 1662, died 1664.

[3] Fuller's "Church History of Britain." There is a copy of the edition of 1656 in the Pepysian Library.

and found him in bed not well, and saw in his chamber his picture,[1] very well done; and am with child[2] till I get it copied out,
which I hope to do when he is gone to sea. To Whitehall again,
where at Mr. Coventry's chamber I met with Sir W. Pen again,
and so with him to Redriffe[3] by water, and from thence walked
over the fields to Deptford (the first pleasant walk I have had a
great while), and in our way had a great deal of merry discourse,
and find him to be a merry fellow and pretty good natured, and
sings very bawdy songs. So we came and found our gentlemen
and Mr. Prin at the pay. About noon we dined together, and were
very merry at table telling of tales. After dinner to the pay of another ship till 10 at night, and so home in our barge, a clear moonshine night, and it was 12 o'clock before we got home, where I
found my wife in bed, and part of our chambers hung to-day by
the upholster, but not being well done I was fretted, and so in a
discontent to bed. I found Mr. Prin a good, honest, plain man,
but in his discourse not very free or pleasant. Among all the
tales that passed among us to-day, he told us of one Damford,
that, being a black man, did scald his beard with mince-pie, and
it came up again all white in that place, and continued to his
dying day. Sir W. Pen told us a good jest about some gentlemen
blinding of the drawer, and who he catched was to pay the reckoning, and so they got away, and the master of the house coming
up to see what his man did, his man got hold of him, thinking it
to be one of the gentlemen, and told him that he was to pay the
reckoning.

[10th]. Office day all the morning. In the afternoon with the
upholster seeing him do things to my mind, and to my content he
did fit my chamber and my wife's. At night comes Mr. Moore,
and staid late with me to tell me how Sir Hards. Waller[4] (who

---

[1] Lord Sandwich's portrait by Lely, see *post*, 22nd of this same month.

[2] A figurative expression for an eager longing desire, used by Udall and by
Spenser. The latest authority given by Dr. Murray in the "New English Dictionary," is Bailey in 1725.

[3] The usual corruption of the name Rotherhithe.

[4] Sir Hardress Waller, Knt., one of Charles I.'s judges. His sentence was com-
muted to imprisonment for life.

only pleads guilty), Scott,[1] Coke,[2] Peters,[3] Harrison,[4] &c. were this day arraigned at the bar at the Sessions House, there being upon the bench the Lord Mayor, General Monk, my Lord of Sandwich, &c., such a bench of noblemen as had not been ever seen in England! They all seem to be dismayed, and will all be condemned without question. In Sir Orlando Bridgman's charge,[5] he did wholly rip up the unjustness of the war against the King from the beginning, and so it much reflects upon all the Long Parliament, though the King had pardoned them, yet they must hereby confess that the King do look upon them as traitors. To-morrow they are to plead what they have to say. At night to bed.

[11th]. In the morning to my Lord's, where I met with Mr. Creed, and with him and Mr. Blackburne to the Rhenish wine house, where we sat drinking of healths a great while, a thing which Mr. Blackburne formerly would not upon any terms have done. After we had done there Mr. Creed and I to the Leg in King Street, to dinner, where he and I and my Will had a good udder to dinner, and from thence to walk in St. James's Park, where we observed the several engines at work to draw up water, with which sight I was very much pleased.[6] Above all the rest, I liked

---

[1] Thomas Scott, the regicide Secretary of State. See *ante*, January 10th (note).

[2] John Cook, a member of Gray's Inn, appointed Solicitor-General for the Commonwealth, and ordered to prepare the charge against Charles I. Owing to the illness of the Attorney-General, the conduct of the prosecution fell chiefly upon him. He was rewarded for his services by being made Master of the Hospital of St. Cross. In 1655 appointed Justice of the Court of Upper Bench in Ireland. He was excluded by name from the Act of Indemnity, and executed October 16th, 1660. He wrote several pamphlets, some of which were very scurrilous in language.

[3] See *ante*, September 5th.

[4] General Thomas Harrison, son of a butcher at Newcastle-under-Lyme, appointed by Cromwell to convey Charles I. from Windsor to Whitehall, in order to his trial. He signed the warrant for the execution of the King. He was hanged, drawn, and quartered on the 13th.

[5] Second son of John Bridgeman, Bishop of Chester, became, after the Restoration, successively Chief Baron of the Exchequer, Chief Justice of the Common Pleas, and Lord Keeper of the Great Seal (1667). He was created a baronet in 1660. In 1672 he was removed from the office of Lord Keeper, and he died June 25th, 1674.

[6] It is said that Le Notre, the architect of the groves and grottos at Versailles, was engaged by Charles II. to arrange the improvements in St. James's Park, but Dr. Morison seems to have been the King's chief adviser.

best that which Mr. Greatorex brought, which is one round thing going within all with a pair of stairs round; round which being laid at an angle of 45°, do carry up the water with a great deal of ease. Here, in the Park, we met with Mr. Salisbury, who took Mr. Creed and me to the Cockpitt[1] to see "The Moore of Venice," which was well done. Burt acted the Moore;[2] by the same token, a very pretty lady that sat by me, called out, to see Desdemona smothered. From thence with Mr. Creed to Hercules Pillars,[3] where we drank and so parted, and I went home.

[12th]. Office day all the morning, and from thence with Sir W. Batten and the rest of the officers to a venison pasty of his at the Dolphin, where dined withal Col. Washington, Sir Edward Brett, and Major Norwood,[4] very noble company. After dinner I went home, where I found Mr. Cooke, who told me that my Lady Sandwich is come to town to-day, whereupon I went to Westminster to see her, and found her at supper, so she made me sit down all alone with her, and after supper staid and talked with her, she showing me most extraordinary love and kindness, and do give me good assurance of my uncle's resolution to make me his heir. From thence home and to bed.

[13th]. To my Lord's in the morning, where I met with Captain Cuttance, but my Lord not being up I went out to Charing Cross, to see Major-general Harrison hanged, drawn, and quartered; which was done there, he looking as cheerful as any man could do in that condition. He was presently cut down, and his head and heart shown to the people, at which there was great shouts of joy. It is said, that he said that he was sure to come shortly at the right hand of Christ to judge them that now had judged him; and that his wife do expect his coming again. Thus it was my

---

[1] The Cockpit theatre in Drury Lane.

[2] Nicholas Burt ranked in the list of good actors after the Restoration, though he resigned the part of Othello to Hart, who had previously acted Cassio when Burt took the Moor.—Davies' *Dramatic Miscellanies*, vol. i. p. 221.

[3] In Fleet Street, opposite Clifford's Inn Passage. The keeper of the tavern appears to have been Edward Oldham, who issued a token (see "Boyne's Trade Tokens," ed. Williamson, vol. i., 1889, p. 604).

[4] Major (afterwards Colonel) Norwood, Deputy Governor of Tangier.

chance to see the King beheaded at White Hall, and to see the
first blood shed in revenge for the blood of the King at Charing
Cross. From thence to my Lord's, and took Captain Cuttance and
Mr. Sheply to the Sun Tavern, and did give them some oysters.
After that I went by water home, where I was angry with my
wife for her things lying about, and in my passion kicked the
little fine basket, which I bought her in Holland, and broke it,
which troubled me after I had done it. Within all the afternoon
setting up shelves in my study. At night to bed.

[14th] (Lord's day). Early to my Lord's, in my way meeting
with Dr. Fairbrother, who walked with me to my father's back
again, and there we drank my morning draft, my father having
gone to church and my mother asleep in bed. Here he caused me
to put my hand among a great many honorable hands to a paper
or certificate in his behalf. To White Hall chappell, where one
Dr. Crofts[1] made an indifferent sermon, and after it an anthem,
ill sung, which made the King laugh. Here I first did see the Prin- •
cess Royal since she came into England. Here I also observed,
how the Duke of York and Mrs. Palmer did talk to one another
very wantonly through the hangings that parts the King's closet
and the closet where the ladies sit. To my Lord's, where I found
my wife, and she and I did dine with my Lady (my Lord dining
with my Lord Chamberlain), who did treat my wife with a good
deal of respect. In the evening we went home through the rain
by water in a sculler, having borrowed some coats of Mr. Sheply.
So home, wet and dirty, and to bed.

[15th]. Office all the morning. My wife and I by water; I landed
her at Whitefriars, she went to my father's to dinner, it being my
father's wedding day, there being a very great dinner, and only
the Fenners and Joyces there. This morning Mr. Carew[2] was

---

[1] Dr. Herbert Croft, Dean of Hereford, consecrated Bishop of Hereford, February 9th, 1661-2. He succeeded Bishop Morley as Dean of the Chapel. Burnet
says, "Crofts was a warm devout man, but of no discretion in his conduct; so
he lost ground quickly. He used much freedom with the King, but it was in
the wrong place, not in private but in the pulpit." Bishop Croft died at Hereford, May 18th, 1691.

[2] John Carew signed the warrant for the execution of Charles I. He held the
religion of the Fifth Monarchists, and was tried October 12th, 1660. He

hanged and quartered at Charing Cross; but his quarters, by a great favour, are not to be hanged up. I was forced to go to my Lord's to get him to meet the officers of the Navy this afternoon, and so could not go along with her, but I missed my Lord, who was this day upon the bench at the Sessions house. So I dined there, and went to White Hall, where I met with Sir W. Batten and Pen, who with the Comptroller, Treasurer, and Mr. Coventry (at his chamber) made up a list of such ships as are fit to be kept out for the winter guard, and the rest to be paid off by the Parliament when they can get money, which I doubt will not be a great while. That done, I took coach, and called my wife at my father's, and so homewards, calling at Thos. Pepys the turner's for some things that we wanted. And so home, where I fell to read "The Fruitless Precaution" (a book formerly recommended by Dr. Clerke at sea to me), which I read in bed till I had made an end of it, and do find it the best writ tale that ever I read in my life. After that done to sleep, which I did not very well do, because that my wife having a stopping in her nose she snored much, which I never did hear her do before.

[16th]. This morning my brother Tom came to me, with whom I made even for my last clothes to this day, and having eaten a dish of anchovies with him in the morning, my wife and I did intend to go forth to see a play at the Cockpit this afternoon, but Mr. Moore coming to me, my wife staid at home, and he and I went out together, with whom I called at the upholster's and several other places that I had business with, and so home with him to the Cockpit, where, understanding that "Wit without money"[1] was acted, I would not stay, but went home by water, by the way reading of the other two stories that are in the book that I read last night, which I do not like so well as it. Being come home, Will. told me that my Lord had a mind to speak with me to-night; so I returned by water, and, coming there, it was only to enquire how the ships were provided with victuals that are to

refused to avail himself of many opportunities of escape, and suffered death with much composure.

[1] A comedy by Beaumont and Fletcher, first printed in 1639, and again in 1661.

go with him to fetch over the Queen, which I gave him a good account of. He seemed to be in a melancholy humour, which, I was told by W. Howe, was for that he had lately lost a great deal of money at cards, which he fears he do too much addict himself to now-a-days. So home by water and to bed.

[17th]. Office day. At noon came Mr. Creed to me, whom I took along with me to the Feathers in Fish Street, where I was invited by Captain Cuttance to dinner, a dinner made by Mr. Dawes and his brother. We had two or three dishes of meat well done; their great design was to get me concerned in a business of theirs about a vessel of theirs that is in the service, hired by the King, in which I promise to do them all the service I can. From thence home again with Mr. Crew, where I finding Mrs. The. Turner and her aunt Duke I would not be seen but walked in the garden till they were gone, where Mr. Spong came to me and Mr. Creed, Mr. Spong and I went to our music to sing, and he being gone, my wife and I went to put up my books in order in closet, and I to give her her books. After that to bed.

[18th]. This morning, it being expected that Colonel Hacker[1] and Axtell[2] should die, I went to Newgate, but found they were reprieved till to-morrow. So to my aunt Fenner's, where with her and my uncle I drank my morning draft. So to my father's, and did give orders for a pair of black baize linings to be made me for my breeches against to-morrow morning, which was done. So to my Lord's, where I spoke with my Lord, and he would have had me dine with him, but I went thence to Mr. Blackburne, where I met my wife and my Will's father and mother (the first time that I ever saw them), where we had a very fine dinner. Mr. Creed was also there. This day by her high discourse I found Mrs. Blackburne to be a very high dame and a costly one. Home with my wife by coach. This afternoon comes Mr. Chaplin and N. Osborn to my house, of whom I made very much, and kept them with me till late, and so to bed. At my coming home I did find that The. Turner hath sent for a pair of doves that my wife

---

[1] Col. Francis Hacker commanded the guards at the King's execution.
[2] Axtell had guarded the High Court of Justice.

had promised her; and because she did not send them in the best cage, she sent them back again with a scornful letter, with which I was angry, but yet pretty well pleased that she was crossed.

[19th]. Office in the morning. This morning my dining-room was finished with green serge hanging and gilt leather, which is very handsome. This morning Hacker and Axtell were hanged and quartered, as the rest are. This night I sat up late to make up my accounts ready against to-morrow for my Lord. I found him to be above £80 in my debt, which is a good sight, and I bless God for it.

[20th]. This morning one came to me to advise with me where to make me a window into my cellar in lieu of one which Sir W. Batten had stopped up, and going down into my cellar to look I stepped into a great heap of ——, by which I found that Mr. Turner's house of office is full and comes into my cellar, which do trouble me, but I shall have it helped. To my Lord's by land, calling at several places about business, where I dined with my Lord and Lady; when he was very merry, and did talk very high how he would have a French cook, and a master of his horse, and his lady and child to wear black patches; which methought was strange, but he is become a perfect courtier; and, among other things, my Lady saying that she could get a good merchant for her daughter Jem., he answered, that he would rather see her with a pedlar's pack at her back, so she married a gentleman, than she should marry a citizen. This afternoon, going through London, and calling at Crowe's the upholster's, in Saint Bartholomew's,[1] I saw the limbs of some of our new traitors set upon Aldersgate,[2] which was a sad sight to see; and a bloody week this and the last have been, there being ten hanged, drawn, and quartered. Home, and after writing a letter to my uncle by the post, I went to bed.

---

[1] Crowe was fined for Alderman in 1663, see *post*, December 1st of that year, but he appears to have taken the office subsequently, see October 15th, 1668.

[2] The old gate was taken down in 1617, and rebuilt in the same year from a design by Gerard Christmas. The gate was injured in the Great Fire, but was repaired and remained until 1761.

[21st] (Lord's day). To the Parish church in the morning, where
a good sermon by Mr. Mills. After dinner to my Lord's, and from
thence to the Abbey, where I met Spicer and D. Vines and others
of the old crew. So leaving my boy at the Abbey against I came
back, we went to Prior's by the Hall back door, but there being
no drink to be had we went away, and so to the Crown in the
Palace Yard, I and George Vines by the way calling at their
house, where he carried me up to the top of his turret, where
there is Cooke's head set up for a traytor, and Harrison's set up
on the other side of Westminster Hall. Here I could see them
plainly, as also a very fair prospect about London. From the
Crown to the Abbey to look for my boy, but he was gone thence,
and so he being a novice I was at a loss what was become of him.
I called at my Lord's (where I found Mr. Adams, Mr. Sheply's
friend) and at my father's, but found him not. So home, where I
found him, but he had found the way home well enough, of
which I was glad. So after supper, and reading of some chapters,
I went to bed. This day or two my wife has been troubled with
her boils in the old place, which do much trouble her. To-day at
noon (God forgive me) I strung my lute, which I had not touched
a great while before.

[22nd]. Office day; after that to dinner at home upon some ribs
of roast beef from the Cook's (which of late we have been forced
to do because of our house being always under the painters' and
other people's hands, that we could not dress it ourselves). After
dinner to my Lord's, where I found all preparing for my Lord's
going to sea to fetch the Queen to-morrow. At night my Lord
came home, with whom I staid long, and talked of many things.
Among others I got leave to have his picture, that was done by
Lilly,[1] copied, and talking of religion, I found him to be a perfect
Sceptic, and said that all things would not be well while there
was so much preaching, and that it would be better if nothing but
Homilies[2] were to be read in Churches. This afternoon (he told

---

[1] Peter Lely, afterwards knighted. He lived in the Piazza, Covent Garden.
This portrait was bought by Lord Braybrooke at Mr. Pepys Cockerell's sale
in 1848, and is now at Audley End.

[2] The edition in the Pepysian Library of "Certain Sermons or Homilies appointed to be read in Churches" is dated 1673.

me) there hath been a meeting before the King and my Lord
Chancellor, of some Episcopalian and Presbyterian Divines; but
what had passed he could not tell me. After I had done talk with
him, I went to bed with Mr. Sheply in his chamber, but could
hardly get any sleep all night, the bed being ill made and he a
bad bedfellow.

[23rd]. We rose early in the morning to get things ready for my
Lord, and Mr. Sheply going to put up his pistols (which were
charged with bullets) into the holsters, one of them flew off, and
it pleased God that, the mouth of the gun being downwards, it
did us no hurt, but I think I never was in more danger in my life,
which put me into a great fright. About eight o'clock my Lord
went; and going through the garden my Lord met with Mr. William Montagu, who told him of an estate of land lately come
into the King's hands, that he had a mind my Lord should beg.
To which end my Lord writ a letter presently to my Lord Chancellor to do it for him, which (after leave taken of my Lord at
White Hall bridge) I did carry to Warwick House to him; and
had a fair promise of him, that he would do it this day for my
Lord. In my way thither I met the Lord Chancellor and all the
Judges riding on horseback and going to Westminster Hall, it
being the first day of the term, which was the first time I ever
saw any such solemnity. Having done there I returned to Whitehall, where meeting with my brother Ashwell and his cozen
Sam. Ashwell and Mr. Mallard, I took them to the Leg in King
Street and gave them a dish of meat for dinner and paid for it.
From thence going to Whitehall I met with Catan Stirpin in
mourning, who told me that her mistress was lately dead of the
small pox, and that herself was now married to Monsieur Petit,[1]
as also what her mistress had left her, which was very well. She
also took me to her lodging at an Ironmonger's in King Street,
which was but very poor, and I found by a letter that she shewed
me of her husband's to the King, that he is a right Frenchman,
and full of their own projects, he having a design to reform the
universities, and to institute schools for the learning of all lan-
guages, to speak them naturally and not by rule, which I know

[1] See *ante*, August 8th.

will come to nothing. From thence to my Lord's, where I went forth by coach to Mrs. Parker's with my Lady, and so to her house again. From thence I took my Lord's picture, and carried it to Mr. de Cretz to be copied. So to White Hall, where I met Mr. Spong, and went home with him and played, and sang, and eat with him and his mother. After supper we looked over many books, and instruments of his, especially his wooden jack in his chimney, which goes with the smoke, which indeed is very pretty. I found him to be as ingenious and good-natured a man as ever I met with in my life, and cannot admire him enough, he being so plain and illiterate a man as he is. From thence by coach home and to bed, which was welcome to me after a night's absence.

[24th]. I lay and slept long to-day. Office day. I took occasion to be angry with my wife before I rose about her putting up of half a crown of mine in a paper box, which she had forgot where she had lain it. But we were friends again as we are always. Then I rose to Jack Cole, who came to see me. Then to the office, so home to dinner, where I found Captain Murford, who did put £3 into my hands for a friendship I had done him, but I would not take it, but bade him keep it till he has enough to buy my wife a necklace. This afternoon people at work in my house to make a light in my yard into my cellar. To White Hall, in my way met with Mr. Moore, who went back with me. He tells me, among other things, that the Duke of York is now sorry for his lying with my Lord Chancellor's daughter, who is now brought to bed of a boy.[1] From Whitehall to Mr. De Cretz, who I found about my Lord's picture. From thence to Mr. Lilly's,[2] where, not finding Mr. Spong, I went to Mr. Greatorex, where I met him, and so to an alehouse, where I bought of him a drawing pen; and he did show me the manner of the lamp-glasses, which carry the light a great way, good to read in bed by, and I intend to have one of them. So to Mr. Lilly's with Mr. Spong, where well received, there being a

[1] The child was born October 22nd.
[2] William Lilly, the astrologer and almanack-maker, born 1602. He lived in the Strand, and died in 1681. His "Merlinus Anglicus Junior" was read to the Parliament's troops in Scotland as promising victory.

club to-night among his friends. Among the rest Esquire Ashmole,[1] who I found was a very ingenious gentleman. With him we two sang afterward in Mr. Lilly's study. That done, we all parted; and I home by coach, taking Mr. Booker[2] with me, who did tell me a great many fooleries, which may be done by nativities, and blaming Mr. Lilly for writing to please his friends and to keep in with the times (as he did formerly to his own dishonour), and not according to the rules of art, by which he could not well err, as he had done. I set him down at Lime-street end, and so home, where I found a box of Carpenter's tools sent by my cozen, Thomas Pepys, which I had bespoke of him for to employ myself with sometimes. To bed.

[25th]. All day at home doing something in order to the fitting of my house. In the evening to Westminster about business. So home and to bed. This night the vault at the end of the cellar was emptied.

[26th] (Office). My father and Dr. Thomas Pepys dined at my house, the last of whom I did almost fox with Margate ale. My father is mightily pleased with my ordering of my house. I did give him money to pay several bills. After that I to Westminster to White Hall, where I saw the Duke de Soissons[3] go from his audience with a very great deal of state: his own coach all red velvet covered with gold lace, and drawn by six barbes, and attended by twenty pages very rich in clothes. To Westminster Hall, and bought, among other books, one of the life of our Queen,[4] which I read at home to my wife; but it was so sillily

---

[1] Elias Ashmole, the antiquary, born May 23rd, 1617. He was for a time in the royal army, but subsequently he settled in London, and became associated with the astrologers. He was made Windsor Herald on June 18th, 1660. Died May 18th, 1692.

[2] John Booker, astrologer (born 1603, died 1667); mentioned in "Hudibras," part ii., canto iii., line 1093.

[3] Eugene Maurice of Savoy, youngest son of Thomas of Savoy, by Marie de Bourbon, Countess of Soissons, whose title he inherited. He married Olympia Mancini, one of the nieces of Cardinal Mazarin, more than suspected of poisoning practices (like the Brinvilliers). His youngest son was the celebrated general, Prince Eugene of Savoy.—B.

[4] "The History of the thrice Illustrious Princess Henrietta Maria de Bourbon Queen of England. London 1660." Dedicated "to the Paragon of Vertue and

writ, that we did nothing but laugh at it: among other things it is dedicated to that paragon of virtue and beauty, the Duchess of Albemarle. Great talk as if the Duke of York do now own the marriage between him and the Chancellor's daughter.

[27th]. In London and Westminster all this day paying of money and buying of things for my house. In my going I went by chance by my new Lord Mayor's house (Sir Richard Browne), by Goldsmith's Hall, which is now fitting, and indeed is a very pretty house.[1] In coming back I called at Paul's Churchyard and bought Alsted's Encyclopædia,[2] which cost me 38s. Home and to bed, my wife being much troubled with her old pain.

[28th] (Lord's day). There came some pills and plaister this morning from Dr. Williams for my wife. I to Westminster Abbey, where with much difficulty, going round by the cloysters, I got in; this day being a great day for the consecrating of five Bishopps, which was done after sermon; but I could not get into Henry the Seventh's chappell. So I went to my Lord's, where I dined with my Lady, and my young Lord, and Mr. Sidney,[3] who was sent for from Twickenham to see my Lord Mayor's show to-morrow. Mr. Child did also dine with us. After dinner to White Hall chappell; my Lady and my Lady Jemimah and I up to the King's closet (who is now gone to meet the Queen). So meeting with one Mr. Hill, that did know my Lady, he did take us into the King's closet, and there we did stay all service-time, which I did think a great honour. We went home to my Lord's lodgings afterwards, and there I parted with my Lady and went home, where I did find my wife pretty well after her physic. So to bed.

[29th]. I up early, it being my Lord Mayor's day[4] (Sir Richd.

Beauty, her Grace the Duchess of Aubemarle, &c.," by John Dauncy. The dedication ends with the wish "that the Rising Sun of your Grace's Vertues and Honours may still soar higher, but never know a declension."

[1] Alderman Sir Richard Browne was one of the commissioners sent to Charles II. at Breda to desire his speedy return to England. See *ante*, Feb. 22nd (note).

[2] "Johannis Henrici Alstedii Encyclopædia," 1630, bound in two volumes folio, is in the Pepysian Library.

[3] Lord Hinchinbroke and Sidney Montagu.

[4] When the calendar was reformed in England by the act 24 Geo. II. c. 23,

Browne), and neglecting my office I went to the Wardrobe, where I met my Lady Sandwich and all the children; and after drinking of some strange and incomparable good clarett of Mr. Rumball's[1] he and Mr. Townsend[1] did take us, and set the young Lords at one Mr. Nevill's, a draper in Paul's churchyard; and my Lady and my Lady Pickering and I to one Mr. Isaacson's, a linen draper at the Key in Cheapside; where there was a company of fine ladies, and we were very civilly treated, and had a very good place to see the pageants, which were many, and I believe good, for such kind of things, but in themselves but poor and absurd. After the ladies were placed I took Mr. Townsend and Isaacson to the next door, a tavern, and did spend 5s. upon them. The show being done, we got as far as Paul's with much ado, where I left my Lady in the coach, and went on foot with my Lady Pickering to her lodging, which was a poor one in Blackfryars, where she never invited me to go in at all, which methought was very strange for her to do. So home, where I was told how my Lady Davis[2] is now come to our next lodgings, and has locked up the leads door from me, which puts me into so great a disquiet that I went to bed, and could not sleep till morning at it.

different provisions were made as regards those anniversaries which affect directly the rights of property and those which do not. Thus the old quarter days are still noted in our almanacs, and a curious survival of this is brought home to payers of income tax. The fiscal year still begins on old Lady-day, which now falls on April 6th. All ecclesiastical fasts and feasts and other commemorations which did not affect the rights of property were left on their nominal days, such as the execution of Charles I. on January 30th and the restoration of Charles II. on May 29th. The change of Lord Mayor's day from the 29th of October to the 9th of November was not made by the act for reforming the calendar (c. 23), but by another act of the same session (c. 48), entitled "An Act for the Abbreviation of Michaelmas Term," by which it was enacted, "that from and after the said feast of St. Michael, which shall be in the year 1752, the said solemnity of presenting and swearing the mayors of the city of London, after every annual election into the said office, in the manner and form heretofore used on the 29th day of October, shall be kept and observed on the ninth day of November in every year, unless the same shall fall on a Sunday, and in that case on the day following."

[1] Officers of the Wardrobe.

[2] Wife of Mr. Davis, belonging to the Navy Office. The appellation of my Lady is used in the same sense as the French word Madame.—B.

[30th]. Within all the morning and dined at home, my mind being so troubled that I could not mind nor do anything till I spoke with the Comptroller to whom the lodgings belong. In the afternoon, to ease my mind, I went to the Cockpit all alone, and there saw a very fine play called "The Tamer tamed;"[1] very well acted. That being done, I went to Mr. Crew's, where I had left my boy, and so with him and Mr. Moore (who would go a little way with me home, as he will always do) to the Hercules Pillars to drink, where we did read over the King's declaration in matters of religion, which is come out to-day, which is very well penned, I think to the satisfaction of most people. So home, where I am told Mr. Davis's people have broken open the bolt of my chamber door that goes upon the leads, which I went up to see and did find it so, which did still trouble me more and more. And so I sent for Griffith, and got him to search their house to see what the meaning of it might be, but can learn nothing to-night. But I am a little pleased that I have found this out. I hear nothing yet of my Lord, whether he be gone for the Queen from the Downs or no; but I believe he is, and that he is now upon coming back again.

[31st]. Office day. Much troubled all this morning in my mind about the business of my walk on the leads. I spoke of it to the Comptroller and the rest of the principal officers, who are all unwilling to meddle in anything that may anger my Lady Davis. And so I am fain to give over for the time that she do continue therein. Dined at home, and after dinner to Westminster Hall, where I met with Billing the quaker at Mrs. Michell's shop, who is still of the former opinion he was of against the clergymen of all sorts, and a cunning fellow I find him to be. Home, and there I had news that Sir W. Pen is resolved to ride to Sir W. Batten's country house[2] to-morrow, and would have me go with him, so I sat up late, getting together my things to ride in, and was fain to cut an old pair of boots to make leathers for those I was to wear.

---

[1] "The Woman's Prize, or Tamer Tamed," a comedy by John Fletcher, and a sort of sequel to Shakespeare's "Taming of the Shrew," published in the folio edition of Beaumont and Fletcher, 1647.

[2] At Walthamstow.

This month I conclude with my mind very heavy for the loss of the leads, as also for the greatness of my late expenses, insomuch that I do not think that I have above £150 clear money in the world, but I have, I believe, got a great deal of good household stuff. I hear to-day that the Queen is landed at Dover, and will be here on Friday next, November 2nd. My wife has been so ill of late of her old pain that I have not known her this fortnight almost, which is a pain to me.

[November 1st]. This morning Sir W. Pen and I were mounted early, and had a very merry discourse all the way, he being very good company. We came to Sir W. Batten's, where he lives like a prince, and we were made very welcome. Among other things he showed us my Lady's closet, where was great store of rarities; as also a chair, which he calls King Harry's chair, where he that sits down is catched with two irons, that come round about him, which makes good sport. Here dined with us two or three more country gentlemen; among the rest Mr. Christmas, my old school-fellow, with whom I had much talk. He did remember that I was a great Roundhead when I was a boy, and I was much afraid that he would have remembered the words that I said the day the King was beheaded (that, were I to preach upon him, my text should be—"The memory of the wicked shall rot"); but I found afterwards that he did go away from school before that time.[1] He did make us good sport in imitating Mr. Case,[2] Ash,[3] and Nye,[4] the ministers, which he did very well, but a deadly drinker he is, and grown exceeding fat. From his house to an ale-house near the church, where we sat and drank and were merry, and so we mounted for London again, Sir W. Batten with us. We called at Bow and drank there, and took leave of Mr. Johnson of

[1] Pepys might well be anxious on this point, for in October of this year Phineas Pett, assistant master shipwright at Chatham, was dismissed from his post for having when a child spoken disrespectfully of the King. See *ante*, August 23rd.

[2] Rev. Thomas Case, see *ante*, May 15th.

[3] Rev. Simeon Ash, one of the leading Presbyterian ministers.

[4] Philip Nye, minister of Kimbolton and rector of Acton, Middlesex. He succeeded Daniel Featley in the latter living in 1642, and was turned out at the Restoration. He died in 1672.

Blackwall, who dined with us and rode with us thus far. So home by moonlight, it being about 9 o'clock before we got home.

[2nd]. Office. Then dined at home, and by chance Mr. Holliard[1] called at dinner time and dined with me, with whom I had great discourse concerning the cure of the King's evil, which he do deny altogether any effect at all. In the afternoon I went forth and saw some silver bosses put upon my new Bible, which cost me 6s. 6d. the making, and 7s. 6d. the silver, which, with 9s. 6d, the book, comes in all to £1 3s. 6d. From thence with Mr. Cooke that made them, and Mr. Stephens the silversmith to the tavern, and did give them a pint of wine. So to White Hall, where when I came I saw the boats going very thick to Lambeth, and all the stairs to be full of people. I was told the Queen was a-coming;[2] so I got a sculler for sixpence to carry me thither and back again, but I could not get to see the Queen; so come back, and to my Lord's, where he was come; and I supt with him, he being very merry, telling merry stories of the country mayors, how they entertained the King all the way as he come along; and how the country gentlewomen did hold up their heads to be kissed by the King, not taking his hand to kiss as they should do. I took leave of my Lord and Lady, and so took coach at White Hall and carried Mr. Childe as far as the Strand, and myself got as far as Ludgate by all the bonfires, but with a great deal of trouble; and there the coachman desired that I would release him, for he durst not go further for the fires. So he would have had a shilling or 6d. for bringing of me so far; but I had but 3d. about me and did give him it. In Paul's church-yard I called at Kirton's,[3] and there they

---

[1] Thomas Holliard or Hollier was appointed in 1638 surgeon for scald heads at St. Thomas's Hospital, and on January 25th, 1643-4, he was chosen surgeon in place of Edward Molins. In 1670 his son of the same name was allowed to take his place during his illness. Ward, in his Diary, p. 235, mentions that the porter at St. Thomas's Hospital told him, in 1661, of Mr. Holyard's having cut thirty for the stone in one year, who all lived.

[2] "Nov. 2. The Queen-mother and the Princess Henrietta came into London, the Queen having left this land nineteen years ago. Her coming was very private, Lambeth-way, where the King, Queen, and the Duke of York, and the rest, took water, crossed the Thames, and all safely arrived at Whitehall." —Rugge's *Diurnal*.

[3] The bookseller's, see *ante*, February 12th, 1659-60.

had got a mass book for me, which I bought and cost me twelve shillings; and, when I came home, sat up late and read in it with great pleasure to my wife, to hear that she was long ago so well acquainted with. So to bed. I observed this night very few bonfires in the City, not above three in all London, for the Queen's coming; whereby I guess that (as I believed before) her coming do please but very few.

[3d]. Saturday. At home all the morning. In the afternoon to White Hall, where my Lord and Lady were gone to kiss the Queene's hand. To Westminster Hall, where I met with Tom Doling, and we two took Mrs. Lane to the alehouse, where I made her angry with commending of Tom Newton and her new sweetheart to be both too good for her, so that we parted with much anger, which made Tom and me good sport. So home to write letters by the post, and so to bed.

[4th] (Lord's day). In the morn to our own church,[1] where Mr.

---

[1] St. Olave's, Hart Street.

Mills did begin to nibble at the Common Prayer, by saying "Glory be to the Father, &c." after he had read the two psalms; but the people had been so little used to it, that they could not tell what to answer. This declaration of the King's do give the Presbyterians some satisfaction, and a pretence to read the Common Prayer, which they would not do before because of their former preaching against it. After dinner to Westminster, where I went to my Lord's, and having spoke with him, I went to the Abbey, where the first time that ever I heard the organs in a cathedral.[1] Thence to my Lord's, where I found Mr. Pierce, the surgeon, and with him and Mr. Sheply, in our way calling at the Bell to see the seven Flanders mares that my Lord has bought lately, where we drank several bottles of Hull ale. Much company I found to come to her, and cannot wonder at it, for she is very pretty and wanton. Hence to my father's, where I found my mother in greater and greater pain of the stone. I staid long and drank with them, and so home and to bed. My wife seemed very pretty to-day, it being the first time I had given her leave to wear a black patch.[2]

[5th] (Office day). Being disappointed of money, we failed of going to Deptford to pay off the Henrietta[3] to-day. Dined at home, and at home all day, and at the office at night, to make up an account of what the debts of nineteen of the twenty-five ships that should have been paid off, is increased since the adjournment of the Parliament, they being to sit again to-morrow. This 5th of November is observed exceeding well in the City; and at night great bonfires and fireworks. At night Mr. Moore came and sat with me, and there I took a book and he did instruct me in many law notions, in which I took great pleasure. To bed.

[6th]. In the morning with Sir W. Batten and Pen by water to Westminster, where at my Lord's I met with Mr. Creed. With him to see my Lord's picture (now almost done), and thence to

---

[1] Dr. Rimbault says that Father Smith built his organ in Westminster Abbey in 1662, and that it cost £120 ("Hopkins on the Organ," 1855, p. 82). The organ which Pepys heard must therefore have been one put in temporarily.

[2] See ante, August 30th.

[3] The "Henrietta" was formerly the "Lambert," see ante, May 23rd.

Westminster Hall, where we found the Parliament met to-day, and thence meeting with Mr. Chetwind, I took them to the Sun, and did give them a barrel of oysters, and had good discourse; among other things Mr. Chetwind told me how he did fear that this late business of the Duke of York's would prove fatal to my Lord Chancellor. From thence Mr. Creed and I to Wilkinson's, and dined together, and in great haste thence to our office, where we met all, for the sale of two ships by an inch of candle[1] (the first time that ever I saw any of this kind), where I observed how they do invite one another, and at last how they all do cry,[2] and we have much to do to tell who did cry last. The ships were the Indian, sold for £1,300, and the Half-moon, sold for £830. Home, and fell a-reading of the tryalls of the late men that were hanged for the King's death, and found good satisfaction in reading thereof. At night to bed, and my wife and I did fall out about the dog's being put down into the cellar, which I had a mind to have done because of his fouling the house, and I would have my will, and so we went to bed and lay all night in a quarrel. This night I was troubled all night with a dream that my wife was dead, which made me that I slept ill all night.

[7th] (Office day). This day my father came to dine at my house, but being sent for in the morning I could not stay, but went by water to my Lord, where I dined with him, and he in a very merry humour (present Mr. Borfett[3] and Childe) at dinner: he, in discourse of the great opinion of the virtue—gratitude (which he did account the greatest thing in the world to him, and had, therefore, in his mind been often troubled in the late times how to answer his gratitude to the King, who raised his father), did say it was that did bring him to his obedience to the King; and did also bless himself with his good fortune, in comparison to what it was when I was with him in the Sound, when he durst not own his correspondence with the King; which is a thing that I never did hear of to this day before; and I do from this raise

---

[1] The old-fashioned custom of sale by auction by inch of candle was continued in sales by the Admiralty to a somewhat late date. See September 3rd, 1662.
[2] To cry was to bid.
[3] Mr. Borfett was Lord Sandwich's chaplain, see *ante*, July 29th.

an opinion of him, to be one of the most secret men in the world, which I was not so convinced of before. After dinner he bid all go out of the room, and did tell me how the King had promised him £4,000 per annum for ever, and had already given him a bill under his hand (which he showed me) for £4,000 that Mr. Fox[1] is to pay him. My Lord did advise with me how to get this received, and to put out £3,000 into safe hands at use, and the other he will make use of for his present occasion. This he did advise with me about with much secresy. After all this he called for the fiddles and books, and we two and W. Howe, and Mr. Childe, did sing and play some psalmes of Will. Lawes's,[2] and some songs; and so I went away. So I went to see my Lord's picture, which is almost done, and do please me very well. Hence to Whitehall to find out Mr. Fox, which I did, and did use me very civilly, but I did not see his lady, whom I had so long known when she was a maid, Mrs. Whittle. From thence meeting my father Bowyer, I took him to Mr. Harper's, and there drank with him. Among other things in discourse he told me how my wife's brother had a horse at grass with him, which I was troubled to hear, it being his boldness upon my score. Home by coach, and read late in the last night's book of Trials, and told my wife about her brother's horse at Mr. Bowyer's, who is also much troubled for it, and do intend to go to-morrow to inquire the truth. Notwithstanding this was the first day of the King's proclamation[3] against hackney coaches coming into the streets to stand to be hired, yet I got one to carry me home.

[1] Afterwards Sir Stephen Fox, see *ante*, May 24th.

[2] William Lawes, elder brother of the more celebrated Henry Lawes, and educated under the same master, John Cooper. For a time he held the situation of a gentleman of the chapel, but at the outbreak of the Civil War he entered the royal army and obtained the rank of captain. He was killed at the siege of Chester, in 1645. Charles I. regretted his loss greatly, and went into mourning for him. The chief work of Lawes was "Choice Psalmes put into Musick for three voices." The Psalms were set to the well-known paraphrase of Sandys, and this volume was published in 1648 by Henry Lawes.

[3] "A Proclamation to restrain the abuses of Hackney Coaches in the Cities of London and Westminster and the Suburbs thereof." This is printed in "Notes and Queries," First Series, vol. viii. p. 122. "In April, 1663, the poor widows of hackney-coachmen petitioned for some relief, as the parliament had reduced the number of coaches to 400; there were before, in and about London, more than 2,000."—Rugge's *Diurnal*.

[8th]. This morning Sir Wm. and the Treasurer and I went by barge with Sir Wm. Doyley and Mr. Prin to Deptford, to pay off the Henrietta, and had a good dinner. I went to Mr. Davys's and saw his house (where I was once before a great while ago) and I found him a very pretty man. In the afternoon Commissioner Pett and I went on board the yacht, which indeed is one of the finest things that ever I saw for neatness and room in so small a vessel. Mr. Pett is to make one to outdo this for the honour of his country, which I fear he will scarce better.[1] From thence with him as far as Ratcliffe, where I left him going by water to London, and I (unwilling to leave the rest of the officers) went back again to Deptford, and being very much troubled with a sudden looseness, I went into a little alehouse at the end of Ratcliffe, and did give a groat for a pot of ale, and there I did . . . So went forward in my walk with some men that were going that way a great pace, and in our way we met with many merry seamen that had got their money paid them to-day. We sat very late doing the work and waiting for the tide, it being moonshine we got to London before two in the morning. So home, where I found my wife up, she shewed me her head which was very well dressed to-day, she having been to see her father and mother. So to bed.

[9th]. Lay long in bed this morning though an office day, because of our going to bed late last night. Before I went to my office Mr. Creed came to me about business, and also Mr. Carter, my old Cambridge friend, came to give me a visit, and I did give them a morning draught in my study. So to the office, and from thence to dinner with Mr. Wivell at the Hoop Tavern, where we had Mr. Shepley, Talbot, Adams, Mr. Chaplin and Osborne, and our dinner given us by Mr. Ady and another, Mr. Wine, the King's fishmonger. Good sport with Mr. Talbot, who eats no sort of fish, and there was nothing else till we sent for a neat's tongue. From thence to Whitehall where I found my Lord, who had an organ set up to-day in his dining-room, but it seems an ugly one in the form of Bridewell. Thence I went to Sir Harry Wright's where

---

[1] This Dutch pleasure boat is mentioned on August 15th, 1660 (see *ante*). On January 13th, 1660-61, Pepys comes to the conclusion that Pett's yacht is much superior to the Dutch boat.

my Lord was busy at cards, and so I staid below with Mrs. Carter and Evans (who did give me a lesson upon the lute), till he came down, and having talked with him at the door about his late business of money, I went to my father's and staid late talking with my father about my sister Pall's coming to live with me if she would come and be as a servant (which my wife did seem to be pretty willing to do to-day), and he seems to take it very well, and intends to consider of it. Home and to bed.

[10th]. Up early. Sir Wm. Batten and I to make up an account of the wages of the officers and mariners at sea, ready to present to the Committee of Parliament this afternoon. Afterwards came the Treasurer and Comptroller, and sat all the morning with us till the business was done. So we broke up, leaving the thing to be wrote over fair and carried to Trinity House for Sir Wm. Batten's hand. When staying very long I found (as appointed) the Treasurer and Comptroller at Whitehall, and so we went with a foul copy to the Parliament house, where we met with Sir Thos. Clarges and Mr. Spry, and after we had given them good satisfaction we parted. The Comptroller and I to the coffee-house, where he shewed me the state of his case; how the King did owe him about £6,000. But I do not see great likelihood for them to be paid, since they begin already in Parliament to dispute the paying of the just sea-debts, which were already promised to be paid, and will be the undoing of thousands if they be not paid. So to Whitehall to look but could not find Mr. Fox, and then to Mr. Moore at Mr. Crew's, but missed of him also. So to Paul's Churchyard, and there bought Montelion,[1] which this year do not prove so good as the last was; so after reading it I burnt it. After reading of that and the comedy of the Rump,[2] which is also very silly, I went to bed. This night going home, Will and I bought a goose.

[11th] (Lord's day). This morning I went to Sir W. Batten's

---

[1] "Montelion, the Prophetical Almanac for the year 1660, 8vo., with frontispiece, by John Phillips." The Montelions for 1661 and 1662 were written by Thomas Flatman. It would appear that Pepys bought the Montelion for 1661.
[2] "The Rump, or the Mirror of the late Times," a comedy by John Tatham, acted at Dorset Court, and printed in 1660 and 1661.

about going to Deptford to-morrow, and so eating some hog's pudding of my Lady's making, of the hog that I saw a fattening the other day at her house, he and I went to Church into our new gallery, the first time it was used, and it not being yet quite finished, there came after us Sir W. Pen, Mr. Davis, and his eldest son. There being no woman this day, we sat in the foremost pew, and behind us our servants, and I hope it will not always be so, it not being handsome for our servants to sit so equal with us. This day also did Mr. Mills begin to read all the Common Prayer, which I was glad of. Home to dinner, and then walked to Whitehall, it being very cold and foul and rainy weather. I found my Lord at home, and after giving him an account of some business, I returned and went to my father's where I found my wife, and there we supped, and Dr. Thomas Pepys, who my wife told me after I was come home, that he had told my brother Thomas that he loved my wife so well that if she had a child he would never marry, but leave all that he had to my child, and after supper we walked home, my little boy carrying a link, and Will leading my wife. So home and to prayers and to bed. I should have said that before I got to my Lord's this day I went to Mr. Fox's at Whitehall, when I first saw his lady, formerly Mrs. Elizabeth Whittle, whom I had formerly a great opinion of, and did make an anagram or two upon her name when I was a boy. She proves a very fine lady, and mother to fine children. To-day I agreed with Mr. Fox about my taking of the £4,000 of him that the King had given my Lord.

[12th]. Lay long in bed to-day. Sir Wm. Batten went this morning to Deptford to pay off the Wolf. Mr. Comptroller and I sat a while at the office to do business, and thence I went with him to his house in Lime Street, a fine house, and where I never was before, and from thence by coach (setting down his sister at the new Exchange) to Westminster Hall, where first I met with Jack Spicer and agreed with him to help me to tell money this afternoon. Hence to De Cretz, where I saw my Lord's picture finished, which do please me very well. So back to the Hall, where by appointment I met the Comptroller, and with him and three or four Parliament men I dined at Heaven, and after dinner called at

Will's on Jack Spicer, and took him to Mr. Fox's, who saved me the labour of telling me the money by giving me £3,000 by consent (the other £1,000 I am to have on Thursday next), which I carried by coach to the Exchequer, and put it up in a chest in Spicer's office. From thence walked to my father's, where I found my wife, who had been with my father to-day, buying of a table-cloth and a dozen of napkins of diaper, the first that ever I bought in my life. My father and I took occasion to go forth, and went and drank at Mr. Standing's, and there discoursed seriously about my sister's coming to live with me, which I have much mind for her good to have, and yet I am much afeard of her ill-nature. Coming home again, he and I, and my wife, my mother and Pall, went all together into the little room, and there I told her plainly what my mind was, to have her come not as a sister in any respect, but as a servant, which she promised me that she would, and with many thanks did weep for joy, which did give me and my wife some content and satisfaction. So by coach home and to bed. The last night I should have mentioned how my wife and I were troubled all night with the sound of drums in our ears, which in the morning we found to be Mr. Davys's jack,[1] but not knowing the cause of its going all night, I understand to-day that they have had a great feast to-day.

[13th]. Early going to my Lord's I met with Mr. Moore, who was going to my house, and indeed I found him to be a most careful, painful,[2] and able man in business, and took him by water to the Wardrobe, and shewed him all the house; and indeed there

---

[1] The date of the origin of smoke-jacks does not appear to be known, but the first patent taken out for an improved smoke-jack by Peter Clare is dated December 24th, 1770. The smoke-jack consists of a wind-wheel fixed in the chimney, which communicates motion by means of an endless band to a pulley, whence the motion is transmitted to the spit by gearing. In the valuable introduction to the volume of "Abridgments of Specifications relating to Cooking, 1634-1866" (Patent Office), mention is made of an Italian work by Bartolomeo Scappi, published first at Rome in 1572, and afterwards reprinted at Venice in 1622, which gives a complete account of the kitchens of the time and the utensils used in them. In the plates several roasting-jacks are represented, one worked by smoke or hot air and one by a spring.

[2] Painful, *i.e.* painstaking or laborious. Latimer speaks of the "painful magistrates."

is a great deal of room in it, but very ugly till my Lord hath bestowed great cost upon it. So to the Exchequer, and there took Spicer and his fellow clerks to the Dog tavern, and did give them a peck of oysters, and so home to dinner, where I found my wife making of pies and tarts to try her oven with, which she has never yet done, but not knowing the nature of it, did heat it too hot, and so a little overbake her things, but knows how to do better another time. At home all the afternoon. At night made up my accounts of my sea expenses in order to my clearing off my imprest bill of £30 which I had in my hands at the beginning of my voyage, which I intend to shew to my Lord to-morrow. To bed.

[14th] (Office day). But this day was the first that we do begin to sit in the afternoon, and not in the forenoon, and therefore I went into Cheapside to Mr. Beauchamp's, the goldsmith, to look out a piece of plate to give Mr. Fox from my Lord, for his favour about the £4,000, and did choose a gilt tankard. So to Paul's Churchyard and bought "Cornelianum dolium."[1] So home to dinner, and after that to the office till late at night, and so Sir W. Pen, the Comptroller, and I to the Dolphin, where we found Sir W. Batten, who is seldom a night from hence, and there we did drink a great quantity of sack and did tell many merry stories, and in good humours we were all. So home and to bed.

[15th]. To Westminster, and it being very cold upon the water I went all alone to the Sun and drank a draft of mulled white wine, and so to Mr. de Cretz, whither I sent for J. Spicer (to appoint him to expect me this afternoon at the office, with the other £1,000 from Whitehall), and here we staid and did see him give some finishing touches to my Lord's picture, so at last it is complete to my mind, and I leave mine with him to copy out another for himself, and took the original by a porter with me to my Lord's, where I found my Lord within, and staid hearing him and Mr. Child playing upon my Lord's new organ, the first time

---

[1] "Cornelianum dolium" is a Latin comedy, by T. R., published at London in 1638. Douce attributed it to Thomas Randolph (d. 1635). The book has a frontispiece representing the sweating tub which, from the name of the patient, was styled Cornelius's tub. There is a description of the play in the "European Magazine," vol. xxxvii. (1800), p. 343.

I ever heard it. My Lord did this day show me the King's picture,
which was done in Flanders, that the King did promise my Lord
before he ever saw him, and that we did expect to have had at sea
before the King came to us; but it came but to-day, and indeed it
is the most pleasant and the most like him that ever I saw picture
in my life. As dinner was coming on table, my wife came to my
Lord's, and I got her carried in to my Lady, who took physic to-
day, and was just now hiring of a French maid that was with
her, and they could not understand one another till my wife
came to interpret. Here I did leave my wife to dine with my Lord,
the first time he ever did take notice of her as my wife, and did
seem to have a just esteem for her. And did myself walk homewards (hearing that Sir W. Pen was gone before in a coach) to
overtake him and with much ado at last did in Fleet Street, and
there I went in to him, and there was Sir Arnold Brames,[1] and we
all three to Sir W. Batten's to dinner, he having a couple of servants married to-day; and so there was a great number of merchants, and others of good quality on purpose after dinner to
make an offering, which, when dinner was done, we did, and I
did give ten shillings and no more, though I believe most of the
rest did give more, and did believe that I did so too. From thence
to Whitehall again by water to Mr. Fox and by two porters carried away the other £1,000. He was not within himself, but I
had it of his kinsman, and did give him £4 and other servants
something; but whereas I did intend to have given Mr. Fox himself a piece of plate of £50 I was demanded £100, for the fee of
the office at 6d. a pound, at which I was surprised, but, however,
I did leave it there till I speak with my Lord. So I carried it to the
Exchequer, where at Will's I found Mr. Spicer, and so lodged it
at his office with the rest. From thence after a pot of ale at Will's I
took boat in the dark and went for all that to the old Swan, and so
to Sir Wm. Batten's, and leaving some of the gallants at cards I
went home, where I found my wife much satisfied with my

---

[1] Sir Arnold Breames, Brahams, or Brames, of Bridge Court, Kent, was son
of Charles Breames, of Dover, and was knighted at Canterbury, May 27th,
1660. He married, first Joanna, daughter of Walter Henflete (or Septvans),
secondly, Elizabeth, daughter of Sir Dudley Digges, Master of the Rolls, and
thirdly, Margaret, daughter of Sir Thomas Palmer, of Wingham, Bart.

Lord's discourse and respect to her, and so after prayers to bed.

[16th]. Up early to my father's, where by appointment Mr. Moore came to me, and he and I to the Temple, and thence to Westminster Hall to speak with Mr. Wm. Montagu about his looking upon the title of those lands which I do take as security for £3,000 of my Lord's money. That being done Mr. Moore and I parted, and in the Hall I met with Mr. Fontleroy (my old acquaintance, whom I had not seen a long time), and he and I to the Swan, and in discourse he seems to be wise and say little, though I know things are changed against his mind. Thence home by water, where my father, Mr. Snow, and Mr. Moore did dine with me. After dinner Mr. Snow and I went up together to discourse about the putting out of £80 to a man who lacks the money and would give me £15 per annum for 8 years for it, which I did not think profit enough, and so he seemed to be disappointed by my refusal of it, but I would not now part with my money easily. He seems to do it as a great favour to me to offer to come in upon a way of getting of money, which they call Bottomry,[1] which I do not yet understand, but do believe there may be something in it of great profit. After we were parted I went to the office, and there we sat all the afternoon, and at night we went to a barrel of oysters at Sir W. Batten's, and so home, and I to the setting of my papers in order, which did keep me up late. So to bed.

[17th]. In the morning to Whitehall, where I inquired at the Privy Seal Office for a form for a nobleman to make one his Chaplain. But I understanding that there is not any, I did draw up one, and so to my Lord's, and there I did give him it to sign for Mr.

---

[1] "The contract of bottomry is a negotiable instrument, which may be put in suit by the person to whom it is transferred; it is in use in all countries of maritime commerce and interests. A contract in the nature of a mortgage of a ship, when the owner of it borrows money to enable him to carry on the voyage, and pledges the keel or bottom of the ship as a security for the repayment. If the ship be lost the lender loses his whole money; but if it returns in safety, then he shall receive back his principal, and also the premium stipulated to be paid, however it may exceed the usual or legal rate of interest."— Smyth's *Sailor's Word-Book*.

Turner[1] to be his first Chaplain. I did likewise get my Lord to sign my last sea accounts, so that I am even to this day when I have received the balance of Mr. Creed. I dined with my Lady and my Lady Pickering, where her son John dined with us, who do continue a fool as he ever was since I knew him. His mother would fain marry him to get a portion for his sister Betty,[2] but he will not hear of it. Hither came Major Hart this noon, who tells me that the Regiment is now disbanded, and that there is some money coming to me for it. I took him to my Lord to Mr. Crew's, and from thence with Mr. Shepley and Mr. Moore to the Devil Tavern,[3] and there we drank. So home and wrote letters by the post. Then to my lyra viall,[4] and to bed.

[18th] (Lord's day). In the morning to our own church, where Mr. Powel (a crook legged man that went formerly with me to Paul's School), preached a good sermon. In the afternoon to our own church and my wife with me (the first time that she and my Lady Batten[5] came to sit in our new pew), and after sermon my Lady took us home and there we supped with her and Sir W. Batten, and Pen, and were much made of. The first time that ever my wife was there. So home and to bed.

[1] Rev. John Turner, rector of Eynesbury.

[2] Elizabeth Pickering, who married John Creed in 1668.

[3] A celebrated place of entertainment in the Strand, by Temple Bar, largely associated with the fame of Ben Jonson. The Royal Society held its dinners here for many years. In 1787 Messrs. Child, the bankers, bought the freehold, and pulling the building down erected Child's Place on the site. This was destroyed in 1879.

[4] The lyre viol is a viol with extra open bass strings, holding the same relation to the viol as the theorbo does to the lute. A volume entitled "Musick's Recreation on the Lyra Viol," was printed by John Playford in 1650.

[5] "Elizabeth Woodcock, evidently his second wife, as his daughter Martha is often mentioned, married February 3rd, 1658-59, to Sir W. Batten; and, secondly, in 1671, to a foreigner called, in the register of Battersea parish, Lord Leyonberg. Lady Leighenberg was buried at Walthamstow, September 16th, 1681."—Lysons' *Environs*. Sir James Barkman Leyenberg, the envoy from Sweden, was resident in England till 1682, or later. See January 21st, 1666-67. His name occurs in "The Intelligencer," March 12th, 1663-64, as delayed at Stockholm by a fever, though his despatches were ready. A hostile message appears to have passed between him and Pepys, in November, 1670, but the duel was prevented. Perhaps they quarrelled about the money due from Sir W. Batten to Pepys, for which the widow was liable.—B.

[19th] (Office day). After we had done a little at the office this morning, I went with the Treasurer in his coach to White Hall, and in our way, in discourse, do find him a very good-natured man; and, talking of those men who now stand condemned for murdering the King, he says that he believes that, if the law would give leave, the King is a man of so great compassion that he would wholly acquit them. Going to my Lord's I met with Mr. Shepley, and so he and I to the Sun, and I did give him a morning draft of Muscadine.[1] And so to see my Lord's picture at De Cretz, and he says it is very like him, and I say so too. After that to Westminster Hall, and there hearing that Sir W. Batten was at the Leg in the Palace,[2] I went thither, and there dined with him and some of the Trinity House men who had obtained something to-day at the House of Lords concerning the Ballast Office. After dinner I went by water to London to the Globe in Cornhill,[3] and there did choose two pictures to hang up in my house, which my wife did not like when I came home, and so I sent the picture of Paris back again. To the office, where we sat all the afternoon till night. So home, and there came Mr. Beauchamp to me with the gilt tankard, and I did pay him for it £20. So to my musique and sat up late at it, and so to bed, leaving my wife to sit up till 2 o'clock that she may call the wench up to wash.

[20th]. About two o'clock my wife wakes me, and comes to bed, and so both to sleep and the wench to wash. I rose and with Will to my Lord's by land, it being a very hard frost, the first we have had this year. There I staid with my Lord and Mr. Shepley, looking over my Lord's accounts and to set matters straight between him and Shepley, and he did commit the viewing of these ac-

---

[1] Muscadine or muscadel, a rich sort of wine. *Vinum muscatum quod moschi odorem referat.*

> "Quaffed off the muscadel, and threw the sops
> All in the sexton's face."

Shakespeare, *Taming of the Shrew*, act iii. sc. 2.—M. B.

[2] There is a token of the Leg in New Palace Yard, which was a famous tavern at this time (see "Boyne's Trade Tokens," ed. Williamson, vol. i., 1889, p. 684).

[3] The Globe is given as one of the taverns in Cornhill in the list of taverns in London and Westminster, 1698 (Harl. MS. 4716).

counts to me, which was a great joy to me to see that my Lord do look upon me as one to put trust in. Hence to the organ, where Mr. Child and one Mr. Mackworth (who plays finely upon the violin) were playing, and so we played till dinner and then dined, where my Lord in a very good humour and kind to me. After dinner to the Temple, where I met Mr. Moore and discoursed with him about the business of putting out my Lord's £3,000 and that done, Mr. Shepley and I to the new Play-house near Lincoln's-Inn-Fields (which was formerly Gibbon's tennis-court),[1] where the play of "Beggar's Bush"[2] was newly begun; and so we went in and saw it, it was well acted: and here I saw the first time one Moone,[3] who is said to be the best actor in the world, lately come over with the King, and indeed it is the finest play-house, I believe, that ever was in England. From thence, after a pot of ale with Mr. Shepley at a house hard by, I went by link home, calling a little by the way at my father's and my uncle Fenner's, where all pretty well, and so home, where I found the house in a washing pickle, and my wife in a very joyful condition when I told her that she is to see the Queen next Thursday, which puts me in mind to say that this morning I found my Lord in bed late, he having been with the King, Queen, and Princess, at the Cockpit[4] all night, where General Monk treated them; and after supper a play, where the King did put a great affront upon Singleton's[5]

[1] This was Killigrew's, or the King's House, opened for the first time November 8th, 1660.

[2] The "Beggar's Bush," a comedy by Beaumont and Fletcher, published in the 1647 edition of their plays.

[3] Michael Mohun, or Moone, the celebrated actor, who had borne a major's commission in the King's army. The period of his death is uncertain, but he is known to have been dead in 1691. Downes relates that an eminent poet [Lee] seeing him act Mithridates "vented suddenly this saying: "Oh, Mohun, Mohun, thou little man of mettle, if I should write a 100, I'd write a part for thy mouth.' "—*Roscius Anglicanus*, p. 17.

[4] The Cockpit at Whitehall. The plays at the Cockpit in Drury Lane were acted in the afternoon.

[5] John Singleton, appointed, 1660, one of the musicians of the sackbuts in place of William Lanier. From the sackbut he advanced to the violin, and lastly to the flute. He is mentioned by Dryden in "MacFlecknoe," and by Shadwell in "Bury Fair." He was one of the King's twenty-four fiddlers in 1674; see North's "Memoirs of Musick," ed. Rimbault, 1846, p. 99 (note). He died 1686, and was buried (April 7th), in the churchyard of St. Paul's, Covent Garden.

musique, he bidding them stop and bade the French musique play, which, my Lord says, do much outdo all ours. But while my Lord was rising, I went to Mr. Fox's, and there did leave the gilt tankard for Mrs. Fox, and then to the counting-house to him, who hath invited me and my wife to dine with him on Thursday next, and so to see the Queen and Princesses.

[21st]. Lay long in bed. This morning my cozen Thomas Pepys, the turner, sent me a cupp of lignum vitæ[1] for a token. This morning my wife and I went to Paternoster Row, and there we bought some green watered moyre for a morning wastecoate. And after that we went to Mr. Cade's[2] to choose some pictures for our house. After that my wife went home, and I to Pope's Head,[3] and bought me an aggate hafted knife, which cost me 5s. So home to dinner, and so to the office all the afternoon, and at night to my viallin (the first time that I have played on it since I came to this house) in my dining room, and afterwards to my lute there, and I took much pleasure to have the neighbours come forth into the yard to hear me. So down to supper, and sent for the barber, who staid so long with me that he was locked into the house, and we were fain to call up Griffith to let him out. So up to bed, leaving my wife to wash herself, and to do other things against to-morrow to go to court.

[22d]. This morning came the carpenters to make me a door at the other side of my house, going into the entry, which I was much pleased with. At noon my wife and I walked to the Old Exchange, and there she bought her a white whisk[4] and put it on, and I a pair of gloves, and so we took coach for Whitehall to Mr. Fox's, where we found Mrs. Fox within, and an alderman of London paying £1,000 or £1,400 in gold upon the table for the

---

[1] A hard, compact, black-green wood, obtained from *Guaiacum officinale,* from which pestles, ship-blocks, rollers, castors, &c., are turned.

[2] Mr. Cade was a stationer in Cornhill.

[3] Pope's Head Alley, a footway from Cornhill to Lombard Street, named after the Pope's Head Tavern, was at this time famous for its cutlers.

[4] A gorget or neckerchief worn by women at this time. "A woman's neck whisk is used both plain and laced, and is called of most a gorget or falling whisk, because it falleth about the shoulders."—*Randle Holme* (quoted by Planché).

King, which was the most gold that ever I saw together in my life. Mr. Fox came in presently and did receive us with a great deal of respect; and then did take my wife and I to the Queen's presence-chamber, where he got my wife placed behind the Queen's chair, and I got into the crowd, and by and by the Queen and the two Princesses came to dinner. The Queen a very little plain old woman, and nothing more in her presence in any respect nor garb than any ordinary woman. The Princess of Orange I had often seen before. The Princess Henrietta is very pretty, but much below my expectation; and her dressing of herself with her hair frized short up to her ears, did make her seem so much the less to me. But my wife standing near her with two or three black patches on, and well dressed, did seem to me much handsomer than she. Dinner being done, we went to Mr. Fox's again, where many gentlemen dined with us, and most princely dinner, all provided for me and my friends, but I bringing none but myself and wife, he did call the company to help to eat up so much good victuals. At the end of dinner, my Lord Sandwich's health was drunk in the gilt tankard that I did give to Mrs. Fox the other day. After dinner I had notice given me by Will my man that my Lord did inquire for me, so I went to find him, and met him and the Duke of York in a coach going towards Charing Cross. I endeavoured to follow them but could not, so I returned to Mr. Fox, and after much kindness and good discourse we parted from thence. I took coach for my wife and me homewards, and I light at the Maypole in the Strand,[1] and sent my wife home. I to the new playhouse[2] and saw part of the "Traitor,"[3] a very good Tragedy; Mr. Moon[4] did act the Traitor very well. So to my Lord's, and sat there with my Lady a great while talking. Among other things, she took occasion to inquire (by Madame Dury's late discourse with her) how I did treat my wife's father and

---

[1] There is a token of "Robert Chamberlaine at the Maypole in the Strand," so that it may have been at this house that Pepys alighted (see "Boyne's Trade Tokens," ed. Williamson, vol. i., 1889, p. 755).

[2] The King's House, near Lincoln's Inn Fields, see *ante*, November 20th.

[3] "The Traitor," a tragedy by James Shirley, licensed May 4th, 1631, and first printed in 1635.

[4] Michael Mohun, see *ante*, November 20th (note).

mother. At which I did give her a good account, and she seemed
to be very well opinioned of my wife. From thence to White Hall
at about 9 at night, and there, with Laud[1] the page that went
with me, we could not get out of Henry the Eighth's gallery into
the further part of the boarded gallery, where my Lord was walking with my Lord Ormond; and we had a key of Sir S. Morland's,
but all would not do; till at last, by knocking, Mr. Harrison the
door-keeper did open us the door, and, after some talk with my
Lord about getting a catch to carry my Lord St. Alban's[2] goods
to France, I parted and went home on foot, it being very late and
dirty, and so weary to bed.

[23rd]. This morning standing looking upon the workmen doing
of my new door to my house, there comes Captain Straughan the
Scot (to whom the King has given half of the money that the two
ships lately sold do bring), and he would needs take me to the
Dolphin, and give me a glass of ale and a peck of oysters, he and I.
He did talk much what he is able to advise the King for good hus-
bandry in his ships, as by ballasting them with lead ore and many
other tricks, but I do believe that he is a knowing man in sea-
business. Home and dined, and in the afternoon to the office,
where till late, and that being done Mr. Creed did come to speak
with me, and I took him to the Dolphin, where there was Mr.
Pierce the purser and his wife and some friends of theirs. So I did
spend a crown upon them behind the bar, they being akin to the
people of the house, and this being the house where Mr. Pierce
was apprentice. After they were gone Mr. Creed and I spent an
hour in looking over the account which he do intend to pass in
our office for his lending moneys, which I did advise about and
approve or disapprove of as I saw cause. After an hour being
serious at this we parted about 11 o'clock at night. So I home and
to bed, leaving my wife and the maid at their linen to get up.

[24th]. To my Lord's, where after I had done talking with him

---

[1] Laud Crisp.

[2] Henry Jermyn, second son of Sir Thomas Jermyn, born about 1604, created
Baron Jermyn of St. Edmondsbury about 1643; advanced to the earldom of
St. Albans, 1660, K.G. 1672. Died January 2nd, 1683-4. He was supposed to be
married to the Queen Dowager, Henrietta Maria.

Mr. Townsend, Rumball, Blackburn, Creed and Shepley and I to the Rhenish winehouse, and there I did give them two quarts of Wormwood wine,[1] and so we broke up. So we parted, and I and Mr. Creed to Westminster Hall and looked over a book or two, and so to my Lord's, where I dined with my lady, there being Mr. Child and Mrs. Borfett, who are never absent at dinner there, under pretence of a wooing. From thence I to Mr. de Cretz and did take away my Lord's picture, which is now finished for me, and I paid £3 10s. for it and the frame, and am well pleased with it and the price. So carried it home by water, Will being with me. At home, and had a fire made in my closet, and put my papers and books and things in order, and that being done I fell to entering these two good songs of Mr. Lawes, "Helpe, helpe, O helpe," and "O God of Heaven and Hell" in my song book,[2] to which I have got Mr. Child to set the base to the Theorbo, and that done to bed.

[25th] (Lord's day). In the forenoon I alone to our church, and after dinner I went and ranged about to many churches, among the rest to the Temple, where I heard Dr. Wilkins[3] a little (late Maister of Trinity in Cambridge). That being done to my father's to see my mother who is troubled much with the stone, and that being done I went home, where I had a letter brought me from my Lord to get a ship ready to carry the Queen's things over to

---

[1] Wormwood (*Artemisia absinthium*) is celebrated for its intensely bitter, tonic, and stimulating qualities, which have caused it to be used in various medicinal preparations, and also in the making of liqueurs, as wormwood wine and *crème d'absinthe*.

[2] Both these songs by Henry Lawes have been mentioned before. "Help, Help, O Help, Divinity of Love" (see June 5th, 1660). "O King of Heaven and Hell" (not "O God") is the same as "Orpheus' Hymn" (see March 4th, 1659-60). Henry Lawes was the friend of Milton and composed the music for "Comus," performed at Ludlow Castle in 1634. He set the anthem, "Zadok the Priest," for the coronation of Charles II. He died October 21st, 1662, and was buried in the Cloisters, Westminster Abbey.

[3] John Wilkins, D.D., born 1614, took the Parliament side, and was made warden of Wadham College, Oxford. In 1656 he married Robina, the widow of Dr. French and sister of Oliver Cromwell. He was appointed Master of Trinity College, Cambridge, in 1659, but was ejected in 1660. Consecrated Bishop of Chester, November 15th, 1668. He died November 19th, 1672. He was one of the founders of the Royal Society, and jokes were often made respecting the publication of his work, "The Discovery of a New World."

France, she being to go within five or six days. So to supper and to bed.

[26th] (Office day). To it all the morning, and dined at home where my father come and dined with me, who seems to take much pleasure to have a son that is neat in his house. I being now making my new door into the entry, which he do please himself much with. After dinner to the office again, and there till night. And that being done the Comptroller and I to the Mitre to a glass of wine, when we well into a discourse of poetry, and he did repeat some verses of his own making which were very good. Home, there hear that my Lady Batten had given my wife a visit (the first that ever she made her), which pleased me exceedingly. So after supper to bed.

[27th]. To Whitehall, where I found my Lord gone abroad to the Wardrobe, whither he do now go every other morning, and do seem to resolve to understand and look after the business himself. From thence to Westminster Hall, and in King Street there being a great stop of coaches, there was falling out between a drayman and my Lord Chesterfield's coachman, and one of his footmen killed. At the Hall I met with Mr. Creed, and he and I to Hell to drink our morning draught, and so to my Lord's again, where I found my wife, and she and I dined with him and my Lady, and great company of my Lord's friends, and my Lord did show us great respect. Soon as dinner was done my wife took her leave, and went with Mr. Blackburne and his wife to London to a christening of a Brother's child of his on Tower Hill, and I to a a play, "The Scornfull Lady,"[1] and that being done, I went homewards, and met Mr. Moore, who had been at my house, and took him to my father's, and we three to Standing's to drink. Here Mr. Moore told me how the House had this day voted the King to have all the Excise for ever. This day I do also hear that the Queen's going to France is stopt, which do like me well, because then the King will be in town the next month, which is my month again at the Privy Seal. From thence home, where when I come

---

[1] A comedy by Beaumont and Fletcher, first printed in 1616. After the Restoration it was one of the plays acted by Killigrew's company.

I do remember that I did leave my boy Waineman at Whitehall with order to stay there for me in the court, at which I was much troubled, but about 11 o'clock at night the boy came home well, and so we all to bed.

[28th]. This morning went to Whitehall to my Lord's, where Major Hart did pay me £23 14s. 9d., due to me upon my pay in

THE COUNTESS OF SANDWICH

my Lord's troop at the time of our disbanding, which is a great blessing to have without taking any law in the world for. But now I must put an end to any hopes of getting any more, so that I bless God for this. From thence with Mr. Shepley and Pinkney to the Sun, and did give them a glass of wine and a peck of oysters for joy of my getting this money. So home, where I found that Mr. Creed had sent me the £11 5s. that is due to me upon the remains of account for my sea business, which is also so much clear money

287

to me, and my bill of impresse[1] for £30 is also cleared, so that I am wholly clear as to the sea in all respects. To the office, and was there till late at night, and among the officers do hear that they may have our salaries allowed by the Treasurer, which do make me very glad, and praise God for it. Home to supper, and Mr. Hater supped with me, whom I did give order to take up my money of the Treasurer to-morrow if it can be had. So to bed.

[29th]. In the morning seeing a great deal of foul water come into my parlour from under the partition between me and Mr. Davis, I did step thither to him and tell him of it, and he did seem very ready to have it stopt, and did also tell me how thieves did attempt to rob his house last night, which do make us all afraid. This noon I being troubled that the workmen that I have to do my door were called to Mr. Davis's away, I sent for them, when Mr. Davis sent to inquire a reason of, and I did give him a good one, that they were come on purpose to do some work with me that they had already begun, with which he was well pleased, and I glad, being unwilling to anger them. In the afternoon Sir W. Batten and I met and did sell the ship Church for £440, and we asked £391, and that being done, I went home, and Dr. Petty came to me about Mr. Barlow's money, and I being a little troubled to be so importuned before I had received it, and that they would have it stopt in Mr. Fenn's hands, I did force the Doctor to go fetch the letter of attorney that he had to receive it only to make him some labour, which he did bring, and Mr. Hales came along with him from the Treasury with my money for the first quarter (Michaelmas last) that ever I received for this employment. So I paid the Dr. £25 and had £62 10s. for myself, and £7 10s. to myself also for Will's salary, which I do intend yet to keep for myself. With this my heart is much rejoiced, and do bless Almighty God that he is pleased to send so sudden and unexpected payment of my salary so soon after my great disbursements. So that now I am worth £200 again. In a great ease of mind and spirit I fell about the auditing of Mr.

---

[1] For "bill of imprest." In Italian *imprestare* means "to lend." In the ancient accounts of persons officially employed by the crown, money advanced, paid on account, was described as "de prestito," or "in prestitis."—M. B.

Shepley's last accounts with my Lord by my Lord's desire, and about that I sat till 12 o'clock at night, till I began to doze, and so to bed, with my heart praising God for his mercy to us.

[30th] (Office day). To the office, where Sir G. Carteret did give us an account how Mr. Holland[1] do intend to prevail with the Parliament to try his project of discharging the seamen all at present by ticket,[2] and so promise interest to all men that will lend money upon them at eight per cent., for so long as they are unpaid; whereby he do think to take away the growing debt, which do now lie upon the kingdom for lack of present money to discharge the seamen. But this we are troubled at as some diminution to us. I having two barrels of oysters at home, I caused one of them and some wine to be brought to the inner room in the office, and there the Principal Officers did go and eat them. So we sat till noon, and then to dinner, and to it again in the afternoon till night. At home I sent for Mr. Hater, and broke the other barrel with him, and did afterwards sit down discoursing of sea terms to learn of him. And he being gone I went up and sat till twelve at night again to make an end of my Lord's accounts, as I did the last night. Which at last I made a good end of, and so to bed.

[December 1st]. This morning, observing some things to be laid up not as they should be by the girl, I took a broom and basted her till she cried extremely, which made me vexed, but before I went out I left her appeased. So to Whitehall, where I found Mr. Moore attending for me at the Privy Seal, but nothing to do to-day. I went to Lord St. Alban's lodgings, and found him in bed, talking to a priest (he looked like one) that leaned along over the side of the bed, and there I desired to know his mind about making the catch stay longer, which I got ready for him the other day. He seems to be a fine civil gentleman. To my Lord's, and did give up my audit of his accounts, which I had been then two days

---

[1] John Holland was secretary to Sir G. Carteret, then Treasurer of the Navy, and was author of "A Brief Discourse on the Navy," written in 1638. See July 25th, 1662.

[2] The system of tickets afterwards gave great trouble, and caused much discontent.—B.

about, and was well received by my Lord. I dined with my Lord
and Lady, and we had a venison pasty. Mr. Shepley and I went
into London, and calling upon Mr. Pinkney,[1] the goldsmith, he
took us to the tavern, and gave us a pint of wine, and there fell
into our company old Mr. Flower and another gentleman, who
tell us how a Scotch knight was killed basely the other day at the
Fleece in Covent Garden,[2] where there had been a great many
formerly killed. So to Paul's Churchyard, and there I took the
little man at Mr. Kirton's and Mr. Shepley to Ringstead's at the
Star, and after a pint of wine I went home, my brains somewhat
troubled with so much wine, and after a letter or two by the post I
went to bed.

[2d] (Lord's day). My head not very well, and my body out of
order by last night's drinking, which is my great folly. To church,
and Mr. Mills made a good sermon; so home to dinner. My wife
and I all alone to a leg of mutton, the sawce of which being made
sweet, I was angry at it, and eat none, but only dined upon the
marrow bone that we had beside. To church in the afternoon,
and after sermon took Tom Fuller's Church History and read
over Henry the 8th's life in it, and so to supper and to bed.

[3rd]. This morning I took a resolution to rise early in the morning, and so I rose by candle, which I have not done all this winter,
and spent my morning in fiddling till time to go to the office,
where Sir G. Carteret did begin again discourse on Mr. Holland's

---

[1] Henry Pinckney (sometimes called Major Pinckney) of the Three Squirrels
in Fleet Street over against St. Dunstan's Church. He was founder of the
banking firm now known as Messrs. Goslings and Sharpe (see Hilton Price's
"Handbook of London Bankers," 1876, p. 63). He must not be confounded
with Leonard Pinckney, one of the Four Tellers of the Receipt of the Exchequer.

[2] "The Fleece Tavern, in York Street, Covent Garden," observes John Aubrey,
in his "Miscellanies," p. 31, "was very unfortunate for homicides; there have
been several killed; three in my time. It is now (1692) a private house." In
Rugge's "Diurnal" is the following entry:—"Nov. 1660. One Sir John Goos-
call was unfortunately killed in the Fleece Tavern, Covent Garden, by one
Balendin, a Scotchman, who was taken, and committed to the Gatehouse in
this month." The tavern was on the west side of Bridges Street, about six
doors south of Russell Street. If Aubrey did not blunder there may have been a
back entrance from York Street. William Clifton was the keeper of the tavern.

proposition, which the King do take very ill, and so Sir George in lieu of that do propose that the seamen should have half in ready money and tickets for the other half, to be paid in three months after, which we judge to be very practicable. After office home to dinner, where come in my cozen Snow by chance, and I had a very good capon to dinner. So to the office till night, and so home, and then come Mr. Davis, of Deptford (the first time that ever he was at my house), and after him Mons. L'Impertinent, who is to go to Ireland to-morrow, and so came to take his leave of me. They both found me under the barber's hand; but I had a bottle of good sack in the house, and so made them very welcome. Mr. Davis sat with me a good while after the other was gone, talking of his hard usage and of the endeavour to put him out of his place in the time of the late Commissioners, and he do speak very highly of their corruption. After he was gone I fell a reading Cornelianum dolium till 11 o'clock at night with great pleasure, and after that to bed.

[4th]. To Whitehall to Sir G. Carteret's chamber, where all the officers met, and so we went up to the Duke of York, and he took us into his closet, and we did open to him our project of stopping the growing charge of the fleet by paying them in hand one moyety, and the other four months hence. This he do like, and we returned by his order to Sir G. Carteret's chamber, and there we did draw up this design in order to be presented to the Parliament. From thence I to my Lord's, and dined with him and told him what we had done to-day. Sir Tho. Crew dined with my Lord to-day, and we were very merry with Mrs. Borfett, who dined there still as she has always done lately. After dinner Sir Tho. and my Lady to the Playhouse to see "The Silent Woman."[1] I home by water, and with Mr. Hater in my chamber all alone he and I did put this morning's design into order, which being done I did carry it to Sir W. Batten, where I found some gentlemen with him (Sir W. Pen among the rest pretty merry with drink) playing at cards, and there I staid looking upon them till one o'clock in the morning, and so Sir W. Pen and I went away, and I to bed. This day the Parliament voted that the bodies of Oliver, Ireton,

[1] Ben Jonson's "Epicœne," first published in 1609.

Bradshaw, &c., should be taken up out of their graves in the Abbey,[1] and drawn to the gallows, and there hanged and buried under it: which (methinks) do trouble me that a man of so great courage as he was, should have that dishonour, though otherwise he might deserve it enough.

[5th]. This morning the Proposal which I wrote the last night I showed to the officers this morning, and was well liked of, and I wrote it fair for Sir. G. Carteret to show to the King, and so it is to go to the Parliament. I dined at home, and after dinner I went to the new Theatre[2] and there I saw "The Merry Wives of Windsor" acted, the humours of the country gentleman and the French doctor very well done, but the rest but very poorly, and Sir J. Falstaffe[3] as bad as any. From thence to Mr. Will. Montagu's chamber to have sealed some writings to-night between Sir R. Parkhurst and myself about my Lord's £2,000, but he not coming, I went to my father's and there found my mother still ill of the stone, and had just newly voided one, which she had let drop into the chimney, and looked and found it to shew it me. From thence home and to bed.

[6th]. This morning some of the Commissioners of Parliament and Sir W. Batten went to Sir G. Carteret's office here in town, and paid off the Chesnut. I carried my wife to White Friars and landed her there, and myself to Whitehall to the Privy Seal, where abundance of pardons to seal, but I was much troubled for it because that there are no fees now coming for them to me. Thence Mr. Moore and I alone to the Leg in King Street, and dined together on a neat's tongue and udder. From thence by

---

[1] The names of Cromwell, Ireton, and Bradshaw are not found in the Registers of Westminster Abbey. Colonel Chester, in his edition of the "Registers" (p. 521), prints the royal warrant for a further exhumation of Commonwealth personages, dated September 9th, 1661. This warrant contains twenty-one names, and these bodies were re-interred on the green on the north side of the Abbey, between the north transept and the west end.

[2] Killigrew's house, see ante, November 20th and 22nd, and above on the 4th of this month. Pepys sometimes calls it the Theatre and at others the Playhouse.

[3] Falstaff was acted by Cartwright, but neither Downes nor Genest give the names of the actors who took the characters of Justice Shallow and Dr. Caius.

coach to Mr. Crew's to my Lord, who told me of his going out of town to-morrow to settle the militia in Huntingdonshire, and did desire me to lay up a box of some rich jewels and things that there are in it, which I promised to do. After much free discourse with my Lord, who tells me his mind as to his enlarging his family, &c., and desiring me to look him out a Master of the Horse and other servants, we parted. From thence I walked to Greatorex (he was not within), but there I met with Mr. Jonas Moore,[1] and took him to the Five Bells,[2] and drank a glass of wine and left him. To the Temple, when Sir R. Parkhurst (as was intended the last night) did seal the writings, and is to have the £2,000 told to-morrow. From thence by water to Parliament Stairs, and there at an alehouse to Doling (who is suddenly to go into Ireland to venture his fortune); Simonds (who is at a great loss for £200 present money, which I was loth to let him have, though I could now do it, and do love him and think him honest and sufficient, yet lothness to part with money did dissuade me from it); Luellin (who was very drowsy from a dose that he had got the last night), Mr. Mount and several others, among the rest one Mr. Pierce, an army man, who did make us the best sport for songs and stories in a Scotch tone (which he do very well) that ever I heard in my life. I never knew so good a companion in all my observation. From thence to the bridge by water, it being a most pleasant moonshine night, with a waterman who did tell such a company of bawdy stories, how once he carried a lady from Putney in such a night as this, and she bade him lie down by her, which he did, and did give her content, and a great deal more roguery. Home and found my girl knocking at the door (it being 11 o'clock at night), her mistress having sent her out for some trivial business, which did vex me when I came in, and so I took occasion to go up

---

[1] Jonas Moore was born at Whitley, Lancashire, February 8th, 1617, and was appointed by Charles I. tutor to the Duke of York. Soon after the Restoration he was knighted and made Surveyor-General of the Ordnance. He was famous as a mathematician, and was one of the founders of the Royal Society. He died August 27th, 1679, and at his funeral sixty pieces of ordnance were discharged at the Tower.

[2] There were taverns with this sign in the Strand and Fleet Street. They are registered in the list of taverns in London and Westminster in 1698 (Harl. MS. 4716).

and to bed in a pet. Before I went forth this morning, one came
to me to give me notice that the Justices of Middlesex do meet to-
morrow at Hicks Hall,[1] and that I as one am desired to be there,
but I fear I cannot be there though I much desire it.

[7th]. This morning the Judge Advocate Fowler came to see me,
and he and I sat talking till it was time to go to the office. To the
office and there staid till past 12 o'clock, and so I left the Comptroller and Surveyor and went to Whitehall to my Lord's, where
I found my Lord gone this morning to Huntingdon, as he told me
yesterday he would. I staid and dined with my Lady, there being
Laud the page's mother[2] there, and dined also with us, and
seemed to have been a very pretty woman and of good discourse.
Before dinner I examined Laud in his Latin and found him a
very pretty boy and gone a great way in Latin. After dinner I
took a box of some things of value that my Lord had left for me to
carry to the Exchequer, which I did, and left them with my
Brother Spicer, who also had this morning paid £1,000 for me by
appointment to Sir R. Parkhurst. So to the Privy Seal, where I
signed a deadly number of pardons, which do trouble me to get
nothing by. Home by water, and there was much pleased to see
that my little room is likely to come to be finished soon. I fell
a-reading Fuller's History of Abbeys,[3] and my wife in Great
Cyrus[4] till twelve at night, and so to bed.

[8th]. To Whitehall to the Privy Seal, and thence to Mr. Pierce's
the Surgeon to tell them that I would call by and by to go to
dinner. But I going into Westminster Hall met with Sir G. Carteret and Sir W. Pen (who were in a great fear that we had committed a great error of £100,000 in our late account gone into the
Parliament in making it too little), and so I was fain to send

---

[1] The Middlesex Sessions House in St. John Street, Clerkenwell, named after
Sir Baptist Hicks, one of the justices, and afterwards Viscount Campden, at
whose cost it was built in 1612. The Sessions House was removed to the present building on Clerkenwell Green in 1782.

[2] Mrs. Crisp.

[3] Which forms part of his "Church History," book vi.

[4] "Artamine ou Le Grand Cyrus," by Magdelaine de Scudery, the second of
her works, which was published in 1650.

order to Mr. Pierce's to come to my house, and also to leave the key of the chest with Mr. Spicer, wherein my Lord's money is, and went along with Sir W. Pen by water to the office, and there with Mr. Huchinson we did find that we were in no mistake. And so I went to dinner with my wife and Mr. and Mrs. Pierce the Surgeon to Mr. Pierce the Purser (the first time that ever I was at his house) who does live very plentifully and finely. We had a lovely chine of beef and other good things very complete and drank a great deal of wine, and her daughter played after dinner upon the virginals,[1] and at night by lanthorn home again, and Mr. Pierce and his wife being gone home I went to bed, having drunk so much wine that my head was troubled and was not very well all night, and the wind I observed was rose exceedingly before I went to bed.

[9th] (Lord's day). Being called up early by Sir W. Batten I rose and went to his house and he told me the ill news that he had this morning from Woolwich, that the Assurance[2] (formerly Captain Holland's ship, and now Captain Stoakes's,[3] designed for Guiny and manned and victualled), was by a gust of wind sunk down to the bottom. Twenty men drowned. Sir Williams both went by barge thither to see how things are, and I am sent to the Duke of York to tell him, and by boat with some other company going to Whitehall from the Old Swan. I went to the Duke. And first calling upon Mr. Coventry at his chamber, I went to the Duke's bed-side, who had sat up late last night, and lay long this morning, who was much surprised therewith. This being done I went to chappell, and sat in Mr. Blagrave's pew, and there did sing my part along with another before the King, and with much ease. From thence going to my Lady I met with a letter from my Lord (which Andrew had been at my house to bring me and missed me), commanding me to go to Mr. Denham,[4] to get a man

---

[1] All instruments of the harpsichord and spinet kind were styled virginals.

[2] The "Assurance" was a fourth-rate of forty guns, built at Deptford in 1646 by P. Pett, sen.

[3] John Stoakes, late captain of the "Royal Henry."

[4] John Denham, son of Sir John Denham, Lord Chief Justice of the King's Bench in Ireland, born at Dublin in 1615, appointed at the Restoration Sur-

to go to him to-morrow to Hinchinbroke, to contrive with him about some alterations in his house, which I did and got Mr. Kennard.[1] Dined with my Lady and staid all the afternoon with her, and had infinite of talk of all kind of things, especially of beauty of men and women, with which she seems to be much pleased to talk of. From thence at night to Mr. Kennard and took him to Mr. Denham, the Surveyor's. Where, while we could not speak with him, his chief man (Mr. Cooper) did give us a cup of good sack. From thence with Mr. Kennard to my Lady who is much pleased with him, and after a glass of sack there, we parted, having taken order for a horse or two for him and his servant to be gone to-morrow. So to my father's, where I sat while they were at supper, and I found my mother below stairs and pretty well. Thence home, where I hear that the Comptroller had some business with me, and (with Giffin's lanthorn) I went to him and there staid in discourse an hour till late, and among other things he showed me a design of his, by the King's making an Order of Knights of the Sea,[2] to give an encouragement for persons of honour to undertake the service of the sea, and he had done it with great pains and very ingeniously. So home and to prayers and to bed.

[10th]. Up exceedingly early to go to the Comptroller, but he not being up and it being a very fine, bright, moonshine morning I went and walked all alone twenty turns in Cornhill, from Gracious Street corner to the Stocks[3] and back again, from 6 o'clock till past 7, so long that I was weary, and going to the Comptroller's thinking to find him ready, I found him gone, at which I was troubled, and being weary went home, and from thence with

veyor-General of the Works, and created a Knight of the Bath at the Coronation of Charles II.; better known as the author of "Cooper's Hill." He was one of the original Fellows of the Royal Society. His troubles with his second wife are related further on in the Diary. He died March, 1668-9, and was buried in Westminster Abbey.

[1] Kennard was master-joiner at Whitehall, see February 11th, 1660-61.

[2] Nothing further appears to have been done in respect to Sir Robert Slingsby's scheme of an Order of Knights of the Sea.

[3] The Stocks originally stood on the site of the Mansion House. At this time the place was occupied by a market.

my wife by water to Westminster, and put her to my father Bowyer's (they being newly come out of the country), but I could not stay there, but left her there. I to the Hall and there met with Col. Slingsby. So hearing that the Duke of York is gone down this morning to see the ship sunk yesterday at Woolwich, he and I returned by his coach to the office, and after that to dinner. After dinner he came to me again and sat with me at my house, and among other discourse he told me that it is expected that the Duke will marry the Lord Chancellor's daughter at last, which is likely to be the ruin of Mr. Davis and my Lord Barkley, who have carried themselves so high against the Chancellor; Sir Chas. Barkley swearing that he and others had lain with her often, which all believe to be a lie.[1] He and I in the evening to the Coffee House in Cornhill, the first time that ever I was there, and I found much pleasure in it, through the diversity of company and discourse. Home and found my wife at my Lady Batten's, and have made a bargain to go see the ship sunk at Woolwich, where both the Sir Williams are still since yesterday, and I do resolve to go along with them. From thence home and up to bed, having first been into my study, and to ease my mind did go to cast up how my cash stands, and I do find as near as I can that I am worth in money clear £240, for which God be praised. This afternoon there was a couple of men with me with a book in each of their hands, demanding money for poll-money,[2] and I overlooked the book and saw myself set down Samuel Pepys, gent. 10s. for himself and for his servants, 2s., which I did presently pay without any dispute, but I fear I have not escaped so, and therefore I have long ago laid by £10 for them, but I think I am not bound to discover myself.

[11th]. My wife and I up very early this day, and though the

---

[1] Sir Charles Berkeley, in the "Memoirs of Grammont" improperly called Sir George Berkeley, created Baron Berkeley of Rathdown and Viscount Fitzharding of Bearhaven (in Ireland) in 1663, and Earl of Falmouth in 1665, was the confidant and favourite of the king. He was killed at Southwold Bay, in the seafight, June 2nd, 1665, and the earldom became extinct. The Duke of York had married Anne Hyde on the 3rd September before.

[2] Pepys seems to have been let off very easily, for, by Act of Parliament 18 Car. II. cap. I (1666), servants were to pay one shilling in the pound of their wages, and others from one shilling to three shillings in the pound.

weather was very bad and the wind high, yet my Lady Batten and her maid and we two did go by our barge to Woolwich (my Lady being very fearfull) where we found both Sir Williams and much other company, expecting the weather to be better, that they might go about weighing up the Assurance, which lies there (poor ship, that I have been twice merry in, in Capt. Holland's time,) under water, only the upper deck may be seen and the masts. Captain Stoakes is very melancholy, and being in search for some clothes and money of his, which he says he hath lost out of his cabin. I did the first office of a Justice of Peace to examine a seaman thereupon, but could find no reason to commit him. This last tide the Kingsale was also run aboard and lost her mainmast, by another ship, which makes us think it ominous to the Guiny voyage, to have two of her ships spoilt before they go out. After dinner, my Lady being very fearfull she staid and kept my wife there, and I and another gentleman, a friend of Sir W. Pen's, went back in the barge very merry by the way, as far as Whitehall in her. To the Privy Seal, where I signed many pardons and some few things else. From thence Mr. Moore and I into London to a tavern near my house, and there we drank and discoursed of ways how to put out a little money to the best advantage, and at present he has persuaded me to put out £250 for £50 per annum for eight years, and I think I shall do it. Thence home, where I found the wench washing, and I up to my study, and there did make up an even £100, and sealed it to lie by. After that to bed.

[12th]. Troubled with the absence of my wife. This morning I went (after the Comptroller and I had sat an hour at the office) to Whitehall to dine with my Lady, and after dinner to the Privy Seal and sealed abundance of pardons and little else. From thence to the Exchequer and did give my mother Bowyer a visit and her daughters, the first time that I have seen them since I went last to sea. From thence up with J. Spicer to his office and took £100, and by coach with it as far as my father's, where I called to see them, and my father did offer me six pieces of gold,[1] in lieu of six

---

[1] By the proclamation of January 27th, 1660-61, a double ducat was valued at 18s. and a golden rider at £1 2s. 6d.

pounds that he borrowed of me the other day, but it went against me to take it of him and therefore did not, though I was afterwards a little troubled that I did not. Thence home, and took out this £100 and sealed it up with the other last night, it being the first £200 that ever I saw together of my own in my life. For which God be praised. So to my Lady Batten, and sat an hour or two, and talked with her daughter and people in the absence of her father and mother and my wife to pass away the time. After that home and to bed, reading myself asleep, while the wench sat mending my breeches by my bedside.

[13th]. All the day long looking upon my workmen who this day began to paint my parlour. Only at noon my Lady Batten and my wife came home, and so I stepped to my Lady's, where were Sir John Lawson and Captain Holmes, and there we dined and had very good red wine of my Lady's own making in England.

[14th]. Also all this day looking upon my workmen. Only met with the Comptroller at the office a little both forenoon and afternoon, and at night step a little with him to the Coffee House[1] where we light upon very good company and had very good discourse concerning insects and their having a generative faculty as well as other creatures. This night in discourse the Comptroller told me among other persons that were heretofore the principal officers of the Navy, there was one Sir Peter Buck,[2] a Clerk of the Acts, of which to myself I was not a little proud.

[15th]. All day at home looking upon my workmen, only at noon Mr. Moore came and brought me some things to sign for the Privy Seal and dined with me. We had three eels that my wife and I bought this morning of a man, that cried them about, for our dinner, and that was all I did to-day.

[16th]. In the morning to church, and then dined at home. In the afternoon I to White Hall, where I was surprised with the news

---

[1] Probably the Coffee House in Exchange Alley which had for its sign, Morat, or the Turk's Head. It is frequently referred to in subsequent pages.

[2] Sir Peter Buck was Clerk of the Cheque at Chatham before his appointment as Clerk of the Acts about 1600. He died in 1625, and was succeeded as Clerk of the Acts by Dennis Fleming.

of a plot against the King's person and my Lord Monk's; and that since last night there are about forty taken up on suspicion; and, amongst others, it was my lot to meet with Simon Beale,[1] the Trumpeter, who took me and Tom Doling into the Guard in Scotland Yard, and showed us Major-General Overton, where I heard him deny that he is guilty of any such things; but that whereas it is said that he is found to have brought many arms to town, he says it is only to sell them, as he will prove by oath. From thence with Tom Doling and Boston and D. Vines (whom we met by the way) to Price's, and there we drank, and in discourse I learnt a pretty trick to try whether a woman be a maid or no, by a string going round her head to meet at the end of her nose, which if she be not will come a great way beyond. Thence to my Lady's and staid with her an hour or two talking of the Duke and his lady, the Chancellor's daughter, between whom, she tells me, that all is agreed and he will marry her. But I know not how true yet. It rained hard, and my Lady would have had me have the coach, but I would not, but to my father's, where I met my wife, and there supped, and after supper by link home and to bed.

[17th]. All day looking after my workmen, only in the afternoon to the office where both Sir Williams were come from Woolwich, and tell us that, contrary to their expectations, the Assurance is got up, without much damage to her body, only to the goods that she hath within her, which argues her to be a strong, good ship. This day my parlour is gilded, which do please me well.

[18th]. All day at home, without stirring at all, looking after my workmen.

[19th]. At noon I went and dined with my Lady at Whitehall, and so back again to the office, and after that home to my workmen. This night Mr. Gauden sent me a great chine of beef and half a dozen of tongues.

---

[1] Simon Beale is mentioned again on September 26th, 1668, where he is said to have been one of Oliver's guards.

[20th]. All day at home with my workmen, that I may get all done before Christmas. This day I hear that the Princess Royal has the small pox.

[21st]. By water to Whitehall (leaving my wife at Whitefriars going to my father's to buy her a muff and mantle), there I signed many things at the Privy Seal, and carried £200 from thence to the Exchequer, and laid it up with Mr. Hales, and afterwards took him and W. Bowyer to the Swan and drank with them. They told me that this is St. Thomas's [day], and that by an old custom, this day the Exchequer men had formerly, and do intend this night to have a supper; which if I could I promised to come to, but did not. To my Lady's, and dined with her: she told me how dangerously ill the Princess Royal is: and that this morning she was said to be dead. But she hears that she hath married herself to young Jermyn,[1] which is worse than the Duke of York's marrying the Chancellor's daughter, which is now publicly owned. After dinner to the office all the afternoon. At seven at night I walked through the dirt to Whitehall to see whether my Lord be come to town, and I found him come and at supper, and I supped with him. He tells me that my aunt at Brampton has voided a great stone (the first time that ever I heard she was troubled therewith) and cannot possibly live long, that my uncle is pretty well, but full of pain still. After supper home and to bed.

[22nd]. All the morning with my painters, who will make an end of all this day I hope. At noon I went to the Sun tavern, on Fish Street hill, to a dinner of Captn. Teddimans, where was my Lord Inchiquin[2] (who seems to be a very fine person), Sir W. Pen, Captn. Cuttance, and one Mr. Lawrence[3] (a fine gentleman now going to Algiers), and other good company, where we had a very fine dinner, good musique, and a great deal of wine. We

---

[1] Henry Jermyn, second son of Thomas Jermyn and nephew of the Earl of St. Alban's, born 1636; Master of the Horse to the Duke of York, 1660-1675; created Baron Dover of Dover, 1685, and Earl of Dover, 1689; succeeded as third Baron Jermyn of St. Edmondsbury, 1703. He died, April 6th, 1708. The report in the text was of course false.

[2] Murrough O'Brien, sixth Baron of Inchiquin, in Ireland, advanced to the earldom of Inchiquin in 1654.

[3] Afterwards Sir John Lawrence.

staid here very late, at last Sir W. Pen and I home together, he so overcome with wine that he could hardly go; I was forced to lead him through the streets and he was in a very merry and kind mood. I home (found my house clear of the workmen and their work ended), my head troubled with wine, and I very merry went to bed, my head akeing all night.

[23rd] (Lord's day). In the morning to Church, where our pew all covered with rosemary and baize. A stranger made a dull sermon. Home and found my wife and maid with much ado had made shift to spit a great turkey sent me this week from Charles Carter, my old colleague, now minister in Huntingdonshire, but not at all roasted, and so I was fain to stay till two o'clock, and after that to church with my wife, and a good sermon there was, and so home. All the evening at my book, and so to supper and to bed.

[24th]. In the morning to the office and Commissioner Pett (who seldom comes there) told me that he had lately presented a piece of plate (being a couple of flaggons) to Mr. Coventry, but he did not receive them, which also put me upon doing the same too; and so after dinner I went and chose a payre of candlesticks to be made ready for me at Alderman Backwell's. To the office again in the afternoon till night, and so home, and with the painters till 10 at night, making an end of my house and the arch before my door, and so this night I was rid of them and all other work, and my house was made ready against to-morrow being Christmas day. This day the Princess Royal died at Whitehall.

[25th] (Christmas day). In the morning very much pleased to see my house once more clear of workmen and to be clean, and indeed it is so, far better than it was that I do not repent of my trouble that I have been at. In the morning to church, where Mr. Mills made a very good sermon. After that home to dinner, where my wife and I and my brother Tom (who this morning came to see my wife's new mantle put on, which do please me very well), to a good shoulder of mutton and a chicken. After dinner to church again, my wife and I, where we had a dull sermon of a stranger, which made me sleep, and so home, and I, before and

after supper, to my lute and Fuller's History, at which I staid all alone in my chamber till 12 at night, and so to bed.

[26th]. In the morning to Alderman Backwell's for the candlesticks for Mr. Coventry, but they being not done I went away, and so by coach to Mr. Crew's, and there took some money of Mr.

THE PRINCESS OF ORANGE

Moore's for my Lord, and so to my Lord's, where I found Sir Thomas Bond[1] (whom I never saw before) with a message from the Queen about vessells for the carrying over of her goods, and so with him to Mr. Coventry, and thence to the office (being soundly washed going through the bridge) to Sir Wm. Batten

---

[1] Sir Thomas Bond was a Roman Catholic; Comptroller of the Household to the Queen Dowager; created a baronet in 1658 by Charles II., to whom, whilst in exile, he had advanced large sums. He died in 1685, and lies buried at Camberwell, in which parish he had purchased an estate at Peckham, and built a house alienated by his son, Sir Henry, to Chief Justice Trevor.—B.

and Pen (the last of whom took physic to-day), and so I went up to his chamber, and there having made an end of the business I returned to White Hall by water, and dined with my Lady Sandwich, who at table did tell me how much fault was laid upon Dr. Frazer[1] and the rest of the Doctors, for the death of the Princess.[2] My Lord did dine this day with Sir Henry Wright, in order to his going to sea with the Queen. Thence to my father Bowyer's where I met my wife, and with her home by water.

[27th]. In the morning to Alderman Backwell's again, where I found the candlesticks done, and went along with him in his coach to my Lord's and left the candlesticks with Mr. Shepley. I staid in the garden talking much with my Lord, who do show me much of his love and do communicate his mind in most things to me, which is my great content. Home and with my wife to Sir W. Batten's to dinner, where much and good company. My wife not very well went home, I staid late there seeing them play at cards, and so home to bed. This afternoon there came in a strange lord to Sir William Batten's by a mistake and enters discourse with him, so that we could not be rid of him till Sir Arn. Breames and Mr. Bens and Sir W. Pen fell a-drinking to him till he was drunk, and so sent him away. About the middle of the night I was very ill—I think with eating and drinking too much—and so I was forced to call the maid, who pleased my wife and I in her running up and down so innocently in her smock, and vomited in the bason, and so to sleep, and in the morning was pretty well, only got cold, and so had pain . . . as I used to have.

[28th]. Office day. There all the morning. Dined at home alone with my wife, and so staid within all the afternoon and evening, at my lute, with great pleasure, and so to bed with great content.

[29th]. Within all the morning. Several people to speak with me;

---

[1] Alexander Fraizer, M.D. (of Montpelier), was physician in ordinary to Charles II., and was knighted by the king, with whom he was a great favourite. In 1651 and 1652 he had been in attendance on the royal family at St. Germains. He died May 3rd, 1681. Dr. Munk says, "His character was never of the highest."—*Roll of the Royal College of Physicians*, 1878, vol. ii., p. 232.
[2] The Princess Royal died on December 24th.

Mr. Shepley for £100; Mr. Kennard and Warren,[1] the merchant, about deals for my Lord. Captain Robert Blake lately come from the Straights about some Florence wine for my Lord, and with him I went to Sir W. Pen, who offering me a barrel of oysters I took them both home to my house (having by chance a good piece of roast beef at the fire for dinner), and there they dined with me, and sat talking all the afternoon—good company. Thence to Alderman Backwell's and took a brave state-plate and cupp in lieu of the candlesticks that I had the other day and carried them by coach to my Lord's and left them there. And so back to my father's and saw my mother, and so to my uncle Fenner's, whither my father came to me, and there we talked and drank, and so away, I home with my father, he telling me what bad wives both my cozen Joyces make to their husbands, which I much wondered at. After talking of my sister's coming to me next week, I went home and to bed.

[30th] (Lord's day). Lay long in bed, and being up, I went with Will to my Lord's, calling in at many churches in my way. There I found Mr. Shepley, in his Venetian cap, taking physique in his chamber, and with him I sat till dinner. My Lord dined abroad and my Lady in her chamber, so Mr. Hetly, Child and I dined together, and after dinner Mr. Child and I spent some time at the lute, and so promising to prick me some lessons to my theorbo he went away to see Henry Laws, who lies very sick. I to the Abbey and walked there, seeing the great confusion of people that come there to hear the organs. So home, calling in at my father's, but staid not, my father and mother being both forth. At home I fell a-reading of Fuller's Church History till it was late, and so to bed.

[31st]. At the office all the morning and after that home, and not staying to dine I went out, and in Paul's Churchyard I bought the play of "Henry the Fourth,"[2] and so went to the new Theatre

---

[1] William Warren, a rich tradesman of Wapping, was knighted in 1661, see *post*, April 17th, 1661. Le Neve says he was "a great builder of ships for King Charles II." A square built on the site of his residence was named "Sir William Warren's Square."

[2] Shakespeare's "King Henry IV.," presumably the first part, is given by Downes as one of the plays acted by the King's Servants, and he gives the

(only calling at Mr. Crew's and eat a bit with the people there at dinner) and saw it acted; but my expectation being too great, it did not please me, as otherwise I believe it would; and my having a book, I believe did spoil it a little. That being done I went to my Lord's, where I found him private at cards with my Lord Lauderdale and some persons of honour. So Mr. Shepley and I over to Harper's, and there drank a pot or two, and so parted. My boy taking a cat home with him from my Lord's, which Sarah had given him for my wife, we being much troubled with mice. At Whitehall inquiring for a coach, there was a Frenchman with one eye that was going my way, so he and I hired the coach between us and he set me down in Fenchurch Street. Strange how the fellow, without asking, did tell me all what he was, and how he had ran away from his father and come into England to serve the King, and now going back again. Home and to bed.

following cast—"King: Mr. Wintersel; Prince: Mr. Burt; Hotspur: Mr. Hart, Falstaff: Mr. Cartwright; Poyns: Mr. Shatterel."